Beginning Direct3D® Game Programming 2ND Edition

PREMIER PRESS

GAME DEVELOPMENT

Beginning Direct3D® Game Programming
2ND Edition

Wolfgang F. Engel

PREMIER PRESS

GAME DEVELOPMENT

Premier
Press

Publisher: Stacy L. Hiquet

Senior Marketing Manager: Martine Edwards

Marketing Manager: Heather Hurley

Associate Marketing Manager: Kristin Eisenzopf

Manager of Editorial Services: Heather Talbot

Acquisitions Editor: Mitzi Foster-Koontz

Project Editor/Copy Editor: Cathleen D. Snyder

Technical Reviewer: André LaMothe

Retail Market Coordinator: Sarah Dubois

Interior Layout: Shawn Morningstar

Cover Designer: Mike Tanamachi

CD-ROM Producer: Brandon Penticuff

Indexer: Katherine Stimson

Proofreader: Lorraine Gunter

ISBN: 1-931841-39-x

Library of Congress Catalog Card Number: 2003101212

Printed in the United States of America

03 04 05 06 07 BH 10 9 8 7 6 5 4 3 2 1

Premier Press, a division of Course Technology
25 Thomson Place
Boston, MA 02210

Für meine Frau Katja und unsere Tochter Anja

Acknowledgments

This book couldn't have been completed without the help of many people. In particular, I want to thank my parents, who gave me a wonderful and warm childhood; my wife, Katja, for being patient with a spare-time author; and our nearly two-year-old daughter, Anna, for showing me the important things in life.

Additionally I would like to thank those people who also helped to make this book possible: Heather Hurley, Mitzi Koontz, Emi Smith, Cathleen Snyder, Heather Talbot, and André LaMothe. Thanks for your patience with me and for a great time at GDC 2003.

About the Author

Wolfgang F. Engel is the editor and coauthor of several programming books. He has also written several online tutorials published on http://www.gamedev.net, http://www.direct3d.info, and other Web sites. He held lectures at GDC 2003 and at Vision Days in Copenhagen. Wolfgang is also a faculty advisor for the Academy of Game Entertainment Technology (http://www.academyofget.com/html/advisors.html).

Contents at a Glance

Contents

Chapter 6
First Steps to Animation 77

Part Three
Hard-Core DirectX
Graphics Programming 175

Chapter 9
Shader Programming with the High-Level Shader Language 177

Chapter 10
More Advanced Shader Effects 197

Appendix C
Mathematics Primer 353

Appendix D
Creating a Texture with
D3DXCreateTextureFromFileEx() 371

LETTER FROM THE SERIES EDITOR

The first edition of *Beginning Direct 3D Game Programming* was such a great success that we thought we would follow it up with a new edition that covers slightly more advanced material, such as shader and vertex programming, and at the same time update the text for DirectX 9.0. This second edition still starts off slowly and explains the key elements of Direct3D programming, but it takes the material a little further and shows you how to create some more advanced effects based on shader programming with the new shader programming languages, such as Microsoft's High-Level Shader Language (HLSL). Additionally, we thought we would throw in some new material on *Quake 2* and *Quake 3* file formats for animated meshes.

If you're looking for a beginner book on Direct3D and you don't want to wade through a lot of general DirectX coverage or Windows programming, then this book is for you.

Sincerely,

André LaMothe

Game Development Series Editor

Introduction

When I finished my first degree in law back in 1993, I was very proud and a little bit exhausted from the long learning period. So I decided to relax by playing a new game by NovaLogic called *Comanche*.

I started the night of January 11th and finished about three days later with only a few hours of sleep. With the new experience in my head, I decided to start computer game programming. My goal was to program a terrain engine like *Comanche*. My then-girlfriend—now my wife—looked a little bit confused when a young, recently-graduated lawyer told her that he was going to be a game programmer.

About two years later, after becoming a member of the Gamedev Forum on CompuServe and reading a few books on game programming by André La Mothe and a good article by Peter Freese on height-mapping engines, I got my own engine up and running under OS/2. I wrote a few articles on OpenGL and OS/2 game programming for German journals, coauthored a German book, and started on Windows game programming.

In 1997, I wrote my first online tutorials on DirectX programming and published them on my own Web site. After communicating with John Munsch and the other administrators of http://www.gamedev.net, I decided to make my tutorials accessible through their Web site as well. In the summer of 1998, as a beta-tester of the DirectX 6.0 SDK, I decided to write the first tutorial on the Direct3D Immediate Mode framework. At that time I used http://www.netit.net as my URL. There was a mailing list with a lot of interested people, and I got a lot of e-mails with positive feedback.

It started to be really fun. In 1999 I fired up my new Web site, at http://www.direct3d.net (now http://www.direct3d.info), with the sole purpose of providing understandable and instructive tutorials on Direct3D programming.

This was also my goal in writing the first edition of the book—to help readers understand and learn DirectX Graphics programming. Now it's been more than two years since I wrote the first edition of the book. Two years is a long time in the real-time graphics industry, and also in my private life.

In the meantime, my wife and I had a daughter, and this little baby grabs her father even when tight deadlines are looming on the horizon. I wrote an advanced series of articles on vertex and pixel shader programming, which were published at http://www.gamedev.net, and I edited and coauthored a book called *ShaderX—Vertex and Pixel Shader Tips and Tricks*, which features advanced shader programming material by 27 authors. The tremendous success of *Beginning Direct3D Game Programming* and *ShaderX* led to a number of new challenges. One of them was speaking at the 2003 Game Developers Conference on the topic "Introduction to Shader Programming with HLSL/Cg." Additionally, I regularly contribute shaders to several ongoing software projects. But let's get back to business....

Nowadays, there are graphics cards like the ATI RADEON 9800 PRO and the NVIDIA GeForce FX which have a much higher performance rate than the cards of two years ago. Vertex and pixel shaders are an integral part of every upcoming game, and therefore they are an integral part of the game development process. This fact and a huge number of e-mails led me to rethink the didactical structure of the second edition of this book. First of all, many e-mails suggested that the explanation on how to install the development environment and the DirectX SDK wasn't detailed enough in the first edition. Furthermore, the new must-have features of vertex and pixel shaders add an additional level of complexity to the development of even the simplest 3D example program. Therefore, this edition of the book has an extended introduction to the preparation of a development system, and the first chapters stick to the fixed-function pipeline to reduce the level of detail. I explain vertex and pixel shader programming later, in Part Three. Unfortunately, Amir Geva was not able to contribute his chapters on physics and collision detection to this edition. If you are interested in using his collision detection library (ColDet) with DirectX, I would suggest reading the first edition of the book or going to his Web site, at http://www.photoneffect.com.

I wish you as much fun reading this book as I had writing it. Don't stop sending me e-mails. As you know, many improvements and new features in the book were implemented with e-mails from you in mind...and getting e-mails is what will drive me to improve this book further in upcoming editions.

Wolf (wolf@direct3d.net)

What You're Going to Learn

This book covers all of the elements necessary to create a Windows 95/98/Me/NT/2000/XP or short Windows-based Direct3D/DirectX Graphics game for the PC, including:

- 3D graphics and algorithms
- Game programming techniques and data structures
- Using 3D files to construct game worlds
- Programming your own character engine with a character animation system
- DirectX Graphics programming
- And more!

What You Need to Know

This book assumes that you can program in C with a dash of C++. I will use the less-esoteric features of C++, the way the Microsoft guys who programmed the Direct3D Immediate Mode samples in the DirectX SDK did. In case you need a refresher, there's a decent C++ primer in Appendix B, so check it out.

You aren't taking a stab at graphics/game programming to learn the math. If you can add, subtract, multiply, divide, and maybe square a number, you will be able to understand 90 percent of the math and what's going on in this book. There's a math primer provided in Appendix C just to be absolutely sure that you won't miss anything.

How This Book Is Organized

This book consists of four parts. The first part will show you the essentials of Direct3D game programming. It deals with the programming conventions, basic algorithms, texture-mapping basics, 3D math, transformation pipeline, lighting, and depth buffers.

In the second part, you will learn how to use the transformation and lighting pipeline to map textures onto objects with different effects. All of the buzzwords, such as bump mapping, environment mapping, and procedural textures, are explained, and the effects are shown in sample programs.

In the third part of this book, you'll deal with file formats and how to integrate them into your game engine. The file formats used are the greatly enhanced .X file format, introduced with the DirectX 8.0 SDK, and the MD3 file format used in most of the games driven by the *Quake 3* engine. Additionally, an enhanced MD3 file format is shown in a character engine.

This part of the book also features vertex- and pixel-shader programming from the ground up. It shows you how to use the new High-Level Shader Language (HLSL) from DirectX 9.

The fourth part contains appendixes, which should be useful if you want to refresh your Windows programming, C++, or math skills.

Using the CD-ROM

There is an appendix devoted to using the CD-ROM, but I'll give you a brief overview here. The companion CD for this book includes all the code in the book, the Microsoft DirectX 9.0 SDK for C/C++, and the DirectX 9 Developer Runtime, which you need to install in order to compile and run the example programs discussed in the book. (See the installation instructions in the following section.) The DirectX SDK contains the run-time files, headers, and libraries you need to compile the book examples, and it provides many example programs for every component of DirectX.

You will find the example code from the book in directories named after the chapters of the book. In every example directory, you'll find the graphics and source files. There's also a readme.txt file, which provides you with additional information on compiling the application.

You'll need a system that fulfills the requirements of DirectX to run the example programs. The minimum requirements are

- Windows 2000 with at least Service Pack 2 or higher. (I recommend Windows XP Professional with the latest service pack because only the Professional version will let you install the Debug run-time you need to develop DirectX applications.)

- Visual C/C++ 6.0 with at least Service Pack 5. (I recommend Visual C++ .NET with the latest service pack.)

- At least 256 MB of RAM.

- At least 600 MB of free hard drive storage space. (Usually a lot more is a better bet.)

- A hardware-accelerated 3D graphics card. To get the maximum visual experience for the examples, you need relatively new graphics hardware. The pixel shader examples will only run on DirectX 8.1-capable hardware. Some of the examples need a graphics card that is capable of supporting some features of DirectX 9 in hardware.

- The newest graphics card device driver.

Please download the newest graphics card device drivers. Usually newer driver versions have less bugs and higher performance. On three computers, I am using Windows XP Professional with 256, 512, and 1000 MB of RAM and a Pentium III 1 GHZ, Pentium IV 2 GHz, and an Athlon 1700+ processor, respectively. The examples are developed with Visual C/C++ 6 with Service Pack 5 and Visual C++ .NET. I test all examples on NVIDIA GeForce 3 and GeForce 4 TI, and ATI RADEON 8500, 9000 Mobility, and 9700 PRO graphics cards.

Installing the DirectX SDK

To install DirectX, look for the folder labeled DirectX on the CD that comes with this book. The two files in the directory should resemble Figure I.1.

Name ▲	Size	Type	Date Modified
dx9sdkcp.exe	99,996 KB	Application	12/20/2002 7:09 AM
dx90_sdk_devruntime.exe	87,072 KB	Application	12/20/2002 7:52 AM

Figure I.1

The two necessary files to install DirectX 9

When you click on the file named dx90_sdk_devruntime.exe, the files will be decompressed into the selected temporary directory, shown in Figure I.2.

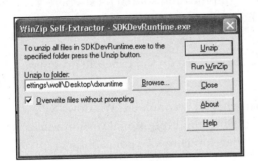

Figure I.2

The creation of the temporary dxruntime folder

I chose a folder named dxruntime on the Desktop. After unzipping the files into the appropriate folder, you will find within that folder another folder named SDKDev, as shown in Figure I.3.

The SDKDev folder contains two folders named Debug and Retail. You should choose the Debug folder to get as much debug info as possible. The Retail builds are stripped of many debug checks and are also compiled to run faster. If you plan to simply play DirectX games and not write your own, the Retail builds are the best choice. The Debug builds help coders get their DirectX applications up and running. They help you track down bugs by giving you debug messages. The tradeoff, however, is that they run slower than the Retail builds.

In the Debug folder, you will find a file named dxdevrtm.exe. When you click on this file, the installation process starts, as shown in Figure I.4.

You don't get many choices from now on. All you have to do is accept the usual license agreement and start the process. At the end, you will be forced to reboot your computer after you click on Finish in the dialog box.

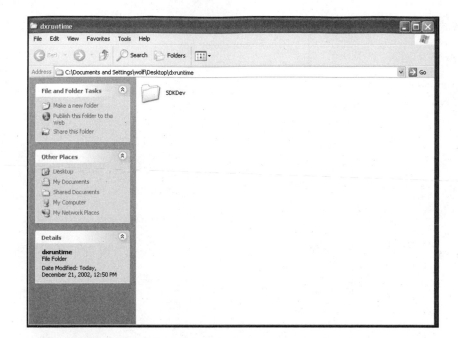

Figure I.3

The SDKDev directory

Figure I.4

The first steps of the DX9 run-time installation process

After the reboot, it might be a good idea to delete the temporary dxruntime folder from the Desktop.

The next step to installing DirectX 9 on your computer is to install the SDK. Click on the second file with the name dx9sdkcp.exe. Again choose a temporary folder name. I suggest using the name dx9sdktemp on your Desktop, as shown in Figure I.6.

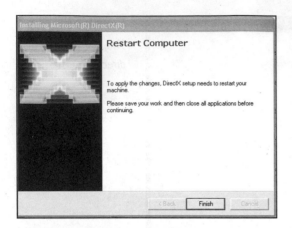

Figure I.5

The reboot dialog box in the installation process

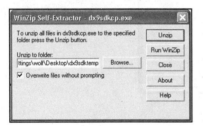

Figure I.6

Unzipping the SDK files into dx9sdktemp

Then click on the folder in the temporary directory named SDK (C++), as shown in Figure 1.7.

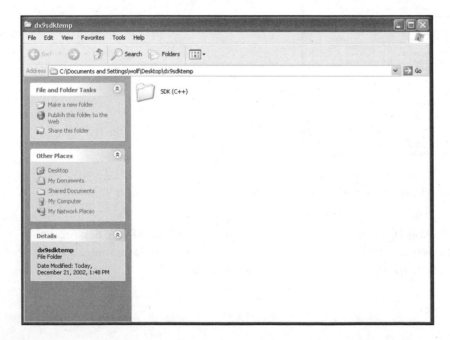

Figure I.7

Click on SDK (C++)

The contents of this folder look like Figure I.8.

Figure I.8

Contents of SDK (C++)

Click on setup.exe to start the installation procedure. During the setup process, you have to accept the license agreement, and you can choose different components. I suggest using all components and specifying your directory (see Figure I.9). The default directory should be C:\DXSDK. Choosing this directory makes it easier to compile examples developed by others.

After you complete the installation procedure by clicking on Finish in the final dialog box of the Installation wizard, you can delete the temporary directory dx9sdktemp from your Desktop.

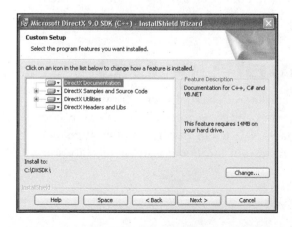

Figure I.9

Choose the appropriate features and the directory for the DirectX 9 SDK

After you finish installing DirectX, take a look at all of the directories and get to know the location of the libraries, include files, help, and samples (see Figure I.10). You need these locations to set up the Visual C++ compiler.

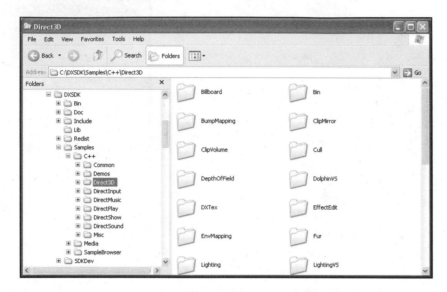

Figure I.10

Important directories in the DirectX 9 SDK

You will find the Direct3D programming files in C:\DXSDK\Samples\C++\Direct3D. The include files are in C:\DXSDK9\Include and in C:\DXSDK9\Samples\C++\Common\Include. The library files are in C:\DXSDK9\Lib.

All of the materials and concepts are compatible with all future versions of DirectX, so keep an eye out for updates at http://msdn.microsoft.com/directx.

You also need to install the newest drivers for your video card. You can pick them up on the Web site of your video card manufacturer. The newest drivers often offer speed and stability improvements and sometimes new features. Take a look at the always-provided readme file to get the proper installation instructions.

Setting Up Visual C++ 6.0

After you have installed DirectX, you need to consider the rest of your software. The most important piece of software is your IDE (*Integrated Development Environment*), or your compiler. I suggest that you use the Microsoft Visual C/C++ 6.x or better compiler. It generates really good Windows code, and you can get it from your local bookstore or software store for a couple of bucks. This is the path of least resistance.

If you install the DirectX 9 SDK after Visual C++ 6.0, its installation routine sets all of the proper paths for you. Nevertheless, in case anything goes wrong, you should be able to check the right paths. The following lines lead you step-by-step through the configuration process of an already-installed Visual C++ 6.0.

First, select Tools, Options and choose the Directories tab (see Figure I.11).

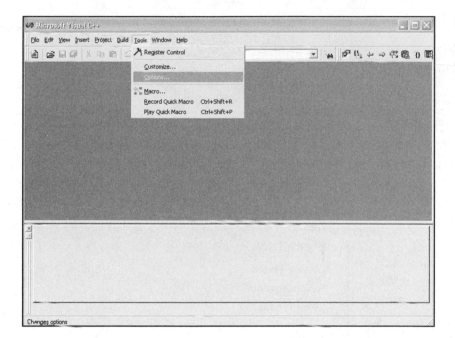

Figure I.11

Click on Tools, Options, Directories

You should see something like the dialog box in Figure I.12.

The include file directories are C:\dxsdk\include and C:\DXSDK9\Samples\C++\Common\ Include. You should point your Visual C++ IDE to these directories by clicking on the New button (see Figure I.13).

These directories should always be at the top of the list because the compiler will search for the files beginning there.

After providing the include file path, you must point the IDE to the Linker Search Paths. These library files are usually in C:\dxsdk\lib (see Figure I.14).

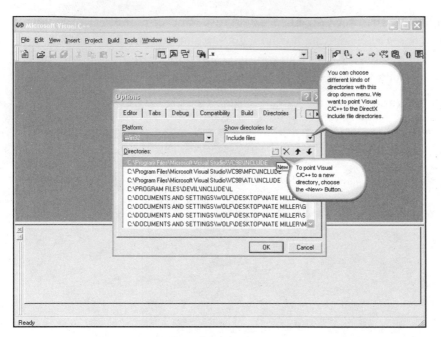

Figure I.12

The Options dialog box

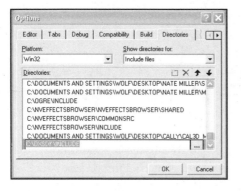

Figure I.13

Clicking on the New button and typing a path

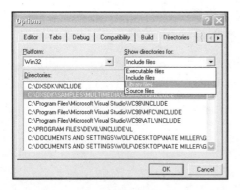

Figure I.14

Configuring the path to the library files

After you have configured Visual C/C++ 6, make sure it is configured correctly by compiling one of the examples in the C:\DXSDK\Samples\C++\Direct3D directory. You might see something like the following message if you haven't configured the include path properly:

```
d:\book\source\part 1\chapter6\animated objects\objects.cpp(68) : error C2146: syntax
error : missing ';' before 'g_Keyboard_pDI'
```

Even if you provided the correct path to the header and library files, you might have to feed the names of these files to the linker of your development environment. The proper path to these object/library modules should be listed in your Link dialog box. To reach this dialog box, select Project, Settings and then choose the Link tab. In the General category, there is an entry field called Object/Library Modules. It holds all of the library files, which should be linked to the application you're currently developing. It should look like Figure I.15.

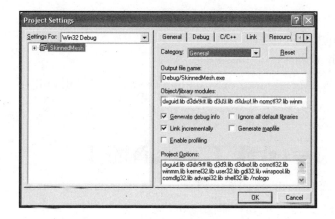

Figure I.15

Configuring the Linker Path

In this entry field, you will need to name at least the following:

- d3dx9.lib
- 3dxof.lib
- d3d9.lib
- winmm.lib
- dxguid.lib

If you missed a file, an error message that might look like this will appear:

```
d3dapp.obj : error LNK2001: unresolved external symbol _Direct3DCreate9@4
Debug/SkinnedMesh.exe : fatal error LNK1120: 1 unresolved externals
Error executing link.exe.
```

Here, d3d9.lib is missing. The unresolved external symbols are part of the COM (*Component Object Model*) interfaces of Direct3D. (I will explain COM in detail later in the book.)

You should also check another include path, the one that holds the path to the directories of the common include files for the C/C++ compiler. If you change your machine or you are working on another machine with a different DirectX directory, normally you have to add the common files using Project, Add Files to Project, Files.

Now let's compile our first project.

1. Fire up your Visual C++ configured development environment.
2. Click on Open Workspace.
3. Choose basics.dsp.
4. Check whether you've configured the paths to the directories as described previously.
5. Choose the Build/basics.exe build.
6. When everything works correctly, choose run basics.exe.

That's it. If something went wrong, reread the sections on installing the DirectX SDK and Visual C++, and consult the provided documentation.

Setting Up Visual C++ .NET

Similar to Visual C/C++ 6, the DirectX 9 SDK will set all paths for you if you install it after you install Visual C++ .NET. Nevertheless, in case anything went wrong, this section tells you what you have to do if you need to configure DirectX 9 in the Visual C++ .NET IDE manually.

You start by clicking on Tools, Options in the Visual C++ .NET IDE, as shown in Figure I.16.

There is a project section that holds all the paths to the relevant directories, as shown in Figure I.17.

If you have seen the dialog box that is used by Visual C/C++ 6 Studio, you should feel comfortable because this dialog box uses the same logic. You can see that at the top-right of the dialog box, the Show Directories For drop-down menu offers the different kinds of files that you can reference (see Figure I.18).

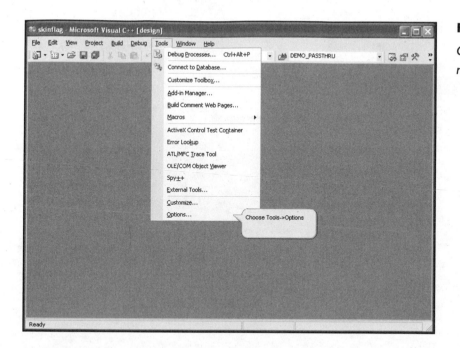

Figure I.16

Choose the Options menu item

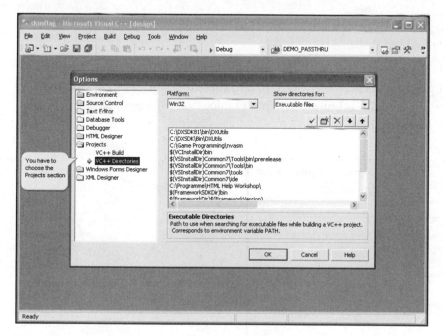

Figure I.17

Choose the Project, VC++ Directories section

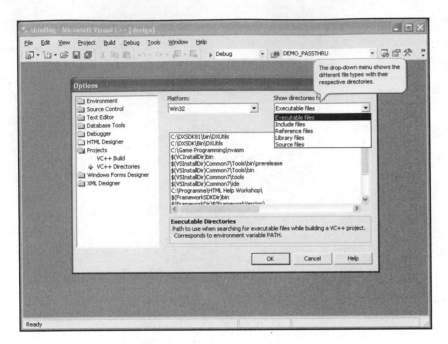

Figure I.18

Choose the type of file to reference

After you choose a type of file, the referenced directories will appear in the large area in the middle of the dialog box.

The include file directories are C:\dxsdk\include and C:\DXSDK9\Samples\C++\Common\Include. You should point your Visual C++ .NET IDE to these directories by clicking on the New button and then on the ellipsis button. A default dialog box will open, allowing you to choose a directory (see Figure I.19).

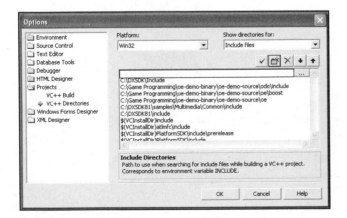

Figure I.19

Choose a directory

Now put this directory at the top of the list by using the arrow buttons.

After you have referenced the directories to the include files, choose the path to C:\dxsdk\lib to reference the library files correctly. Don't forget to bring them to the top of the list using the arrow buttons.

The proper path to the additional dependencies files should be listed in the Additional Dependencies field at Project, Properties, Linker, Input. In this entry field, you will need to name at least the following (see Figure I.20):

- d3dx9.lib
- d3dxof.lib
- d3d9.lib
- winmm.lib
- dxguid.lib

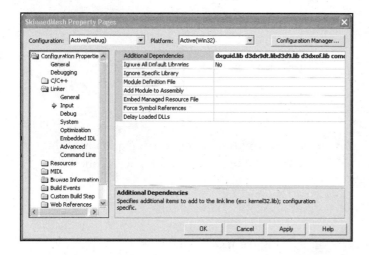

Figure I.20

Choose additional dependencies

If any problem occurs, check out the end of the "Setting Up Visual C++ 6.0" section for solutions to common problems. The solutions are the same for Visual C++ .NET.

Now let's compile our first project.

1. Fire up your Visual C++ .NET configured development environment.
2. Click on Open Solution.
3. Choose basics.sln.
4. Check whether you've configured the paths to the directories as described previously.
5. Choose Debug, Start Without Debugging.
6. When everything works correctly, basics.exe will start.

That's it. If something went wrong, reread the sections on installing the DirectX SDK and Visual C++ .NET, and study the provided documentation.

DirectX Shader Debugger

To debug vertex and pixel shaders, you need to install the DirectX shader debugger. This debugger is only provided for Visual C++ .NET. You can find it in the dialog box of the DirectX installation routine, as shown in Figure I.21.

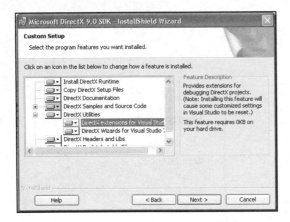

Figure I.21

Choose the shader debugger by clicking on DirectX Extensions for Visual Studio 7

By default, the shader debugger is not selected, so you have to choose it explicitly. If the computer only hosts a Visual C/C++ 6 installation, you don't get this choice at all. The dialog box will look like Figure I.22.

Please note that only Visual C++ .NET users can use the shader debugger.

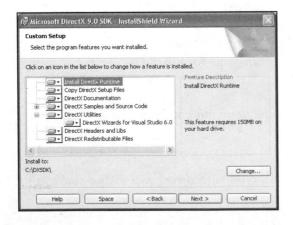

Figure I.22

Installable DirectX utilities under Visual C/C++ 6

Other Tools

Two plug-and-play compilers (provided by Intel and Codeplay) can be switched into the Visual C/C++ 6 or Visual C++ .NET IDE. They offer higher performance for game programmers than the compilers provided with these IDEs. However, I don't recommend that beginners use these compilers because they overcomplicate some things. You can find more information at http://www.intel.com/software/products/compilers and at http://www.codeplay.com. While on Intel's Web site, don't forget to check out VTune, a profiler that helps you to optimize your game. These and the Visual C++ compilers from Microsoft are the fundamental development tools that the majority of PC game programmers use nowadays.

Additional Resources

The CD-ROM provided with this book includes a directory called Movies. These movies interactively show you how to configure the default paths of Visual C/C++ 6 and Visual C++ .NET.

You should visit the Microsoft MSDN site for DirectX (http://msdn.microsoft.com/directx) at regular intervals, and also the mailing list at http://discuss.microsoft.com/SCRIPTS/ WA-MSD.EXE?S1=DIRECTXDEV. You can find daily news about the game developer community at http://www.gamedev.net or http://www.flipcode.com. I'll also provide additional information on http://www.direct3d.info.

PART ONE

DirectX Graphics: Don't Hurt Me

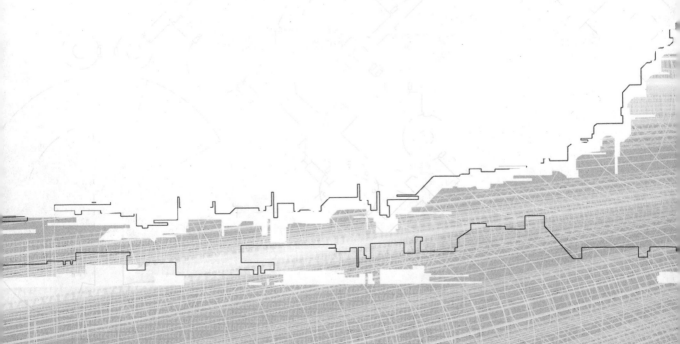

CHAPTER 1

THE HISTORY OF DIRECT3D/ DIRECTX GRAPHICS

This chapter covers the history of Direct3D and its functional development over time. It starts with DOS and PC history, and it discusses how three British students changed the world of 3D programming.

Before Windows, DOS was the most popular operating system for the PC. Games were programmed exclusively in DOS for many years. Game developers resisted developing for Windows because of its unacceptable graphics and audio performance at the time.

The direct access to hardware that DOS afforded came with its own complications, however. DOS games had to support the full range of video and audio hardware. This forced developers to write complex code to support dozens of different configurations just to provide consistent graphics and audio across all PCs.

In this chapter, you will learn about:

- The history and earlier versions of DirectX, leading up to the current version
- The introduction of point sprites and vertex and pixel shaders in DirectX 8
- The basics of 3D textures

DirectX 2.0

With the advent of DirectX in 1995, Microsoft provided within Windows the performance previously available only through DOS, without the complexity of supporting each vendor's particular hardware. Now every hardware vendor delivers its product with Windows drivers.

Direct3D, part of DirectX, appeared in 1996 in DirectX 2.0. Direct3D is designed to give access to the advanced graphics capabilities of 3D hardware accelerators, while promoting device independence and hardware abstraction by providing a common interface to the programmer. Code properly written for Direct3D will work on Direct3D devices now and in the future.

Let's dive a little bit deeper into history. In the early 1990s, many 3D engines for PCs were built in Great Britain. There was the well-known Renderware (http://www.renderware.com) and the BRender from Argonaut (http://www.argonaut.com), which was ported in 1994 to OS/2 and a small British company called RenderMorphics. RenderMorphics was founded in 1993 by Servan Keondjian, Kate Seekings, and Doug Rabson, and they produced a product called Reality Lab. Keondjian played piano in a band at night and programmed his 3D engine by day. Seekings subsequently upped her credentials with a quick master's degree in computer graphics at Middlesex University. It's interesting to note that her 3D rendering library, developed with input from Keondjian and Rabson, was submitted as a school project that she flunked for not following the assigned specs closely enough. Microsoft spotted the team at the first trade show they attended (SIGGRAPH 94), and RenderMorphics was acquired in February 1995.

After the acquisition of RenderMorphics, Microsoft integrated Reality Lab into its DirectX family of APIs (*Application Programming Interfaces*). The Immediate Mode component of Reality Lab absorbed the standard 3D Windows API of the time, 3-D-DDI, which was created by Michael Abrash, who later helped create the *Quake 1* engine at id Software.

DirectX 6/7

Until the advent of DirectX 8.0, Direct3D consisted of two distinct APIs: Retained Mode and Immediate Mode. At the time, the Immediate Mode API was difficult to use, but it was a flexible, low-level API that ran as efficiently as possible. Retained Mode was built on top of Immediate Mode and provided additional services, such as frame hierarchy and animation. Retained Mode was easier to learn and use than Immediate Mode, but programmers wanted the added performance and flexibility that Immediate Mode provided. Development of the Retained Mode API has been frozen with the release of DirectX 6.0.

The major changes between Direct3D Immediate Mode versions 6.0 and 7.0 affected the support of hardware-accelerated transformation and lighting and the reorganization of the lights, materials, and viewport objects, which now are set directly by calling the methods of IDirect3DDevice7. Direct3D 7 dropped the special interface used in Direct3D 6 to access textures. The IDirect3DDrawSurface7 interface also provided an easier way to manage the textures.

DirectX 8

The advent of the DirectX 8.0 SDK brought the biggest improvements in the history of Direct3D. Direct3D got a fundamentally new architecture with version 8.0. The initialization, allocation, and management of data were simplified by the integration of DirectDraw and Direct3D into one interface, called DirectX Graphics, which led to a smaller memory footprint and a simpler programming model. It is safe to say that these changes made DirectX 8 easier to use and more consistent than OpenGL for the first time.

Some of the new features in DirectX 8 included

- Point sprites (hardware-supported sprite objects)
- 3D volumetric textures (textures with three dimensions)
- An improved Direct3DX library (which provided many useful and highly optimized routines)
- N-patches (which add an algorithm and vertices to a model to get a higher-tessellated model)
- Vertex and pixel shaders (which interface to program the graphics processor directly)

Point Sprites

A new feature of DirectX 8 was the ability to use hardware sprites for a particle system to generate sparks, explosions, rain, snow, and so on. So-called *point sprites* are supported by their own programming interface to help you accomplish this.

3D Textures

With 3D volumetric textures, you can accomplish exact per-pixel lighting effects, point- and spot-light effects, and atmospheric effects.

Direct3DX Utility Library

DirectX 8 also enhanced the `Direct3DX` utility library, which was introduced in DirectX 7. This library provides helper functionality for:

- Enumerating device configurations
- Setting up a device
- Running full-screen or windowed mode uniformly
- Running resizing operations
- Calculating vector and matrix operations
- Simplifying image-file loading and texture creation
- Drawing simple shapes, sprites, and cube maps

With the release of DirectX 8, the utility library offered support for skinned meshes, multi-resolution level-of-detail (LOD) geometry, and higher-order surface data for .X files. The `D3DX` image file loader functions now support BMP, TGA, PNG, JPG, DIB, PPM, and DDS files. DirectX 8.0 also introduced helper methods to port OpenGL applications to DirectX Graphics, as well as the only higher-order surfaces that are used in current games— N-patches. These are used to tessellate models higher with the help of the graphics processor, which means you send in the data for a low-polygon model and it is tessellated (polygons are added) in the graphics card.

Vertex and Pixel Shaders

The big bang in DirectX 8.0 that changed the overall development process and the appearance of modern games was the introduction of vertex and pixel shaders. Whereas DirectX 8.0 supported the vertex and pixel shader standards vs_1_1 and ps_1_1, DirectX 8.1 added the pixel shader standards ps_1_2, ps_1_3, and ps_1_4. The last pixel shader standard, in particular, exposed the advanced capabilities of the ATI RADEON 8500–9200 cards, and ps_1_4 pointed the syntactical way for the upcoming pixel shader standards in DirectX 9.0, such as ps_2_0, ps_2_x, ps_2_a, and ps_3_0. (ps_2_0 pixel shaders are used in most examples in Chapter 9, "Shader Programming with the High-Level Shader Language.")

DirectX 9

The overall API has not changed much from DirectX 8.1 to DirectX 9.0. The new version introduced new and very much improved vertex shader and pixel shader standards, including the vs_2_0, vs_2_x, and vs_3_0 vertex shader standards and the ps_2_0, ps_2_x, and ps_3_0 pixel shader standards. Although these three pixel shader standards correspond to three hardware designs, in the past the ps_1_1 standard that was initially designed for the NVIDIA GeForce 3 was adopted by all major graphic card manufacturers, for example. There are now more equivalent software implementations for the vertex and pixel shader 2_0 and 3_0 versions, called vs_2_sw, vs_3_sw, ps_2_sw, and ps_3_sw.

To be able to write shaders in the most efficient way, an HLSL (*High-Level Shader Language*) was introduced in DirectX 9. This HLSL helps you write shaders faster and easier in a C-like syntax instead of the old assembly syntax. All shader examples in this book use HLSL.

To keep up with OpenGL, a scissor test and line anti-aliasing were introduced with DirectX 9.0. The scissor test is performed after the fragment color is computed but before alpha testing. It determines whether the screen coordinates of a value are within the scissor rectangle defined by four values, and it discards fragments that are lying outside this rectangle. Additionally, there is a new render state that supports the OpenGL-style sphere map texgen. (Texgen is a nickname for *automatic texture-coordinate generation.*) Two-sided stencil support was implemented to enable programmers to add shadow volumes to occlude geometry. (Please see the two-sided stencil example in Chapter 10, "More Advanced Shader Effects," which shows the usage of shadow volumes.)

One feature that should soon make it into DirectX 9.0 games is the ability to render from one pixel shader to multiple render targets. (This is called a G-buffer.) You can then blend up to four render targets in another pass. A feature that is comparable but less useful than the multiple render targets is the multi-element texture. The pixel shader can store up to four textures in one multi-element texture, and it can read them from there. Displacement maps were added as a new class of higher-order surfaces, but at the time of this writing, it looks like only the Matrox Parhelia and the ATI RADEON 9700 PRO are supporting them in hardware.

Two long-awaited features of DirectX 9.0 are the support of up to 24-bit color precision and the ability to change the gamma values depending on your monitor's gamma support. This gamma support uses very simple filters that are applied to data as it leaves a surface and before it is rendered on the screen. The so-called gamma controls don't change the contents of the surface itself.

The DirectX 9.0 SDK provides a programming framework that has been used in versions since DirectX 6 and is used in all examples in this book. Starting with DirectX 8.0, this framework is called *common files*. You will find these files in the C:\DXSDK9\Samples\C++\Common directory.

The common files give you the direct access you need and encapsulate the details of setting up Direct3D, which is great for your learning curve. You can concentrate on the essentials while still being able to see everything on the lowest level. This framework gives you a common ground on which you can implement your individual features. As a beginner, you can avoid a lot of basic mistakes with the fast and well-tested framework code, allowing you to concentrate on learning. Intermediate and professional programmers might use the framework as a good testing platform, and professional programmers might write their own framework that better suits their needs by looking at the DirectX Graphics common files source code.

Summary

This chapter showed the long way the DirectX API progressed from its beginning in DirectX 2 to the first really superior incarnation in DirectX 8. Although not many changes to the API interface were made between DirectX 8 and 9, the shader capabilities of modern cards were exposed in several new shader versions. Having a stable API with evolving shader capabilities is the future of DirectX, which means users of the API don't have to learn a new API each year—which makes learning DirectX 9 a long-term investment.

CHAPTER 2

Overview of HAL and COM

This chapter gives you a rough overview of why the HAL (*Hardware Abstraction Layer*) exists, how it is used, why Microsoft used the COM (*Component Object Model*) interface to encapsulate the DirectX code, and how it is accessed from within the application.

Both techniques enable Direct3D to provide maximum speed on different hardware, with a common interface and backward compatibility in mind. The introduction of both techniques addressed the following demands:

- The API needs consistency to be viable.
- If hardware doesn't support some features of Direct3D, there must be fallback mechanisms.
- Interface innovation must be possible with the lowest possible learning curve for programmers.
- All games developed in early versions of DirectX must be guaranteed to run in future versions of DirectX.

Hardware Abstraction Layer

Along with the graphics card driver provided by the hardware vendor, Direct3D provides a very thin software layer around your graphics card. HAL makes up one part of this thin layer.

If you've ever played a game driven by DirectX, you've seen HAL. Every game includes a drop-down menu that gives you the option to pick a device or driver. Depending on the graphics hardware, in DirectX 7.0 games you can choose a HAL, TnLHAL (*Transformation and Lighting HAL*), RGB, or a reference rasterizer driver from this dialog box. In DirectX 8.0/8.1/9.0 games, you might choose between a HAL, a pluggable software device, or a reference rasterizer; or the application might select one automatically. You will find this device selection box, called the Direct3D Settings dialog box, in every Direct3D example program delivered with the DirectX 9.0 SDK (see Figure 2.1). Just start an example and press F2.

Even if a HAL is available, the game will usually switch features on and off, depending on the features the HAL is able to provide. The process works like this:

1. The game checks the HAL's capabilities.
2. The game switches features on or off as appropriate.
3. If features are switched off, a fallback method might be implemented, which might emulate the feature. This usually leads to reduced image quality.

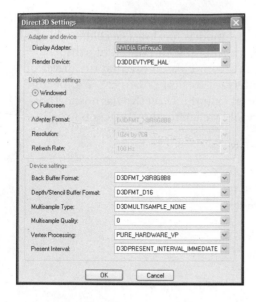

Figure 2.1

Device selection in the Direct3D Settings dialog box

In the past, a HEL (*Hardware Emulation Layer*) could emulate certain features in software. However, HELs have not been provided since DirectX 8.0. If you want your games to run on ancient hardware, it would make sense to use DirectX 7.0 with its HEL (which is called an RGB device).

Like its predecessor, DirectX 9 provides an interface to use a HEL written by a software developer. This type of HEL is now called a *pluggable software device*. As far as I know, nobody has done that so far, which supports the fact that DirectX 8.0/8.1/9.0 games are very dependent on what the hardware is able to provide.

The overview in Figure 2.2 shows the relationships among the Direct3D API, HAL, and GDI (*Graphics Device Interface*) APIs.

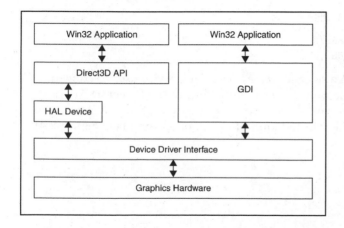

Figure 2.2

The relationship between DDI, HAL, and GDI

As you can see, Direct3D uses HAL to access the graphics hardware through the DDI (*Device Driver Interface*). HAL is the primary device type, and it supports hardware-accelerated rasterization and both hardware and software vertex processing. If your computer's display adapter supports Direct3D, HAL will exist on your computer. Please note that the driver of your graphics card has to support at least the DDI interface version of DirectX 7 to be able to run DirectX 9.0 applications. To check the DDI level, run the DirectX Diagnostic Tool and examine the saved text file. You can access this tool by clicking the DxDiag button in the DirectX Properties dialog box (see Figure 2.3).

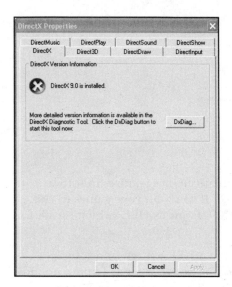

Figure 2.3

The DirectX Properties dialog box contains the DxDiag button.

Therefore, a graphics card that will run DirectX 9.0 games must have a driver that is at least compatible with DirectX 7.

HAL is also able to emulate vertex processing in software completely or in parts. The following flags control vertex-processing behavior for HAL and reference devices:

- D3DCREATE_SOFTWARE_VERTEXPROCESSING
- D3DCREATE_HARDWARE_VERTEXPROCESSING
- D3DCREATE_MIXED_VERTEXPROCESSING

Additionally, HAL is able to switch on a so-called *pure device*. This device uses a reduced number of state checks and is available only if specific functions of the Direct3D API are not used. It is a bit faster than the non-pure hardware vertex-processing device. The examples in the DirectX 9.0 SDK display the selected kind of vertex processing (see Figure 2.4).

Figure 2.4

HAL shows its method of vertex processing.

HAL has four different methods of vertex processing. These include

- SW VP (*Software Vertex Processing*)
- Mixed VP (*Mixed Vertex Processing*)
- HW VP (*Hardware Vertex Processing*)
- Pure VP (*Pure Vertex Processing*)

The behaviors of the pluggable software device and the reference device must be identical to that of the HAL device. Application code to work with the HAL device should work with the software or reference devices without modification. In fact, the reference device is the reference implementation that sets the standards, and the software device and HAL have to be measured at its functionality.

You must check the capabilities for each device, of course. The reference rasterizer supports all of the Direct3D 9.0 features, whereas a pluggable software device might not even support texturing.

If there's no hardware accelerator in a user's machine, attempting to create a HAL device will fail.

Pluggable Software Devices

It is possible to write a hardware emulation layer (now called a pluggable software device) that runs even if the user's computer hardware doesn't provide all of the 3D operations required to play the game. Nowadays, the software/game manufacturer must develop the hardware emulation device, whereas in former incarnations of the DirectX run-time environment, Microsoft provided it as the RGB device. Software devices are loaded by the application and registered with the Direct3D object. The function to register a pluggable software device is `IDirect3D9::RegisterSoftwareDevice`. The DirectX 9 DDK (*Device Driver Kit*) provides more information on how to program a pluggable software device.

Reference Rasterizer

The reference device is supplied only with the installation of the SDK. When an application requests the reference device on a machine on which the SDK is not installed, a NULL reference device is supplied. This NULL reference device does nothing, and all rendering results in a black screen.

The reference rasterizer supports all Direct3D features. You should only use it to test features that your card doesn't support. This device is optimized for accuracy, not for speed. Direct3D does not enumerate it by default. The DirectX SDK installer will set the `EnumReference` value in the HKEY_LOCAL_MACHINE\SOFTWARE\Microsoft\Direct3D\Drivers registry key to a non-zero `DWORD` value. Hardware, software, and the reference device cannot render to 8-bit render-target surfaces.

Controlling Devices

You can configure all controlling devices in the DirectX Properties dialog box, which you will find in the DirectX option in your computer's Control Panel (see Figure 2.5).

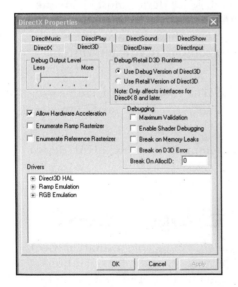

Figure 2.5

Configure all controlling devices in the DirectX Properties dialog box.

Note the Enable Shader Debugging check box in the dialog box, which might be useful later. Additionally, the Debug/Retail D3D Runtime section lets you choose between the debug and retail builds, which might be useful if you want to jump back and forth between the debug and retail builds to measure retail performance.

With this HAL/pluggable software driver/reference driver approach, Microsoft guarantees a consistent API on which you can fall back if specialized 3D hardware is absent. That's great, isn't it? OK, what about the other two demands specified in the beginning of this chapter: How does Direct3D handle version changes? Are they easy to learn, and are they handled so that they're transparent to the programmer? This is where the COM interface design of the DirectX SDK helps.

COM

If you've used other Microsoft APIs, there's a good chance that you're an old COM freak and you can skip over this section. The rest of you must invest a small learning effort, but you will get a good return on your investment by learning to use the COM interface, which has been used by DirectX since its inception.

In COM terms, a software component is simply a chunk of code that provides services through interfaces, and an interface is a group of related methods. A COM component is normally a .DLL (*Dynamic Link Library*) file that can be accessed in a consistent and defined way. Period. It doesn't sound like something you could write a thousand-page book about, does it?

COM has many advantages. I'd like to highlight three that I think are important for Direct3D programmers like us.

- COM interfaces can never change.
- COM is language-independent.
- You can only access a COM component's methods, never its data.

C++ and many other languages are source-based; therefore, they do not have a versioning strategy. COM was designed to be a binary-based programming model. COM interfaces can never be modified in any way.

For an example of why COM is necessary, consider this scenario. Non-COM DLL A is produced by software company C, whereas non-COM DLL B is produced by software company D. DLLs A and B might be compatible as long as one of the companies does not change the interface of its DLL. However, if company D changes the interface of DLL B, it will be incompatible with DLL A unless company C made the same changes to the interface of DLL A.

This scenario cannot occur with a COM DLL. When a COM object is changed, a completely new interface with a new name is added to the DLL. Therefore, every COM DLL has to support the interfaces since its release. If both companies in the aforementioned scenario used a COM DLL, a change in the interface of DLL A would lead to the addition of a new interface to A. Because A would then have two interfaces, DLL B would still be able to connect to the old interface.

This is exactly how DirectX implements its interfaces. Direct3D 9.0 or DirectX Graphics support the following interfaces:

- IDirect3D
- IDirect3D2
- IDirect3D3

- IDirect3D7
- IDirect3D8
- IDirect3D9

Table 2.1 shows the interfaces that were added to the corresponding versions of DirectX.

Table 2.1 DirectX Interfaces and Versions

DirectX Version	Interface
DirectX 2	IDirect3D
DirectX 3	IDirect3D2
DirectX 6	IDirect3D3
DirectX 7	IDirect3D7
DirectX 8	IDirect3D8
DirectX 9	IDirect3D9

The newest DirectX version at the time of this writing therefore supports IDirect3D through IDirect3D9. This means that older games that use IDirect3D2 can still run on current hardware because this interface is still supported in the newest DirectX version. In other words, if a company produces a game that is compatible with Windows NT 4.0, which only supports the IDirect3D2 interface of the DirectX 3.0 SDK, the company will have to use the IDirect3D2 interface for everything to work. The IDirect3D2 interface has been implemented in every Direct3D DLL since the advent of DirectX 3.0, and it will be implemented in any future versions. The aforementioned game will run on every platform that runs at least the DirectX 3.0 run-time.

COM is language-independent. Whether your favorite language is Visual Basic, Pascal, or something else, you can access COM objects with your favorite compiler package. Delphi users are especially fond of this feature, but Visual Basic gurus have been provided with a fine implementation of their own in all DirectX SDKs since the arrival of DirectX 7.0. Language independence matters when parts of the game—for example, the world editor— are written in Delphi and other parts (perhaps different places in the world) are written with the Visual C++ compiler.

COM can only be accessed via methods. You cannot access data objects directly. This is a good object-oriented design. As you will see in the next chapter, you can't call a method directly. Instead, you have to use double indirection through a virtual function table, called the *v-table* or *VTBL*. These v-tables are also the key to a language-independent interface. With these advantages, COM helps you get language-independent, guaranteed access to the legacy and current Direct3D interfaces. Now get access!

Summary

This chapter introduced the ideas behind HAL and COM. HAL is the main device driver of the graphics card. If HAL does not support a feature, there must be a fallback mechanism that gives the user a comparable visual experience. Alternatively, the game should run with a pluggable software device written by the game's manufacturer.

COM provides a versioning strategy, which guarantees that all games developed in earlier versions of DirectX are guaranteed to run in future versions. It helps you encapsulate data and provides a consistent interface to different languages.

CHAPTER 3

Programming Conventions

This chapter introduces the programming conventions that are used throughout the book. In this chapter, you will learn:

- How to access a COM object
- The naming convention (Hungarian notation) used in the DirectX SDK and throughout this book
- Useful debugging tips for Direct3D applications
- How and why to use return codes

Accessing COM Objects

When you call a method in a COM component, you have to use a v-table. When you're deciding whether to develop your code in C or C++, you need to consider a few issues. I'll start with an example. Suppose you want to set a light in a scene of your world-class 3D game. With C, you would use the following line of code:

```
hr = m_pd3dDevice->lpVtbl->SetLight(m_pd3dDevice, 0, &light );
```

You call the COM interface methods by passing the this pointer, called lpdd, as the first parameter of the method and by referencing the interface's method by using it as a pointer to the interface v-table, which is called lpVtbl here (see Figure 3.1).

Although there are macros that help make C programmers' lives easier (for example, in ddraw.h), C++ is much simpler for using COM objects. COM objects and C++ objects are binary-compatible so that compilers handle COM interfaces and C++ abstract classes in the same way. The in-memory layout in C++ of a class instance that inherits from a pure virtual base class (a class with only methods that are virtual and equal to zero) has the same memory representation as a COM interface. Therefore, in C++ the lpVtbl pointer is implicitly dereferenced, and the parameter is implicitly passed. Thus, the previously described call for C would look like this in C++:

```
hr = m_pd3dDevice->SetLight(0, &light );
```

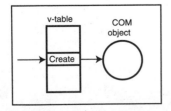

Figure 3.1

The v-table

In general, most DirectX calls in C++ look like this:

```
lpinterface->methodname
```

As you saw in the Introduction to this book, you have to include a number of import libraries to compile a DirectX program.

- d3dx9.lib
- d3dxof.lib
- d3d9.lib
- winmm.lib
- dxguid.lib

Most of these libraries are import libraries that provide the interface names to the linker of your development environment.

Now that you understand that COM objects are collections of interfaces, which are simply method pointers and, more specifically, v-tables, you need to see an example of how to work with COM. There are three things of which you should be aware.

- Direct3D run-time COM objects and DLLs must be registered to and loaded by Windows. The DirectX installer will do this for you.
- You must include the previously mentioned libraries in your Windows project so that the wrapper methods you call are linked. (For more information, see the "Setting Up Visual C++ 6.0" and "Setting Up Visual C++ .NET" sections in the Introduction to this book.)
- You must include the proper include files in your source file and in the include path entry forms of your IDE (for example, Visual C++) so the compiler can see header information, prototypes, and data types for DirectX Graphics. (Again, for more information see the "Setting Up Visual C++ 6.0" and "Setting Up Visual C++ .NET" sections in the Introduction.)

The data type for an `IDirect3D9` interface pointer is

```
LPDIRECT3D9 g_pD3D = NULL;
```

To create an `IDirect3D8` COM object and retrieve an interface pointer for it, you simply need to use the `Direct3DCreate9()` method.

```
m_pD3D = Direct3DCreate9( D3D_SDK_VERSION );
```

The only parameter passed to `Direct3DCreate9()` should be `D3D_SDK_VERSION`. This informs Direct3D that the correct header files are being used. This value is incremented whenever a header or other change requires applications to be rebuilt. If the version does not match, `Direct3DCreate9()` will fail.

The retrieved interface pointer gives you access to the interface of `IDirect3D9`. You might call a method in that interface, for example:

```
// Create the device
```

```
hr = m_pD3D->CreateDevice( m_d3dSettings.AdapterOrdinal(),
                           pDeviceInfo->DevType, m_hWndFocus,
                           behaviorFlags,
                           &m_d3dpp, &m_pd3dDevice );
```

That's it for COM. You will use COM throughout this book. If you're wondering about the strange and cryptic parameter names, read on for an explanation.

Naming Conventions

I use a simple variable tagging scheme that has its roots in the so-called Hungarian notation used by Microsoft for its own development projects. The name came from its inventor, Charles Simonyi, a now-legendary Microsoft programmer who happened to be Hungarian. It's helpful to supply variables in the right format to help others read your code, but it can be confusing to people who haven't seen the Hungarian convention.

Table 3.1 shows the prefixes I use and their respective types. You might occasionally come across other prefixes, but this table shows the common ones. Hungarian notation simply consists of prefixing variables with their types.

Although the variable-naming convention is to prefix the variables with their types, the naming convention for *methods* just clarifies readability and the purpose of the method. In all methods, the first letters of subnames are capitalized; an underscore is illegal.

```
HRESULT ConfirmDevice( D3DCAPS9* pCaps, DWORD dwBehavior, D3DFORMAT adapterFormat,
                                        D3DFORMAT backBufferFormat )
```

```
HRESULT EnumerateDevices( D3DAdapterInfo* pAdapterInfo, CArrayList* pAdapterFormatList )
```

As you can see, parameters for *functions* follow the same naming conventions as normal variables. The parameter pCaps points to a D3DCAPS9 structure. The third and fourth parameters of ConfirmDevice() use the same type to describe a surface format. You can tell that the two parameters of EnumerateDevices() are not provided by Direct3D because they are not capitalized.

Types and *constants* begin with an uppercase letter, but you can use underscores in the names, for example:

```
#define D3DPRESENT_BACK_BUFFERS_MAX    3L
```

You must prefix all C++ *classes* with a capital C, and you must capitalize the first name of each subname, for example:

```
class CD3DMesh
{
    public:
};
```

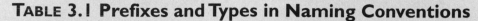

TABLE 3.1 Prefixes and Types in Naming Conventions

Prefix	Type	Example
w	WORD	wSpeed
dw	DWORD	dwHitList
f	FLOAT	fSpeed
d	DOUBLE	dDirection
p	Pointer	pArray
v	D3DVECTOR3	vLight
l	LONG	lPitch
s	String	sQuestion
sz	String terminated by 0	szQuestion
h	Handle	hResult
I	COM interface	IDirect3D
m_p	Member class pointer	m_pFloorVertices
m_f	Member class float	m_fStartTimeKey
c	Constant	cText
b	BOOL	bCheck

The CD3DMesh class handles the loading of .X files. It's implemented in d3dfile.h of the common files. Why don't you try it? Take a look at a typical Direct3D application class:

```
class CMyD3DApplication : public CD3DApplication
{
    CD3DFont*           m_pFont;
    CUSTOMVERTEX        m_QuadVertices[4];
    LPDIRECT3DTEXTURE9  m_pCustomNormalMap;
    LPDIRECT3DTEXTURE9  m_pFileBasedNormalMap;
    D3DXVECTOR3         m_vLight;
    BOOL                m_bUseFileBasedTexture;
    BOOL                m_bShowNormalMap;
    HRESULT CreateFileBasedNormalMap();
```

```
    HRESULT CreateCustomNormalMap();
    HRESULT ConfirmDevice( D3DCAPS9*, DWORD, D3DFORMAT );
    LRESULT MsgProc( HWND hWnd, UINT uMsg, WPARAM wParam, LPARAM lParam );
protected:
    HRESULT OneTimeSceneInit();
    HRESULT InitDeviceObjects();
    HRESULT RestoreDeviceObjects();
    HRESULT InvalidateDeviceObjects();
    HRESULT DeleteDeviceObjects();
    HRESULT Render();
    HRESULT FrameMove();
    HRESULT FinalCleanup();
public:
    CMyD3DApplication();
};
```

There is a member class pointer on a font class at the beginning of the code. There is also another member in the class, which uses a custom vertex structure for a quad array of vertices. Two member class pointers are pointing to Direct3D texture objects. A light vector is stored in D3DXVECTOR3. If a file-based texture is used, m_bUseFileBasedTexture will indicate this. If the user likes to see the normal map, the m_bShowNormalMap switch has to be set to TRUE. As you can see in this class (taken from a file from the common files directory), the Hungarian naming convention is used for all files used in the DirectX SDK.

Debugging DirectX

Debugging DirectX applications can be challenging. Following are a few tips to get you started.

- Define STRICT at the beginning of your *.cpp file before including windows.h. This leads to strict type checking, which will help you find bugs.
- Use the DXDiag utility from the DirectX SDK to report your bugs, but be sure that you know exactly what is on your system.
- The DirectX Control Panel allows you to set the debug output level from 0 to 5. To access the Control Panel, select Start, Settings, Control Panel, DirectX, Direct3D. On the same tab, you can switch from the retail to debug run-time version or vice versa.
- The D3DX library is a static library. To help you debug, there's a debug-only dynamic library of D3DX. To use it, link to d3dx9d.lib, which is an import library corresponding to the D3DX9D.DLL.
- Using a memory manager can reduce memory allocation and de-allocation problems. Visual C++ provides a memory manager called CRT. On the Internet, you can also find memory managers that are more suitable for game development. Just do a search at http://www.flipcode.com or http://www.gamedev.net. BoundsChecker (http://www.compuware.com) is a commercial solution.

- You can debug vertex and pixel shaders with a plug-in for Visual .NET. I will cover this debugger in more detail in the shader section of this book.

- If you want to measure the performance of your application with something like Intel's VTune, you should download the release symbol files from the Microsoft Web site. Usually you will use the default debug symbol files.

- The OutputDebugString() function is a useful debugging aid. It outputs debug messages in the debug window of your IDE while your program is running.

- Using a simple log file class is helpful in larger applications to show problems while the program is initializing. You can find a couple of very useful log file classes on the Internet. The example in Chapter 12, "Using *.md3 Files," uses such a log file class.

- It is quite common to use a debug texture to see whether problems with texture alignment or filtering are occurring. Usually you try to paint such a texture with a different color or you use some text so you can see how it is aligned. Figure 3.2 provides an example.

- The Visual C++ GUI debugger can debug full-screen exclusive applications only when you are using a multi-monitor system or remote debugging. Using a multi-monitor system is pretty common nowadays, and remote debugging is explained in the DirectX SDK help file. If you don't have a multi-monitor system or the ability to debug remotely, it's usually wise to build the application in a windowed mode, like the one provided by the framework that is implemented in the common files.

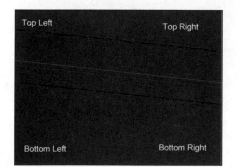

Figure 3.2

Using a texture to test the layout

Return Codes

A return code is the value returned when the method is complete. It indicates the success or failure of a call and, if applicable, the reason why the call failed. Checking the return codes is simplified by the SUCCEEDED() and FAILED() macros provided with the DirectX 9.0 SDK. They take an HRESULT as an argument and return whether it indicates a success code or a failure code. Don't try to check HRESULT against S_OK; not every method returns S_OK if it succeeds. A function might return S_FALSE to indicate that it did nothing because there was no need to do anything.

Because every DirectX method returns an HRESULT, you need to structure your code to check for and handle all potential errors. This work is frustrating at first, but it soon becomes second nature. Having a program that is more resistant to crashing is a good reward for the work.

Summary

This chapter should have provided you with some general knowledge of Direct3D programming. The rules and the conventions will help you to build examples consistently. Such rule files are quite common in game development teams. This might be a starting point to build up one on your own.

CHAPTER 4

3D FUNDAMENTALS, GOURAUD SHADING, AND TEXTURE-MAPPING BASICS

This chapter will give you a brief introduction to the most important 3D concepts, show you the difference between Gouraud and flat shading, and provide you with an overview of how a texture is mapped to an object. In this chapter, you'll learn how to:

- Work with vertices and orientation
- Work with faces and polygons
- Use Gouraud shading
- Put into practice the basics of texture mapping

3D Fundamentals

The Direct3D engine uses a left-handed coordinate system by default. Every positive axis (x, y, or z) is pointing away from the viewer. To make things a little bit clearer, Figure 4.1 shows the world coordinate system.

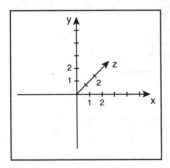

Figure 4.1

The Direct3D coordinate system

The positive y-axis is up, the positive x-axis is to the right, and the positive z-axis is into the screen, away from the user. The OpenGL coordinate system uses a positive z-axis that points out of the screen. This is called a right-handed coordinate system. The Direct3DX utility library has built-in functions that can help you port an application that uses the OpenGL coordinate system to the Direct3D left-handed system. As you will see in Chapter 12, "Using *.md3 Files," *Quake 3* and its .md3 file format use their own coordinate system, where the positive z-axis points up and the positive y-axis points out of the screen. However, most games use the coordinate systems used by OpenGL or Direct3D. Because we are using floating-point coordinate values, you don't lose any precision by using numerically small units. Now on to vertices. Let's face a square, as shown in Figure 4.2.

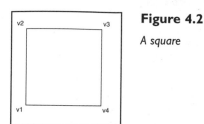

Figure 4.2

A square

The square uses four vertices, v1 through v4. A *vertex* defines the point of intersection of one or more lines; these are straight lines as far as we are concerned. What's the point of all this business about coordinate systems and vertices? The point is that Direct3D needs a way to place these primitives in a scene. You need something to measure distance and space, so go ahead and place your square in the coordinate system (see Figure 4.3).

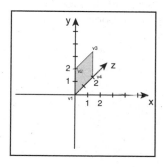

Figure 4.3

A square in the Direct3D coordinate system

To define a vertex in 3D space, you must specify three coordinate values: x, y, and z. The origin of your coordinate system is 0, 0, 0. The position of the vertices of the square could be described as

> v1 (0, 0, 0)
> v2 (0, 2, 0)
> v3 (0, 2, 2)
> v4 (0, 0, 2)

And there you are. You can define the location of a vertex by specifying a vector from the origin to another point in 3D space. This is the so-called *free vector*, or *zero vector*, used by game programmers. Its initial point is assumed to be the origin, and only the final point is described (see Figure 4.4).

Vectors are one of the most important concepts in 3D games. They are mathematical entities that describe a direction and a magnitude (which can be used for velocity, for example). Vectors are usually denoted by a bold-faced letter, such as **a**. Thus you could say the vector **v** = (1, 0, 1). The first value denotes units in the x direction, the second value denotes units in the y direction, and the third value denotes units in the z direction.

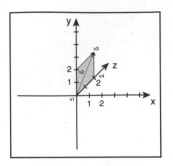

Figure 4.4

A free or zero vector describing the third vertex of a square

Vectors are not only used to define the position of the vertices, they are also used to define a direction. For example, the vector vUp (0, 1, 0) defines the up direction (see Figure 4.5). Note that the actual length of a vector is not important when the vector is used to define a direction or a vertex. However, the length of a vector is important sometimes, such as in the case of a normal or a light vector. You will deal with these kinds of vectors later in the book.

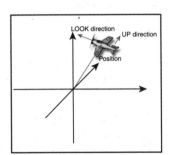

Figure 4.5

Orientation of an aircraft

As you might expect, Direct3D provides two default structures for defining vectors. You'll find the enhanced D3DXVECTOR3 version of Direct3DX--the utility library—in d3dx9math.h, and the default D3DVECTOR version in d3d9types.h, which handles all the math routines you need when you use vectors. Vector v3 would be defined as

```
D3DVECTOR v3( 0, 2, 2);    // or ...
D3DXVECTOR3 v3(0, 2, 2);   // used by the utility library
```

Understanding Vertices

A free, or zero, vector is often used to describe the position of a vertex. Nevertheless, a vertex consists of much more data than the position. If the vertex has a color, then there is a variable for the color. If it has a normal, then there is a variable that holds the vertex normal vector. If a texture is used, the vertex has variables to hold the texture coordinates. A vertex structure might look like this:

```
Struct Vertex
{
    D3DVECTOR3 vPosition;
    DWORD dwDiffuse;          // diffuse  vertex color
    D3DVECTOR3 vNormal;       // vertex normal
    FLOAT u, v;               // texture coordinates of vertex
}
```

I will explain the idea behind the terms *vertex normal* and *texture coordinates* in the next chapter. It is important to note that a vertex is usually a structure that holds more data than the position. The Direct3D run-time is used to receive data this way. All vertices are stored in a vertex buffer that allows your example application to allocate and access memory that's usually only accessible by the driver. I will discuss vertex buffers in more detail in Chapter 5, "The Basics."

Working with Orientation

Measuring and organizing space in a virtual world is important for every game, but you also need a way to define the orientation of objects.

You might describe the orientation of an object by using at least four vectors—LOOK, UP, RIGHT, and POSITION. The POSITION vector defines the position of the object. The LOOK vector defines the way the object is pointing. The RIGHT vector defines where the right side of the object is pointing. The UP vector is necessary if the object is rotated around the LOOK vector. The UP vector tells you when the object is considered up or down.

You can rotate the object around the vectors. If you want to change the pitch of an aircraft, you might rotate it around the RIGHT vector. If you want to roll the aircraft, you might rotate it around the LOOK vector. If you want to change the direction the aircraft is facing (the yaw), you might rotate it around the UP vector. If you want to move the object in the direction the LOOK vector is facing, you might change the POSITION vector.

Understanding Faces

Any 3D object consists of faces, as shown in Figure 4.6.

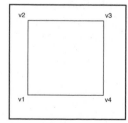

Figure 4.6

The face of a square

To create a smooth-looking object, you need hundreds or even thousands of faces or surfaces, as shown in Figure 4.7.

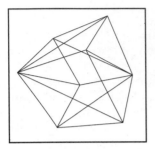

Figure 4.7

A cube constructed of triangles

Every model and 3D world is broken down into points, lines, and triangles, the only primitives Direct3D is able to render. If you design your shapes using polygons with four or more vertices to reduce the number of faces, Direct3D will divide every face into triangles. To get optimal performance, you should make every object easily divisible into triangles. Therefore, you should usually use triangles to construct your object. An object consisting of several triangles like the cube shown in Figure 4.7 is called a *mesh*.

Figure 4.8 shows a more complex mesh, which consists of nine faces from ten triangles.

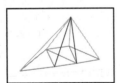

Figure 4.8

Faces of a more complex object

One final point you need to be aware of is that Direct3D can cull back faces. The Backface Culling feature removes all triangles that are facing away from the viewer or camera. These are by default the vertices that are grouped counter-clockwise. On average, half of your game world triangles will be facing away from the camera at any given time, so this helps to reduce rendering time. Depending on what is going to be rendered, you can switch off Backface Culling with the D3DCULL_NONE flag. Backface Culling uses the cross-product of two sides of a triangle to calculate a vector that is perpendicular to the plane that is formed by the two sides. This vector is the face normal, and the direction of this normal determines whether the triangle faces frontward or backward. Because the Direct3D API always uses the same vertex order to calculate the cross-product, you know whether a triangle's vertices are "wound" clockwise or counter-clockwise. You can read more about the cross-product in Appendix C, "Mathematics Primer."

Understanding Polygons

A polygon can be defined in either 2D or 3D space; in our case, we will refer to polygons as n-sided closed figures defined by at least three vertices. The simplest polygon is a triangle. Direct3D uses triangles to compose most polygons because all three vertices in a triangle are guaranteed to be co-planar; rendering non-planar vertices would be inefficient.

Understanding Normals

Normals are perpendicular vectors that can be used to define the direction a face is pointing or the visible side of a face (see Figure 4.9).

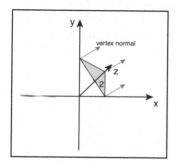

Figure 4.9

A triangle's vertex normals

A *vertex normal* is often perpendicular to a face, and it usually sits upon the vertex as one unit long. The other type of normal is a *face normal*. It is usually perpendicular to a face and sits in the middle of the face. You don't have to worry about this kind of normal because Direct3D calculates them automatically. Vertex normals are important for lighting calculations, as you will see in Chapter 9, "Shader Programming with the High-Level Shader Language." Furthermore, face and vertex normals are also important for the shading mode. Whereas face normals are used for flat shading, for example, vertex normals are used for Gouraud shading.

Understanding Normals and Gouraud Shading

The vertex normal vector is used in Gouraud shading mode (the default shading mode since the advent of Direct3D 6.0) to control lighting and to make some texturing effects. So what's a shading mode? Shading is the process of performing lighting computations and determining pixel colors from them. These pixel colors are later drawn on the object. (More technically, shading is the way the rasterizer "shades" pixels.) Flat shading lights per polygon or face, and Gouraud shading lights per vertex (see Figure 4.10).

Figure 4.10

A teapot as a wireframe model, a flat shaded model, and a Gouraud shaded model

As you can see in Figure 4.10, the user might see the faces of the teapot with flat shading, but he can get the illusion of a round teapot by using the Gouraud model. How does that work? Let's build a simpler example using the triangle from Figure 4.9. It will appear as a flat triangle when it's shaded with Gouraud shading because all of the vertex normals point the same way, so all the points in the faces between the vertices get the same lighting. The triangle would look the same with flat shading because flat shading shades per face, which means that the face normal sitting in the middle of the triangle is used to calculate the lighting. This should lead to a similar result as when you use the vertex normals. Now change the normals to be non-perpendicular, as shown in Figure 4.11.

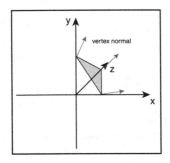

Figure 4.11

A triangle with non-perpendicular vertex normals

Using flat shading, nothing would change because the face normal in the middle of the triangle is still perpendicular. Using Gouraud shading, the face appears rounded at the corners because the direction of the vertex normals varies from vertex to vertex, making the geometry look as if it's rounded when in fact the lighting artificially creates this effect.

Gouraud shading mode is the default mode in Direct3D, so you don't have to do anything extra to set it. So...no code.

Texture-Mapping Basics

The 3D objects in the games of the '80s and early '90s tended to have a shiny plastic look. These solid-colored objects looked rather bland and uninteresting. They lacked the types of details that give 3D objects realistic visual complexity, such as bullet holes, irregularities, rusted parts, cracks, fingerprints, screws that hold steel plates, and so on. These markings are created with textures. With texturing, you can provide complex visual detail using an image instead of geometry. At its most basic, a texture is simply a bitmap of pixel colors that you can produce with the help of Adobe Photoshop or a similar program. In this context, texture refers to a special kind of image that you can map onto a face or multiple faces (see Figure 4.12).

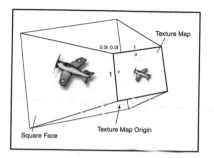

Figure 4.12

Mapping a texture onto

a square

In Figure 4.12, you can see how a texture map is mapped onto a square. In this case the texture map has to be scaled because the square is bigger than the texture map. In order to map texels (texture elements) onto primitives, Direct3D requires a uniform address range for all texels in a texture. Therefore, it uses a generic addressing scheme in which all texel addresses are in the range of 0.0 to 1.0, inclusive. The texture space coordinates are represented by u for the horizontal direction and v for the vertical direction. The bottom-right corner is (1.0f, 1.0f) and the upper-left corner is (0.0f, 0.0f), regardless of the actual size of the texture—even if the texture is wider than it is tall. By assigning texture coordinates outside that range, you can create certain special texturing effects. You'll read more about this concept in Chapter 7, "Texture-Mapping Fundamentals."

Texture coordinates are assigned to the vertices of a mesh. Therefore, the coordinates can be included directly as vertex components, as shown in the vertex structure in the "Understanding Vertices" section.

The square in Figure 4.12 has the same aspect ratio (the ratio of width to height) as the texture. In this case the texture coordinates (0.0, 0.0), (1.0, 0.0), (1.0, 1.0), and (0.0, 1.0) are assigned to the primitve's vertices, causing Direct3D to stretch the texture over the entire square. That might work like this:

```
cvVertices [0] = {0.0f, 0.0f, 0.5f, 1.0f, 0.0f, 0.0f};    // x, y, z, rhw, tu, tv
cvVertices [1] = {1.0f, 0.0f, 0.5f, 1.0f, 1.0f, 0.0f};
cvVertices [2] = {1.0f, 1.0f, 0.5f, 1.0f, 1.0f, 1.0f};
cvVertices [3] = {0.0f, 1.0f, 0.5f, 1.0f, 0.0f, 1.0f};
```

This is a typical vertex structure. It consists of the position vector, an RHW (*Reciprocal of Homogeneous W*) value, and the tu and tv coordinates of the texture. (I will explain RHW in more detail in Chapter 5.) For now I want to concentrate on the last two variables—the texture coordinates. The value 1.0f stretches the textures over the entire object. If you choose to apply the texture to a rectangle that's half as wide instead, you have to decide how to apply it. You can apply the entire texture to the rectangle, which requires you to change the texture's aspect ratio; otherwise, the texture will be squashed so that it fits the rectangle. The second option is to apply the left or right half of the texture to the rectangle. For this option, you have to assign the texture coordinates (0.0, 0.0), (0.5, 0.0), (0.5, 1.0), and (0.0, 1.0) to the vertices.

You can assign parts of a texture to a primitive by using texture coodinates. If you want to texture a triangle, it could work something like Figure 4.13.

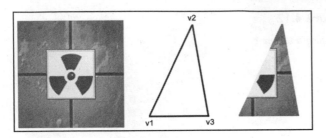

Figure 4.13

Mapping parts of a texture onto a triangle

That's the easy part. Now take a look at a more advanced level of texture mapping. Examine the texture of an .md2 file from *Quake 2*, shown in Figure 4.14.

Figure 4.14

The texture of an .md2 model

Figure 4.15 shows the whole knight as an .md2 model.

Figure 4.15

A textured .md2 model

As you can see, different parts of the texture are mapped on different polygons on this model. You can use a specialized program to paint the texture and set the texture coordinates on the model. MilkShape 3D is a wonderful tool to develop such models. You can find it at http://www.swissquake.ch/chumbalum-soft.

Summary

I hope you got the big picture on texture mapping. And now you're ready to rock…let's get your feet wet with DirectX (try to rap that).

CHAPTER 5

THE BASICS

This chapter will provide you with your first DirectX 9.0 programming experience. It will introduce the common files framework and show you how a vertex structure is built, how the vertex buffer is populated, and how the geometry stored in the vertex buffer is displayed. Additionally, you will learn about texture mapping by mapping a texture on a simple quad. I'll start with the features and then move on to how to use the example programs in this chapter.

All example programs have the following features:

- They work in windowed and full-screen modes. Press Alt+Enter to switch between these modes.
- Pressing F2 brings up a Direct3D Settings dialog box that allows you to change many device-specific features.
- They offer a step-by-step mode in case an animation is occurring, which allows the user to step through the animation by pressing Enter and then the spacebar.
- They shut down when the Esc key is pressed.

Compiling the Examples

To get your feet wet, I want to go through the necessary steps to compile the first example, named basic, which displays a rainbow-like color spectrum (see Figure 5.1).

All the files you need are located in the \chapter 5\basic directory on the CD-ROM. You might want to copy the basic directory into the default DirectX directory that stores the DirectX SDK examples. (On my computer, the path is C:\DXSDK\Samples\C++\Direct3D.) After you do so, the path to the basic directory should be C:\DXSDK\Samples\C++\ Direct3D\Basic.

The directory should contain the following files (see Figure 5.2).

- **basic.cpp**. The main file
- **winmain.rc**. The resource file (menu, accelerator, icon information, and so on)
- **resource.h**. The header of winmain.rc
- **basic.dsw**. The "workspace" file needed for Visual C/C++ 6.0
- **basic.dsp**. The "project" file needed for Visual C/C++ 6.0
- **basic.sln**. The "solution" file needed for Visual C++ .NET
- **basic.vcproj**. The "project" file needed for Visual C++ .NET
- **readme.txt**. An explanation of the example

Figure 5.1

Vertex colors

Figure 5.2

The source directory displaying the files you need for the first example

basic.cpp	9 KB
Basic.dsp	5 KB
basic.dsw	1 KB
basic.sln	1 KB
basic.vcproj	5 KB
readme.txt	1 KB
resource.h	2 KB
winMain.rc	7 KB

Visual C and C++ 6.0 use the basic.dsw and basic.dsp files to remember the paths and options you chose for the application. The main file is the "workspace" file. Its name corresponds to an option in Visual C/C++ 6.0 that you can find by selecting File, Open Workspace. You can open a workspace by choosing this option or by clicking on the *.dsw file.

Visual C++ .NET uses the basic.sln and basic.vcproj files to remember the paths and options you chose for the application. The main file is the "solution" file. Its name corresponds to an option in Visual C++ .NET that you can find by selecting File, Open Solution. You can open a solution by choosing this option or by clicking on the *.sln file.

To compile this example program successfully, you must link it with the following lib files:

- d3dx9dt.lib
- d3dxof.lib
- d3d9.lib

- winmm.lib
- dxguid.lib
- comctl32.lib

Most of these lib files are COM wrappers, as described in Chapter 4. The release version of the Direct3DX static link library is called d3dx9.lib. There is also a *.dll version of the debug build called d3dx9dt.dll in the system32 directory. To use it, simply link it to the d3dx9dt.lib COM wrapper.

All of the example programs in this book use the common files framework provided by the DirectX 9 SDK. The following pages will present this framework.

The DirectX Graphics Common Architecture

The common files have been well accepted by the game programming community since they first appeared in the beta versions of the DirectX 6.0 SDK. The common files framework helps developers get up to speed because:

- It helps to avoid how-tos for Direct3D in general, so the focus is on the real stuff.
- It has a common and tested foundation that helps reduce the debug time.
- All of the Direct3D samples in the DirectX SDK use it, so the learning curve is shorter.
- Its window mode makes debugging easier.
- Self-developed production code can be based on the common files, so knowing how to use them is always a winning solution.

A high-level view of the common files shows 17 *.cpp files in C:\DXSDK\Samples\C++\ Common\Src. These files encapsulate the basic functionality you need to start programming a Direct3D application. The most important d3dapp.cpp file contains the CD3DApplication class. It provides seven functions that you can override.

- `virtual HRESULT OneTimeSceneInit() { return S_OK; }`
- `virtual HRESULT InitDeviceObjects() { return S_OK; }`
- `virtual HRESULT RestoreDeviceObjects() { return S_OK; }`
- `virtual HRESULT DeleteDeviceObjects() { return S_OK; }`
- `virtual HRESULT Render() { return S_OK; }`
- `virtual HRESULT FrameMove( FLOAT ) { return S_OK; }`
- `virtual HRESULT FinalCleanup() { return S_OK; }`

To create an application based on this framework code, all you have to do is create a new project and new implementations of these functions in the main source file. This is also demonstrated in all Direct3D examples in the DirectX SDK.

These seven functions can be called the *public interface* of the common files framework (see Figure 5.3).

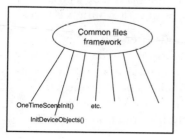

Figure 5.3

The public interface of the common files framework

The Basic Example

The most important thing is the base class of the application. It is called CD3DApplication.

```
class CMyD3DApplication : public CD3DApplication
{
   LPDIRECT3DVERTEXBUFFER9 m_pVB; // Buffer to hold vertices
   DWORD m_dwSizeofVertices;
protected:
    HRESULT OneTimeSceneInit();
    HRESULT InitDeviceObjects();
    HRESULT RestoreDeviceObjects();
    HRESULT InvalidateDeviceObjects();
    HRESULT DeleteDeviceObjects();
    HRESULT FinalCleanup();
    HRESULT Render();
    HRESULT FrameMove();
    HRESULT ConfirmDevice (D3DCAPS9* pCaps,
                           DWORD dwBehavior,
                           D3DFORMAT adapterFormat,
                           D3DFORMAT backBufferFormat );
public:
    CMyD3DApplication();
};
```

The first two variables hold the vertex buffer and the size of the vertices. In all of the upcoming examples, I'll use one of the top features of Direct3D to store vertices—vertex buffers. Normally the driver copies the data from a Direct3D buffer, which is held by the application in its own buffer. With vertex buffers, the data is originally copied in the driver buffer. Therefore, you might save the CPU cycles that are needed to copy from the

Direct3D app buffer to the driver buffer by storing the data in the memory that the graphics cards can access, which is a big performance enhancement. In other words, managing a vertex buffer means allowing the application to allocate and access memory that's usually only accessible by the driver. This occurs via the Lock() or Unlock() functions.

Especially with the common graphics hardware that supports transformation and lighting in hardware, vertex buffers give you a huge performance boost. This support will be a basic feature of all upcoming graphics cards, so starting the basic example with vertex buffers is a must.

Now back to the application class. There are a number of methods after the vertex buffer variables. One of them, which is executed before all other methods, is called ConfirmDevice(). This method checks the capabilities of the graphics hardware. It's used in every sample in this book and in the SDK. You can specify capabilities here to allow the framework to switch to the reference rasterizer or to vertex software processing in case some of the needed capabilities are not supported. Additionally, this function provides a way to implement fallback paths for unsupported features.

The following code checks to see whether vertex shader version 1.1 is supported by the graphics hardware.

```
HRESULT CMyD3DApplication::ConfirmDevice( D3DCAPS9* pCaps, DWORD dwBehavior,
                                          D3DFORMAT adapterFormat,
                                          D3DFORMAT backBufferFormat )
{
    // check hardware support for vertex shaders
    if( (dwBehavior & D3DCREATE_HARDWARE_VERTEXPROCESSING ) ||
        (dwBehavior & D3DCREATE_MIXED_VERTEXPROCESSING ) )
      {
          // if there is no support choose software vertex shaders
          if( pCaps->VertexShaderVersion < D3DVS_VERSION(1,1) )
                return E_FAIL;
      }

    return S_OK;
}
```

If hardware or mixed vertex processing is not supported by the graphics hardware, the hardware also will not support a programmable vertex shader. In that case, the framework will switch on software vertex processing, and the vertex shader will be executed in a software emulation mode.

After ConfirmDevice() is called, the framework will execute the following functions to start the application.

1. ConfirmDevice()

2. OneTimeSceneInit()

3. InitDeviceObjects()

4. RestoreDeviceObjects()

When the application is running, the following functions are executed in a loop:

- FrameMove()
- Render()

This is the main loop of every framework application. While the program is running, the user might want to resize the window. In that case, the framework would call

- InvalidateDeviceObjects()
- RestoreDeviceObjects()

If the user wanted to change the device (HAL or REF) by pressing F2 or clicking on File, Change Device, the framework would call

- InvalidateDeviceObjects()
- DeleteDeviceObjects()
- InitDeviceObjects()
- RestoreDeviceObjects()

If the user quits the application, the framework will call

- InvalidateDeviceObjects()
- DeleteDeviceObjects()
- FinalCleanup()

There are matching functional pairs. InvalidateDeviceObjects() destroys what RestoreDeviceObjects() has built up, and DeleteDeviceObjects() destroys what InitDeviceObjects() has built up. The FinalCleanup() function destroys what OneTimeSceneInit() has built up. The idea is to give every functional pair its own tasks. The OneTimeSceneInit()/FinalCleanup() pair is called at the beginning and the end of the lifecycle of the game. Both functions are used to load or delete data that is device-independent. A good candidate might be geometry data. OneTimeSceneInit() is invoked once per application execution cycle for all things that need a permanent initialization. You can load geometry data, set up calculated values, and so on. Basically, any one-time resource allocation should be performed here.

The target of the InitDeviceObjects()/ DeleteDeviceObjects() pair is data that is device-dependent, like the name implies. If the already-loaded data has to be changed when the device changes, it should be loaded here. The following examples, named Basic2, Basic3, and so on, will load, recreate, or destroy their vertex buffers, index buffers, and textures in these functions.

NOTE

The word *device* is used here in the context of a "device driver," meaning a piece of software that controls some hardware or software device in the system. However, "device" in most other cases refers to the graphics card.

The InvalidateDeviceObjects()/RestoreDeviceObjects() pair has to react to changes in the window size. For example, you might place code that handles the projection matrix here. Additionally, the following examples will set most of the render states in RestoreDeviceObjects(). There is one thing you should note: InvalidateDeviceObjects() is called when the window is resized or the device is changed by the user, whereas the response to this call, RestoreDeviceObjects(), is called when the application starts, the window is resized, or the device has changed. So InvalidateDeviceObjects() is not called before RestoreDeviceObjects() when your game starts. In all other cases, these methods build a functional pair.

The Render() method is self-explanatory. It is called once per frame and is the entry point for 3D rendering. It can set up render states, clear the viewport, and render a scene. In an animated program, the FrameMove() method is used to hold the entire animation code, including updating matrices, texture coordinates, object coordinates, and other time-varying activities. FinalCleanup(), the last framework function, destroys the allocated memory for the geometry data, deletes the file objects, and so on.

To give you a deeper understanding of the inner workings of every common files method, I'll now go through basic.cpp from beginning to end.

The ConfirmDevice(), OneTimeSceneInit(), and InitDeviceObjects() Functions

Because this example does not require any special device capabilities, the ConfirmDevice() function is empty. This example only uses four vertices to display the colored window client area. To make it simpler to handle, these vertices will be loaded in the RestoreDeviceObjects() method along with the vertex buffer creation. Therefore, the OneTimeSceneInit() function can be empty as well, although normally you might use it to load the geometry data of models that are part of a scene. Furthermore, in this example you do not need to initialize device-related things such as font classes or textures. For this reason, InitDeviceObjects() can stay empty as well.

```
HRESULT CMyD3DApplication::ConfirmDevice( D3DCAPS9* pCaps, DWORD dwBehavior,
                                          D3DFORMAT adapterFormat,
                                          D3DFORMAT backBufferFormat )

{
    return S_OK;
}


HRESULT CMyD3DApplication::OneTimeSceneInit()
{
    return S_OK;
}
```

```
HRESULT CMyD3DApplication::InitDeviceObjects()
{
    return S_OK;
}
```

Please note that all of these functions return an S_OK HRESULT value to show you that everything went well.

The RestoreDeviceObjects() Method

The RestoreDeviceObjects() method is called after InitDeviceObjects() when the application starts. When the user resizes the application window, this method is called after a call to InvalidateDeviceObjects(). Most of the real stuff in the first example happens here.

```
HRESULT CMyD3DApplication::RestoreDeviceObjects()
{
    // fill the vertex buffer with the data for a quad
    VERTEX Vertices[] =
    {
        {  0.0f,  0.0f, 0.5f, 1.0f, 0x00ff0000, }, // x, y, z, rhw, color
        {(float)m_d3dsdBackBuffer.Width,  0.0f, 0.5f, 1.0f, 0x00ff0000, },
        {(float)m_d3dsdBackBuffer.Width, (float)m_d3dsdBackBuffer.Height, 0.5f,
                1.0f, 0x0000ff00, },
        {0.0f, (float)m_d3dsdBackBuffer.Height, 0.5f, 1.0f, 0x0000ffff, },
    };

    m_dwSizeofVertices = sizeof(Vertices);

    // sixth parameter is new in DX9
    if( FAILED( m_pd3dDevice->CreateVertexBuffer(m_dwSizeofVertices,
                                            D3DUSAGE_WRITEONLY, FVF,
                                            D3DPOOL_MANAGED, &m_pVB, NULL ) ) )
                    return E_FAIL;

    VERTEX* pVertices;
    // DX9: the third parameter has changed from BYTE** to VOID**
    if( FAILED( m_pVB->Lock( 0, m_dwSizeofVertices, (VOID**)&pVertices, 0 ) ) )
        return E_FAIL;
    memcpy( pVertices, Vertices, m_dwSizeofVertices);
    m_pVB->Unlock();

    return S_OK;
}
```

The vertex structure shows the layout of the data that is stored in the vertex buffer later.

```
// A structure for our custom vertex type
struct VERTEX
{
    FLOAT x, y, z, rhw; // The transformed position for the vertex
    DWORD color;        // The vertex color
};
```

```
// Fixed-Function Vertex structure
// In DX8: #define D3DFVF_CUSTOMVERTEX (D3DFVF_XYZRHW|D3DFVF_DIFFUSE)
const DWORD FVF = (D3DFVF_XYZRHW | D3DFVF_DIFFUSE);
```

Four structures are filled with position data, an RHW value, and a color value in RestoreDeviceObjects() (see Figure 5.4).

```
    // fill the vertex buffer with the data for a quad
    VERTEX Vertices[] =
    {
      {  0.0f,  0.0f, 0.5f, 1.0f, 0xffff0000, }, // x, y, z, rhw, color
      { (float)m_d3dsdBackBuffer.Width,  0.0f, 0.5f, 1.0f, 0xffff0000, },
      { (float)m_d3dsdBackBuffer.Width, (float)m_d3dsdBackBuffer.Height, 0.5f,
            1.0f, 0xff00ff00, },
      {  0.0f, (float)m_d3dsdBackBuffer.Height, 0.5f, 1.0f, 0xff00ffff, },
    };
```

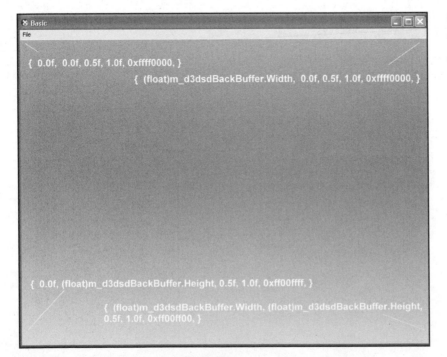

Figure 5.4

Vertex layout of the basic example

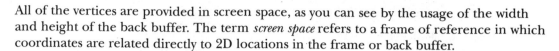

All of the vertices are provided in screen space, as you can see by the usage of the width and height of the back buffer. The term *screen space* refers to a frame of reference in which coordinates are related directly to 2D locations in the frame or back buffer.

Because it is not necessary to transform the vertices in any way, you do not need another frame of reference, such as a world coordinate system or a model coordinate system. This is the most efficient way to handle these vertices in Direct3D.

No transformation from world, view, or projection space happens, and the first vertex (as the first member of the vertex array) lies at the top-left of the window's client area. The vertex's x, y coordinates are (0.0f, 0.0f). The second member of the vertex array describes the second vertex, which is positioned in the top-right corner. The third member describes the third vertex, which lies in the bottom-right corner, and the fourth vertex array member describes the fourth vertex, which lies in the bottom-left corner. Every vertex has a z-value of 0.5f. Changing this value should not lead to any differences because this example doesn't use a z-buffer, as shown in the `CMyD3DApplication` constructor with:

```
m_d3dEnumeration.AppUsesDepthBuffer = FALSE
```

The fourth entry in each line in the aforementioned vertex array is called an *RHW value*. It shows the Direct3D pipeline in which the vertices are already transformed in homogenous space, which is the case here, because they are in screen space. (You'll learn more about this in Chapter 6, "First Steps to Animation.") The last entry is a color value. As you can see from the use of 0x, hexadecimal values are used here. This is quite handy because the four color values (ARGB) are each represented by a pair of hexadecimal values. The first `ff` pair stands for alpha, the second pair stands for red, and so on. Therefore, the top-left and top-right corner vertexes should both be red. Most paint programs, such as Adobe Photoshop or Jasc Paint Shop Pro, offer a color selection dialog that shows you the 0x values of RGB (see Figure 5.5).

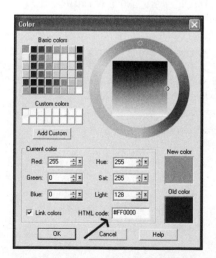

Figure 5.5

The Color Picker in Jasc Paint Shop Pro

The vertex buffer that should hold these values is created with the following code:

```
if( FAILED( m_pd3dDevice->CreateVertexBuffer(
                                            // size of vertex
                                            m_dwSizeofVertices,
                                            // buffer usage
                                            D3DUSAGE_WRITEONLY,
                                            // description of vertex buffer
                                            FVF,
                                            // memory pool
                                            D3DPOOL_MANAGED,
                                            // pointer to vertex buffer
                                            &m_pVB, NULL ) ) )
            return E_FAIL;
```

Creating the right kind of vertex buffer is important for the performance of the application. The CreateVertexBuffer() function helps you do just that. m_dwSizeofVertices holds the size of the vertices, FVF holds the vertex description, and m_pVB holds the returned pointer to the interface of the vertex buffer. Whereas the size of vertices is self-explanatory, you must take a closer look at the vertex description. This parameter is a flag that describes the vertex format used for this set of primitives. In other words, it tells Direct3D something about the structure that holds the vertex information. It's defined at the beginning of the basic.cpp file with the following command:

```
// Fixed-Function Vertex structure
// In DX8: #define D3DFVF_CUSTOMVERTEX (D3DFVF_XYZRHW|D3DFVF_DIFFUSE)
const DWORD FVF = (D3DFVF_XYZRHW | D3DFVF_DIFFUSE);
```

These flags tell the Direct3D engine how the data is organized in the vertex buffer. The syntax has changed from DirectX 8 to DirectX 9, as shown in the comments for this piece of source. These changes are easy to handle. Instead of a #define, a const DWORD variable now holds the vertex flags. The d3d9types.h header file declares these flags to explicitly describe a vertex format and also provides helper macros that act as common combinations of such flags. Each of the drawing functions (DrawPrimitive*()) or CreateVertexBuffer() functions of IDirect3DDevice9 accepts a combination of these flags and uses them to determine how a vertex buffer is structured and how to render primitives. Basically, these flags tell the system which vertex components—position, normal, colors, and the number of texture coordinates— your application uses. In other words, the presence or absence of a particular vertex format flag communicates to the system

> **NOTE**
>
> Defining the vertex flags this way is only useful when you are using the fixed-function pipeline. A program that uses vertex shaders does not need these flags because the vertex declaration for vertex shaders has a similar task. I will demonstrate this concept in one of the upcoming example programs.

which vertex component fields are present in memory and which you've omitted. By using only the needed vertex components, your application can conserve memory and minimize the processing bandwidth required to render your 3D world.

D3DFVF_XYZRHW tells your system that your game engine has already transformed the vertices so Direct3D doesn't have to do it. Therefore, Direct3D doesn't transform your vertices with the world, view, or projection matrices. The vertices have to be delivered in screen space in this example program.

Unlike D3DFVF_XYZRHW, the D3DFVF_XYZ flag tells your system that your game has not transformed vertices and calls for help from Direct3D to do so.

D3DFVF_DIFFUSE indicates that the vertex format includes a diffuse color component. The use of D3DFVF_SPECULAR indicates that the vertex format includes a specular color component.

> **NOTE**
>
> It's a different story when you are using vertex shaders instead of the fixed-function pipeline. In that case, the vertices have to be delivered in HCLIP space, which means in a range of -1.0f..1.0f. See Chapter 6 for examples of this.

Mapping of the vertex input registers is fixed while you are using the fixed-function pipeline, so specific vertex elements such as position or normals must be placed in specified registers located in the vertex input memory. Therefore, you have to format all the vertex structures in a specific order, shown here.

1. Position of the transformed/untransformed vertex—float x, y, and z coordinates
2. RHW as the reciprocal of the homogenous w coordinate (only for already transformed vertices)
3. Blending weight values 1–5 floats
4. The vertex normal as float x, y, and z normal coordinates
5. The vertex point size
6. The diffuse color as diffuse RGBA
7. The specular color as specular RGBA
8. Texture coordinate sets 1–8 as float u and v coordinates

For example, your vertex structure could look like this:

```
typedef struct
{
     FLOAT x,y,z;        // position
     DWORD diffuse;      // diffuse color
     FLOAT u,v;          // one pair of texture coordinates
} MYVERTEX;
```

You have to define the flags for this vertex structure as follows:

```
const DWORD D3DFVF_CUSTOMVERTEX = (D3DFVF_XYZ | D3DFVF_DIFFUSE | D3DFVF_TEX1)
```

Another sample could be

```
struct LineVertex
{
  FLOAT x, y, z;          // position
};
const DWORD LINE_VERTEX = ( D3DFVF_XYZ )
```

A more complex example might be

```
typedef struct SObjVertex
{
    FLOAT x, y, z;          // position
    FLOAT nx, ny, nz;       // normal
    DWORD diffuse;          // diffuse color
    DWORD specular;         // specular color
    FLOAT tu, tv;           // first pair of texture coordinates
    FLOAT tu2, tv2, tw2;    // second pair of texture coordinates
    FLOAT tu3, tv3;         // third pair of texture coordinates
    FLOAT tu4, tv4;         // fourth pair of texture coordinates
} SObjVertex;
...
const DWORD gSObjVertexFVF = (D3DFVF_XYZ | D3DFVF_DIFFUSE | D3DFVF_SPECULAR |
                             D3DFVF_NORMAL | D3DFVF_TEX4 |
                             D3DFVF_TEXCOORDSIZE2(0) | D3DFVF_TEXCOORDSIZE3(1) |
                             D3DFVF_TEXCOORDSIZE2(2) | D3DFVF_TEXCOORDSIZE2(3));
```

The D3DFVF_TEX4 flag instructs the Direct3D engine that four texture coordinates will be used. The D3DFVF_TEXCOORDSIZE* flags specify the number of texture coordinate values—two or three—and their order. For example, the second texture uses three texture coordinates consisting of three floating-point values. This might be useful in the case of a cube or volume texture.

Another important concept is the management of resources by Direct3D. With the advent of Direct3D 8.0, a unified resource manager was introduced for textures and geometry. This resource manager is used for mipmaps, volume maps, cube maps, and vertex and index buffers.

The resource manager is indicated by the D3DPOOL_MANAGED flag in the CreateVertexBuffer() method call. This flag defines the memory class that holds the vertex buffers. Now, you might ask why we use different memory classes. There's memory that is located in your graphics card (for example, 128-MB DDRAM II), and there's memory that is located in your system memory (for example, 1024-MB RAM). Direct3D can manage your application memory requirements in a way that uses the right memory for the right task, but you have to give it a sign indicating what you would like to do with the resource. Only resources with the memory pool D3DPOOL_MANAGED are managed by the resource manager.

Choosing a way to manage the resources (or defining the memory class that holds the resources) is called *choosing a pool* in Direct3D. There are four different kinds of pools in DirectX 9.

```
typedef enum _D3DPOOL {
    D3DPOOL_DEFAULT = 0,            // AGP, graphics card memory
    D3DPOOL_MANAGED = 1,           // AGP, graphics card memory && copy in sys memory
    D3DPOOL_SYSTEMMEM = 2,         // system memory, re-creatable
    D3DPOOL_SCRATCH = 3,           // system memory, not re-creatable
    D3DPOOL_FORCE_DWORD = 0x7fffffff
} D3DPOOL;
```

If you specify a scratch pool, the resource is stored in system memory and cannot be recreated when a device is lost. This occurs, for example, when you switch between windowed and full-screen modes or when you change the resolution in one of these modes. These resources cannot be accessed by the Direct3D device nor set as textures or render targets. However, they can always be created, locked, and copied. This memory pool was introduced to DirectX 9 because the CreateImageSurface() function was removed from the API. D3DPOOL_SCRATCH, together with CreateOffscreenPlainSurface(), will return a surface that has identical characteristics to a surface created by the former CreateImageSurface(). Therefore, it is used mainly for the creation of image surfaces.

If you specify a system pool, the resource is stored in system memory. The advantage of this pool is that the resources do not need to be recreated after the device is lost. Additionally, you can lock and update resources in this pool. Therefore, this pool is recommended for data that undergoes frequent software processing.

When you specify a managed pool, the resource is stored in AGP/graphics card memory, and a copy is stored in the system memory. The advantage to this kind of pool compared to the system pool is that the resource is lying in the AGP/graphics card memory, and a copy of the memory needs to be made only if changes are made in the system memory.

When you specify a default pool, the resource is typically stored in graphics card or AGP memory. This is the most accessible memory to the rendering device. You must use it when the vertex and index buffers have to be updated frequently, because the system or managed pools would be too slow with their ongoing system-to-AGP/graphics card copies. You must allocate all of the default pool resources prior to creating the managed resources. Not doing so can result

NOTE

AGP (*Accelerated Graphics Port*) is a PCI-based interface that was designed specifically for the demands of 3D graphics applications. The 32-bit AGP channel directly links the graphics controller to the main memory. Although the channel runs at only 66 MHz, it supports data transmission during both the rising and falling ends of the clock cycle, yielding an effective speed of 133 MHz.

in significant performance loss. The disadvantage of a default pool is that it has to be managed by the application.

Every pool has its own tasks. You might say that dynamic vertex and index buffers can be updated more efficiently in a default pool. This might be also the pool of choice for textures that do not have to be changed by the application. On the other hand, textures that *do* have to be changed frequently can only be accessed via a scratch, system, or managed pool.

If performance does not matter, you are always on the safe side when you use a managed pool. This is the easiest and best way to map memory to devices. The resources are copied automatically to device-accessible memory as needed. Managed resources are backed by system memory and do not need to be recreated when a device is lost. Rule of thumb: Use managed unless you know a better way. It works for any class of driver and must be used with Unified Memory Architecture mainboards. In these boards, graphics card memory is located in the same hardware as the system memory or RAM.

This is why I chose the managed pool for the vertex buffer in the CreateVertexBuffer() function we discussed. The fifth parameter of this function returns a pointer to the vertex buffer. In DirectX 9, the newly introduced sixth parameter is reserved and should be set to NULL. In other words, it has no underlying functionality today, but it might in the next DirectX release.

After you create the vertex buffer and lock it using Lock(), you can fill it with memcpy().

```
VERTEX* pVertices;
// DX9: the third parameter has changed from BYTE** to VOID**
if( FAILED( m_pVB->Lock( 0, m_dwSizeofVertices, (VOID**)&pVertices, 0 ) ) )
        return E_FAIL;
memcpy( pVertices, Vertices, m_dwSizeofVertices);
m_pVB->Unlock();
```

Locking a resource means granting CPU access to its storage. In addition to granting processor access, any other operations involving that resource are serialized for the duration of a lock. Only a single lock for a resource is allowed, even for non-overlapping regions, and no ongoing accelerator operations on a surface are allowed while there is an outstanding lock operation on that surface. The syntax of the Lock() function is

```
HRESULT Lock(
    UINT OffsetToLock,      // offset into the vertex buffer
    UINT SizeToLock,        // == vertices * SizeOfVertex
    VOID **ppbData,         // pointer to memory buffer
    DWORD Flags             // hints on the usage of the vertex buffer
);
```

The first parameter lets the programmer provide an offset for the vertex buffer. Together with the second parameter, this allows you to put several models into one vertex buffer and lock only the area where the geometry of a specific model resides, for example.

The size is specified by the number of vertices multiplied by the size of one vertex. The third parameter returns the pointer to a memory buffer. The last parameter lets the programmer provide the following hints on how the vertex buffer will be used:

- D3DLOCK_DISCARD. The application overwrites every location in the vertex buffer.
- D3DLOCK_READONLY. The application does not write to the vertex buffer.
- D3DLOCK_NOOVERWRITE. The data in the vertex buffer is not overwritten.
- D3DLOCK_NOSYSLOCK. Enables the possibility of display mode changes during lock().
- D3DLOCK_NO_DIRTY_UPDATE. There is no dirty region to the locked vertex buffer.

The D3DLOCK_DISCARD and D3DLOCK_NOOVERWRITE flags are valid only on buffers that are updated regularly (indicated by the D3DUSAGE_DYNAMIC flag), which is not the case here. The D3DLOCK_READONLY flag is only useful when the application will not write to the buffer. This enables resources stored in non-native formats to save the recompression step when unlocking. Therefore, it makes sense to provide 0 as the last parameter here because the program can't provide a useful flag that might provide the driver with a hint to optimize the vertex buffer.

After the vertex buffer is filled with the vertices' data, it's unlocked with a call to m_pVB->Unlock();. This is the last step in initializing and restoring the device-dependent objects. Up until now, the game has gone through the whole initialization process via ConfirmDevice(), OneTimeSceneInit(), InitDeviceObjects(), and RestoreDeviceObjects(). The next function call enters into the ongoing rendering loop, which consists of the FrameMove() and Render() function calls.

The FrameMove() Function

Because you're not animating a scene, you don't need to include any code inside FrameMove(). A lot of things will happen here in the upcoming examples.

```
HRESULT CMyD3DApplication::FrameMove()
{
    return S_OK;
}
```

The Render() Function

The Render() method is called once per frame and is the entry point for 3D rendering. It can set up render states, clear the render target, and render a scene.

```
HRESULT CMyD3DApplication::Render()
{
    // Begin the scene
    if( SUCCEEDED( m_pd3dDevice->BeginScene() ) )
    {
        // In DX8: m_pd3dDevice->SetVertexShader( D3DFVF_CUSTOMVERTEX );
```

```
          // Passing an FVF to IDirect3DDevice9::SetFVF specifies a legacy FVF with stream 0.
          m_pd3dDevice->SetFVF(FVF ); // new in DX9
          // DX8: only three parameters. In DX9 the third parameter is new
          m_pd3dDevice->SetStreamSource( 0, m_pVB, 0, sizeof(VERTEX) );
          m_pd3dDevice->DrawPrimitive( D3DPT_TRIANGLEFAN, 0, 2 );
          // End the scene.
          m_pd3dDevice->EndScene();
      }
      return S_OK;
}
```

Render() calls the BeginScene()/EndScene() pair. The first method is called before you perform the rendering; the second is called after rendering. BeginScene() causes the system to
check its internal data structures and the availability and validity of rendering surfaces. It
also sets an internal flag to signal that a scene is in progress. Attempts to call rendering
methods when a scene is not in progress fail, returning D3DERR_SCENE_NOT_IN_SCENE. When
your rendering is complete, you need to call EndScene(), which clears the internal flag that
indicates that a scene is in progress, flushes the cached data, and makes sure the rendering
surfaces are okay.

Direct3D can assemble each vertex that is
fed into the processing portion of the
Direct3D pipeline from one or more data
streams. For example, one data stream can
hold the positions and normals, while a
second holds color values and a third holds
texture coordinates. The SetStreamSource()
function delivers this functionality. The
declaration of this method is

> **NOTE**
> You should omit multiple
> BeginScene()/EndScene() **pairs in one
> application because scene-capture
> graphic chips such as the PowerVR
> Kyro and Kyro II (http://www.
> powervr.com) will not work with
> multiple pairs.**

```
HRESULT SetStreamSource(
    UINT StreamNumber,
    IDirect3DVertexBuffer9 *pStreamData,
    UINT OffsetInBytes,
    UINT Stride
);
```

The first parameter defines the data stream. Depending on the underlying hardware, there
can be up to 16 different data streams. DirectX 7-compatible hardware will only support
one stream, but newer hardware supports up to 16.

The second parameter provides the stream data. Usually this is a pointer to the vertex
buffer, which is m_pVB here.

When you use a fixed-function pipeline like I have done here, the stride of the vertex
stream must match the vertex size computed from the FVF. In this example, that means that
you must provide the size of the VERTEX structure in the fourth parameter. Therefore, when
you use the fixed-function pipeline you cannot use one vertex buffer for several streams.

The Fur demo in the DirectX 9 SDK shows a nice example of how to use streams with vertex shaders. Following is some pseudocode that demonstrates how the demo uses streams:

```
All passes: stream 0: Position, Normal, Diffuse vertex color
if (finpass)
    fin pass stream 1: texture coordinates for fins
if (shellpass)
    shells pass stream 2: texture coordinates for shells
```

In every pass, SetStreamSource() sets stream 0 to use the position, normal, and diffuse color values. You can choose these values if you add another pass in which SetStreamSource() sets stream 1 to use a texture coordinate for the fins. Additionally, you can let SetStreamSource() set stream 2 to use a texture coordinate for the shells in a second pass. Switching on and off the fin and shell pass makes the whole system scalable. For example, if the object with fur is far away, it wouldn't make sense to show its fur because it wouldn't be visible from that distance.

NOTE

When you are using vertex shaders with a vertex declaration, the stride should be greater than or equal to the stream size computed from the declaration, which makes it possible to use one vertex buffer for several streams.

Please note that the new version of SetStreamSource() in DirectX 9 adds the ability to set an offset, similar to the Lock() function that you used to lock the vertex buffer. This makes it easier to have several game objects reside in one vertex buffer.

Another change in DirectX 9 is the introduction of the SetFVF() function, which is used only for the fixed-function pipeline. If you are using a vertex shader, you must use SetVertexShader() instead. You aren't using vertex shaders here, so you should use the SetFVF() function. The only parameter to this function is the vertex format.

```
m_pd3dDevice->SetFVF(FVF ); // new in DX9
```

The most important function call in Render() goes out to:

```
m_pd3dDevice->DrawPrimitive( D3DPT_TRIANGLEFAN, 0, 2 );
```

DrawPrimitive() has changed quite a bit since version 7.0. It renders non-indexed, geometric primitives of the specified type from the current set of data input streams—in this case, from the one and only data stream declared by SetStreamSource(). Its syntax is

```
HRESULT DrawPrimitive(
    D3DPRIMITIVETYPE PrimitiveType,
    UINT StartVertex,
    UINT PrimitiveCount
);
```

The first parameter defines the primitive type you want to use. There are six different primitive types—D3DPT_POINTLIST, D3DPT_LINELIST, D3DPT_LINESTRIP, D3DPT_TRIANGLELIST, D3DPT_TRIANGLESTRIP, and D3DPT_TRIANGLEFAN.

```
typedef enum _D3DPRIMITIVETYPE {
D3DPT_POINTLIST = 1,
D3DPT_LINELIST = 2,
D3DPT_LINESTRIP = 3,
D3DPT_TRIANGLELIST = 4,
D3DPT_TRIANGLESTRIP = 5,
D3DPT_TRIANGLEFAN = 6
D3DPT_FORCE_DWORD = 0x7fffffff,
} D3DPRIMITIVETYPE;
```

In a TRIANGLEFAN, which is used in this example, all of the triangles generally share one vertex (see Figure 5.6).

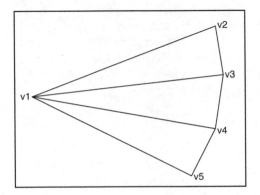

Figure 5.6

A fan of four triangles

Because we are only using two triangles, it is not obvious at first glance that we used a triangle fan because it is difficult to see the vertex that both share (see Figure 5.7).

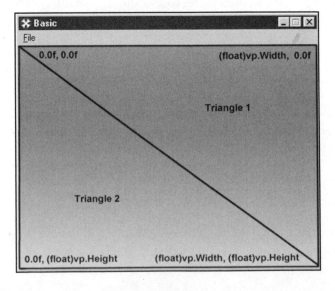

Figure 5.7

A fan of two triangles used by the example program

The second parameter of DrawPrimitive() lets the user choose a starting index for the vertices. This corresponds to the starting indices of Lock() and SetStreamSource(). In the last parameter, you must set the number of primitives. Table 5.1 helps you calculate the number of primitives in the case of non-indexed vertices.

TABLE 5.1 Number of Primitives

D3D Primitive Type	Number of Primitives
D3DPT_POINTLIST	PrimitiveCount = n
D3DPT_LINELIST	PrimitiveCount = n/2
D3DPT_LINESTRIP	PrimitiveCount = n*1
D3DPT_TRIANGLELIST	PrimitiveCount = n/3
D3DPT_TRIANGLESTRIP	PrimitiveCount = n*2
D3DPT_TRIANGLEFAN	PrimitiveCount = n*2

In this case the number of vertices is four, so the number of primitives is 2. As another example, if you were building the quad out of a triangle fan of four triangles, you would need six vertices.

Now that I have explained this last parameter of the DrawPrimitive() function, we end our travels through the main rendering loop (= FrameMove() / Render()) of a typical common files framework application.

The framework will leave this rendering loop in case the user changes the device or the resolution or exits the application. Then the cleanup code of the InvalidateDeviceObjects() and DeleteDeviceObjects() functions will be processed. This code is shown in the following sections.

The InvalidateDeviceObjects() Function

InvalidateDeviceObjects() is called when your game shuts down, the user resizes the window, or the device is changed; it's not called in your application's startup phase.

When the user resizes the window of this example, the InvalidateDeviceObjects() function is called, and then RestoreDeviceObjects() builds up what the function destroyed. This happens to the vertex buffer all the time (for example, every time the user resizes the window). It is released in the InvalidateDeviceObjects() function and recreated in the RestoreDeviceObjects() function shown earlier.

```
HRESULT CMyD3DApplication::InvalidateDeviceObjects()
{
    SAFE_RELEASE( m_pVB );
   return S_OK;
}
```

The SAFE_RELEASE macro is defined in dxutil.h, like this:

```
#define SAFE_RELEASE(p)        { if(p) { (p)->Release(); (p)=NULL; } }
```

It is the standardized release function that every DirectX COM object implements. It releases all system resources occupied by the object.

The DeleteDeviceObjects() Function

DeleteDeviceObjects() is the functional pair to InitDeviceObjects(). Therefore, it deletes what the InitDeviceObjects() function has created. However, because you're not initializing any device-dependent stuff in InitDeviceObjects(), you don't have to delete it here.

```
HRESULT CMyD3DApplication::DeleteDeviceObjects()
{
   return S_OK;
}
```

The FinalCleanup() Function

The last framework call goes out to FinalCleanup(). It's the last chance to deallocate memory you've grabbed or to destroy any resources you've occupied.

```
HRESULT CMyD3DApplication::FinalCleanup()
{
   return S_OK;
}
```

No resources (such as geometry data or textures) were occupied in OneTimeSceneInit()—the matching pair to FinalCleanup()—so there's nothing to release here.

Tada...you've worked through your first Direct3D example. Congratulations!

The Basic2 Example

This example demonstrates the following additional features compared to the previous example:

- How to apply textures to objects
- How to use the framework font class

Because of the usage of the font class provided by the framework, this example can display useful data on the underlying hardware and its performance (see Figure 5.8).

Figure 5.8

The Basic2 example

Frames per second

Width × height of window

Back buffer format

Graphics card format

Device type

The frames per second counter shows how many frames the example can display. To the right of the frames per second counter, you will find the size of the window. In this case, the window is 800×600 pixels. You can change that value by resizing the window. To the right of the window size, you will see the format of the back buffer. This helps you identify problems with textures or resources that are not compatible with the back buffer format.

The second row shows the type of HAL selected by this program. I presented the different kinds of HALs in Chapter 2. If the reference rasterizer was chosen, this value will be REF. The last piece of information in the second row is the name of the graphics card vendor that programmed the HAL. My display shows NVIDIA because I use the reference graphics drivers from that company, although my card is from Leadtek.

In addition to these text messages, which are made possible by the font class, a texture is visible in the client area of the window. I have used a texture from the media folder of the DirectX 9.0 SDK. I must admit that the texture looks a little bit pixelated in this example (see Figure 5.9). However, you will learn how to filter textures in Chapter 8, "Using Multiple Textures."

Figure 5.9

Texture mapping

To use a 2D texture map in a framework example, you must

- Use two additional texture coordinate variables in the vertex structure and fill the vertex buffer with them.
- Create the texture in the InitDeviceObjects() function with D3DUtil_CreateTexture().
- Set the texture in the Render() function using SetTexture() with some corresponding states.
- Release the texture in DeleteDeviceObjects() with the SAFE_RELEASE() macro.

To remember these steps, just think of the lifecycle of a texture. You have to create the texture, use it (set it), and delete it (release it) to free occupied memory. Because a texture must suit the capabilities of the graphics hardware, it is very device-specific. Therefore, the creation process must occur in a device-specific context. The InitDeviceObjects()/DeleteDeviceObjects() functions are the ideal place to do it.

Using the framework font class in d3dfont.cpp should be even easier than building up the texture. The following steps allow you to use a font to display text:

1. Create the font class in the constructor of the application class.
2. Call the font class function InitDeviceObjects() in the application class function InitDeviceObjects().
3. Call the font class function RestoreDeviceObjects() in the application class function RestoreDeviceObjects().

4. Call the font class function `DrawText()` in the application class function `Render()`, which is part of the rendering loop of the application class.

5. Call the font class function `InvalidateDeviceObjects()` in the application class function `InvalidateDeviceObjects()`.

6. Call the font class function `DeleteDeviceObjects()` in the application class function `DeleteDeviceObjects()`.

7. Delete the font class in the application destructor.

As you can see, the functions used by the font class in d3dfont.cpp have the same names as the functions used by the framework. Therefore, the only thing you have to do to utilize the font class is put the corresponding functions into the framework functions.

Now let's see how all this was accomplished in the Basic2 example program. Because this small example program does not need any special graphics card capabilities, the `ConfirmDevice()` function of Basic2 is empty. Additionally, the `OneTimeSceneInit()` function is empty because the amount of geometry that must be loaded is not larger than in the previous example. Therefore, I will not mention those functions here.

The first new thing occurs in the application class constructor. To create the font class, you must call the font class constructor in the application class constructor. Use a bold Arial font with the point size of 12.

```
CMyD3DApplication::CMyD3DApplication()
{
    m_strWindowTitle = _T("Basic");
    m_d3dEnumeration.AppUsesDepthBuffer = FALSE;
    m_dwCreationWidth          = 800;    // Width used to create window
    m_dwCreationHeight         = 600;
    m_pVB = NULL;
    m_pFont = new CD3DFont( _T("Arial"), 12, D3DFONT_BOLD );
}
```

I did not cover the application class constructor in the previous example in order to reduce the amount of new info that you had to absorb. Therefore, you have to do it now because this class initializes a few default values of the application class. The class constructor defines the width and height of the application window and sets the window's title to the string "Basic." It does not request a depth buffer by setting the Boolean value to FALSE, and it initializes the vertex buffer by setting it to NULL. Additionally, the `new()` function allocates the necessary memory for the font class. Just play around with it a little bit. You might set the window's width and height to 640×480, or you might change the title text, size, or font.

Now that you have initialized the application class, you can move on to the first relevant framework function in this example—the `InitDeviceObjects()` function.

The InitDeviceObjects() Function

You can use the InitDeviceObjects() function to initialize device-dependent objects. This function is called when the application starts up and the user changes the device by pressing F2. To use the font class, you have to call the font class function InitDeviceObjects().

```
HRESULT CMyD3DApplication::InitDeviceObjects()
{
    m_pFont->InitDeviceObjects( m_pd3dDevice );

    // Load the texture for the background image
    if( FAILED( D3DUtil_CreateTexture( m_pd3dDevice, _T("Lake.bmp"),
                                        &m_pBackgroundTexture) ) )
        return D3DAPPERR_MEDIANOTFOUND;

    return S_OK;
}
```

To create the background texture, you use the D3DUtil_CreateTexture() utility function. It accepts a pointer to the Direct3D device in its first parameter and the name of the texture in its second parameter, and it returns a pointer to an LPDIRECT3DTEXTURE9 texture object in its last parameter. This function does all the complicated initialization steps for you and searches for a texture with the name you provided. This is very handy. A much more powerful function to create textures is presented in Appendix D, "Creating a Texture with D3DXCreateTextureFromFileEx()."

So far, you have allocated the memory for the font class, created the texture, and provided a handle.

The RestoreDeviceObjects() Function

The RestoreDeviceObjects() function did not change much from the first example. It is called when the user changes the window size and when the device is changed. The font class function RestoreDeviceObjects() is called to handle the functionality necessary to react to this kind of user interaction.

```
HRESULT CMyD3DApplication::RestoreDeviceObjects()
{
// we don't need any transformation -> position will be delivered in screen coordinates

    m_pFont->RestoreDeviceObjects();

    // fill the vertex buffer with the new data
    // Initialize to render a quad
    VERTEX Vertices[] =
    {
```

```
                    {  0.0f,  0.0f, 0.5f, 1.0f, 0.0f, 0.0f, }, // x, y, z, rhw, tu, tv
                    {  (float)m_d3dsdBackBuffer.Width,  0.0f, 0.5f, 1.0f, 1.0f, 0.0f, },
                    {  (float)m_d3dsdBackBuffer.Width, (float)m_d3dsdBackBuffer.Height,
                              0.5f, 1.0f, 1.0f,1.0f, },
                    {  0.0f, (float)m_d3dsdBackBuffer.Height, 0.5f, 1.0f, 0.0f,1.0f, },
        };

        m_dwSizeofVertices = sizeof(Vertices);

        // sixth parameter is new in DX9
        // Create a square for rendering the background
        if( FAILED( m_pd3dDevice->CreateVertexBuffer(m_dwSizeofVertices,
                                                     D3DUSAGE_WRITEONLY, FVF,
                                                     D3DPOOL_MANAGED, &m_pVB, NULL ) ) )
            return E_FAIL;

        VERTEX* pVertices;
          // the third parameter changed from BYTE** to VOID** in DX9
        if( FAILED( m_pVB->Lock( 0, m_dwSizeofVertices, (VOID**)&pVertices, 0 ) ) )
            return E_FAIL;
        memcpy( pVertices, Vertices, m_dwSizeofVertices);
        m_pVB->Unlock();

        return S_OK;
}
```

You must change the vertex structure to handle texture mapping.

```
// A structure for our custom vertex type
struct VERTEX
{
    FLOAT x, y, z, rhw; // The transformed position for the vertex
    FLOAT tu, tv;       // texture coordinates
};
```

This example uses two texture coordinates per vertex instead of a color to lay out the texture map.

```
            {  0.0f,  0.0f, 0.5f, 1.0f, 0.0f, 0.0f, }, // x, y, z, rhw, tu, tv
            {  (float)m_d3dsdBackBuffer.Width,  0.0f, 0.5f, 1.0f, 1.0f, 0.0f, },
            {  (float)m_d3dsdBackBuffer.Width, (float)m_d3dsdBackBuffer.Height,
                      0.5f, 1.0f, 1.0f,1.0f, },
            {  0.0f, (float)m_d3dsdBackBuffer.Height, 0.5f, 1.0f, 0.0f,1.0f, },
```

The last two values of every vertex are the tu and tv values, which are shortcuts for texture coordinates u and v. To map texels onto primitives, Direct3D requires a uniform address range for all texels in all textures. Therefore, it uses a generic addressing scheme in which all texel addresses are in the range of 0.0 to 1.0, inclusive.

The texture is "fixed" to the top-left vertex by using 0.0f for the u value and 0.0f for the v value. You use 1.0f for the u value and 1.0f for the v value to fix the bottom-right edge of the texture to the bottom-right vertex. As in screen space, the top-left corner is the origin, as shown in Figure 5.10.

Figure 5.10

Texture layout

The vertex flags reflect the different layout of the vertex structure.

```
// Fixed-Function Vertex structure
const DWORD FVF = (D3DFVF_XYZRHW | D3DFVF_TEX1);
```

The Direct3D engine can expect four floating-point values that describe the position of the vertex and one pair of floating-point values that holds the texture coordinates of a texture.

The rest of the RestoreDeviceObjects() function has not changed compared to the previous example. The vertex buffer is created, locked, and filled in the same way as in the previous example.

You can skip the framework function, FrameMove(), here because you don't have to animate anything and therefore it is empty. You can move on to the Render() function of the application's main loop.

The Render[] Function

In this example, the Render() function has two new additions to the previous example. It handles the font class drawing code and the mapping of the texture onto the four vertices.

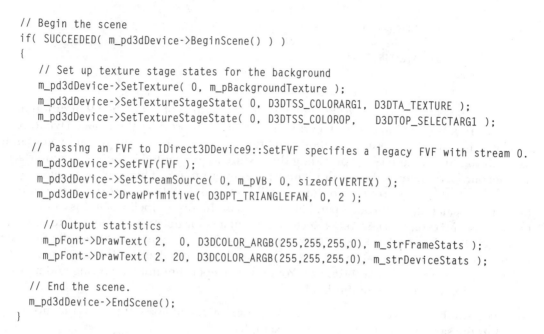

```
    // Begin the scene
    if( SUCCEEDED( m_pd3dDevice->BeginScene() ) )
    {
        // Set up texture stage states for the background
        m_pd3dDevice->SetTexture( 0, m_pBackgroundTexture );
        m_pd3dDevice->SetTextureStageState( 0, D3DTSS_COLORARG1, D3DTA_TEXTURE );
        m_pd3dDevice->SetTextureStageState( 0, D3DTSS_COLOROP,   D3DTOP_SELECTARG1 );

        // Passing an FVF to IDirect3DDevice9::SetFVF specifies a legacy FVF with stream 0.
        m_pd3dDevice->SetFVF(FVF );
        m_pd3dDevice->SetStreamSource( 0, m_pVB, 0, sizeof(VERTEX) );
        m_pd3dDevice->DrawPrimitive( D3DPT_TRIANGLEFAN, 0, 2 );

        // Output statistics
        m_pFont->DrawText( 2,  0, D3DCOLOR_ARGB(255,255,255,0), m_strFrameStats );
        m_pFont->DrawText( 2, 20, D3DCOLOR_ARGB(255,255,255,0), m_strDeviceStats );

        // End the scene.
        m_pd3dDevice->EndScene();
    }
```

Compared to the previous example, there are two new code blocks in this example. The first one sets the texture with the main function SetTexture(), and the second one uses DrawText() to position the text and set the text that is later displayed in the client region of the window. I'll start with the texture mapping code.

The IDirect3DDevice9::SetTexture() method assigns a texture to a given stage for a device. Direct3D provides eight texture stages, which means that you can set up to eight textures for one DrawPrimitive() call. (However, you can use more DrawPrimitive() calls, which is called *multi-pass rendering*. One pass equals one DrawPrimitive() call.) You can choose the texture stage you like by providing its number in the first parameter of SetTexture(). It is common to start with the texture stage 0 and to increment this number for every additional texture stage for which a texture should be assigned. That's why the background texture is assigned to the 0 texture stage here.

When an application selects a texture as the current texture, it instructs the Direct3D device to apply the texture to all primitives that are rendered from that time until the current texture is changed again. If each primitive in a 3D scene has its own texture, the texture must be set before each primitive is drawn, which means just before the DrawPrimitive() function is called.

After you set the texture, you have to set the proper texture stages with the following SetTextureStageState() calls:

```
m_pd3dDevice->SetTextureStageState( 0, D3DTSS_COLORARG1, D3DTA_TEXTURE );
m_pd3dDevice->SetTextureStageState( 0, D3DTSS_COLOROP,   D3DTOP_SELECTARG1);
...
```

```
HRESULT SetTextureStageState(
  DWORD Stage,
  D3DTEXTURESTAGESTATETYPE Type,
  DWORD Value
);
```

SetTextureStageState() is responsible for the color and alpha blending between different materials (textures, color, and alpha values of textures). It provides the Direct3D texture or pixel engine with the chosen operation and arguments. You choose the texture you want to use with the first parameter by providing the texture stage that holds the texture interface. The second parameter is the texture state type you want to use. There are two main types—D3DTSS_COLORx states control the flow of an RGB vector, and D3DTSS_ALPHAx states govern the flow of the scalar alpha through parallel segments of the pixel pipeline. In this example, the second SetTextureStageState() selects the use of a color operation render state by using D3DTSS_COLOROP. The D3DTOP_SELECTARG1 parameter tells the texturing unit to use the first argument as output. The first SetTextureStageState() call indicates that this first argument is the color of the texture set by SetTexture(). You'll dive deeper into multi-texturing and multipass texturing in Part Two of this book.

After you set the texture, the SetFVF(), SetStreamSource(), and DrawPrimitive() functions are called in the same way as in the previous example.

After you call these functions, you must call the draw function of the font class using DrawText(). This is a very handy function that can do all the things necessary to display text.

```
m_pFont->DrawText( 2,  0, D3DCOLOR_ARGB(255,255,255,0), m_strFrameStats );
m_pFont->DrawText( 2, 20, D3DCOLOR_ARGB(255,255,255,0), m_strDeviceStats );
```

The first two parameters determine the place where the text should be displayed. These x and y values have their origin in the upper-left corner (just like the texture mapping values and screen space values provided for the vertices). The next parameter is the text color. The alpha, red, and green channels are set to 255, whereas the blue channel is set to 0. If you lower the alpha value, the characters will become transparent.

The last parameters, m_strFrameStats and m_strDeviceStats, are arrays that are put together in d3dapp.cpp. m_strFrameStats shows the frames per second, the width and height of the window, and the format of the background buffer, whereas m_strDeviceStats shows the device type and description (for example, hw vp, which means hardware vertex processing and the device name). You'll recall that I explained the content of these arrays at the beginning of this section.

The InvalidateDeviceObjects() Function

InvalidateDeviceObjects() holds the font class function with the same name. It releases the vertex buffer that its functional match (RestoreDeviceObjects()) created.

```
HRESULT CMyD3DApplication::InvalidateDeviceObjects()
{
```

```
        m_pFont->InvalidateDeviceObjects();
        SAFE_RELEASE( m_pVB );
    return S_OK;
}
```

The DeleteDeviceObjects() Function

DeleteDeviceObjects() is the functional match to InitDeviceObjects(), and it is used to delete the objects previously created with InitDeviceObjects().

```
HRESULT CMyD3DApplication::DeleteDeviceObjects()
{
    m_pFont->DeleteDeviceObjects();
    SAFE_RELEASE( m_pBackgroundTexture );
    return S_OK;
}
```

The FinalCleanup() Function

As usual, the last call goes out to FinalCleanup(). This is where you should redo the things that you started in OneTimeSceneInit().

```
HRESULT CMyD3DApplication::FinalCleanup()
{
    return S_OK;
}
```

You haven't occupied anything in OneTimeSceneInit(), so there is no work to do there.

Now you should have the big picture on how to use texture mapping in Direct3D and how to use the font class provided in d3dfont.cpp. The Basic3 example will present a new kind of primitive to display geometry via Direct3D—a triangle strip.

The Basic3 Example

The Basic3 example has only one small change compared to the previous example. Instead of a triangle fan, it uses a triangle strip as the rendering primitive in DrawPrimitive(). This primitive is more cache-friendly on some newer graphics cards. Therefore, it might perform better, but you will not see a speed difference by using only four vertices, as in these example programs. There are only two changes compared to the previous example. First, the values for the vertices are set in a different order in the vertex buffer in RestoreDeviceObjects().

```
{  0.0f, 0.0f, 0.5f, 1.0f, 0.0f, 0.0f, },
{  (float)m_d3dsdBackBuffer.Width, 0.0f, 0.5f, 1.0f, 1.0f,0.0f, },
```

```
{ 0.0f, (float)m_d3dsdBackBuffer.Height, 0.5f, 1.0f, 0.0f, 1.0f, }, // x, y, z, rhw, tu, tv
{ (float)m_d3dsdBackBuffer.Width, (float)m_d3dsdBackBuffer.Height, 0.5f, 1.0f, 1.0f,1.0f,},
```

This example provides the vertices in the same way that Zorro rips his Z into the forehead of his enemies. First the top-left vertex is provided, then the top-right, and then the bottom-left and bottom- right vertices. Figure 5.11 shows the Z.

Figure 5.11

Execution order of vertices ordered as triangle strips

Top-right vertex

Top-left vertex

Bottom-left vertex

Bottom-right vertex

The previous example used the following order of vertices for a triangle fan:

```
{  0.0f,  0.0f, 0.5f, 1.0f, 0.0f, 0.0f, }, // x, y, z, rhw, tu, tv
{ (float)m_d3dsdBackBuffer.Width,  0.0f, 0.5f, 1.0f, 1.0f, 0.0f, },
{(float)m_d3dsdBackBuffer.Width, (float)m_d3dsdBackBuffer.Height, 0.5f, 1.0f, 1.0f,1.0f, },
{  0.0f, (float)m_d3dsdBackBuffer.Height, 0.5f, 1.0f, 0.0f,1.0f, },
```

Here the order of vertices moved around the quad, starting at the top-left, then the top-right, and then the bottom-right. The bottom-left is the last vertex set. This "moving around the corner" behavior is typical for a triangle fan primitive. For example, if you use six vertices, the order of execution would be top-middle, top-right, bottom-right, bottom-middle, bottom-left, and top-left, whereas the order of execution in a triangle strip would be bottom-left, top-left, top-middle, bottom-middle, top-right, and bottom-right. Note that in a triangle strip any three consecutive vertices form a triangle.

In these examples, you only used four vertices that can be set "by hand." Nowadays, entire 3D models commonly consist of thousands of vertices. These models are constructed with the help of 3D modeling programs such as discreet's 3ds max or Caligari's trueSpace. It is not a trivial task to rearrange the vertices produced by such a program from triangle fans to triangle strips or vice versa. This is usually accomplished with the help of primitive libraries. You will find one of these libraries, which reorders all vertices of a model to triangle strips, on the NVIDIA Web site at http://developer.nvidia.com.

The second change to the source of the previous example specifies the correct primitive type in the DrawPrimitive() call in the Render() function.

```
HRESULT CMyD3DApplication::Render()
{
…

            m_pd3dDevice->DrawPrimitive (D3DPT_TRIANGLESTRIP, 0, 2);
…

    return S_OK;
}
```

That's all for this example. The next example will introduce the idea behind index buffers and will use a new primitive type called *indexed triangle lists*.

The Basic4 Example

The Basic4 example highlights the following Direct3D features:

- Index buffers
- Primitive type indexed triangle lists

As usual, I will focus on the new features that are added to the previous example. Using index buffers together with indexed primitives will lead to a performance gain on most current graphics cards, compared to using non-indexed primitives.

To use an index buffer in its simplest form, you must complete the following steps:

1. Create and fill the index buffer at the same place where the vertex buffer is created (in this case, RestoreDeviceObjects()).

2. Set the indices in the rendering loop with SetIndices() and use an indexed primitive such as an indexed triangle list to display geometry.

3. Release the index buffer at the same place where the vertex buffer is released (in this case, InvalidateDeviceObjects()).

To be able to use an index buffer, you must declare an index buffer object as a member of the application class and initialize it with NULL in the application class constructor.

```
LPDIRECT3DINDEXBUFFER9  m_pIB;
DWORD m_dwSizeofIndices;
...
CMyD3DApplication::CMyD3DApplication()
{
```

```
m_strWindowTitle    = _T("Basic");
m_d3dEnumeration.AppUsesDepthBuffer = FALSE;
m_dwCreationWidth          = 800;    // Width used to create window
m_dwCreationHeight         = 600;
m_pVB = NULL;
m_pIB = NULL;
m_pFont = new CD3DFont( _T("Arial"), 12, D3DFONT_BOLD );
}
```

The creation of the index buffer occurs in a call to CreateIndexBuffer() in the RestoreDeviceObjects() function.

```
HRESULT CMyD3DApplication::RestoreDeviceObjects()
{
    // we don`t need any transformation -> position will be delivered in screen coordinates

    m_pFont->RestoreDeviceObjects();

    // fill the vertex buffer with the new data
    // Initialize to render a quad
    VERTEX Vertices[] =
    {
            {  0.0f,  0.0f, 0.5f, 1.0f, 0.0f, 0.0f, }, // x, y, z, rhw, tu, tv
            { (float)m_d3dsdBackBuffer.Width,  0.0f, 0.5f, 1.0f, 1.0f, 0.0f, },
            { (float)m_d3dsdBackBuffer.Width, (float)m_d3dsdBackBuffer.Height, 0.5f,
                1.0f, 1.0f,1.0f, },
            {  0.0f, (float)m_d3dsdBackBuffer.Height, 0.5f, 1.0f, 0.0f,1.0f, },
    };

    m_dwSizeofVertices = sizeof(Vertices);

    // sixth parameter is new in DX9
    // Create a square for rendering the background
    if( FAILED( m_pd3dDevice->CreateVertexBuffer( m_dwSizeofVertices,
                                                    D3DUSAGE_WRITEONLY, FVF,
                                                    D3DPOOL_MANAGED, &m_pVB, NULL ) ) )
        return E_FAIL;

    VERTEX* pVertices;
    // the third parameter changed from BYTE** to VOID** in DX9
    if( FAILED( m_pVB->Lock( 0, m_dwSizeofVertices, (VOID**)&pVertices, 0 ) ) )
        return E_FAIL;
    memcpy( pVertices, Vertices, m_dwSizeofVertices);
    m_pVB->Unlock();

    // Initialize the Index buffer
    WORD wIndices[] = {0, 1, 2, 0, 2, 3};
```

```
m_wSizeofIndices = sizeof(wIndices);

// Create the index buffer
// six parameter new in DX9
if( FAILED( m_pd3dDevice->CreateIndexBuffer( m_wSizeofIndices,
                                        0, D3DFMT_INDEX16,
                               D3DPOOL_MANAGED, &m_pIB, NULL ) ) )
    return E_FAIL;

VOID* pIndices;
// DX9 third parameter changed from BYTE** to VOID **
if( FAILED( m_pIB->Lock( 0, m_wSizeofIndices, (VOID**)&pIndices, 0 ) ) )
        return E_FAIL;
memcpy( pIndices, wIndices, sizeof(wIndices) );
m_pIB->Unlock();

    return S_OK;
}
```

This example uses the same order of vertices as the first example, but there is one fundamental difference. An un-indexed triangle list consists of two isolated triangles that do not need to be connected in any way (see Figure 5.12).

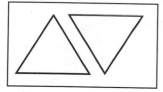

Figure 5.12

Two triangles from a triangle list

Figure 5.12 shows two triangles that are not connected in any way. In a triangle list, every triangle is a standalone polygon in a mesh. Consider an example of two triangles that overlap at two vertices (see Figure 5.13).

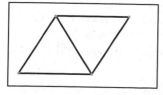

Figure 5.13

Two overlapping triangles

An entire model consisting of non-indexed triangle lists would have many overlapping vertices because there shouldn't be a gap between triangles. This might lead to weak performance because a lot of redundant work would be required. Additionally, gaps between triangles might occur because the arithmetic precision of computers might not be able to calculate the position of the vertices precisely enough.

The solution to this problem is to use an index buffer. This buffer indexes the vertices in such a way that only four vertices have to be provided to the vertex buffer, and two of them are reused for each of the two triangles. Therefore, the index buffer helps you reuse vertices.

In this process, every vertex gets a number from 0 to 3. The numbers correspond to the order of the vertices in the vertex buffer (top-left, top-right, bottom-right, and bottom-left). Therefore, the top-left vertex is 0, the top-right is 1, the bottom-right is 2, and the bottom-left is 3 (see Figure 5.14).

Figure 5.14

The numbered vertices

By numbering the vertices, the index buffer is able to reuse two vertices by feeding the rendering engine of Direct3D the same vertex numbers for the two overlapping edges of the two triangles. The layout of the index buffer is

```
WORD wIndices[] = {0, 1, 2, 0, 2, 3};
```

As you can see, every vertex has its own number from 0 to 3. The first triangle uses the vertices 0, 1, and 2, and the second triangle uses the vertices 0, 2, and 3. Vertices 0 and 2 are used in both triangles. Thus it's an integer offset in the vertex buffer. This tells DrawIndexedPrimitive() that it should use vertices 0, 1, and 2 for the first triangle and vertices 0, 2, and 3 for the second triangle.

Now the basic question: Which type of primitive should you use? In many applications multiple polygons share vertices. You'll get maximum performance when you reduce the duplication in vertices transformed and sent across the bus to the rendering device. A non-indexed triangle list does not share vertices, so it's the least optimal method. Strips and fans imply a specific connectivity relationship between polygons. When the structure of the data falls naturally into strips and fans, this is the most appropriate choice because they minimize the data sent to the driver.

Additionally, using an index buffer can improve performance if your geometry is reused by indices. If you use more than two indices per vertex, there should be a visible gain. It seems like indexed triangle strips are slightly faster than indexed triangle lists on some graphics hardware, whereas they have the same speed as indexed triangle lists on other graphics hardware. However, you should measure this very thoroughly in every case.

There are several limitations that can lead to reduced performance. For an overview, it is sufficient to differentiate between three kinds of possible restrictions—CPU limited, vertex throughput limited, and fill rate limited. CPU limited and vertex throughput limited are self-explanatory, and fill rate limited means that the application causes a bottleneck in the area between the rasterization stage and the end of the Direct3D pipeline. (I will cover the Direct3D pipeline in Chapter 9, "Shader Programming with the High-Level Shader Language.") Measuring things correctly to find your limitation is a tough task that requires some experience. Just know that using the right kind of primitive might help to reduce the burden of vertex throughput limitation, although it will not help with the other two limiting factors. Now back to the code.

The index buffer is created with a call to `CreateIndexBuffer()`.

```
HRESULT CreateIndexBuffer(
                    // size of index buffer in bytes
                    UINT Length,
                    // usage flags
                    DWORD Usage,
                     // index buffer format
                    D3DFORMAT Format,
                    // memory pool
                    D3DPOOL Pool,
                    // pointer to index buffer
                    IDirect3DIndexBuffer9** ppIndexBuffer,
                    // reserved for future DX versions
                    HANDLE* pHandle)
```

This function needs the length of the index buffer as the first parameter, a list of usage hints as the second parameter, and the appreciated format as the third parameter. The flags that indicate to the driver the usage of the index buffer are similar to the flags that you can choose for the `CreateVertexBuffer()` function. Because you have no special needs here, you can provide 0 as the parameter. The format parameter lets the user choose between two different index buffer formats—16-bit (`D3DFMT_INDEX16`) and 32-bit (`D3DFMT_INDEX32`). The larger index buffer format can store more indices and therefore is able to store the indices of models with a higher number of vertices, but it is slower than the 16-bit format on some graphics hardware.

The fourth parameter requires the kind of pool you want to choose. Remember the four different kinds of pools available in DirectX 9.0 and the rule of thumb that says the managed pool is right in most cases. Therefore, you'll want to specify a managed pool here.

The fifth parameter returns the pointer to the buffer region that should store the indices. This pointer will fill the buffer area with memcpy() after locking it with the Lock() command, much like the fill process of the vertex buffer.

```
VOID* pIndices;
// DX9 third parameter changed from BYTE** to VOID **
if( FAILED( m_pIB->Lock( 0, m_wSizeofIndices, (VOID**)&pIndices, 0 ) ) )
            return E_FAIL;
memcpy( pIndices, wIndices, sizeof(wIndices) );
m_pIB->Unlock();
```

The sixth parameter is new in DirectX 9.0. You should set it to NULL and reserve it for future functionality.

The parameters of the Lock() and Unlock() functions are similar to their vertex buffer equivalents. The only difference is that you need to specify the size of the indices as the second parameter instead of the size of the vertices.

To use the index buffer, you must set it in the Render() function.

```
HRESULT CMyD3DApplication::Render()
{
    // Begin the scene
    if( SUCCEEDED( m_pd3dDevice->BeginScene() ) )
    {
      // Set up texture stage states for the background
      m_pd3dDevice->SetTexture( 0, m_pBackgroundTexture );
      m_pd3dDevice->SetTextureStageState( 0, D3DTSS_COLORARG1, D3DTA_TEXTURE );
      m_pd3dDevice->SetTextureStageState( 0, D3DTSS_COLOROP,   D3DTOP_SELECTARG1 );

      // Passing an FVF to IDirect3DDevice9::SetFVF specifies a legacy FVF with stream 0.
       m_pd3dDevice->SetFVF(FVF );
      m_pd3dDevice->SetStreamSource( 0, m_pVB, 0, sizeof(VERTEX) );
            m_pd3dDevice->SetIndices( m_pIB ); // new in DX9 only takes one parameter
      // second parameter new in DX9
      m_pd3dDevice->DrawIndexedPrimitive( D3DPT_TRIANGLELIST,
                                 0,
                                 0,
                                 4,  // number of vertices
                                 0,
                                 2); // number of primitives

        // Output statistics
        m_pFont->DrawText( 2,  0, D3DCOLOR_ARGB(255,255,255,0), m_strFrameStats );
        m_pFont->DrawText( 2, 20, D3DCOLOR_ARGB(255,255,255,0), m_strDeviceStats );
```

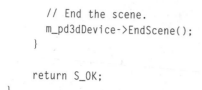

```
        // End the scene.
        m_pd3dDevice->EndScene();
    }

    return S_OK;
}
```

You set the index buffer with `SetIndices()`, which accepts only one parameter—the index buffer itself. Because you built up the index buffer in the `RestoreDeviceObjects()` function, you have to release it in the `InvalidateDeviceObjects()` function.

```
HRESULT CMyD3DApplication::InvalidateDeviceObjects()
{
    m_pFont->InvalidateDeviceObjects();
    SAFE_RELEASE( m_pVB );
    SAFE_RELEASE( m_pIB );
    return S_OK;
}
```

The rest of the fourth example is the same as the third example. Therefore, you can proceed to the fifth example.

The Basic5 Example

The only difference between the previous example and the Basic5 example is the use of indexed triangle strips. Therefore, you only need to change three things:

- The order of the vertices (strips)
- The order of the indices (Zorro's Z)
- The first parameter in `DrawIndexedPrimitive()` (the primitive type)

The following code sets the vertices in the order of a stripe. You will find it in the `RestoreDeviceObjects()` function in the example source code.

```
...
{  0.0f, 0.0f, 0.5f, 1.0f, 0.0f, 0.0f, },
{  (float)m_d3dsdBackBuffer.Width, 0.0f, 0.5f, 1.0f, 1.0f,0.0f, },
{ 0.0f, (float)m_d3dsdBackBuffer.Height, 0.5f, 1.0f, 0.0f, 1.0f, }, // x, y, z, rhw, tu, tv
{(float)m_d3dsdBackBuffer.Width, (float)m_d3dsdBackBuffer.Height, 0.5f, 1.0f, 1.0f,1.0f, },
...
```

This is the same order that you used in the Basic3 example, which used non-indexed triangle strips. You must change the order of indices to get the Z form, like this:

```
        WORD wIndices[] = {0, 1, 2, 3, 2, 0};
```

The index numbers 0, 1, 2, and 3 index into the first, second, third, and fourth vertices. The remaining numbers (2 and 0) lead the renderer back to its starting point. After preparing the correct vertices and indices, the `DrawIndexPrimitive()` function has to be instructed to accept this kind of primitive with the `D3DPT_TRIANGLESTRIP` flag.

Summary

So that just about wraps up the basics. Ready to move on? In the next chapter, you'll learn the first steps to using animation. Sounds like fun, doesn't it?!

CHAPTER 6

FIRST
STEPS TO
ANIMATION

You might recall that in the last chapter you saw that all samples built with the help of the common files in the DirectX SDK are created with overloaded versions of the CD3DApplication methods.

```
HRESULT OneTimeSceneInit()       { return S_OK; }
HRESULT InitDeviceObjects()      { return S_OK; }
HRESULT RestoreDeviceObjects     { return S_OK; }
HRESULT DeleteDeviceObjects()    { return S_OK; }
HRESULT Render()                 { return S_OK; }
HRESULT FrameMove( FLOAT )       { return S_OK; }
HRESULT FinalCleanup()           { return S_OK; }
```

You also learned the task of every method in this class. In this chapter, you will step into the world of animating objects and creating a virtual camera system. You will learn how to:

- Work with transformations
- Move objects in a 3D world
- Move your camera
- Concatenate transformations
- Work with projection transformations
- Use viewports
- Work with the depth buffer

Understanding Transformations and Viewports

To best understand how you use transformations to build the impression of real-world motion, consider this scenario. Imagine you are standing in your living room with your video camera, taking a video of your girlfriend. She has a position and orientation in the room, as does the camera you are holding. When she starts moving, you try to follow her with the camera in your hand. You change the lens properties to get a sharp picture, and perhaps you zoom in or out of the scene to show her smile a little bit better. It can be pretty difficult to handle this situation in real-time, but this is also what you try to handle in real-time graphics.

You mimic all these movements in a computer game by using transformations. You change your girlfriend's position and orientation and that of the camera by using *world* and *view transformations*. You zoom in and out and change the properties of the camera lens to get a sharp picture by using a *projection transformation*.

The whole scene is happening in three dimensions. At the end, you need to map these three dimensions to the two dimensions of the film. You do this using the viewport.

NOTE

There is one additional transformation that I don't cover in this chapter called *model transformation*. A real-life equivalent would be when your girlfriend starts dancing but doesn't change her position or orientation.

The World Transformation

You move an object in a 3D world using a world transformation. Figure 6.1 shows two cubes that are the same size but have different positions and orientations.

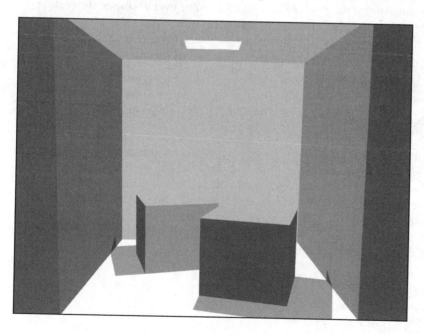

Figure 6.1

Two cubes with different positions and orientations

Figure 6.2 shows the transformations necessary to move one of the cubes into position.

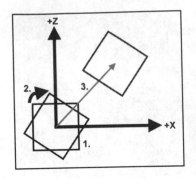

Figure 6.2

World transformations of a cube shown from above

The following steps detail the transformations necessary to move the cubes into place.

1. The cube is standing with its origin in the origin of the world coordinate system.
2. Rotate the cube.
3. Move the cube to its new position.

The position for Step 1 comes from the vertex buffer data, which you remember from the previous chapter. In the case of a static object like this, the data never changes. Therefore, everything always begins with this default position and orientation. The cube is rotated in Step 2 and moved into position in Step 3. All this happens every frame, so each time a scene is displayed, all objects are first moved into their places and oriented correctly.

The order of these steps is very important. If steps 2 and 3 are exchanged, the object might behave in an unexpected way. If the cube is moved and then rotated, it will rotate around the center of the world coordinate system instead of around its own geometrical center or its center of gravity, as shown in Figure 6.3.

It is common to transform the vertices of the cubes using a world transformation matrix or short world matrix. (Please read Appendix C, "Mathematics Primer," to learn more about matrices.) One of the benefits of using matrices is that you can easily draw several instances of the same object using one vertex buffer with several different transformation matrixes. The application that displayed the cubes in Figures 6.2 and 6.3 uses only one set of geometry, which means one vertex buffer. That saves memory and bandwidth because in terms of the geometry data sent to the video card, there is only one model.

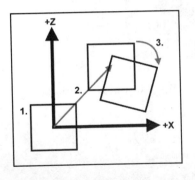

Figure 6.3

World transformations of a cube with steps 2 and 3 exchanged

As I mentioned earlier, the order in which the transformations occur is important. In other words, matrix multiplication is not commutative. That means [a] * [b] <> [b] * [a]. The order of transformations depends on what you try to achieve, as you will see in the second example program of this chapter. A 4×4 world matrix contains four vectors, which might represent the orientation and position of an object.

```
ux uy uz 0
vx vy vz 0
wx wy wz 0
tx ty tz 1
```

The u, v, and w vectors describe the orientation of the object's vertices compared to the world coordinate system. The t vector describes the position of the object's vertex compared to the world coordinate system. Figure 6.4 shows these four vectors describing the orientation and position of a cube.

Every vertex of the cube gets the correct orientation and position by being multiplied by this matrix. To desribe the position of the cube in Figure 6.4, you must multiply the following matrix by every vertex of the cube.

```
1, 0, 0, 0
0, 1, 0, 0
0, 0, 1, 0
2, 2, 2, 1
```

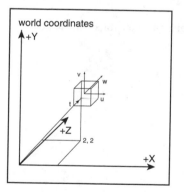

Figure 6.4

*One cube in the world
coordinate system*

This matrix doesn't change the orientation of the cube. It just translates the origin of the cube to 2, 2, 2. You can access a 4×4 matrix with:

```
D3DMATRIX mat;
mat._11 = 1.0f; mat._12 = 0.0f; mat._13 = 0.0f; mat._14 = 0.0f;
mat._21 = 0.0f; mat._22 = 1.0f; mat._23 = 0.0f; mat._24 = 0.0f;
mat._31 = 0.0f; mat._32 = 0.0f; mat._33 = 1.0f; mat._34 = 0.0f;
mat._41 = 2.0f; mat._42 = 2.0f; mat._43 = 2.0f; mat._44 = 1.0f;
```

To access the third row in the first column, you might use mat._31. To change the location of the cube on the x-axis, you might change the matrix element mat._41.

You build up a translation matrix using the D3DXMatrixTranslation() function. Translation can best be described as a linear change in position. This change can be represented by a delta vector (tx, ty, tz), where tx—or often dx—represents the change in the object's x position; ty or dy represents the change in its y position; and tz or dz represents the change in its z position. We don't have the source code for D3DXMatrixTranslation(), but it might look like this:

```
inline VOID D3DXMatrixTranslation (D3DXMATRIX* m, FLOAT tx, FLOAT ty, FLOAT tz )
{
  D3DXMatrixIdentity(m );
  m._41 = tx; m._42 = ty; m._43 = tz;
}
=
1  0  0  0
0  1  0  0
0  0  1  0
tx ty tz 1
```

You build up a rotation matrix using functions provided by Direct3D. A rotation can be described as circular motion around an axis. The incremental angles used to rotate the object represent rotation from the current orientation. To rotate by 1 degree around the z-axis using the three steps discussed previously, you tell your object to rotate 1 degree around its z-axis, regardless of its current orientation and how you got that orientation. This is how the real world operates.

D3DXMatrixRotationY() rotates the objects around the y-axis, where fRads equals the desired amount of rotation. The source of this method could look like this:

```
VOID D3DXMatrixRotationY( D3DXMATRIX* mat, FLOAT fRads )
{
    D3DXMatrixIdentity(mat);
    mat._11 =  cosf( fRads );
    mat._13 = -sinf( fRads );
    mat._31 =  sinf( fRads );
    mat._33 =  cosf( fRads );
}
=
cosf fRads      0      -sinf fRads      0
0               0      0                0
sinf fRads      0      cosf fRads       0
0               0      0                0
```

If you want to rotate an object around its x-axis, you need to use D3DXMatrixRotationX( ), where fRads equals the desired amount of rotation.

```
VOID D3DXMatrixRotationX( D3DXMATRIX* mat, FLOAT fRads )
{
    D3DXMatrixIdentity(mat);
```

```
    mat._22 =  cosf( fRads );
    mat._23 =  sinf( fRads );
    mat._32 = -sinf( fRads );
    mat._33 =  cosf( fRads );
}
=
```

1	0	0	0
0	cos fRad	sin fRads	0
0	-sin fRads	cos fRads	0
0	0	0	0

D3DXMatrixRotationZ() rotates the objects around the z-axis, where fRads equals the desired amount of rotation.

```
VOID D3DXMatrixRotationZ( D3DXMATRIX* mat, FLOAT fRads )
{
    D3DXMatrixIdentity(mat);
    mat._11 =  cosf( fRads );
    mat._12 =  sinf( fRads );
    mat._21 = -sinf( fRads );
    mat._22 =  cosf( fRads );
}
=
```

cosf fRads	sinf fRads	0	0
-sinf fRads	cos fRads	0	0
0	0	0	0
0	0	0	0

Another function that is useful for transformations is D3DXMatrixMultiply(). The prototype of D3DXMatrixMultiply() looks like D3DXMATRIX * D3DXMatrixMultiply (D3DXMATRIX* pOut, CONST D3DXMATRIX* pM1, CONST D3DMATRIX* pM2). In other words, pOut=pM1*pM2. The return value for this function is the same value returned in the pOut parameter. This way, you can use the D3DXMatrixMultiply() function as a parameter for another function. Matrix multiplication is the operation by which one matrix is transformed by another. A matrix multiplication stores the results of the sum of the products of matrix rows and columns.

```
a b c d      A B C D
e f g h  *   E F G H =
i j k l      I J K L
m n o p      M N O P
mat._11 = a*A+b*E+c*I+d*M
mat._12 = a*B+b*F+c*J+d*N
mat._13 = a*C+b*G+c*K+d*O
mat._14 = a*D+b*H+c*L+d*P
mat._21 = e*A+f*E+g*I+h*M
mat._22 = e*B+f*F+g*J+h*N etc.
```

A matrix multiplication routine could look like this:

```
D3DXMATRIX* D3DXMatrixMultiply (D3DXMATRIX* pOut,
                                CONST D3DXMATRIX* pM1,
                                CONST D3DMATRIX* pM2)
{
    FLOAT  pM[16];
    ZeroMemory( pM, sizeof(D3DXMATRIX) );
    for( WORD i=0; i<4; i++ )
        for( WORD j=0; j<4; j++ )
            for( WORD k=0; k<4; k++ )
                pM[4*i+j] +=  pM1[4*i+k] * pM2[4*k+j];
    memcpy( pOut, pM, sizeof(D3DXMATRIX) );
  return (pOut);
}
```

This function might be optimized highly for different processors, but there is an even better way to multiply matrices.

```
D3DXMATRIX matRotX, matRotY;
matWorld = matTrans * matRotX * matRotY;
```

This method is possible using the operator overloading C++ feature. You will read more about this feature in Appendix B, "C++ Primer."

Another matrix function that might be useful is D3DXMatrixScaling(). This function accepts x, y, and z scaling factors and the matrix that should be scaled. The source of this function might look like this in C:

```
D3DXMATRIX * D3DXMatrixScaling (D3DXMATRIX *pOut, FLOAT sx, FLOAT sy,FLOAT sz)
{
    pOut->_11 = sx; pOut->_22 = sy; pOut->_33 = sz;

    return pOut;
}
=
```

sx	0	0	0
0	sy	0	0
0	0	sz	0
0	0	0	0

You can use this function to change the appearance of your geometry. For example, to place several cubes of different sizes in a scene, just scale the height of the same geometry and place it with different scaling factors in the scene. Using this method, you might use one vertex buffer with the cube geometry several times.

One of the pros of using matrix multiplication is that scaling, rotation, and translation all take the same amount of time to perform, so the performance of a dedicated transformation engine is predictable and consistent. This allows game developers to make informed decisions regarding performance and quality.

So far you have seen how transformations are performed using matrices, but you haven't seen how Direct3D is involved in matrix transformation. The following line of code provides the world matrix to Direct3D for further execution:

```
m_pd3dDevice->SetTransform( D3DTS_WORLD,  &m_matWorld );
```

Using the D3DTS_WORLD flag, it sets the device world-transformation-related state. The D3DTS_VIEW or D3DTS_PROJECTION flags set the device state regarding the view or projection transformation. I will demonstrate this concept later in the chapter.

The 1steps Example

The 1steps.exe example program, located in the \1steps directory on the CD-ROM, demonstrates how Direct3D executes the world matrix. It rotates a quad around its y-axis (see Figure 6.5).

```
75.03 fps (1024x768), X8R8G8B8 (D16) (4x Multisample)
HAL (pure hw vp): RADEON 9700/9500 SERIES
```

Figure 6.5

A quad rotated around its y-axis

The previous chapter showed a similar rectangle with a texture mapped on it, but this time the rectangle should be animated with the help of Direct3D. To provide this information to the Direct3D engine, you have to change some code. The first step for involving the Direct3D transformation engine is to remove the RHW position flag in the vertex flags.

```
// A structure for our custom vertex type
struct VERTEX
{
    FLOAT x, y, z; // The untransformed position for the vertex
    FLOAT tu, tv;
```

```
};
```

```
// Fixed-Function Vertex structure
const DWORD FVF = (D3DFVF_XYZ | D3DFVF_TEX1);
```

Without an RHW value, the values in the vertex buffer look like this:

```
VERTEX Vertices[] =
{
     { -1.0f,-1.0f, 0.0f, 1.0f, 1.0f, }, // x, y, z, tu, tv
     {  1.0f,-1.0f, 0.0f, 0.0f, 1.0f, },
     {  1.0f, 1.0f, 0.0f, 0.0f, 0.0f, },
     { -1.0f, 1.0f, 0.0f, 1.0f, 0.0f, },
};
```

The x and y position values are not chosen in screen space, as in the previous examples where the size of the back buffer was provided. If you use the transformation unit of Direct3D, the origin of the world lies by default in the middle of the window's client area. Therefore, -1.0, -1.0 is the bottom-left vertex of the quad; 1.0f, -1.0f is the bottom-right vertex; 1.0f, 1.0f is the top-right vertex; and -1.0f, 1.0f is the top-left vertex. The index buffer shows that these vertices are set in the following order:

```
     WORD wIndices[]={3, 2, 0, 2, 1, 0};
```

In other words, top-left, top-right, bottom-left, top-right, bottom-right, bottom-left. The first triangle that is drawn lies in the upper-left corner, and the second one lies in the bottom-right corner.

The main transformation is done in the framework function FrameMove().

```
HRESULT CMyD3DApplication::FrameMove()
{
     // rotates the object about the y-axis
     D3DXMATRIX matRotY;
     D3DXMatrixRotationY( &matRotY, m_fTime * 1.5f);

     D3DXMATRIX matTrans;
     D3DXMatrixTranslation(&matTrans, 0.0f, 0.0f, 0.0f);

     m_pd3dDevice->SetTransform( D3DTS_WORLD, &(matRotY * matTrans));
     return S_OK;
}
```

The utility function D3DXMatrixRotationY() builds up a matrix that rotates around the y-axis. You use the matrix type provided by the Direct3D utility library here. All of the names of variable types provided by this library start with D3DX*. The framework provides the m_fTime variable. You can call it everywhere in your application, and you will get the time since the application started. It starts with the 0.0f. The time variable is multiplied by 1.5f to accelerate the rotation a bit. Then, D3DXMatrixTranslation() sets the ._41, ._42, ._42 members of the `matTrans` matrix. To concatenate the rotation and transformation matrices, you multiply them in such a way that the transformation matrix follows the rotation matrix. The result is provided to the `SetTransform()` function, which delivers the world matrix almost directly to the transformation unit of the hardware, if transformation is supported in the hardware. Otherwise, Direct3D must do software vertex processing.

The Direct3D engine does the rest of the work. What I left out here are the view, projection matrix, and usage of the depth buffer. I will present the view and projection transformations later in this chapter in the sections titled "The View Transformation" and "The Projection Transformation," and I will cover the concept behind depth buffers and how to use them at the end of this chapter.

To extend the 1steps example, you might copy the following source code into `FrameMove()`. That way you can rotate the quad around its x and y axes.

```
HRESULT CMyD3DApplication::FrameMove()
{
        D3DXMATRIX matRotY, matRotX;
        D3DXMatrixRotationY( &matRotY, m_fTime * 1.5f);
        D3DXMatrixRotationX( &matRotX, m_fTime * 1.5f);

        D3DXMATRIX matTrans;
        D3DXMatrixTranslation(&matTrans, 0.0f, 0.0f, 0.0f);
        m_pd3dDevice->SetTransform( D3DTS_WORLD, &(m_RotY * m_RotX * matTrans));

        return S_OK;
}
```

As you can see, you concatenate the two rotation matrices by multiplying them.

The 1steps2 Example

The 1steps2.exe example program, located in the \1steps directory on the CD-ROM, shows the importance of the order of transformations (see Figure 6.6).

It uses four viewports that display different scenes in which different matrices are involved in the transformation of the textured quad. This program is heavily inspired by an example program used in Kelly Dempski's *Real-Time Rendering Tricks and Techniques in DirectX* (Premier Press, 2002).

NOTE

This example also shows the effect of back-face culling. The Direct3D engine does not process the quad's back face, which is more efficient. This makes sense, for example, in the case of a cube, where you don't see the back face anyway. There are flags for the `SetRenderState()` function that can alter the behavior of back-face culling. For example, the following line switches off back-face culling:

```
d3dDevice->SetRenderState
(D3DRS_CULLMODE, D3DCULL_NONE);
```

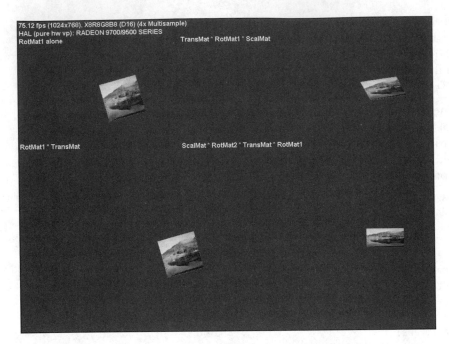

Figure 6.6

Order of transformations

All the matrices used by the program are created once in the `Render()` function. Normally I would place them into the `FrameMove()` function, but I think it is easier to get the whole picture by putting them into the rendering function. The program uses four different matrices.

```
D3DXMATRIX RotationMatrix1;
D3DXMATRIX RotationMatrix2;
D3DXMATRIX TranslationMatrix;
D3DXMATRIX ScalingMatrix;
```

The first and the second rotation matrices (`RotationMatrix1` and `RotationMatrix2`) rotate around the z-axis.

```
D3DXMatrixRotationZ(&RotationMatrix1, m_fTime * 1.5f);
D3DXMatrixRotationZ(&RotationMatrix2, -m_fTime * 1.5f);
```

The first rotation matrix rotates counterclockwise, and the second one rotates clockwise. `TranslationMatrix` sets the rotating quad three units to the right using the `D3DXMatrixTranslation()` function.

```
D3DXMatrixTranslation(&TranslationMatrix, 3.0f, 0.0f, 0.0f);
```

Additionally, a scaling matrix appropriately called `ScalingMatrix` is used.

```
D3DXMatrixScaling(&ScalingMatrix, 1.0f, 0.5f, 1.0f);
```

This matrix scales the height to 0.5f.

So far I have described all of the different transformations used by the 1steps2 example program. The following sections will show you how these transformation matrices produce the output in the viewport.

Top-Left Viewport

The first rotation matrix, RotationMatrix1, is featured in the top-left viewport, in which the quad rotates around the z-axis in the middle of the viewport window. You don't have to pay attention to the order of matrix multiplication because only one matrix is used.

Bottom-Left Viewport

The bottom-left viewport also shows a scene in which the quad rotates around the z-axis. This time it is translated by the TranslationMatrix three units to the right by using the D3DXMatrixTranslation() function. The translation matrix is standing in the multiplication order after the first rotation matrix.

Top-Right Viewport

The top-right viewport shows a quad that rotates around the z-axis and the center of the viewport. At the same time, it is scaled in its height relative to the x-axis.

Because the order of the rotation matrix and the translation matrix are changed compared to the bottom-left viewport, the quad rotates around the z-axis and also around its own z-axis in three units' distance. By letting the scale matrix follow the other matrices, scaling occurs relative to the x-axis of the world coordinate system, so the quad changes its height all the time.

Bottom-Right Viewport

The bottom-right viewport shows a quad that rotates around the center of the viewport in three units' distance, but not around its own z-axis. Additionally, it is scaled to half its size. Scaling occurs this way because the scaling matrix is the first matrix used in the order of multiplication. Additionally, an anti-rotation matrix prevents the rotation of the quad. This is accomplished by using the second rotation matrix, which rotates in the opposite direction of the first rotation matrix. Therefore, the rotations cancel each other. This method is how a planet might orbit around another planet, for example.

Note that rotating an object in three dimensions by using the three rotation functions mentioned might result in a lost dimension. This well-known phenomenon is called *gimbal lock*. Nevertheless, these functions are quite suitable for most games today, in which two and a half dimensions are enough. One solution, which involves rotating an object in three dimensions, can be realized with vectors; another solution uses quaternions.

The 1steps3 Example

The 1steps3.exe example demonstrates a technique for rotating an object around all three axes with the help of vectors. Figure 6.7 shows two simple models that you can rotate and position wherever you want. It is a very basic space flight simulator without physics or lighting.

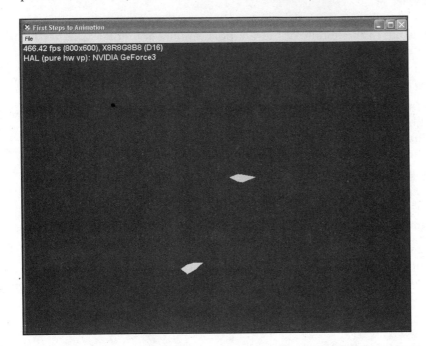

Figure 6.7

Two spaceships

There is a small help system that you can call by pressing 1. To rotate the first ship, use the Q/E keys to yaw the ship, W/S to pitch it, A/D to roll it, and F/V to move it. You can rotate the second ship using the U/O, I/K, and J/L keys, and you can move it using the H/N keys.

All of the upcoming example programs use a simple object. Because they do not use lighting, the form of the object needs to help identify its orientation. Figure 6.8 shows a wireframe view of the spaceship.

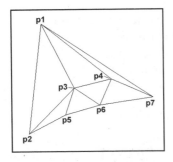

Figure 6.8

Wireframe view of the spaceship

The whole model is created in the `OneTimeSceneInit()` function.

```
// Points which make up an object geometry
D3DXVECTOR3 p1 = D3DXVECTOR3( 0.00f, 0.00f, 0.50f );
D3DXVECTOR3 p2 = D3DXVECTOR3( 0.50f, 0.00f,-0.50f );
D3DXVECTOR3 p3 = D3DXVECTOR3( 0.15f, 0.15f,-0.35f );
D3DXVECTOR3 p4 = D3DXVECTOR3(-0.15f, 0.15f,-0.35f );
D3DXVECTOR3 p5 = D3DXVECTOR3( 0.15f,-0.15f,-0.35f );
D3DXVECTOR3 p6 = D3DXVECTOR3(-0.15f,-0.15f,-0.35f );
D3DXVECTOR3 p7 = D3DXVECTOR3(-0.50f, 0.00f,-0.50f );

// vertices for the top
m_pvObjectVertices[0].p = p1;
m_pvObjectVertices[0].tu = 0.0f;
m_pvObjectVertices[0].tv = 0.5f;
m_pvObjectVertices[1].p = p2;
m_pvObjectVertices[1].tu = 0.5f;
m_pvObjectVertices[1].tv = 1.0f;
m_pvObjectVertices[2].p = p3;
m_pvObjectVertices[2].tu = 0.425f;
m_pvObjectVertices[2].tv = 0.575f;
m_pvObjectVertices[3].p = p4;
m_pvObjectVertices[3].tu = 0.425f;
m_pvObjectVertices[3].tv = 0.425f;
m_pvObjectVertices[4].p = p7;
m_pvObjectVertices[4].tu = 0.5f;
m_pvObjectVertices[4].tv = 0.0f;

// vertices for the bottom
...
// vertices for the rear
...

// Vertex indices for the object
m_pwObjectIndices[ 0] =  0; m_pwObjectIndices[ 1] =  1; m_pwObjectIndices[ 2] =  2;
m_pwObjectIndices[ 3] =  0; m_pwObjectIndices[ 4] =  2; m_pwObjectIndices[ 5] =  3;
m_pwObjectIndices[ 6] =  0; m_pwObjectIndices[ 7] =  3; m_pwObjectIndices[ 8] =  4;
m_pwObjectIndices[ 9] =  5; m_pwObjectIndices[10] =  7; m_pwObjectIndices[11] =  6;
m_pwObjectIndices[12] =  5; m_pwObjectIndices[13] =  8; m_pwObjectIndices[14] =  7;
m_pwObjectIndices[15] =  5; m_pwObjectIndices[16] =  9; m_pwObjectIndices[17] =  8;
m_pwObjectIndices[18] = 10; m_pwObjectIndices[19] = 15; m_pwObjectIndices[20] = 11;
m_pwObjectIndices[21] = 11; m_pwObjectIndices[22] = 15; m_pwObjectIndices[23] = 12;
m_pwObjectIndices[24] = 12; m_pwObjectIndices[25] = 15; m_pwObjectIndices[26] = 14;
m_pwObjectIndices[27] = 12; m_pwObjectIndices[28] = 14; m_pwObjectIndices[29] = 13;
```

m_pvObjectVertices[0] and m_pvObjectVertices[5] lie on point 1. m_pvObjectVertices[1] and m_pvObjectVertices[6] lie on point 2. m_pvObjectVertices[3] and m_pvObjectVertices[11] lie on point 3, and so on. Every point is declared as a vector with D3DXVECTOR3. The last two variables of m_pvObjectVertices are the texture coordinates. Most textures, like bitmaps, are two-dimensional arrays of color values. The individual color values are called *texture elements,* or *texels.* Each texel has a texel coordinate—a unique address in the texture. Direct3D programs specify texel coordinates in terms of u, v values, much like 2D Cartesian coordinates are specified in terms of x, y coordinates. The address can be thought of as a column and row number. Direct3D uses a uniform address range for all texels in all textures. Therefore, it uses a generic addressing scheme in which all texel addresses are in the range of 0.0 to 1.0, inclusive. You set the indices with the following code:

```
// Vertex indices for the object
m_pwObjectIndices[ 0] = 0; m_pwObjectIndices[ 1] = 1; m_pwObjectIndices[ 2] = 2;
m_pwObjectIndices[ 3] = 0; m_pwObjectIndices[ 4] = 2; m_pwObjectIndices[ 5] = 3;
m_pwObjectIndices[ 6] = 0; m_pwObjectIndices[ 7] = 3; m_pwObjectIndices[ 8] = 4;
m_pwObjectIndices[ 9] = 5; m_pwObjectIndices[10] = 7; m_pwObjectIndices[11] = 6;
m_pwObjectIndices[12] = 5; m_pwObjectIndices[13] = 8; m_pwObjectIndices[14] = 7;
m_pwObjectIndices[15] = 5; m_pwObjectIndices[16] = 9; m_pwObjectIndices[17] = 8;
m_pwObjectIndices[18] = 10; m_pwObjectIndices[19] = 15; m_pwObjectIndices[20] = 11;
m_pwObjectIndices[21] = 11; m_pwObjectIndices[22] = 15; m_pwObjectIndices[23] = 12;
m_pwObjectIndices[24] = 12; m_pwObjectIndices[25] = 15; m_pwObjectIndices[26] = 14;
m_pwObjectIndices[27] = 12; m_pwObjectIndices[28] = 14; m_pwObjectIndices[29] = 13;
```

This piece of code generates the indices for the D3DPT_TRIANGLELIST call in DrawIndexedPrimitive(). As you learned in the first chapter, Direct3D allows you to define your polygons in one of two ways—by defining their vertices or by defining indices into a list of vertices. The latter approach is often faster and more flexible because it allows objects with multiple polygons to share vertex data.

Our object consists of only seven points, which are used by 15 vertices. Therefore, you index an average of more than two vertices.

The two objects are defined with the help of the m_pObjects structure, which holds only a matrix variable. To implement collision and other nifty stuff, you might store many more variables here.

```
struct Object
{
    D3DXMATRIX    matLocal;
};
```

Three vectors in the matrix keep track of the orientation of the model. These are called the Look, Up, and Right vectors. Figure 6.9 shows all three vectors attached to a model.

In Figure 6.9, you can see the Look, Up, and Right vectors of a plane. The figure is a bit oversimplified because all three vectors should start at the center of the object's gravity.

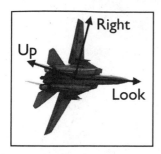

Figure 6.9

The Look, Up, and Right vectors

The Look vector describes the way the object is facing; it's the object's local z-axis. To set the object's direction so that it is facing into the screen, you would have to set the Look vector to D3DVECTOR (0, 0, 1).

The Look vector is not enough to describe the orientation of the object. For example, the object could stand upside down, and the Look vector wouldn't reflect this change in orientation. The Up vector helps here; it points up vertically, relative to the direction the object points, like the object's y-axis. Therefore, the Up vector is defined as D3DVECTOR (0, 1, 0). If you turn the object upside down, the Up vector will be D3DVECTOR (0, -1, 0).

These vectors are stored in the matrix in the following order. The vLook vector is in the third row, a vUp vector is in the second row, and a vRight vector is in the first row. This matrix is filled with default values.

```
// yellow object
D3DXMatrixIdentity(&m_pObjects[0].matLocal);
m_pObjects[0].matLocal._41 = -1.0f; // Position

// red object
D3DXMatrixIdentity(&m_pObjects[1].matLocal);
m_pObjects[1].matLocal._41   = 1.0f;
```

D3DXMatrixIdentity() already defaulted the matrix to the identity matrix, so the vLook vector is (0.0f, 0.0f, 1.0f), the vUp vector is (0.0f, 1.0f, 0.0f), and the vRight vector is (1.0f, 0.0f, 0.0f). The only thing left is to choose a position for the object. You accomplish this by giving the first element of the vector in the fourth row a position for the respective object.

To rotate the object, two of these vectors must always be rotated around the rotation vector. For example, to roll the object, the Up and Right vectors have to be rotated around the Look vector. Figure 6.10 should help you visualize the rotation.

To pitch the object, you must rotate the Up and Look vectors around the Right vector. To yaw the object, you must rotate the Look and Right vectors around the Up vector. You accomplish this rotation of a vector around another vector as the rotation axis using D3DXVec3TransformCoord(). This function transforms a 3D vector by a given matrix. The following code details the core of this source.

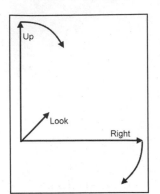

Figure 6.10

*The rotation of the
Up and Right vectors
around the Look vector*

```
// rotate the LOOK & RIGHT Vectors about the UP Vector
D3DXVec3TransformCoord(&vLook, &vLook, &matYaw);
D3DXVec3TransformCoord(&vRight, &vRight, &matYaw);

// rotate the LOOK & UP Vectors about the RIGHT Vector
D3DXVec3TransformCoord(&vLook, &vLook, &matPitch);
D3DXVec3TransformCoord(&vUp, &vUp, &matPitch);

// rotate the RIGHT & UP Vectors about the LOOK Vector
D3DXVec3TransformCoord(&vRight, &vRight, &matRoll);
D3DXVec3TransformCoord(&vUp, &vUp, &matRoll);
```

Every pair of vectors is rotated with the help of a yaw, pitch, or roll matrix. This matrix was produced with the help of the D3DXMatrixRotationAxis() function, which builds a matrix that rotates around an arbitrary axis. This matrix is built before the vectors are rotated.

```
// Matrices for pitch, yaw and roll
D3DXMatrixRotationAxis(&matPitch, &vRight, fPitch );
D3DXMatrixRotationAxis(&matYaw, &vUp, fYaw );
D3DXMatrixRotationAxis(&matRoll, &vLook, fRoll);
```

Before the whole vector rotation can occur, you must re-normalize all vectors. When computers handle floating-point numbers, little accumulation errors occur during the rotation math. After a few rotations, these rounding errors create a state in which the three vectors are no longer perpendicular to each other (see Figure 6.11).

You can re-normalize the vectors with the following code:

```
// base vector regeneration
D3DXVec3Normalize(&vLook, &vLook);
D3DXVec3Cross(&vRight, &vUp, &vLook);   // Cross Product of the UP and LOOK Vector
D3DXVec3Normalize(&vRight, &vRight);
D3DXVec3Cross(&vUp, &vLook, &vRight); // Cross Product of the RIGHT and LOOK Vector
D3DXVec3Normalize(&vUp, &vUp);
```

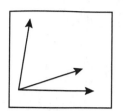

Figure 6.11

Unperpendicular
vectors

Before you can use vectors to create the rotation matrices shown previously, you must always re-normalize them. Re-normalization of vectors is a computationally expensive task. This source code makes the vectors perpendicular to each other through the following steps.

1. Normalize Look.
2. Build the cross-product between Look and Up to get Right.
3. Normalize Right.
4. Build the cross-product between Look and Right to get Up.
5. Normalize Up.

Normalizing a vector means making it one unit long. You need vectors that are one unit long to simplify the rotation calculation. The length of a vector is computed by:

```
||A|| = sqrt(x² + y² + z²)
```

This is the square root of the Pythagorean theorem. The magnitude of a vector has a special symbol in mathematics—a capital letter designated with two vertical bars: ‖A‖. The source code for D3DXVec3Normalize() is not provided, but it might look like this:

```
D3DXVECTOR3* D3DXVec3Normalize(D3DXVECTOR3* v1, D3DXVECTOR3* v2)
{
    D3DXVECTOR3 tv1 = (D3DXVECTOR3)*v1;
    D3DXVECTOR3 tv2 = (D3DXVECTOR3)*v2;
    tv1 = tv2/(float) sqrt(tv2.x * tv2.x + tv2.y * tv2.y + tv2.z * tv2.z);
    v1 = &tv1;
    return (v1);
}
```

This code divides the vector by its magnitude, which is retrieved by the square root of the Pythagorean theorem.

To get perpendicular vectors, you must calculate the cross-product of two vectors to get a third vector that is perpendicular to the first two (see Figure 6.12). For example, in back-face culling, the cross-product determines the direction in which the polygons are facing. It uses two of the polygon's edges to generate a normal. Thus, you can use it to generate a normal for any surface for which you have two vectors that lie within the surface.

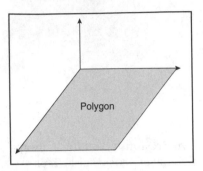

Figure 6.12

Cross-product

The formula for the cross-product is U×V. The source code for `D3DXVec3Cross()` is not publicly available, but it might look like this:

```
D3DXVECTOR3* D3DXVec3Cross (
    D3DXVECTOR3* pOut,
    const D3DXVECTOR3* pV1,
    const D3DXVECTOR3* pV2)
{
    pOut->x = pV1->y * pV2->z - pV1->z * pV2->y;
    pOut->y = pV1->z * pV2->x - pV1->x * pV2->z;
    pOut->z = pV1->x * pV2->y - pV1->y * pV2->x;

    return pOut;
}
```

As you can see from this code, the Look vector creates perpendicular Right and Up vectors via the cross-product. (You'll learn more about the cross-product in Appendix C.) Therefore, this is the "leading" vector in the re-normalization process.

The vectors are stored in a matrix, which is available per-object to rotate the objects independently from each other. The vectors are stored in the following order:

```
m_pObjects[0].matLocal._11 = vRight.x;
m_pObjects[0].matLocal._12 = vRight.y;
m_pObjects[0].matLocal._13 = vRight.z;
m_pObjects[0].matLocal._21 = vUp.x;
m_pObjects[0].matLocal._22 = vUp.y;
m_pObjects[0].matLocal._23 = vUp.z;
m_pObjects[0].matLocal._31 = vLook.x;
m_pObjects[0].matLocal._32 = vLook.y;
m_pObjects[0].matLocal._33 = vLook.z;
m_pObjects[0].matLocal._41 = vPos.x;
m_pObjects[0].matLocal._42 = vPos.y;
m_pObjects[0].matLocal._43 = vPos.z;
```

The first row stores the Right vector, the second row stores the Up vector, and the third row stores the Look vector, whereas the fourth row holds the position.

The following code shows the entire source to rotate and position one object:

```
D3DXVECTOR3 vRight, vUp, vLook, vPos;
FLOAT fRoll, fPitch, fYaw;

FLOAT fspeed = fOneStep;

fRoll = fPitch = fYaw = 0.0f;

if (m_bKey['D']) fRoll -= fOneStep;
if (m_bKey['A']) fRoll += fOneStep;
if (m_bKey['S']) fPitch -= fOneStep;
if (m_bKey['W']) fPitch += fOneStep;
if (m_bKey['Q']) fYaw -= fOneStep;
if (m_bKey['E']) fYaw += fOneStep;

vRight.x = m_pObjects[0].matLocal._11;
vRight.y = m_pObjects[0].matLocal._12;
vRight.z = m_pObjects[0].matLocal._13;
vUp.x = m_pObjects[0].matLocal._21;
vUp.y = m_pObjects[0].matLocal._22;
vUp.z = m_pObjects[0].matLocal._23;
vLook.x = m_pObjects[0].matLocal._31;
vLook.y = m_pObjects[0].matLocal._32;
vLook.z = m_pObjects[0].matLocal._33;
vPos.x = m_pObjects[0].matLocal._41;
vPos.y = m_pObjects[0].matLocal._42;
vPos.z = m_pObjects[0].matLocal._43;

// base vector regeneration
D3DXVec3Normalize(&vLook, &vLook);
D3DXVec3Cross(&vRight, &vUp, &vLook);  // Cross Product of the UP and LOOK Vector
D3DXVec3Normalize(&vRight, &vRight);
D3DXVec3Cross(&vUp, &vLook, &vRight); // Cross Product of the RIGHT and LOOK Vector
D3DXVec3Normalize(&vUp, &vUp);

// Matrices for pitch, yaw and roll
D3DXMATRIX matPitch, matYaw, matRoll;
D3DXMatrixRotationAxis(&matPitch, &vRight, fPitch );
D3DXMatrixRotationAxis(&matYaw, &vUp, fYaw );
D3DXMatrixRotationAxis(&matRoll, &vLook, fRoll);

// rotate the LOOK & RIGHT Vectors about the UP Vector
D3DXVec3TransformCoord(&vLook, &vLook, &matYaw);
D3DXVec3TransformCoord(&vRight, &vRight, &matYaw);
```

```
// rotate the LOOK & UP Vectors about the RIGHT Vector
D3DXVec3TransformCoord(&vLook, &vLook, &matPitch);
D3DXVec3TransformCoord(&vUp, &vUp, &matPitch);

// rotate the RIGHT & UP Vectors about the LOOK Vector
D3DXVec3TransformCoord(&vRight, &vRight, &matRoll);
D3DXVec3TransformCoord(&vUp, &vUp, &matRoll);

 // move forward
if (m_bKey['R'])
{
        vPos.x+=fspeed*vLook.x;
        vPos.y+=fspeed*vLook.y;
        vPos.z+=fspeed*vLook.z;
}

// move back
if (m_bKey['F'])    // Key END
{
        vPos.x-=fspeed*vLook.x;
        vPos.y-=fspeed*vLook.y;
        vPos.z-=fspeed*vLook.z;
}

m_pObjects[0].matLocal._11 = vRight.x;
m_pObjects[0].matLocal._12 = vRight.y;
m_pObjects[0].matLocal._13 = vRight.z;
m_pObjects[0].matLocal._21 = vUp.x;
m_pObjects[0].matLocal._22 = vUp.y;
m_pObjects[0].matLocal._23 = vUp.z;
m_pObjects[0].matLocal._31 = vLook.x;
m_pObjects[0].matLocal._32 = vLook.y;
m_pObjects[0].matLocal._33 = vLook.z;
m_pObjects[0].matLocal._41 = vPos.x;
m_pObjects[0].matLocal._42 = vPos.y;
m_pObjects[0].matLocal._43 = vPos.z;
```

This code shows how the vectors are retrieved from the matrix, renormalized, and rotated. Additionally, you move the object in the direction in which the Look vector points by adding the Look vector multiplied by a speed factor to the position data.

Now that you have seen a consistent way to rotate objects in 3D, the 1steps4 example presents an even more efficient way of doing this by using quaternions.

The 1steps4 Example

The 1steps4.exe example shows a more efficient way to rotate an object in 3D. You can use the same keys as in the previous example to move the objects. The entire source code to accomplish this follows.

```
FLOAT fRoll, fPitch, fYaw;
fRoll = fPitch = fYaw = 0.0f;

if (m_bKey['D']) fRoll -= fOneStep;
if (m_bKey['A']) fRoll += fOneStep;
if (m_bKey['S']) fPitch -= fOneStep;
if (m_bKey['W']) fPitch += fOneStep;
if (m_bKey['Q']) fYaw -= fOneStep;
if (m_bKey['E']) fYaw += fOneStep;

// Update rotation matrix
D3DXQUATERNION qR;
D3DXMATRIX matRot;
D3DXQuaternionRotationYawPitchRoll (&qR, fYaw, fPitch, fRoll);
D3DXMatrixRotationQuaternion (&matRot, &qR);
D3DXMatrixMultiply (&m_pObjects[0].matLocal, &matRot, &m_pObjects[0].matLocal);

// Update position
D3DXVECTOR3 vLook;                      // Look vector
vLook.x = m_pObjects[0].matLocal._31;   // extract Look vector
vLook.y = m_pObjects[0].matLocal._32;
vLook.z = m_pObjects[0].matLocal._33;

// move forward
if (m_bKey['R'])
{
        m_pObjects[0].matLocal._41 += fOneStep * vLook.x;
        m_pObjects[0].matLocal._42 += fOneStep * vLook.y;
        m_pObjects[0].matLocal._43 += fOneStep * vLook.z;
}

// move back
if (m_bKey['F'])
{
        m_pObjects[0].matLocal._41 -= fOneStep * vLook.x;
        m_pObjects[0].matLocal._42 -= fOneStep * vLook.y;
        m_pObjects[0].matLocal._43 -= fOneStep * vLook.z;
}
```

This is really a handy piece of source that rotates the objects. You can reduce the number of lines even further, but I didn't do that for clarity's sake.

Sir William Rowan Hamilton invented quaternions back in 1843 as an extension to the complex numbers, but it was not until 1985 that Ken Shoemake introduced them to the field of computer graphics on SIGGRAPH (http://www.siggraph.org).

Quaternions extend the concept of rotation in three dimensions to rotation in four dimensions. They are useful for representing and processing 3D rotations of points. They can also be used in:

- Skeletal animation
- Inverse cinematics
- 3D physics

NOTE

The official mission statement of SIGGRAPH is: Our mission is to promote the generation and dissemination of information on computer graphics and interactive techniques.

You can use quaternions in a game to replace rotation matrices. They can describe any rotation around any axis in 3D space. Why should you use quaternions instead of matrices?

- They take less space than matrices.
- Some operations, such as interpolation between quaternions, are more pleasant visually.

Let's start with the major question. What is a quaternion?

My favorite answer to this question is that a quaternion is a vector plus rotation. This is a very non-mathematical way to describe it, but this simple description helps me to visualize it in my head (see Figure 6.13).

Quaternions contain a scalar component and a 3D vector component. The scalar component is usually referred to as w. You can refer to the vector component v as a single entity v or as individual components x, y, and z. Both notations are illustrated in the following lines.

```
[w v]
[w (x, y, z)]
```

With the Direct3D quaternion class, you use the w, x, y, and z components by adding .x, .y, .z, and .w to the variable names.

Define a vector v as the axis of rotation. To simplify calculations, v should be unit length. The direction of v defines the "positive" rotation. The scalar q should be the amount of rotation around the axis specified by v. Thus, the pair (q, v) defines an amount of rotation

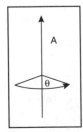

Figure 6.13

A quaternion
representing a rotation
around Axis A

(angular displacement) as a rotation of q radians around the axis specified by v. Unfortunately, q and v are not simply stored directly in the four numbers of the quaternion. The following equation shows how the numbers inside a quaternion q are related to q and v. Both forms of quaternion notation are used.

```
q = [cos(q/2) sin(q/2)v]
q = [cos(q/2) (sin(q/2)vx, sin(q/2)vy, sin(q/2)vz)]
```

Yaw, pitch, and roll are converted to a quaternion here. This is also referred to as converting from Euler angles to a quaternion. This is quite tricky because the order of operations must be correct. Because you can convert the Euler angles to three independent quaternions by setting the arbitrary axis to the coordinate axes, you can then multiply the three quaternions to obtain the final quaternion.

If you have three Euler angles (yaw, pitch, and roll), you can form three independent quaternions.

```
Qx = [ cos(yaw/2), (sin(yaw/2), 0, 0)]
Qy = [ cos(pitch/2), (0, sin(pitch/2), 0)]
Qz = [ cos(roll/2), (0, 0, sin(roll/2))]
```

You obtain the final quaternion by multiplying $Qx * Qy * Qz$. Converting the yaw, pitch, and roll to a quaternion is done via the following function:

```
D3DXQUATERNION * D3DXQuaternionRotationYawPitchRoll (
    D3DXQUATERNION * pOut,
    FLOAT yaw,
    FLOAT pitch,
    FLOAT roll)
{
    FLOAT sinY, cosY, sinP, cosP, sinR, cosR;

    sinY = sin(0.5f * yaw);
    cosY = cos(0.5f * yaw);

    sinP = sin(0.5f * pitch);
    cosP = cos(0.5f * pitch);

    sinR = sin(0.5f * roll);
    cosR = cos(0.5f * roll);

    pOut->x = cosR * sinP * cosY + sinR * cosP * sinY;
    pOut->y = cosR * cosP * sinY - sinR * sinP * cosY;
    pOut->z = sinR * cosP * cosY - cosR * sinP * sinY;
    pOut->w = cosR * cosP * cosY + sinR * sinP * sinY;

    return pOut;
}
```

The multiplication of the three quaternions occurs in the four rows that store their results in pOut.

Because the Direct3D transformation engine awaits matrices, you must convert the quaternion into the matrix format. You accomplish this with the following code:

```
D3DXMATRIX  * D3DXMatrixRotationQuaternion(
    D3DXMATRIX  * pOut,
    CONST D3DXQUATERNION *pQ)
{

    D3DMath_MatrixFromQuaternion (&pOut, *pQ.x, *pQ.y, *pQ.z, *pQ.w);

  return pOut;
}
From d3dmath.cpp:
VOID D3DMath_MatrixFromQuaternion( D3DMATRIX& mat, FLOAT x, FLOAT y, FLOAT z,
                                   FLOAT w )
{
    FLOAT xx = x*x; FLOAT yy = y*y; FLOAT zz = z*z;
    FLOAT xy = x*y; FLOAT xz = x*z; FLOAT yz = y*z;
    FLOAT wx = w*x; FLOAT wy = w*y; FLOAT wz = w*z;

    mat._11 = 1 - 2 * ( yy + zz );
    mat._12 =     2 * ( xy - wz );
    mat._13 =     2 * ( xz + wy );

    mat._21 =     2 * ( xy + wz );
    mat._22 = 1 - 2 * ( xx + zz );
    mat._23 =     2 * ( yz - wx );

    mat._31 =     2 * ( xz - wy );
    mat._32 =     2 * ( yz + wx );
    mat._33 = 1 - 2 * ( xx + yy );

    mat._14 = mat._24 = mat._34 = 0.0f;
    mat._41 = mat._42 = mat._43 = 0.0f;
    mat._44 = 1.0f;
}
```

Please note that the source code for the first two functions is not available, and that the source shown here is just a guess.

With regard to world transformations, you have learned how to

- Use matrices to store rotations and transformations of objects
- Be aware of the order of matrices
- Use orientation vectors to rotate objects in 3D
- Use a quaternion built from yaw, pitch, and roll to rotate objects in 3D

I will show you how to create and use all these viewports later in this chapter, in the "Working with the Viewport" section.

An obvious improvement to the examples that does not fit in the scope of the book is the implementation of time-based physics. You would use this to interpret the user's input as a velocity in the desired direction. Since you have the ship's orthogonal orientation basis vectors (Look, Up, and Right), the implementation is a simple one-dimensional physics problem.

```
Position += deltaTime * InputSpeed * forward
```

You might use this to achieve damping effects. It looks pretty cool when your ship has some momentum while slowing down or rotating. You might be able to give different ships different velocities so the user can "feel" the size of the ship by seeing its velocity. A big ship would be sluggish and a small ship would be very fast.

After reviewing the world transformations, you can go on to the view transformations. The main challenge in this section is to build a camera class.

The View Transformation

View transformations usually describe the position and the orientation of a viewer in a scene. This is normally your position and orientation, looking through the glass of your monitor into the scene. Many people use the example of a camera through which you look into the scene to describe this transformation. You accomplish a view transformation via a view transformation matrix or a short view matrix. Such a matrix is conceptually different from the world matrix but mechanically the same, meaning that the transformation matrices are built the same way for both types of transformations. The main difference between a world and a view matrix is the way the three orientation vectors are stored. Whereas the world matrix stores them in a row order, the view matrix stores them in a column order.

You use the view matrix to build up a solid camera model that allows the player to see the world through a different set of eyes. This section outlines two camera models that might be useful in games.

- A very efficient camera model provided by Direct3D for games, in which the camera does not have to be able to rotate through three dimensions. This model will be useful in most situations.
- A sophisticated camera model that allows you to rotate the camera in 3D, which is useful in flight simulators or space shooters.

The first camera model is provided in Direct3D via the D3DXMatrixLookAtLH() function. This function awaits the position, the Look vector, and the Up vector, and provides a matrix that represents the position and orientation of the camera. Unfortunately the source code is not available for this function, but it might look like the following code.

```
#define MX_EPS5            1e-5f
D3DXMATRIX * D3DXMatrixLookAtLH ( D3DXMATRIX * pOut, const D3DXVECTOR3 * pEye,
                                  const D3DXVECTOR3 * pAt,
                                  const D3DXVECTOR3 * pUp)
{
    // the three orientation vectors of the camera
    D3DXVECTOR3   uAxis, vAxis, nAxis;

    // create look vector and normalize it
    nAxis = (*pAt) - (*pEye);
    if (D3DXVec3Normalize(&nAxis, &nAxis) == NULL) return NULL;

    // create up vector
    vAxis = (*pUp) - nAxis * D3DXVec3Dot(pUp, &nAxis);

    if (D3DXVec3Length(&vAxis) < MX_EPS5)
    {
        vAxis.x =        - nAxis.y * nAxis.x;
        vAxis.y = 1.0f - nAxis.y * nAxis.y;
        vAxis.z =        - nAxis.y * nAxis.z;

        if (D3DXVec3Length(&vAxis) < MX_EPS5)
        {
            vAxis.x =      - nAxis.z * nAxis.x;
            vAxis.y =        - nAxis.z * nAxis.y;
            vAxis.z = 1.0f - nAxis.z * nAxis.z;
            if (D3DXVec3Length(&vAxis) < MX_EPS5) return NULL;
        }
    }

    // normalize up vector
    D3DXVec3Normalize(&vAxis, &vAxis);

    // create right vector
    D3DXVec3Cross(&uAxis, &vAxis, &nAxis);

    pOut->_11 = uAxis.x; pOut->_12 = vAxis.x; pOut->_13 = nAxis.x; pOut->_14 = 0.0f;
    pOut->_21 = uAxis.y; pOut->_22 = vAxis.y; pOut->_23 = nAxis.y; pOut->_24 = 0.0f;
    pOut->_31 = uAxis.z; pOut->_32 = vAxis.z; pOut->_33 = nAxis.z; pOut->_34 = 0.0f;
```

```
pOut->_41 = -D3DXVec3Dot(pEye, &uAxis);
pOut->_42 = -D3DXVec3Dot(pEye, &vAxis);
pOut->_43 = -D3DXVec3Dot(pEye, &nAxis);
pOut->_44 = 1.0f;

    return pOut;
}
```

This function creates three vectors internally. It uses the position of the camera and the position at which the camera is looking to create a Look vector named nAxis. The Up vector is provided via the parameter and is called vAxis after stretching and normalization. The Right vector is calculated from the cross-product of the Look and Up vectors. A camera uses these orientation vectors in a similar way as they were used to orient objects in 3D (see Figure 6.14).

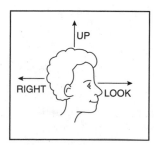
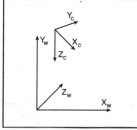

Figure 6.14

The Up, Right, and Look vectors

The Look vector describes the way the camera is facing; it's the camera's local z-axis. Figure 6.14 shows it as z_c. To set the camera's direction so it is facing into the screen, you would have to set the Look vector to D3DVECTOR (0, 0, 1).

The Look vector isn't enough to describe the orientation of the camera. The camera could stand upside down, and the Look vector wouldn't reflect this change in orientation. The Up vector helps here; it points up vertically relative to the direction the camera points. It's like the camera's y-axis, and it's labeled as Y_c in Figure 6.14. Therefore, the Up vector is defined as D3DVECTOR (0, 1, 0). If you turn the camera upside down, the Up vector will be D3DVECTOR (0, -1, 0). You can generate a Right vector from the Look and Up vectors by using the cross-product of the two vectors, which is labeled as X_c in Figure 6.14.

To visualize camera rotation around a camera axis, imagine a player sitting in the cockpit of an F-22. If the player pushes his foot pedals in the F-22 for the left or right, the Look and the Right vectors have to be rotated around the Up vector or y-axis (yaw effect). If he pushes his flight stick to the right or left, the Up and Right vectors have to be rotated around the Look vector or z-axis (roll effect). If he pushes the flight stick forward or backward, you have to rotate the Look and Up vectors around the Right vector or x-axis (pitch effect).

D3DXMatrixLookAtLH() returns the view matrix. You can see how the vectors are filled in the columns. The first three values of the first column store the Up vector, the first three values of the second column store the Right vector, and the first three values of the third column store the Look vector.

D3DXMatrixLookAtLH() is very helpful for building a follow-up camera. The Look vector points to the object the camera should follow. The position vector of the camera is moved around this object or positioned behind or in front of it. Pseudocode for the function might look like this:

```
static FLOAT tic = -200.0f * rand();
tic += 0.01f;


vLook = m_pObjects[0].vLoc; // position of object that should be in the focus of the camera
vPos.z = vLook.z - 5.0f;// position of the camera
vPos.x = vLook.x ;
vPos.y = vLook.y + (FLOAT)(1.0f + 0.3f * sin(tic * 0.33f)); // slightly up and down move:
more lively


D3DXMATRIX view;
D3DXMatrixLookAtLH (&view,&vPos,  // pEye = Position
                    &vLook,  // pAt
                    &vUp);  // pUp
```

This function is designed for simple uses. For example, it is perfect for a head-mounted tracking display or a follow-up camera, but it won't help you build a space shooter or flight simulator camera. Therefore, a second class of camera techniques is more useful for these types of games. There are two implementations—one where the camera is rotated around vectors and one where the camera is rotated around arbitrary axes using quaternions. I will start with the camera class that rotates the camera around its axis.

The 1steps5 Example

Similar to the way you can rotate objects in 3D with the help of vectors, which I demonstrated previously, you can rotate a camera with the help of Up, Right, and Look vectors (refer to Figure 6.14). Whereas the camera technique in Figure 6.14 only used two of the vectors to track the camera orientation (Look and Up), this technique uses all three vectors. Rotating the camera around the Look vector means rolling it. Rotating the camera around the Right vector changes the pitch of the camera, and rotating the camera around the Up vector changes its yaw.

This time, you store the vectors in four vector objects instead of a matrix, and the camera is positioned to face the objects. To control the camera, you use the same technique that you used to control the objects in the 1steps3 example. The source code that is responsible for the camera should look quite familiar to you, now that you have seen the source code for how to rotate the object around a vector.

```
static D3DXVECTOR3 vCameraLook=D3DXVECTOR3(0.0f,0.0f,1.0);        // look vector
static D3DXVECTOR3 vCameraUp=D3DXVECTOR3(0.0f,1.0f,0.0f);         // up vector
static D3DXVECTOR3 vCameraRight=D3DXVECTOR3(1.0f,0.0f,0.0f);      // right vector
static D3DXVECTOR3 vCameraPos=D3DXVECTOR3(0.0f,0.0f,-5.0f);       // position vector


fPitch = fYaw = fRoll = 0.0f;
fspeed = fOneStep * 1.5f;


if (m_bKey[VK_UP])              fPitch=-1.0f * m_fElapsedTime;    // fPitch
if (m_bKey[VK_DOWN])           fPitch=+1.0f * m_fElapsedTime;
if (m_bKey[VK_LEFT])           fYaw=+1.0f * m_fElapsedTime;       // fYaw
if (m_bKey[VK_RIGHT])          fYaw=-1.0f * m_fElapsedTime;
if (m_bKey['C'])               fRoll=-1.0f * m_fElapsedTime;      // fRoll
if (m_bKey['X'])               fRoll=+1.0f * m_fElapsedTime;


// camera forward
if (m_bKey[VK_HOME])   // Key HOME
{
     vCameraPos.x+=fspeed*vCameraLook.x;
     vCameraPos.y+=fspeed*vCameraLook.y;
     vCameraPos.z+=fspeed*vCameraLook.z;
}


// camera back
if (m_bKey[VK_END])    // Key END
{
     vCameraPos.x-=fspeed*vCameraLook.x;
     vCameraPos.y-=fspeed*vCameraLook.y;
     vCameraPos.z-=fspeed*vCameraLook.z;
}


// base vector regeneration
D3DXVec3Normalize(&vCameraLook, &vCameraLook);
D3DXVec3Cross(&vCameraRight, &vCameraUp, &vCameraLook);  // Cross Product of the UP and
LOOK Vector
D3DXVec3Normalize(&vCameraRight, &vCameraRight);
D3DXVec3Cross(&vCameraUp, &vCameraLook, &vCameraRight); // Cross Product of the RIGHT and
LOOK Vector
D3DXVec3Normalize(&vCameraUp, &vCameraUp);


// Matrices for pitch, yaw and roll
D3DXMatrixRotationAxis(&matPitch, &vCameraRight, fPitch );
D3DXMatrixRotationAxis(&matYaw, &vCameraUp, fYaw );
D3DXMatrixRotationAxis(&matRoll, &vCameraLook, fRoll);
```

```
// rotate the LOOK & RIGHT Vectors about the UP Vector
D3DXVec3TransformCoord(&vCameraLook, &vCameraLook, &matYaw);
D3DXVec3TransformCoord(&vCameraRight, &vCameraRight, &matYaw);

// rotate the LOOK & UP Vectors about the RIGHT Vector
D3DXVec3TransformCoord(&vCameraLook, &vCameraLook, &matPitch);
D3DXVec3TransformCoord(&vCameraUp, &vCameraUp, &matPitch);

// rotate the RIGHT & UP Vectors about the LOOK Vector
D3DXVec3TransformCoord(&vCameraRight, &vCameraRight, &matRoll);
D3DXVec3TransformCoord(&vCameraUp, &vCameraUp, &matRoll);

D3DXMATRIX view;
D3DXMatrixIdentity( &view );
view._11 = vCameraRight.x;
view._12 = vCameraUp.x;
view._13 = vCameraLook.x;
view._21 = vCameraRight.y;
view._22 = vCameraUp.y;
view._23 = vCameraLook.y;
view._31 = vCameraRight.z;
view._32 = vCameraUp.z;
view._33 = vCameraLook.z;
view._41 = - D3DXVec3Dot( &vCameraPos, &vCameraRight );
view._42 = - D3DXVec3Dot( &vCameraPos, &vCameraUp );
view._43 = - D3DXVec3Dot( &vCameraPos, &vCameraLook );

m_pd3dDevice->SetTransform(D3DTS_VIEW, &view);
```

You can see how the three orientation vectors and the position vector are stored at the
beginning of the source code snippet. Instead of a matrix, this example holds the orientation and position data in four vectors, which does not make a big difference. The vector
re-normalization, creation of rotation matrices, and rotation of two vectors around a rotation
vector works the same as in the 1steps3.exe example in the section on world transformations.
However, the orientation vectors are stored differently in the view matrix. They are stored
in column order, not in row order as in the previous example. Additionally, the position is
calculated with a dot-product from the camera position and one of the three orientation
vectors. To move the position of the camera to the origin of the three orientation vectors,
the position vector is multiplied by the three orientation vectors and negated.

Now that you have seen how you can rotate a camera around all three axes in 3D by rotating
two vectors around a rotation vector, you are prepared to dive into a more sophisticated
example that does the same thing using a quaternion.

The 1steps6 Example

Perhaps you've played one of the *Tomb Raider* titles. (Who can forget Lara Croft, the girl with the guns?) It was one of the first commercial games that used quaternion rotations to animate all of the camera movements. A lot of third-person games use a virtual camera placed at some distance behind or to the side of the player's character with quaternions. These days, a quaternion orients most of those cameras.

Similar to the way you used a quaternion to rotate a 3D object in the previous section, you can use it to rotate a camera. The example 1steps6 is based on the example 1steps4, and it uses a quaternion to rotate the camera. Additionally, the camera can now slide to the left or right and up or down. Here is the main source code snippet:

```
fRoll = fPitch = fYaw = 0.0f;
D3DXVECTOR3 vPos(0.0f, 0.0f, 0.0f);
static D3DXMATRIX matView = D3DXMATRIX(1.0f, 0.0f, 0.0f, 0.0f,
                                       0.0f, 1.0f, 0.0f, 0.0f,
                                       0.0f, 0.0f, 1.0f, 0.0f,
                                       0.0f, 0.0f,-5.0f, 1.0f);
// Process keyboard input
if (m_bKey[VK_UP])        fPitch += fOneStep; // Pitch Up
if (m_bKey[VK_DOWN])          fPitch -= fOneStep; // Pitch Down
if (m_bKey[VK_LEFT])          fYaw += fOneStep; // Turn Left
if (m_bKey[VK_RIGHT])         fYaw -= fOneStep; // Turn Right
if (m_bKey['C'])               fRoll += fOneStep; // Rotate Left
if (m_bKey['X'])               fRoll -= fOneStep; // Rotate Right
if (m_bKey[VK_HOME])          vPos.z += fOneStep; // Move Forward
if (m_bKey[VK_END])       vPos.z -= fOneStep; // Move Backward
if (m_bKey[VK_NUMPAD4])   vPos.x -= fOneStep; // Slide Left
if (m_bKey[VK_NUMPAD6])   vPos.x += fOneStep; // Slide Right
if (m_bKey[VK_NUMPAD8])        vPos.y += fOneStep; // Slide Down
if (m_bKey[VK_NUMPAD2])        vPos.y -= fOneStep; // Slide Up

// Update position and view matrices
D3DXMATRIX matR, matTemp;
D3DXQuaternionRotationYawPitchRoll (&qR, fYaw, fPitch, fRoll);
D3DXMatrixRotationQuaternion (&matR, &qR);
D3DXMatrixMultiply (&matView, &matR, &matView);
D3DXMatrixTranslation (&matTemp, vPos.x, vPos.y, vPos.z);
D3DXMatrixMultiply (&matView, &matTemp, &matView);
D3DXMatrixInverse (&matTemp, NULL, &matView);

m_pd3dDevice->SetTransform(D3DTS_VIEW, &matTemp );
```

This time you use the `matView` matrix to store the camera's orientation. As you already know, the third column stores the Look vector of the camera, the second column stores the Up vector, and the first column stores the Right vector. Additionally, you keep track of the camera's position change in the `vPos` variable. The functions are accomplishing the following steps:

1. Build a quaternion from yaw, pitch, and roll with the rotation in it.
2. Create a matrix from that quaternion.
3. Multiply this rotation matrix by the view matrix.
4. Translate the view matrix according to the change of position in `vPos`.
5. Get the inverse of the resulting matrix.
6. Provide the matrix to the Direct3D engine.

You already saw the first three steps in the section on world transformations. The result of these three steps is a matrix with the rotation in it. The fourth step is setting the camera's position. In the fifth step, the code uses a Direct3D utility library function to invert the matrix. Why do you need to invert a matrix? You're using a quaternion to rotate the camera. These rotations happen around an arbitrary point because the camera will be translated to other points where the rotation will occur. A rotation around an arbitrary point won't be linear if you don't invert the rotation matrix. Now, *how* do you invert the rotation matrix?

You get the inverse of a rotation matrix by negating the rotation angle. A rotation around the origin through an angle A will be canceled by a rotation through an angle –A. If a matrix has an inverse, it is written A^{-1}, and you have $A A^{-1} = A^{-1} A = I$.

Multiplying the matrix A with its inverse matrix results in the identity matrix I. Inverting a rotation matrix is useful for mapping the origin of a rotation around an arbitrary point onto itself.

This section on view transformations showed you the way the orientation vectors are stored in the view matrix that is awaited by the `SetTransform()` function. Furthermore, it showed you a technique to rotate a camera with the help of three perpendicular vectors that are used to orient the camera. This technique has the disadvantage of requiring you to re-normalize the three vectors before they are used each time. Such inefficiency does not occur when you use a camera control that uses quaternions to rotate the camera. This seems to be the common technique to control cameras nowadays, although quaternions are difficult to understand.

There is still room to improve the camera systems discussed previously. The 1steps7.exe example, which you can find in the \1steps7 directory on the CD-ROM, implements a simple time-based physics system. You can feel the velocity to rotate or move the ship in which you are sitting.

The Projection Transformation

The perspective projection transformation converts the camera's viewing frustum (the pyramid-like shape that defines what the camera can see) into a cube space, as shown in Figure 6.15. (With a cube-shape geometry, clipping is much easier.)

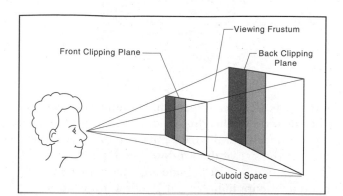

Figure 6.15

Projection space

Objects close to the camera are enlarged greatly, and objects farther away are enlarged less. Here, parallel lines are generally not parallel after projection. This transformation applies perspective to a 3D scene. It projects 3D geometry into a form that can be viewed on a 2D display. The near and far planes define the distances at which objects are visible. Objects that are either too close or too far are not included in the final rendering. The field-of-view (FOV) angle defines the width and height of the view (see Figure 6.16).

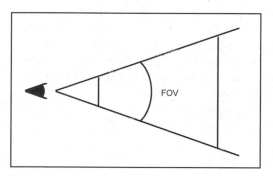

Figure 6.16

Field of view

For instance, a zoom lens has a lower field of view, meaning that a smaller part of the view occupies a larger part of the image, which makes the final zoomed object bigger. The D3DX library contains at least ten different functions for creating projection matrices. There are also right-handed versions to enable you to port an existing engine from OpenGL to Direct3D. I solely use the D3DXMatrixPerspectiveFovLH() function in the examples in this chapter.

```
D3DXMATRIX  matProj;
FLOAT fAspect = m_d3dsdBackBuffer.Width / (FLOAT)m_d3dsdBackBuffer.Height;
D3DXMatrixPerspectiveFovLH( &matProj, D3DX_PI/4, fAspect, 1.0f, 500.0f );
m_pd3dDevice->SetTransform( D3DTS_PROJECTION, &matProj );
```

Its syntax is

```
D3DXMATRIX * D3DXMatrixPerspectiveFovLH(
    D3DXMATRIX *pOut,
```

```
    FLOAT fovY,
    FLOAT Aspect,
    FLOAT zn,
    FLOAT zf
);
```

The first parameter returns the projection matrix. The second parameter awaits the field of view in the y direction, in radians. You must provide the height-to-width ratio to the third parameter. It is useful to provide the height and width of the back buffer so the size of the objects are shown correctly if the user changes the size of the window. The last two parameters are used for the near and far clipping planes. You must provide a z-value for each. You should use a near clipping plane of 1.0f and a far clipping plane of 500.0f to fly around with the objects. You can use the projection matrix for sophisticated things such as solving depth-buffer artifacts, rendering high-resolution screenshots, and rejecting unwanted geometry from rendering, but these concepts are outside the scope of this book. In most cases, a setup for a projection matrix such as the one shown previously is sufficient.

Working with the Viewport

After you have finished the three transformation steps, the device still needs to determine how the data is finally mapped to each pixel. You help the device do this by defining a viewport. By default, the viewport is defined by the size of the window in a windowed application or the resolution of the screen in a full-screen application. Therefore, you often don't need to set it explicitly. However, Direct3D also allows you to specify a portion of the window as a viewport. This is useful when you are rendering multiple views in the same window, as shown earlier in this chapter in the 1steps2.exe example. The four viewports were made visible in Figure 6.17 by painting two white lines.

You define a viewport with the D3DVIEWPORT9 structure.

```
typedef struct _D3DVIEWPORT9 {
    DWORD X;
    DWORD Y;
    DWORD Width;
    DWORD Height;
    float MinZ;
    float MaxZ;
} D3DVIEWPORT9;
```

The X, Y, Width, and Height values correspond to the viewport rectangle (see Figure 6.18).

This structure defines the rectangular position of the viewport within the window or screen, as well as two additional members that indicate the depth ranges into which the scene will be rendered. Direct3D assumes that the x value ranges from -1.0f to 1.0f and that the y value ranges from 1.0f to -1.0f. These values indicate the depth range into which the scene will be rendered, and are not used for clipping. (This change was introduced in DirectX 8;

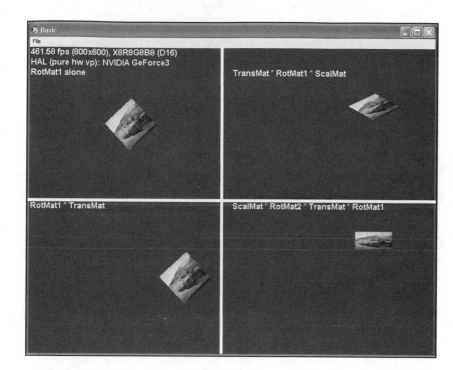

Figure 6.17

Viewports

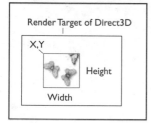

Figure 6.18

The viewport rectangle

in DirectX 7, these members were used for clipping.) Normally these members are set to 0.0f and 1.0f to render to the entire range of depth values in the depth buffer. To render a heads-up display, for example, you might set both values to 0.0f to force the system to render it in the foreground. Before you set a new viewport, you should save the old viewport with GetViewport() so you can reset the viewport when you are finished rendering.

```
HRESULT GetViewport(D3DVIEWPORT9 *pViewport);
```

With a copy of the old viewport, you can set a new one with the SetViewport() function, which has the same syntax as GetViewport().

```
HRESULT SetViewport(D3DVIEWPORT9 *pViewport);
```

This defines a new subsection of the window; drawing occurs in that rectangle. If a new viewport is outside the boundaries of the device, SetViewport() will fail. Please note that the aspect (width-to-height ratio) of the viewport rectangle should match the aspect of the projection matrix, or the objects might look squished.

The source code of the example 1steps2 shows the use of four viewports. These viewports are declared in the application class.

```
D3DVIEWPORT9   m_RViewport;
D3DVIEWPORT9   m_SRTViewport;
D3DVIEWPORT9   m_TRViewport;
D3DVIEWPORT9   m_RTRSViewport;
```

The first viewport will hold the view that shows the quad transformed by the rotation matrix only, as the capital R in the name implies. The second viewport will hold the view that shows the quad transformed by a scale-rotate-translate matrix, as the capital SRT in the name implies. The third viewport will hold the view that shows the quad transformed by a translate-rotate matrix, as the capital TR implies. The fourth viewport will hold the view that shows the quad transformed by a rotate-translate-rotate-scale matrix, as the capital RTRS implies. The size of the four viewports is set in RestoreDeviceObjects(), which means that every change of the window size will recalculate these sizes.

```
// Setup the sub-viewports
D3DVIEWPORT9 MainViewport;
m_pd3dDevice->GetViewport(&MainViewport);

// Each viewport fills a quarter of the window
m_RViewport.Width =
m_SRTViewport.Width =
m_TRViewport.Width =
m_RTRSViewport.Width = MainViewport.Width / 2;
m_RViewport.Height =
m_SRTViewport.Height =
m_TRViewport.Height =
m_RTRSViewport.Height = MainViewport.Height / 2;

m_RViewport.Y = m_SRTViewport.Y = 0;
m_RViewport.X = m_TRViewport.X = 0;

m_TRViewport.Y = m_RTRSViewport.Y = MainViewport.Height / 2;
m_SRTViewport.X = m_RTRSViewport.X = MainViewport.Width / 2;

// Set the full Z range for each viewport
m_RViewport.MinZ =
m_SRTViewport.MinZ =
m_TRViewport.MinZ =
m_RTRSViewport.MinZ = 0.0f;
```

```
m_RViewport.MaxZ =
m_SRTViewport.MaxZ =
m_TRViewport.MaxZ =
m_RTRSViewport.MaxZ = 1.0f;
```

In this code, the current viewport is retrieved first. This viewport should hold the size of the window's client area. Next, the rectangle is divided into four equal rectangles, and the four viewports are provided with the values of these four rectangles. Please note that you must use capitalized variables to provide the .X and .Y values.

The `DrawPrimitiveIndex()` functions draw the quad in `Render()` into the viewport after each viewport is set.

```
// Draw the rotated data
m_pd3dDevice->SetViewport(&m_RViewport);
m_matWorld = RotationMatrix1;
m_pd3dDevice->SetTransform(D3DTS_WORLD, &m_matWorld);
m_pd3dDevice->DrawIndexedPrimitive( D3DPT_TRIANGLELIST,
                                    0,
                                    0,
                                    4,   // number of vertices
                                    0,
                                    2); // number of primitives
```

You are familiar with the `DrawIndexedPrimitive()` function from Chapter 5. After you draw the quad, you draw all the text that displays information about the graphics card or marks the different viewports. You must do this in the original viewport that spans the entire window's client area. You do this with a call to `SetViewport()`.

```
// Set the viewport back to the full window.  This ensures
// that any other processing (such as Clear or the DrawText functions) takes place
// over the full window.
m_pd3dDevice->SetViewport(&MainViewport);

// Output statistics
m_pFont->DrawText( 2,  0, D3DCOLOR_ARGB(255,255,255,0), m_strFrameStats );
m_pFont->DrawText( 2, 20, D3DCOLOR_ARGB(255,255,255,0), m_strDeviceStats );
m_pFont->DrawText( 2, 40, D3DCOLOR_ARGB(255,255,255,255), _T("RotMat1 alone") );
m_pFont->DrawText( m_SRTViewport.X, m_SRTViewport.Y, D3DCOLOR_ARGB(255,255,255,255),
_T("TransMat * RotMat1 * ScalMat") );
m_pFont->DrawText( m_TRViewport.X, m_TRViewport.Y, D3DCOLOR_ARGB(255,255,255,255),
_T("RotMat1 * TransMat") );
m_pFont->DrawText( m_RTRSViewport.X, m_RTRSViewport.Y, D3DCOLOR_ARGB(255,255,255,255),
_T("ScalMat * RotMat2 * TransMat * RotMat1") );
```

I used the viewport dimensions to position the text at the respective viewport edges. You don't need to release the viewports in the `DeleteDeviceObjects()` or `FinalCleanup()` functions because they are not COM objects.

To summarize the usage of viewports in a few words: By retrieving the viewport data via GetViewport(), you fill a viewport structure with the size of the viewport and the MinX and MinY values, which are provided to the depth buffer. You set a viewport with SetViewport() just before the DrawPrimitive*() command. After you have finished drawing, you should restore the original viewport to clear the entire render target in one pass and to enable text drawing with the font class provided by the Direct3D framework.

Now you are coming to an important feature that I used throughout the examples in this chapter but did not present up to this point—depth buffering.

Depth Buffering

Overdrawing is a major problem that all game developers face when designing 3D worlds. Consider a 3D scene in which you are looking through a small window into a room. Some of the walls and objects in the room will be visible through the window, and some will not.

The most efficient way to render the scene would be to render only pixels that are visible to the viewer. If you render pixels that are not visible (for example, for objects in the room that cannot be seen through the window), the redundant operation is called *overdrawing* because a pixel of the object was overdrawn by a pixel of the wall that surrounds the window. Pixels closer to the camera must obscure pixels that are farther away.

Depth complexity is a measure of the amount of overdraw in a scene. This represents the ratio of total pixels rendered to visible pixels. For example, if a scene has a depth complexity of 3, three times as many pixels were rendered as were actually visible on the screen. This also means that you would need three times the fill rate to display the scene at a given frame rate as you would if there were no overdraw. Depending on the complexity of content, the depth complexity can vary from as low as 1 to more than 10, but values around 2 or 3 are most common. Overdraw is a major source of inefficiency in 3D games.

Direct3D supports the creation of a so-called *depth buffer*, which plays an important role in preventing overdraw. This buffer stores depth information for every pixel in the display. Before displaying your virtual world, Direct3D clears every pixel on this depth buffer to the farthest possible depth value. When rasterizing, it determines the depth of each pixel on the polygon. If a pixel is closer to the camera than the one previously stored in the depth buffer, the pixel is displayed and the new depth value is stored in the depth buffer. This process continues until all pixels are drawn.

A depth buffer is created by the Direct3D framework by specifying TRUE to the enumeration class that selects the suitable device solution and depth/stencil buffer support.

```
m_d3dEnumeration.AppUsesDepthBuffer = TRUE;
```

To use the depth buffer on a per-frame basis, you must clear it every frame in the Render() function. This is done in the following code, along with clearing the render target.

```
// Clear the render target | z-buffer
m_pd3dDevice->Clear( OL, NULL, D3DCLEAR_TARGET | D3DCLEAR_ZBUFFER,
            D3DCOLOR_XRGB(0,0,128), 1.0f, OL );
```

The documentation states that the Clear() method clears the viewport. It is my understanding that it clears the render target in the dimensions provided by the viewport. The viewport just maps to the render target. This function can also clear the stencil buffer. The method is declared as:

```
HRESULT Clear(
    DWORD Count,
    const D3DRECT *pRects,
    DWORD Flags,
    D3DCOLOR Color,
    float Z,
    DWORD Stencil
);
```

The method accepts one or more rectangles in pRects. The number of rectangles is stored in Count. The Flags variable indicates the type of memory that should be cleared. You might clear the z-buffer, render target, and stencil buffer. The Z variable holds the z-value, and the Stencil variable holds the stencil value.

That is all you have to do to switch on the depth buffer. Unfortunately, sometimes depth-buffer artifacts show up in a game engine. Ideally, the depth buffer is the same size and shape as the color buffer where your scene is stored for later on-screen drawing. On current hardware the depth buffer typically has 16 or 24 bits for each pixel. The reference rasterizer even exposes 32-bit depth buffer formats. The distance values of world space in a perspective-viewed environment are not proportional to the values, called z-values, of the depth buffer (see Figure 6.19). This means that the distance between any adjacent depth values is not uniform; it's finer at the lower depth values.

If you lose depth-buffer precision, you have a higher possibility of generating rendering errors. Because the depth precision depends on the precision of the color buffer, only 16-bit color resolutions can be affected. These problems normally occur only with the so-called z-buffer. The obvious solution to this problem is to choose a 24-bit depth buffer.

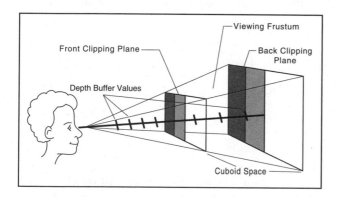

Figure 6.19

Depth buffer values

The w-buffer is another solution provided by Direct3D. The w-buffer reduces the problems that z-buffers exhibit with objects in the distance, and has a constant performance for both near and far objects. The old DirectX 7.0 SDK provided a very instructive example to show the difference between a z-buffer and a w-buffer in action; it showed the rendering errors that occur when you lose depth-buffer precision in 16-bit color mode. If you try that example, you have to choose a 16-bit color mode to see the errors occur (see Figure 6.20).

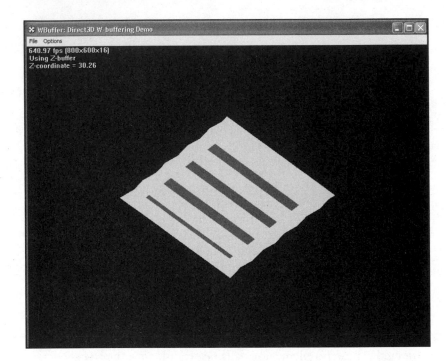

Figure 6.20

Depth-buffer artifacts

When depth buffering works correctly, you can read a small text passage on the green square. Behind the green square is a blue square, which overlaps the text when the z-buffer with greater distance has lost its precision.

You can set the w-buffer using the SetRenderState() function.

```
m_pd3dDevice->SetRenderState( D3DRS_ZENABLE, D3DZB_USEW ); // w-buffer
```

You can check w-buffer support using the following code:

```
if( d3dCaps.RasterCaps & D3DPRASTERCAPS_WBUFFER)
        m_bDeviceSupportsW = TRUE;
else
        m_bDeviceSupportsW = FALSE;
```

A w-based depth buffer is often more evenly distributed between the near and far clip planes than a z-buffer. The key benefit is that the ratio of distances for the near and far clipping planes is no longer an issue. This allows applications to support large maximum ranges while still getting relatively accurate depth buffering close to the eye point (the point where your camera/eye are located). However, a w-based depth buffer isn't perfect and can sometimes exhibit hidden surface artifacts for near objects. Another drawback to the w-buffered approach is that w-buffering isn't supported as widely in hardware as z-buffering. To be on the safe side, use a z-buffer.

Additional Resources

You will find a nice and simple COM tutorial at http://www.gamedev.net/reference/articles/article1299.asp.

I've found good pages on camera orientation at http://crystal.sourceforge.net.

Three excellent articles on quaternions are

- Shoemake, Ken. "Euler Angle Conversion," *Graphics Gems IV*. Ed. Paul S. Heckbert. Toronto: Academic Press Professional. 222–229.
- Void, Sobeit. "Quaternion Powers." <http://www.gamedev.net/reference/articles/article1095.asp>.
- Downs, Laura. "Using Quaternions to Represent Rotation." <http.cs.berkeley.edu/~laura/cs184/quat/quaternion.html>.

There are a couple good pages on math stuff at:

- http://www.sisweb.com/math/tables.htm
- http://www.swin.edu.au/astronomy/pbourke

The Witchlord Web site at http://www.angelcode.com, which moderates the DirectX/OpenGL/Glide/Genesis3D discussion forum, might also be useful.

If you haven't already found it, one of the best sites for game programmers is http://www.gamasutra.com.

For further reading, I recommend *Real-Time Rendering Tricks and Techniques in DirectX* (Premier Press, 2002).

Summary

Whew! This chapter walked you through several example programs to teach you how to use world, view, and projection transformations. You were also introduced to viewports and depth buffering. In the next chapter, you'll learn about texture mapping and filtering. Are you ready? Let's move on!

Part One Quiz

Q: What is the purpose of a pluggable software device?

A: If a feature is not supported in HAL, the pluggable software device can take control and emulate the hardware. It's not provided by the DirectX 9 SDK.

Q: What is the purpose of the reference rasterizer?

A: To test features that your card doesn't support.

Q: What are the most important COM features for game programmers?

A: • COM interfaces can never change
 • Language independence
 • Only access to methods, not data

Q: What is a v-table?

A: A virtual function table references the methods implemented in a COM object. You can't access COM methods directly.

Q: How do you define the location of a vertex in 3D space?

A: By specifying a vector from the origin to the point where the vertex resides.

Q: How do you define the orientation of an object in 3D space?

A: By using the Look, Up, and Right vectors.

Q: Why do you have to specify face vertices in clockwise order?

A: Direct3D does not draw back faces of objects to gain more speed. By default, it only draws faces of objects where the vertices are oriented in clockwise order. This is called back-face culling. Therefore, you must recommend the proper ordering of your vertices.

Q: How are textures mapped on a face?

A: By using a uniform address range for all texels in a texture. The upper-left corner is (0.0f, 0.0f), and the bottom-right corner is (1.0f, 1.0f).

Q: What are the common files?

A: They encapsulate the basic functionality to start a Direct3D game. They are proven code and well tested.

Q: What is the purpose of the `OneTimeSceneInit()`/`InitDeviceObjects()` methods?

A: `OneTimeSceneInit()` performs all of the functions necessary to load the geometry data of a scene. It is called only once. `InitDeviceObjects()` initializes all per-device objects, such as loading texture bits onto a device surface, setting matrices, populating vertex buffers, and setting render states. It's called when the application starts or the device is being changed.

Q: What is the difference between `DeleteDeviceObjects()` and `FinalCleanUp()`?

A: `DeleteDeviceObjects()` is called when the application exits or when the device changes. `FinalCleanup()` is the last framework call in your application before it exits. It destroys allocated memory (for example, for textures) and deletes file objects.

Q: What textures can `D3DUtil_CreateTexture()` load?

A: Bitmaps from *.bmp, *.jpg, *.png, *.ppm, *.dds, and *.tga files.

Q: What is a viewport?

A: In order for Direct3D to know what frustum to clip to, you need the viewport dimensions. These dimensions are used to clip the perspective projection's viewing frustum to the cube shape.

Q: What is the purpose of the `BeginScene()`/`EndScene` pair?

A: `BeginScene()` causes the system to check its internal data structures and the availability and validity of rendering surfaces, and it sets the internal flag to signal that a scene is in progress. `EndScene()` clears the internal flag that indicates that a scene is in progress, flushes the cached data, and makes sure the rendering surfaces are okay.

Q: What happens if you set a texture?

A: A call to `SetTexture()` instructs the Direct3D device to apply the texture to all primitives that are rendered from that time until another texture is set or the texture stage is switched off.

Q: What is the function of a triangle strip?

A: It creates a series of connected triangles.

Q: What is the function of a vertex flag?

A: It tells Direct3D something about the used vertex structure in which the vertex information is stored. The presence or absence of a particular vertex format flag communicates to the system which vertex component fields are present in memory and which you've omitted. By using only the needed vertex components, your application can conserve memory and minimize the processing bandwidth required to render the 3D world.

Q: Do you have to use the Direct3D transformation and lighting pipeline?

A: No, you're free to skip it. Just use the proper vertex flags (`_RHW`) and the proper vertex structure.

Q: What is the purpose of the world, view, and projection transformations?

A: The world transformation stage transforms an object from model to world space, the absolute frame of reference for a 3D world. The view transformation stage transforms your 3D world from world space to camera space by placing the camera at the origin and pointing it directly down its positive z-axis. The projection transformation controls the camera's internals. It's analogous to choosing a lens for the camera.

Q: Why is the use of matrices a good choice in game programming?

A: The performance of a dedicated transform engine is predictable and consistent with matrices. This allows game developers to make informed decisions regarding performance and quality.

Q: Building a concept for a camera system in a game is not trivial; it depends on the vehicle in which the player is sitting. A helicopter pilot needs a different camera system than an X-wing fighter pilot.

Q: What is wrong with the default camera control technique provided by `D3DXMatrixLookAtLH()`?

A: This function is designed for simple uses. For example, it is perfect for a head-mounted tracking display or a follow-up camera, but it won't help you build a space shooter or flight simulator camera.

Q: Describe the rotation of the camera using a quaternion.

A: A quaternion is built from yaw, pitch, and roll (Euler angles). It is converted to a matrix, and the matrix is inverted at the end.

Q: Why do you have to use a depth buffer?

A: A z- or w-buffer is used to reduce the problem of overdraw. These buffers hold the depth of each pixel in the scene. If a pixel is closer to the camera than one previously stored in the depth buffer, the pixel is displayed and the new depth value is stored in the depth buffer.

Q: What is the fastest primitive to use?

A: That depends on the primitive data you use. Index primitive types such as indexed triangle lists or indexed triangle strips should be the fastest primitive type in most cases. If fewer than two of the object's vertices share an index, you should think about using non-indexed primitives. The best way to find the fastest primitive in a specific case is to measure the performance.

Q: What can you accomplish by taking the cross-product of two vectors?

A: The result will form a third vector, which is perpendicular to the plane formed by the first two vectors. It's used to determine which way polygons are facing. It might also be used to derive the plane equation for a plane determined by two intersecting vectors.

PART TWO

KNEE-DEEP
IN DIRECTX
GRAPHICS
PROGRAMMING

CHAPTER 7

TEXTURE-MAPPING FUNDAMENTALS

This chapter will cover texture-mapping techniques that are useful for DirectX 7 and DirectX 8 hardware with the fixed Direct3D multitexturing unit (as opposed to the programmable pixel shader unit, which will be covered in Chapter 9, "Shader Programming with the High-Level Shader Language"). In this chapter, you will learn how to:

- Perform texture color and alpha operations
- Use bump mapping
- Work with environment mapping
- Use texture transformations

What Is the Point of Textures?

Before you dive into any source code, I want to answer a main question: Why do we need a texture? Imagine a wall consisting of bricks. You do not want to place every brick, and then transform and light each one. Instead, you can choose to map a texture on a rectangular polygon several times (or just once, if the texture is large enough), and the wall will appear to consist of multiple bricks.

As you can see, texture mapping helps you reduce geometry because textures mimic the existence of geometry. Furthermore, they are useful for including more colors on an object. Pressing the F1 key in the sample program for this chapter gives you access to a number of different texture-mapping options, which are detailed in Table 7.1.

Figure 7.1 shows the Border Color addressing mode with the Blending with Frame Buffer option selected. The sample program frequently uses the most important method for sampling textures, `SetSamplerState()`, which was introduced in DirectX 9. In previous editions of DirectX, the `SetTextureStageState()` function handled these sampling tasks, as well as additional tasks. Renaming this function was quite useful. All sampler states set with `SetSamplerState()` are available with the fixed-function multitexturing unit and with pixel shaders, whereas all the functionality left over from `SetTextureStageState()` is only usable in conjunction with the multitexturing unit. This chapter and Chapter 8, "Using Multiple Textures," cover the use of the multitexturing unit because many types of installed graphics hardware still do not support the more advanced pixel shaders. The pixel shader performs the same tasks as the multitexturing unit in the Direct3D pipeline, and will be its functional replacement in the future.

Figure 7.1

The example program

TABLE 7.1 Texture-Mapping Options

Option	Key
Dark Mapping	1
Animated Dark Mapping	2
Blending with Material Diffuse Color	3
Darkmap with Material Diffuse Color	4
Glow Mapping	5
Detail Mapping	6
Modulate Alpha	7
Blending with Frame Buffer	8
Trilinear Filtering	F5
Anisotropic Filtering	F6
Clamp Addressing Mode	F9
Mirror Once	F11
Border Color	F12
Exit Menu	F1

`SetSamplerState()` sets the sampler state, including the one used in the tessellator unit to sample displacement maps. (The tessellator is the functional unit in the graphics hardware that is used to handle higher-order surfaces like Bezier patches, N-patches, and so on.) These states have been renamed with a `D3DSAMP_` prefix to enable compile-time error detection when porting from DirectX 8.x. The states include

- `D3DSAMP_ADDRESSU`, `D3DSAMP_ADDRESSV`, `D3DSAMP_ADDRESSW`
- `D3DSAMP_BORDERCOLOR`
- `D3DSAMP_MAGFILTER`, `D3DSAMP_MINFILTER`, `D3DSAMP_MIPFILTER`
- `D3DSAMP_MIPMAPLODBIAS`
- `D3DSAMP_MAXMIPLEVEL`
- `D3DSAMP_MAXANISOTROPY`

`SetSamplerState()` specifies texture filtering, tiling, clamping, MIPLOD, and so on. With the fixed-function multitexturing unit, the device caps `MaxTextureBlendStages` and `MaxSimultaneousTextures` identify the number of texture stages and texture blend stages available to the application. In the case of a GeForce3, there are eight texture-blend stages available, and you can set up to four simultaneous textures. In case of a RADEON 9700 PRO, there are eight texture-blend stages available, and you can set up to eight simultaneous textures. `MaxTextureBlendStages` denotes how many `D3DTSS_` or `D3DSAMP_` blend stages the driver understands, and `MaxSimultaneousTextures` denotes how many different textures you can use at a time. These are not the same thing; you might be able to use extra blend stages without using extra textures. For example, the Dot3 product lighting performed on DirectX 7 hardware is done with three blend stages and two textures.

The syntax of `SetSamplerState()` is

```
HRESULT SetSamplerState(
    DWORD Sampler,
    D3DSAMPLERSTATETYPE Type,
    DWORD Value
);
```

The first parameter is the number of the texture stage. This should be the same number you used in the `SetTexture()` method. The second parameter is one of the sampler state types with the prefix `D3DSAMP_`. The last parameter needs the value that corresponds to the sampler state. For example, the following code switches on anisotropic filtering for texture stage 0. (I will give you more details about this topic later, in the "Texture Filtering and Anti-Aliasing" section.)

```
m_pd3dDevice->SetSamplerState( 0, D3DSAMP_MAGFILTER, D3DTEXF_ANISOTROPIC);
m_pd3dDevice->SetSamplerState( 0, D3DSAMP_MINFILTER, D3DTEXF_ANISOTROPIC);
m_pd3dDevice->SetSamplerState( 0, D3DSAMP_MIPFILTER, D3DTEXF_ANISOTROPIC);
m_pd3dDevice->SetSamplerState( 0, D3DSAMP_MAXANISOTROPY, 8);
```

The `SetTextureStageState()` function provides additional functionality for using the fixed-function multitexturing unit. However, it won't work with pixel shaders. The syntax for this function is

```
HRESULT SetTextureStageState(
  DWORD Stage,
  D3DTEXTURESTAGESTATETYPE Type,
  DWORD Value);
```

As you can see, the syntax is exactly the same as it is for the SetSamplerState() function. The first parameter is the number of the texture stage. This should be the same number you used in the SetTexture() method. The second parameter is one of the stage state types with the prefix D3DTSS_. The last parameter needs the value that corresponds to the stage state. For example, the following code maps the texture colors onto the object unmodified:

```
m_pd3dDevice->SetTexture( 0, m_pBackgroundTexture );
m_pd3dDevice->SetTextureStageState( 0, D3DTSS_COLORARG1, D3DTA_TEXTURE );
m_pd3dDevice->SetTextureStageState( 0, D3DTSS_COLOROP,   D3DTOP_SELECTARG1 );
```

The SetTextureStageState() method is useful for handling:

- Different texture coordinates
- Color operations
- Alpha operations
- Bump/environment mapping operations

Please note that these operations are only valid for the fixed-function multitexturing unit of DirectX 9, not for use in conjunction with pixel shaders. Let's start by examining texture coordinates.

Working with Texture Coordinates

A texture associates color values to two coordinates (u,v) of a polygon's area. This common approach stores color values for each coordinate pair (u=column and v=row) in a two-dimensional array, so that each one has a unique address. This address is called a *texture coordinate*, and it is represented in the texture's own coordinate space. A single element of this array is often called a *texel* (texture element).

You can access each texel in a texture by specifying its coordinates. To do this, Direct3D needs a uniform address range for all of the texels in a texture. Direct3D uses a normalized addressing scheme in which texture addresses consist of texel coordinates that map to the range 0.0 to 1.0. This allows you to deal with texture coordinates without worrying about the dimensions for the texture map you're using. You might assign a texture that looks like a wall of bricks on a rectangular polygon with (0.0f, 0,0f), (1.0f, 0.0f), (1.0f, 1.0f), and (0.0f, 1.0f), causing Direct3D to stretch the texture over the entire rectangle. Or, you might only apply the left or right half of the texture to the polygon. If you choose to apply the left side of the texture, assign the texture coordinates (0.0f, 0.0f), (0.5f, 0.0f), (0.5f, 1.0f), and (0.0f, 1.0f). Keep an eye on the aspect ratio (the ratio of width to height) of the texture and the polygon. You can pick out regions of a texture by specifying coordinates, for example (0.1f, 0.1), (0.5f, 0.4f), (0.3f, 0.8f), and (0.2f, 0.6f). In current games, texture maps for game characters frequently have sizes from 256×256 up to 2048×2048 (see Figure 7.2).

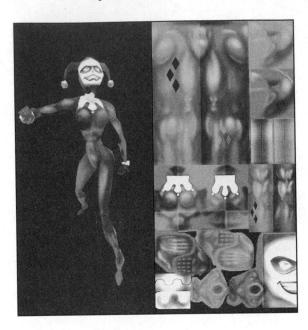

Figure 7.2

Harley Quinn, a model made by Wrath (http://www.polycount. com)

It is quite difficult to map a specific region from the texture on the right side to the model on the left side by providing the texture coordinate values by hand. Usually you use a model tool to do this, but it's useful to have at least the big picture of what the model tool is doing. Suppose the arm of this model has 125 vertices, and each vertex holds a (u,v) coordinate pair for the texture. This coordinate pair is used to map the texture onto the arm.

As you'll recall, you map one texture to a piece of geometry by specifying D3DFVF_TEX1.

```
const DWORD FVF = (D3DFVF_XYZRHW | D3DFVF_TEX1);
```

To provide values to the texture coordinate pairs, you use a vertex structure with a layout that corresponds to these vertex flags.

```
VERTEX Vertices[] =
{
        {  0.0f,  0.0f, 0.5f, 1.0f, 0.0f, 0.0f, }, // x, y, z, rhw, tu, tv
        { (float)m_d3dsdBackBuffer.Width,  0.0f, 0.5f, 1.0f, 1.0f, 0.0f, },
        { (float)m_d3dsdBackBuffer.Width, (float)m_d3dsdBackBuffer.Height,
                0.5f, 1.0f, 1.0f,1.0f, },
        {  0.0f, (float)m_d3dsdBackBuffer.Height, 0.5f, 1.0f, 0.0f,1.0f, },
};
```

Mapping more than one texture onto the same geometry (in this case, the arm) makes sense when you want to achieve special lighting effects, for example. You might use two texture coordinate pairs per vertex with the vertex flag D3DFVF_TEX2.

```
const DWORD FVF = (D3DFVF_XYZRHW | D3DFVF_TEX2);
...
VERTEX Vertices[] =
{
    // x, y, z, rhw, tu, tv, tu2, tv2
    {  0.0f,  0.0f, 0.5f, 1.0f, 0.0f, 0.0f, 0.0f, 0.5f,},
...
};
```

You can choose up to eight texture coordinates in this manner (D3DFVF_TEX1 through D3DFVF_TEX8). The texture coordinate pair is set for a specifc texture with D3DTSS_TEXCOORDINDEX.

```
m_pd3dDevice->SetTexture( 0, m_pWallTexture);
m_pd3dDevice->SetTextureStageState( 0, D3DTSS_TEXCOORDINDEX,  0);
...
m_pd3dDevice->SetTexture(1, m_pEnvTexture);
m_pd3dDevice->SetTextureStageState( 1, D3DTSS_TEXCOORDINDEX, 1 );
...
```

The first texture uses texture coordinate pair #1 of the vertices, and the second texture uses texture coordinate pair #2.

You can also reuse texture coordinate pairs. In the example above, you could set the same texture coordinate pair to both texture stages.

```
m_pd3dDevice->SetTexture( 0, m_pWallTexture);
m_pd3dDevice->SetTextureStageState( 0, D3DTSS_TEXCOORDINDEX,  0);
...
m_pd3dDevice->SetTexture(1, m_pEnvTexture);
m_pd3dDevice->SetTextureStageState( 1, D3DTSS_TEXCOORDINDEX, 0);
...
```

The second texture stage uses the same texture coordinate pair as the first stage. Therefore, you must only have one texture coordinate pair for each vertex stored in the vertex buffer. This method of reusing texture coordinates reduces the amount of data the Direct3D engine sends to the graphics card.

Using Texture-Addressing Modes

Choosing texels of a texture map by setting the texture-coordinate pair of a vertex to a value between 0.0f and 1.0f is pretty straightforward, but what if you provide texture coordinates that lie outside of this range? How values outside the 0.0 to 1.0 range modify the appearance of the texture depends on the texture-addressing mode you choose. The different addressing modes are called wrap, mirror, clamp, border color, and mirroronce. You should check the capabilities of your graphics card carefully to see which addressing mode is supported. Usually graphics cards support some addressing modes, but not all of them. In the example program that accompanies this chapter, the background texture shows the different texture-addressing modes.

Wrap Texture-Addressing Mode

You might use the wrap texture-addressing mode to repeat the texture on every integer junction and addressing mode. This is the default mode used by Direct3D. Insert the following piece of source into the example application:

```
VERTEX Vertices[] =
{
    // x, y, z, rhw, tu, tv
    {  0.0f, (float)m_d3dsdBackBuffer.Height, 0.5f, 1.0f, -0.5f, 1.5f, },
    {  0.0f, 0.0f, 0.5f, 1.0f, -0.5f, -0.5f, },
    {  (float)m_d3dsdBackBuffer.Width, (float)m_d3dsdBackBuffer.Height, 0.5f, 1.0f,
            1.5f,1.5f, },
    {  (float)m_d3dsdBackBuffer.Width, 0.0f, 0.5f, 1.0f, 1.5f,-0.5f, },
};
```

Additionally, you have to switch on the wrap addressing mode using the following code snippet:

```
m_pd3dDevice->SetSamplerState( 0, D3DSAMP_ADDRESSU,  D3DTADDRESS_WRAP);
m_pd3dDevice->SetSamplerState( 0, D3DSAMP_ADDRESSV,  D3DTADDRESS_WRAP);
```

The background texture will be applied three times in the u and v directions, and it should look like Figure 7.3.

If you choose to use the following texture coordinates, the texture will be tiled in another way (see Figure 7.4).

```
VERTEX Vertices[] =
{
        // x, y, z, rhw, tu, tv
    {  0.0f, (float)m_d3dsdBackBuffer.Height, 0.5f, 1.0f, -1.5f, 3.0f, },
    {  0.0f, 0.0f, 0.5f, 1.0f, -1.5f, -3.0f, },
    {  (float)m_d3dsdBackBuffer.Width, (float)m_d3dsdBackBuffer.Height, 0.5f,
        1.0f, 1.5f, 3.0f, },
    {  (float)m_d3dsdBackBuffer.Width, 0.0f, 0.5f, 1.0f, 1.5f, -3.0f, },
};
```

The upper-left texture starts at -1.5f and is repeated two and a half times to the right and five times to the bottom.

Figure 7.3

Wrap texture-addressing mode

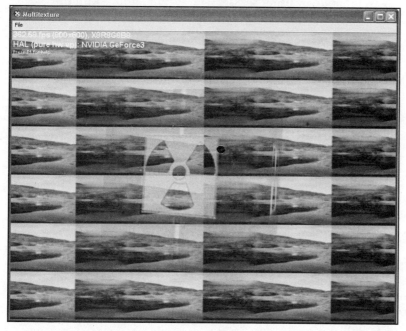

Figure 7.4

Another example of wrap texture-addressing mode

Mirror Texture-Addressing Mode

The mirror texture-addressing mode causes Direct3D to mirror the texture at every integer boundary, so the texels are flipped outside of the 0.0 to 1.0 region. The texture is mirrored along each axis in this manner (see Figure 7.5).

Figure 7.5

Mirror texture-addressing mode

You can set the mirror addressing mode by using `SetSamplerState()` methods with the `D3DTADDRESS_MIRROR` parameter.

```
m_pd3dDevice->SetSamplerState(0, D3DSAMP_ADDRESSU, D3DTADDRESS_MIRROR);
m_pd3dDevice->SetSamplerState(0, D3DSAMP_ADDRESSV, D3DTADDRESS_MIRROR);
```

The following structure is useful to demonstrate the mirror texture-addressing mode:

```
VERTEX Vertices[] =
{
     // x, y, z, rhw, tu, tv
     { 0.0f, (float)m_d3dsdBackBuffer.Height, 0.5f, 1.0f, -0.5f, 1.5f, },
     { 0.0f, 0.0f, 0.5f, 1.0f, -0.5f, -0.5f, },
     { (float)m_d3dsdBackBuffer.Width, (float)m_d3dsdBackBuffer.Height,
         0.5f, 1.0f, 1.5f,1.5f, },
     { (float)m_d3dsdBackBuffer.Width, 0.0f, 0.5f, 1.0f, 1.5f,-0.5f, },
};
```

Clamp Texture-Addressing Mode

The clamp texture-addressing mode applies the texture to the polygon once and then smears the color of the texture's edge pixels. With the same vertices used in the previous example, that might look like Figure 7.6.

The pixel colors at the bottom of the columns and the ends of the rows are extended to the bottom and right of the primitive, respectively. The `SetSampSet()` method might look like the following call:

```
m_pd3dDevice->SetSamplerState( 0, D3DSAMP_ADDRESSU,  D3DTADDRESS_CLAMP);
m_pd3dDevice->SetSamplerState( 0, D3DSAMP_ADDRESSV,  D3DTADDRESS_CLAMP);
```

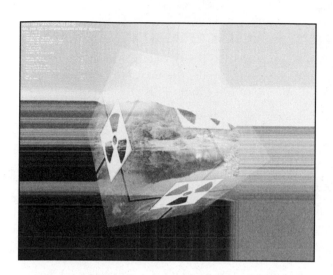

Figure 7.6

Clamp addressing mode

The clamp mode is convenient if you want to stitch multiple textures together over a mesh because the bilinear interpolation at the edges of the default wrap mode introduces artifacts from the opposite edge of the texture. This does not fix things entirely, however; to do that you must modify your texture coordinates.

Border Color Texture-Addressing Mode

When the border color texture-addressing mode is set, a border in the color you choose appears around the texture. You set the border color mode with the following code snippet:

```
m_pd3dDevice->SetSamplerState (0, D3DSAMP_ADDRESSU, D3DTADDRESS_BORDER);
m_pd3dDevice->SetSamplerState (0, D3DSAMP_ADDRESSV, D3DTADDRESS_BORDER);
m_pd3dDevice->SetSamplerState (0, D3DSAMP_BORDERCOLOR, 0x00aaaaaa);
```

Setting the vertices might look like this:

```
VERTEX Vertices[] =
{
    // x, y, z, rhw, tu, tv
      {  0.0f, (float)m_d3dsdBackBuffer.Height, 0.5f, 1.0f, -0.5f, 1.5f, },
      {  0.0f, 0.0f, 0.5f, 1.0f, -0.5f, -0.5f, },
      {  (float)m_d3dsdBackBuffer.Width, (float)m_d3dsdBackBuffer.Height, 0.5f,
          1.0f, 1.5f,1.5f, },
      {  (float)m_d3dsdBackBuffer.Width, 0.0f, 0.5f, 1.0f, 1.5f,-0.5f, },
};
```

You might use this texture mode to fake large textures on walls by using a smaller texture surrounded by the texture's color.

Mirroronce Texture-Addressing Mode

DirectX 8.0 introduced a new texture-addressing mode that is sort of a hybrid of the mirror and clamp modes. In the mirroronce texture-addressing mode, the texture is mirrored within the range of −1.0 to 1.0 and clamped outside of this range. This one is cool.

```
m_pd3dDevice->SetTextureStageState(0, D3DTSS_ADDRESSU, D3DTADDRESS_MIRRORONCE);
m_pd3dDevice->SetTextureStageState(0, D3DTSS_ADDRESSV, D3DTADDRESS_MIRRORONCE);
```

Texture Wrapping

Texture wrapping is different than the wrap texture-addressing mode. Instead of deciding how texel coordinates outside the boundary of (0.0,1.0) should be mapped, it decides how to interpolate between texture coordinates. It affects the way Direct3D rasterizes textured polygons, as well as the way it utilizes the texture coordinates specified for each vertex. Normally, the system treats the texture as a 2D plane. It interpolates new texels by taking the shortest route from point A to point B within a texture, assuming that 0.0 and 1.0 coincide. If point A represents the (u,v) position (0.6,1.0), and point B is at (0.1,0.1), the line of interpolation will look like Figure 7.7.

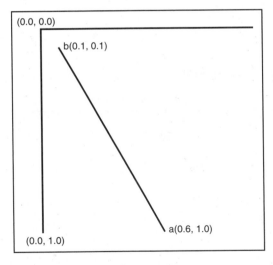

Figure 7.7

Default texture wrapping

The shortest distance between A and B runs roughly through the middle of the texture. If texture wrapping in the v direction is enabled, the rasterizer interpolates in the shortest direction (see Figure 7.8).

Texture wrapping in the u direction would look like Figure 7.9. If you combine both, you might get something like Figure 7.10.

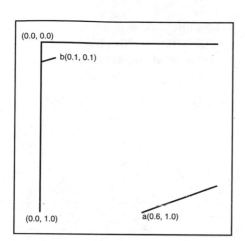

Figure 7.8

Texture wrapping in the v direction

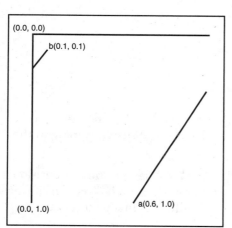

Figure 7.9

Texture wrapping in the u direction

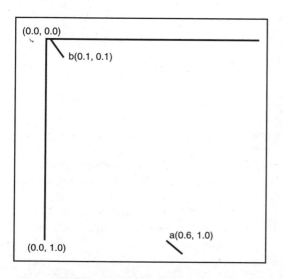

Figure 7.10

Texture wrapping in the u and v directions

To enable texture wrapping for each stage of the texture pipeline, you must set the render state with D3DRS_WRAPx, where x is the desired texture stage (from 0 to 7). To enable the texture-wrapping direction, you include D3DWRAP_U for the u direction and D3DWRAP_V for the v direction.

You can imagine that enabling texture wrapping in one direction causes the system to treat a texture as though it were wrapped around a cylinder (see Figure 7.11).

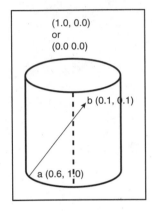

Figure 7.11

Texture wrapping in the u direction on a cylinder

You can see that the shortest route to interpolate the texture is no longer across the middle of the texture. It's now across the border, where 0.0 and 1.0 exist together. Wrapping in the v direction works for a cylinder that is lying on its side.

Wrapping in both the u and v directions is more complex. In this situation, you can envision the texture as a torus or doughnut. You might want to use wrapping in both directions if you map a texture around a sphere, for example. You can enable it for the first texture stage by calling:

```
m_pd3dDevice->SetRenderState( D3DRS_WRAP0, D3DWRAP_U | D3DWRAP_V );
```

Activating texture wrapping makes texture coordinates outside of the 0.0 and 1.0 range invalid and texture addressing modes unavailable.

Texture Filtering and Anti-Aliasing

Imagine a checkerboard that moves away from the viewer. At some point, the projection of the squares becomes smaller than the pixels on the screen. Naturally, if both black and white pixels project to the same pixel, the pixel should appear as some shade of gray. By default a texture mapper will not consider areas, so either black or white pixels will be drawn, depending on the rounding. This can cause the image to look unnatural and can produce artifacts.

Another example is the so-called staircase effect. Lines consisting of different plotted pixels produce edges with the default straightforward rasterization algorithms used in the popular 3D graphic APIs (see Figure 7.12).

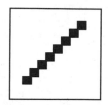

Figure 7.12

Staircase effect

Both examples demonstrate aliasing problems caused by the nature of raster graphics. To overcome these shortcomings, Direct3D provides three texture-filtering methods and the so-called mipmaps. (*MIP* is an acronym for the Latin "multum in parvo," or "many things in a small place." Read on for a more complete explanation.) The texture-filtering methods are

- Nearest point sampling
- Linear texture filtering
- Anisotropic texture filtering

Filtering is the way you get texels from the texture map given a u,v coordinate pair. In the checkerboard example discussed earlier, you can differentiate between two separate issues—magnification and minification.

Magnification, for example, occurs when you try to map a 64×64 texture onto a 400×400-pixel polygon. This will produce the staircase effect. Minification occurs when you do the opposite—for example, when you draw a 64×64 texture onto a 10×10-pixel polygon. This will produce swimming pixels.

Most of the newer hardware supports four different varieties of filtering to alleviate magnification and minification artifacts—point sampling, bilinear filtering (or linear filtering, in Direct3D terms), trilinear filtering (or linear filtering plus mipmapping, in Direct3D terms), and anisotropic filtering.

Mipmaps

Mipmaps consist of a series of textures, each containing a progressively lower resolution of an image that represents the texture (see Figure 7.13).

Each level in the mipmap sequence has a height and a width that is half of the height and width of the previous level. The levels can be either square or rectangular.

Mipmaps are produced and used automatically if you provide the right parameters to the `CreateTexture()` method, which uses the `D3DXCreateTextureFromFileEx()` method explained in Appendix D, "Creating a Texture with D3DXCreateTextureFromFileEx()."

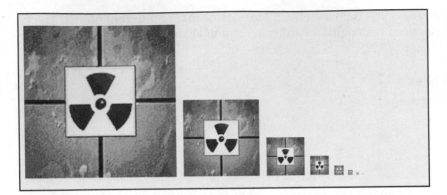

Figure 7.13

*Mipmap (a series
of textures with
progressively lower
resolution)*

Using mipmaps ensures that textures retain their realism and quality as you move closer or further away from them, to alleviate minification or magnification problems, respectively. There are two additional arguments for using mipmaps. Filtering a 256×256 texture onto a 2×2 polygon might look great, but it takes too long; mipmaps provide an effective way to reduce memory traffic for textures.

Direct3D will automatically pick the appropriate mip level from which to texture. It picks the mip level with the texel-to-pixel ratio closest to 1. If a polygon is approximately 128×128 pixels on the screen, Direct3D will use the 128×128 mip level. If the polygon is 95×95 pixels on the screen, Direct3D will pick the 64×64 mip level.

Nearest-Point Sampling

Nearest-point sampling is the simplest kind of filter. It snaps the texture coordinates to the nearest integer, and the texel at that coordinate is used as the final color. It's a fast and efficient way to process textures in a size that is similar to the polygon's image on the screen. The PlayStation 1 console and the first generation of 3D games, such as *Descent* and *Quake*, used it.

Direct3D maps a floating-point texture coordinate ranging from 0.0 to 1.0 to an integer texel space value ranging from −0.5 to n−0.5, where *n* is the number of texels in a given dimension on the texture. The resulting texture index is rounded to the nearest integer, which might introduce inaccuracies at texel boundaries. The system might choose one sample texel or the other, and the result can change abruptly from one texel to the next as the boundary is crossed. This, in turn, can allow visually unpleasant artifacts to occur, which often happens when you map a small texture onto a big polygon (magnification). *Quake* got past some visual artifacts of point sampling by choosing a mipmap based on distance and using point sampling out of that.

Because the majority of graphics hardware today is optimized for linear filtering, applications should avoid using nearest-point sampling whenever possible.

Linear Texture Filtering

Linear texture filtering uses bilinear texture filtering, which averages the four nearest texels based on the relative distances from the sampling point (see Figure 7.14). Okay, let me go through that step by step. Bilinear filtering first computes a texel address, which is usually not an integer address. Next, it finds the texel whose integer address is closest to the computed address. After that, it computes a weighted average of the texels that are immediately above, below, or to the left or right of the nearest sample point.

You invoke linear texture filtering with:

```
m_pd3dDevice->SetTextureStageState( 0, D3DTSS_MINFILTER, D3DTEXF_LINEAR );
m_pd3dDevice->SetTextureStageState( 0, D3DTSS_MAGFILTER, D3DTEXF_LINEAR );
```

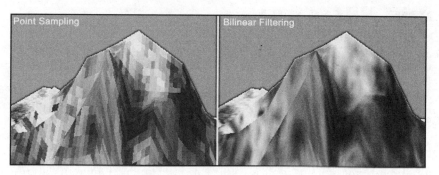

Figure 7.14

Bilinear filtering (courtesy of http://www. reactorcritical.com)

You might also pass D3DTSS_MIPFILTER as a second argument. It indicates the texture filter to use between mipmap levels. The default value is D3DTEXF_NONE. If you provide D3DTEXF_LINEAR, you are using trilinear texture filtering or mipmap filtering.

```
m_pd3dDevice->SetTextureStageState( 0, D3DTSS_MAGFILTER, D3DTEXF_LINEAR );
m_pd3dDevice->SetTextureStageState( 0, D3DTSS_MINFILTER, D3DTEXF_LINEAR );
m_pd3dDevice->SetTextureStageState( 0, D3DTSS_MIPFILTER, D3DTEXF_LINEAR );
```

Trilinear texture filtering looks much better than bilinear filtering, especially as you move through a scene (see Figure 7.15). How does it work? For each pixel, it chooses the two nearest mipmaps, which are bilinear filtered. The two bilinear-filtered pixels are combined using the proximity of each mipmap to the ideal mip level. If the ideal mip level is 3.4, then the combination should be 0.6 (1 minus 0.4) times the bilinear-filtered result from mip level 3, plus 0.4 times the bilinear-filtered result from mip level 4.

In the case of older graphics hardware, you might check out the cap bits for the support of trilinear filtering. Some hardware supports trilinear filtering only in one texture stage.

Figure 7.15

*Trilinear/bilinear filtering
(courtesy of http://www.
reactorcritical.com)*

Anisotropic Filtering

One of the drawbacks of bilinear and trilinear filtering is that texels are sampled using square sampling areas. If a texture is angled sharply away from you, distortion effects called *anisotropy* can occur.

Direct3D measures the anisotropy of a pixel as the elongation—that is, length divided by width—of a screen pixel that is inverse-mapped into texture space. Anisotropic filtering samples more texels when a screen pixel is elongated to reduce the blurriness that the standard linear filtering can produce. The number of texels can be between 16 and 32 from the texture maps. Using more texels requires an even bigger memory bandwidth and is almost impossible on traditional rendering systems, unless you use a very expensive memory architecture. Tile-based rendering (used in PowerVR cards) saves a lot of bandwidth and allows the implementation of anisotropic filtering.

Anisotropic rendering offers a big visual improvement by giving you better depth detail and an accurate representation of texture maps on polygons that are not parallel to the screen. There are different levels of quality available, depending on the number of pixel samples, or *taps*. 64-tap anisotropic filtering offers much higher quality than 8-tap anisotropic filtering, but it's also slower. Anisotropic filtering is the latest filtering type to be implemented in 3D accelerators. Figure 7.16 shows the visual differences between point sampling, bilinear filtering, and trilinear filtering.

You can use anisotropic filtering by setting the following `SetTextureStageState()` methods:

```
m_pd3dDevice->SetTextureStageState( 0, D3DTSS_MAGFILTER, D3DTEXF_ANISOTROPIC);
m_pd3dDevice->SetTextureStageState( 0, D3DTSS_MINFILTER, D3DTEXF_ANISOTROPIC);
m_pd3dDevice->SetTextureStageState( 0, D3DTSS_MIPFILTER, D3DTEXF_ANISOTROPIC);
m_pd3dDevice->SetTextureStageState( 0, D3DTSS_MAXANISOTROPY, 16);
```

An ATI Radeon supports a maximum anisotropy level of 16. A GeForce DDR card supports a maximum anisotropy level of 2. You might get the maximum anisotropy level from the DirectX Caps Viewer or by checking the proper flag in the `ConfirmDevice()` method. You can see the difference in the sample program by pressing the F5 and F6 keys (see Figure 7.17).

Figure 7.16

Point sampling/bilinear filtering/trilinear filtering (courtesy of http://www.reactorcritical.com)

You can see the difference by looking at the sign in the middle of the wall texture. The anisotropic filtering is much sharper. On older hardware, the support quality of anisotropic filtering can be very different. It might make sense to check the visual appearance and switch off anisotropic filtering automatically on some hardware.

Figure 7.17

Trilinear filtering/ anisotropic filtering

Anti-Aliasing

Anti-aliasing is an instant upgrade to all PC games. It has long been the Holy Grail in 3D computer graphics. 3dfx, especially, has promoted full-screen anti-aliasing heavily. It's now a default feature in DirectX Graphics, and it is one of the supported multisampling types. FSAA (*Full Screen Anti-Aliasing*) hides the jagged effect of image diagonals by modulating the intensity on either side of the diagonal boundaries. This creates a local blurring along these edges and reduces the appearance of stepping. So what does it do?

Full-screen multi-sampling samples each pixel multiple times. The various samples recorded for each pixel are blended and output to the screen. This provides improved image quality for anti-aliasing or other effects.

A more advanced method of multisampling is done in the Rasterizer stage; therefore, it only affects triangles and groups of triangles, not lines. It increases the resolution of polygon edges, as well as depth and stencil tests. This kind of multisampling is also called *maskable multisampling,* and it is supported by newer hardware. Check the cap bits or the Direct3D Settings dialog box (see Figure 7.18). The D3DMULTISAMPLE_NONMASKABLE flag shows that this kind of multisampling is not supported, whereas D3DMULTISAMPLE_MASKABLE lets the user choose a multisample quality level in the Multisample Quality field.

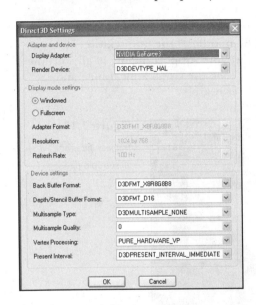

Figure 7.18

Switch on multisampling.

Switching on multisampling provides a much higher-quality visual appearance (see Figure 7.19). The result is a smoother, far more realistic image.

You can use multisampling for special effects, which will be part of the new game generation. For example, you might specify that only some samples are affected by a given rendering pass, enabling simulation of motion blur, depth-of-field focus effects, reflection blur, and so on.

Figure 7.19

With and without multisampling

Alpha Blending

You can use alpha blending to combine the primitive's color with the color previously stored in that pixel of the frame buffer (see Figure 7.20). This is known as blending with the frame buffer. Using this form of alpha blending, you can simulate semitransparent objects; combine two images; and add special effects such as force fields, flames, plasma beams, and light mapping.

Figure 7.20

Alpha blending

The most important advantage of alpha blending is that it allows you to render multiple passes (which means rendering the same geometry with different techniques several times) and to blend these passes together. I will talk more about this concept in Chapter 8.

The alpha-blending step is one of the last in the pixel pipeline. The pixel in the alpha-blending step is combined with the pixel that is currently in the frame buffer using blending factors. You can add the two pixels, multiply them, combine them linearly using the alpha component, and so on.

When you perform alpha blending, you are combining two colors—a source color and a destination color. The source color is the pixel you are attempting to draw to the frame buffer; the destination color is the pixel that already exists in the frame buffer. Alpha blending uses a formula to control the ratio between the source and destination objects.

```
FinalColor = SourcePixelColor * SourceBlendFactor + DestPixelColor * DestBlendFactor
```

`SourcePixelColor` is the contribution from the primitive being rendered at the current pixel location. `DestPixelColor` is the contribution from the frame buffer at the current pixel location.

You can change the `SourceBlendFactor` (D3DRS_SRCBLEND) and `DestBlendFactor` (D3DRS_DESTBLEND) flags to generate the effects you want. `FinalColor` is the color that is written to the frame buffer.

Now think about a few examples. If you want the alpha blending to do nothing, just draw the pixel and don't consider what was already in the frame buffer.

```
FinalColor = SourcePixelColor * 1.0 + DestPixelColor * 0.0
```

With a `DestBlendFactor` of 0.0, the equation reduces to:

```
FinalColor = SourcePixelColor
```

Your source code might look like the following lines:

```
m_pd3dDevice->SetRenderState (D3DRS_ALPHABLENDENABLE, TRUE);
m_pd3dDevice->SetRenderState(D3DRS_SRCBLEND, D3DBLEND_ONE);
m_pd3dDevice->SetRenderState(D3DRS_DESTBLEND, D3DBLEND_ZERO);
```

If you want to multiply the source and destination colors, you have to set `SourceBlendFactor` to 0.0 and `DestBlendFactor` to `SourcePixelColor`.

```
FinalColor = SourcePixelColor * 0.0 + DestPixelColor * SourcePixelColor
```

Your source code might look like the following lines:

```
m_pd3dDevice->SetRenderState (D3DRS_ALPHABLENDENABLE, TRUE);
m_pd3dDevice->SetRenderState(D3DRS_SRCBLEND, D3DBLEND_ZERO);
m_pd3dDevice->SetRenderState(D3DRS_DESTBLEND, D3DBLEND_SRCCOLOR);
```

The code I used in the example program (choose it by pressing F1 and then 8) to get the transparent cube looks like the following lines:

```
if (m_bTex8 == TRUE)
{
 m_pd3dDevice->SetRenderState (D3DRS_ALPHABLENDENABLE, TRUE);
 m_pd3dDevice->SetRenderState(D3DRS_SRCBLEND, D3DBLEND_SRCCOLOR);
 m_pd3dDevice->SetRenderState(D3DRS_DESTBLEND, D3DBLEND_INVSRCCOLOR);
 m_pd3dDevice->SetTexture( 0, m_pWallTexture);
}
// render primitives
if (m_bTex8 == TRUE)
{
 // switch off alpha blending
 m_pd3dDevice->SetRenderState (D3DRS_ALPHABLENDENABLE, FALSE);
}
```

As a result of the calls in the preceding code fragment, Direct3D performs a linear blend between the source color (the color of the primitive being rendered at the current location) and the destination color (the color at the current location in the frame buffer). This gives an appearance similar to tinted glass. Some of the color of the destination object seems to be transmitted through the source object, and the rest of it appears to be absorbed. The equation looks like the following line:

```
FinalColor = SourcePixelColor * SourceColor + DestPixelColor * InverseSourceColor
```

Where `InverseSourceColor` is

$(1 - SourcePixelColor_{red}, 1 - SourcePixelColor_{green}, 1 - SourcePixelColor_{blue}, 1 - SourcePixelColor_{alpha})$.

There are many alpha-blending factors, which are explained in the DirectX 9.0 SDK documentation. Just search for "blending."

Alpha blending requires a fair bit of extra math and memory access, so it is worth the effort to turn it on and off by setting `ALPHABLENDENABLE` to False after the call to `Render()`.

All you have to worry about is whether your graphics hardware supports alpha blending. You can determine this by checking the special caps.

```
if( (0 == ( pCaps->DestBlendCaps & D3DPBLENDCAPS_INVSRCCOLOR)) &&
    (0 == ( pCaps->SrcBlendCaps & D3DPBLENDCAPS_SRCCOLOR)) &&
...
```

`D3DPBLENDCAPS_*` is the flag to check the capability of the graphics card to support `D3DBLEND_*` flags. The `DestBlendCaps` or `SrcBlendCaps` members of the `D3DCAPS8` structure check the capabilities of these flags for the `D3DRS_DESTBLEND`/`D3DRS_SRCBLEND` parameters.

Summary

This chapter covered the fundamentals of texture mapping. You learned how texture coordinates are used and how they affect the visual appearance with different texture-addressing modes such as wrap texture-addressing mode and mirror texture-addressing mode. One of the most important texture topics is texture filtering. Different filtering methods have different impacts on the visual appearance as well as the application's performance. Depending on the graphics hardware, you might have to trade texture quality for speed to get suitable performance.

Alpha blending, which was introduced at the end of this chapter, is an efficient way to blend two textures (one as the source texture and one as the destination texture).

So far I have focused only on using one texture. The next chapter will show you how to juggle more than one texture at a time.

CHAPTER 8

USING MULTIPLE TEXTURES

This chapter will cover the color and alpha operations possible with the multitexturing unit. Using the multitexturing unit was the only way to influence the pixel color via the Direct3D interface until DirectX 8 appeared, with the support of pixel shaders. Nowadays, the legacy multitexturing unit is still used on older graphics hardware which, at the time of this writing, makes up the majority of the games market.

In this chapter, you will learn how to:

- Work with dark mapping
- Blend a texture with a material diffuse color
- Use a dark map blended with material diffuse color

Multipass Rendering

One of the most interesting features at the time the multitexturing unit was introduced in DirectX 6.0 was the ability to map more than one texture on a polygon at a time. The following lines present this procedure step by step, in pseudocode.

```
// texture #1
m_pd3dDevice->SetTextureStageState( 0, D3DTSS_COLORARG1, D3DTA_TEXTURE );
m_pd3dDevice->SetTextureStageState( 0, D3DTSS_COLOROP, D3DTOP_SELECTARG1);
m_pd3dDevice->SetRenderState(D3DRS_ALPHABLENDENABLE, FALSE);
m_pd3dDevice->SetTexture( 0, m_pWallTexture);
m_pd3dDevice->SetStreamSource( 0, m_pCubeVB, 0,  sizeof(CUBEVERTEX) );
m_pd3dDevice->SetFVF( FVF_CUBEVERTEX );
m_pd3dDevice->SetIndices( m_pCubeIB, 0 );
m_pd3dDevice->DrawIndexedPrimitive( D3DPT_TRIANGLELIST, 0, 24, 0, 36/3);
// texture #2
m_pd3dDevice->SetRenderState(D3DRS_ALPHABLENDENABLE, TRUE);
m_pd3dDevice->SetRenderState(D3DRS_SRCBLEND, D3DBLEND_ONE);
m_pd3dDevice->SetRenderState(D3DRS_DESTBLEND, D3DBLEND_ONE);
m_pd3dDevice->SetTexture(0, m_pDetailTexture);
m_pd3dDevice->SetStreamSource( 0, m_pCubeVB, 0, sizeof(CUBEVERTEX) );
m_pd3dDevice->SetFVF( FVF_CUBEVERTEX );
m_pd3dDevice->SetIndices( m_pCubeIB );
m_pd3dDevice->DrawIndexedPrimitive( D3DPT_TRIANGLELIST, 0, 24, 0, 36/3);
```

This is called *multipass rendering*, because you use more than one pass to render the textures. In his Course 29 notes at SIGGRAPH '98, Brian Hook said that *Quake 3* uses 10 passes (see Table 8.1).

TABLE 8.1 Rendering Passes Used in *Quake 3*

Pass	Description
(1–4)	Accumulate bump map
5	Diffuse lighting
6	Base texture (with specular component)
(7)	Specular lighting
(8)	Emissive lighting
(9)	Volumetric/atmospheric effects
(10)	Screen flashes

At that time, only the fastest machines could support 10 passes to render a single frame and still keep up a reasonable frame rate. If the graphics accelerator cannot maintain a reasonable frame rate, you can eliminate the passes in parentheses.

Obviously, the more passes a renderer takes, the lower its overall performance is. To reduce the number of passes, some graphics accelerators support multitexturing, in which two or more textures are accessed during the same pass. The following lines provide a pseudocode representation of multitexturing.

```
// texture #1
m_pd3dDevice->SetTexture( 0, m_pWallTexture);
m_pd3dDevice->SetTextureStageState( 0, D3DTSS_COLORARG1, D3DTA_TEXTURE);
m_pd3dDevice->SetTextureStageState( 0, D3DTSS_COLOROP, D3DTOP_SELECTARG1);

// texture #2
m_pd3dDevice->SetTexture(1, m_pDetailTexture);
m_pd3dDevice->SetTextureStageState(1, D3DTSS_TEXCOORDINDEX, 0 );
m_pd3dDevice->SetTextureStageState(1, D3DTSS_COLORARG1, D3DTA_TEXTURE );
m_pd3dDevice->SetTextureStageState(1, D3DTSS_COLORARG2, D3DTA_CURRENT );
m_pd3dDevice->SetTextureStageState(1, D3DTSS_COLOROP, D3DTOP_ADDSIGNED);
m_pd3dDevice->SetStreamSource( 0, m_pCubeVB, 0, sizeof(CUBEVERTEX) );
m_pd3dDevice->SetFVF( FVF_CUBEVERTEX );
m_pd3dDevice->SetIndices( m_pCubeIB );
m_pd3dDevice->DrawIndexedPrimitive( D3DPT_TRIANGLELIST, 0, 24, 0, 36/3);
```

There's only one render call (one pass) to map the two textures at once on a polygon. If the second texture uses a result produced by the texture operation with the first texture, it is called *texture blending*. You can put together the results of up to eight texture passes. This is called a *texture-blending cascade* (see Figure 8.1).

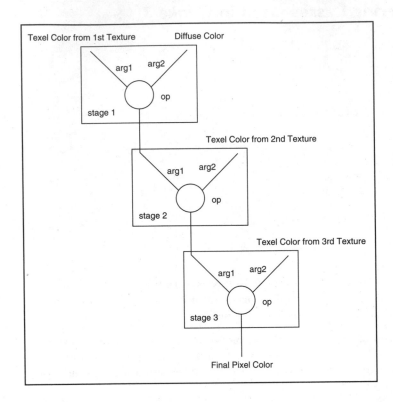

Texel Color from 1st Texture   Diffuse Color

arg1   arg2

op

stage 1

Texel Color from 2nd Texture

arg1   arg2

op

stage 2

Texel Color from 3rd Texture

arg1   arg2

op

stage 3

Final Pixel Color

Figure 8.1

Texture-blending

cascade

Before Direct3D 6.0, the pipeline stages determined the texel color and blended it with the color of the primitive interpolated from the vertices. Since Direct3D 6.0, you can cascade up to eight texture operation units to apply multiple textures to a common primitive in eight passes (multipass) or, if the graphics hardware supports it, in a single pass (multitexturing). The results of each stage are carried over to the next, and the result of the final stage is rasterized on the polygon.

Most of the current 3D hardware only supports applying two textures at the same time to a common primitive. Newer hardware handles up to 16 texture at once.

Now let's examine the color operations of the SetTextureStageState() method.

CAUTION

Old 3D hardware won't support multitexturing at all; this example won't run on those cards. (You'll see an informative message box!)

Color Operations

Color operations are set with D3DTSS_COLOROP. An abstract statement using color operations might look like the following lines:

```
m_pd3dDevice->SetTextureStageState( 1, D3DTSS_COLORARG1, arg );
m_pd3dDevice->SetTextureStageState( 1, D3DTSS_COLORARG2, arg );
m_pd3dDevice->SetTextureStageState( 1, D3DTSS_COLOROP,   op);
```

The ATI RADEON supports the following op parameters, which are located in the D3DTEXTURESTAGESTATETYPE structure.

- D3DTOP_DISABLE
- D3DTOP_SELECTARG1
- D3DTOP_SELECTARG2
- D3DTOP_MODULATE
- D3DTOP_MODULATE2X
- D3DTOP_MODULATE4X
- D3DTOP_ADD
- D3DTOP_ADDSIGNED
- D3DTOP_ADDSIGNED2X
- D3DTOP_SUBTRACT
- D3DTOP_BLENDDIFFUSEALPHA
- D3DTOP_BLENDTEXTUREALPHA
- D3DTOP_BLENDFACTORALPHA
- D3DTOP_BLENDTEXTUREALPHAPM
- D3DTOP_BLENDCURRENTALPHA
- D3DTOP_MODULATEALPHA_ADDCOLOR
- D3DTOP_MODULATEINVALPHA_ADDCOLOR
- D3DTOP_BUMPENVMAP
- D3DTOP_DOTPRODUCT3
- D3DTOP_MULTIPLYADD
- D3DTOP_LERP

Every color operation can accept up to three arguments: D3DTSS_COLORARG0, D3DTSS_COLORARG1, and D3DTSS_COLORARG2. (ATI RADEON supports mapping three textures at once.) You can set these color arguments to any combination of:

- D3DTA_DIFFUSE. Use the diffuse color interpolated from vertex components during Gouraud shading.
- D3DTA_SPECULAR. Use the specular color interpolated from vertex components during Gouraud shading.
- D3DTA_TFACTOR. Use the texture factor set in a previous call to SetRenderState() with the D3DRS_TEXTUREFACTOR render-state value.

- D3DTA_TEXTURE. Use the texture color for this texture stage.
- D3DTA_CURRENT. Use the result of the previous blending stage.
- D3DTA_TEMP. Use a temporary register color for read or write.

You can bitwise or in one or both of the D3DTA_ALPHAREPLICATE and D3DTA_COMPLEMENT modifier flags to alpha-replicate and/or invert the argument. Read on to examine some real-world examples.

Dark Mapping

Most effects that modify the appearance of a surface are calculated on what's called a *per-vertex* basis. This means that the actual calculations are performed for each vertex of a triangle, as opposed to each pixel that gets rendered. Sometimes this technique produces noticeable artifacts. Think of a large triangle with a light source close to the surface. As long as the light is close to one of the triangle's vertices, you can see the lighting effects on the triangle. When it moves toward the center of the triangle, the triangle gradually loses the lighting effect. In the worst case, the light is directly in the middle of the triangle, and you see a triangle with very little shining on it, instead of a triangle with a bright spot in the middle. If no light shines on the vertices, the surface properties are not calculated properly. The best way to generate the illusion of pixel-based lighting is to use a texture map of the desired type of light shining on a dark surface.

Multiplying the colors of two textures is called *light mapping*. (Sometimes this is also called *dark mapping* because it's often used to darken the texture.) To set a dark map, you must use it in the Render() method with the following commands:

```
// Set texture for the cube
m_pd3dDevice->SetTexture( 0, m_pWallTexture);
m_pd3dDevice->SetTextureStageState( 0, D3DTSS_TEXCOORDINDEX, 0 );
m_pd3dDevice->SetTextureStageState( 0, D3DTSS_COLORARG1, D3DTA_TEXTURE );
m_pd3dDevice->SetTextureStageState( 0, D3DTSS_COLOROP,   D3DTOP_SELECTARG1 );


// Set the dark map
m_pd3dDevice->SetTexture(1, m_pEnvTexture);
m_pd3dDevice->SetTextureStageState( 1, D3DTSS_TEXCOORDINDEX, 0 );
m_pd3dDevice->SetTextureStageState( 1, D3DTSS_COLORARG1, D3DTA_TEXTURE );
m_pd3dDevice->SetTextureStageState( 1, D3DTSS_COLORARG2, D3DTA_CURRENT );
m_pd3dDevice->SetTextureStageState( 1, D3DTSS_COLOROP,   D3DTOP_MODULATE );
```

In more detail:

```
// first texture operation unit
// Associate texture with the first texture stage
m_pd3dDevice->SetTexture( 0, m_pWallTexture);
// use texture coordinate pair #1
m_pd3dDevice->SetTextureStageState( 0, D3DTSS_TEXCOORDINDEX, 0 );
// Set the first color argument to the texture associated with this stage
```

```
m_pd3dDevice->SetTextureStageState( 0, D3DTSS_COLORARG1, D3DTA_TEXTURE );
// Use this texture stage's first color unmodified, as the output.
m_pd3dDevice->SetTextureStageState( 0, D3DTSS_COLOROP,   D3DTOP_SELECTARG1 );

// second texture operation unit
// Associate texture with the second texture stage
m_pd3dDevice->SetTexture(1, m_pEnvTexture);
// use texture coordinate pair #1
m_pd3dDevice->SetTextureStageState( 1, D3DTSS_TEXCOORDINDEX, 0 );
// use the texture color from this texture stage.
m_pd3dDevice->SetTextureStageState( 1, D3DTSS_COLORARG1, D3DTA_TEXTURE );
// Set the second color argument to the output of the last texture stage
m_pd3dDevice->SetTextureStageState( 1, D3DTSS_COLORARG2, D3DTA_CURRENT );
// multiply result of stage 1 with result of stage 2
m_pd3dDevice->SetTextureStageState( 1, D3DTSS_COLOROP,   D3DTOP_MODULATE );
```

This code combines the following textures, shown in Figure 8.2.

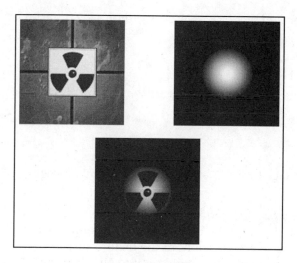

Figure 8.2

D3DTOP_MODULATE

This kind of multitexturing is called dark mapping because the resulting texel is a darker version of the unlit texel of the primary map. This technique is used frequently in 3D shooters; you can see it in *GLQuake1*.

For RGB color, the render states D3DTSS_COLORARG1 and D3DTSS_COLORARG2 control arguments, while D3DTSS_COLOROP controls the operation on the arguments.

The first texture operation unit passes the data from texture 0 to the next stage. The control argument D3DTA_TEXTURE means that the texture argument is the texture color for this texture stage. The second texture operation unit receives these texels via Arg2. It modulates (= D3DTOP_MODULATE) the texels from texture 0 with the texels from texture 1, which were received via Arg1.

There are three other modulation operations, as shown in Table 8.2.

TABLE 8.2 Modulation Operations

Constant	Description	Short Description
D3DTOP_MODULATE	Multiply the components of the arguments.	BaseMap * LightMap
D3DTOP_MODULATE2X	Multiply the components of the arguments and shift the products to the left 1 bit (effectively multiplying them by 2) for brightening.	BaseMap * LightMap << 1
D3DTOP_MODULATE4X	Multiply the components of the arguments and shift the products to the left 2 bits (effectively multiplying them by 4) for brightening.	BaseMap * LightMap << 2

The default value for the first texture stage (stage 0) is D3DTOP_MODULATE; for all other stages, the default is D3DTOP_DISABLE.

The SetTexture() method assigns a texture to a given stage for a device. The first parameter must be a number in the range of 0 to 7, inclusive. Pass the texture interface pointer as the second parameter. This method increments the reference count of the texture surface being assigned. When the texture is no longer needed, you should set it to NULL at the appropriate stage. If you fail to do this, the surface will not be released, which will result in a memory leak. Since version 6.0, Direct3D is capable of blending up to eight current textures at once.

When your application selects a texture as the current texture, it instructs the Direct3D device to apply the texture to all primitives that are rendered from that time until the current texture is changed again. If each primitive in a 3D scene has its own texture, you must set the texture before each primitive is rendered.

The code shown earlier in this chapter showed multitexturing; now take a look at the whole thing with multipass rendering.

```
// Set texture for the cube
m_pd3dDevice->SetTextureStageState( 0, D3DTSS_COLORARG1, D3DTA_TEXTURE);
m_pd3dDevice->SetTextureStageState( 0, D3DTSS_COLOROP, D3DTOP_SELECTARG1);
m_pd3dDevice->SetRenderState(D3DRS_ALPHABLENDENABLE, FALSE);
m_pd3dDevice->SetTextureStageState( 0, D3DTSS_TEXCOORDINDEX, 0 );
m_pd3dDevice->SetTexture( 0, m_pWallTexture);
// draw polygon
// Set darkmap
m_pd3dDevice->SetRenderState(D3DRS_ALPHABLENDENABLE, TRUE);
m_pd3dDevice->SetRenderState(D3DRS_SRCBLEND, D3DBLEND_ZERO);
m_pd3dDevice->SetRenderState(D3DRS_DESTBLEND, D3DBLEND_SRCCOLOR);
m_pd3dDevice->SetTextureStageState( 0, D3DTSS_TEXCOORDINDEX, 0 );
m_pd3dDevice->SetTexture(0, m_pEnvTexture);
// draw polygon
```

The alpha-blending formula looks like this:

```
FinalColor = SourcePixelColor * 0.0 + DestPixelColor * SourcePixelColor
```

It should mimic the modulate color operation used in the multitexture rendering code.

Animating the Dark Map

I created an animated sample with the three modulation types.

```
// animate darkmap
if (i < 40)
{
    m_pd3dDevice->SetTextureStageState(1, D3DTSS_COLOROP, D3DTOP_MODULATE);
}
else if (i < 80)
{
    m_pd3dDevice->SetTextureStageState(1, D3DTSS_COLOROP, D3DTOP_MODULATE2X);
}
else if (i < 120)
{
    m_pd3dDevice->SetTextureStageState(1, D3DTSS_COLOROP, D3DTOP_MODULATE4X);
}
else if (i = 120)
{
    i = 0;
}
i++;
```

This is just a quick hack to show you a simple effect. This effect is not time-based. In the first 40 frames SetTextureStage() uses D3DTOP_MODULATE. In the next 40 frames it uses D3DTOP_MODULATE2X, and in the next 40 frames it uses D3DTOP_MODULATE4X. The effect gets brighter in two steps until 120 frames are shown, and then the whole thing starts again.

Blending a Texture with Material Diffuse Color

Sometimes the sun shines so brightly that the colors on objects get brighter. You can imitate that effect by blending the texture with the material diffuse color (see Figure 8.3).

Figure 8.3

Light color plus texture color

How did I get such an effect? A directional light is reflected by a white material. More reflection means less texture color, so the cube appears white at places where the light shines directly on its side. You set the material with calls to the following methods:

```
D3DMATERIAL9 Material;
D3DUtil_InitMaterial( Material, 1.0f, 1.0f, 1.0f, 1.0f );
m_pd3dDevice->SetMaterial( &Material );
```

You set a directional light that is located above the cube with SetLight() and LightEnable(0, TRUE).

```
HRESULT CMyD3DApplication::SetLights()
{
        if (m_bTex3 == TRUE || m_bTex4 == TRUE)
        {
            m_pd3dDevice->SetRenderState(D3DRS_AMBIENT, 0);
            D3DLIGHT8 light;
              D3DUtil_InitLight( light, D3DLIGHT_DIRECTIONAL, 0.0f, -5.0f, -5.0f );
```

```
                              m_pd3dDevice->SetLight( 0, &light );
                              m_pd3dDevice->LightEnable( 0, TRUE );
                    }
               else if (m_bTex7 == TRUE)
               {
                              m_pd3dDevice->LightEnable( 0, FALSE);
                              // Set the ambient light.
                              m_pd3dDevice->SetRenderState(D3DRS_AMBIENT, 0x00aaffaa);
               }
      return S_OK;
}
```

The code might look like this:

```
// Set texture for the cube
m_pd3dDevice->SetTexture( 0, m_pWallTexture);
m_pd3dDevice->SetTextureStageState( 0, D3DTSS_COLORARG1, D3DTA_TEXTURE );
m_pd3dDevice->SetTextureStageState( 0, D3DTSS_COLORARG2, D3DTA_DIFFUSE);
m_pd3dDevice->SetTextureStageState( 0, D3DTSS_COLOROP, D3DTOP_ADD);
```

In more detail:

```
// Associate texture with the first texture stage
m_pd3dDevice->SetTexture( 0, m_pWallTexture);
// use the texture color from this texture stage.
m_pd3dDevice->SetTextureStageState( 0, D3DTSS_COLORARG1, D3DTA_TEXTURE );
// use the diffuse lighting information produced by gouraud shading
m_pd3dDevice->SetTextureStageState( 0, D3DTSS_COLORARG2, D3DTA_DIFFUSE);
// add texture color and diffuse color
m_pd3dDevice->SetTextureStageState( 0, D3DTSS_COLOROP, D3DTOP_ADD);
```

As you can see, this effect only needs one pass, so there's no multitexture code here. The short description is BaseMap + DiffuseInterpolation.

There are three ways to get a diffuse color in the fixed-function pipeline—from material, diffuse vertex color, or the specular vertex color. (However, there are many more with the programmable vertex and pixel shader.) Where the color is taken from depends on the D3DRS_DIFFUSEMATERIALSOURCE parameter in the RenderState() function.

```
SetRenderState(D3DRS_DIFFUSEMATERIALSOURCE, D3DMCS_MATERIAL);
```

D3DMCS_MATERIAL selects the color from the current material, D3DMCS_COLOR1 selects the color from the diffuse color variable of the vertex, and D3DMCS_COLOR2 selects the specular color variable of the vertex. If you haven't chosen a color, the default color is opaque white. If you haven't set a D3DMCS_* parameter, the default color source is the material color.

A Dark Map Blended with Material Diffuse Color

Imagine that you are standing in a very dark room and you can't see the colors around you. You switch on the light. Suddenly, colors of things appear as if they are lit by the flame. This is the basic idea for the following effect (see Figure 8.4).

Figure 8.4

*(Light color * Wall texture) * Dark map*

In this example, I'm combining the dark mapping with blending a texture with a material diffuse color effect.

```
m_pd3dDevice->SetTexture( 0, m_pWallTexture);
m_pd3dDevice->SetTextureStageState( 0, D3DTSS_TEXCOORDINDEX, 0 );
m_pd3dDevice->SetTextureStageState( 0, D3DTSS_COLORARG1, D3DTA_TEXTURE );
m_pd3dDevice->SetTextureStageState( 0, D3DTSS_COLORARG2, D3DTA_DIFFUSE);
m_pd3dDevice->SetTextureStageState( 0, D3DTSS_COLOROP, D3DTOP_MODULATE);
// Set darkmap
m_pd3dDevice->SetTexture(1, m_pEnvTexture);
m_pd3dDevice->SetTextureStageState(1, D3DTSS_TEXCOORDINDEX, 0 );
m_pd3dDevice->SetTextureStageState(1, D3DTSS_COLORARG1, D3DTA_TEXTURE );
m_pd3dDevice->SetTextureStageState(1, D3DTSS_COLORARG2, D3DTA_CURRENT );
m_pd3dDevice->SetTextureStageState(1, D3DTSS_COLOROP, D3DTOP_MODULATE);
```

In more detail:

```
m_pd3dDevice->SetTexture( 0, m_pWallTexture);
// use texture coordinate pair #1
m_pd3dDevice->SetTextureStageState( 0, D3DTSS_TEXCOORDINDEX, 0 );
// use as first argument the texture color of this texture
m_pd3dDevice->SetTextureStageState( 0, D3DTSS_COLORARG1, D3DTA_TEXTURE );
// use as the second argument the color of the material
m_pd3dDevice->SetTextureStageState( 0, D3DTSS_COLORARG2, D3DTA_DIFFUSE);
// multiply both
m_pd3dDevice->SetTextureStageState( 0, D3DTSS_COLOROP, D3DTOP_MODULATE);
```

If there's no light, the texture color will be multiplied by 0 so the wall texture is not visible. In this case, only the second texture is visible.

```
// Set darkmap
m_pd3dDevice->SetTexture(1, m_pEnvTexture);
m_pd3dDevice->SetTextureStageState(1, D3DTSS_TEXCOORDINDEX, 0 );
// use the texture color of this stage
m_pd3dDevice->SetTextureStageState(1, D3DTSS_COLORARG1, D3DTA_TEXTURE );
// use the result of the previous texture stage = tex color X light color
m_pd3dDevice->SetTextureStageState(1, D3DTSS_COLORARG2, D3DTA_CURRENT );
// multiply the result of the previus texture with the color of this texture
m_pd3dDevice->SetTextureStageState(1, D3DTSS_COLOROP, D3DTOP_MODULATE);
```

If the first texture is invisible, the multiplication of the 0 value of the first stage with the color of the second stage will also result in black. The first texture color fades to black when no light shines on that side of the cube. This might be useful in really dark places where you are not able to see the colors of things because of weak light. You can shorten the description of this process to (Base Map * Light Color) * Dark Map.

The multipass-rendering version might look like this:

```
// Set texture for the cube
m_pd3dDevice->SetTextureStageState( 0, D3DTSS_COLORARG1, D3DTA_TEXTURE );
m_pd3dDevice->SetTextureStageState( 0, D3DTSS_COLORARG2, D3DTA_DIFFUSE);
m_pd3dDevice->SetTextureStageState( 0, D3DTSS_COLOROP, D3DTOP_MODULATE);
m_pd3dDevice->SetRenderState(D3DRS_ALPHABLENDENABLE, FALSE);
m_pd3dDevice->SetTexture( 0, m_pWallTexture);
// draw polygon
// Set darkmap
m_pd3dDevice->SetRenderState(D3DRS_ALPHABLENDENABLE, TRUE);
m_pd3dDevice->SetRenderState(D3DRS_SRCBLEND, D3DBLEND_ZERO);
m_pd3dDevice->SetRenderState(D3DRS_DESTBLEND, D3DBLEND_SRCCOLOR);
m_pd3dDevice->SetTexture(0, m_pEnvTexture);
// draw polygon
```

The alpha-blending part of the process is the same as I used in the dark mapping example.

Glow Mapping

Glow mapping is the opposite of dark mapping. It's useful for creating objects that have glowing parts independent from the base map, such as LEDs, buttons, and lights in buildings or on spaceships (see Figure 8.5).

The glow map should have no effect on the base map except on the glowing area, so you have to add the glow effect and not modulate it.

```
m_pd3dDevice->SetTexture( 0, m_pWallTexture);
m_pd3dDevice->SetTextureStageState( 0, D3DTSS_TEXCOORDINDEX, 0 );
```

Figure 8.5

Glow mapping

```
m_pd3dDevice->SetTextureStageState( 0, D3DTSS_COLORARG1, D3DTA_TEXTURE );
m_pd3dDevice->SetTextureStageState( 0, D3DTSS_COLOROP, D3DTOP_SELECTARG1);
// Set glow map
m_pd3dDevice->SetTexture(1, m_pEnvTexture);
m_pd3dDevice->SetTextureStageState( 1, D3DTSS_TEXCOORDINDEX, 0 );
m_pd3dDevice->SetTextureStageState(1, D3DTSS_COLORARG1, D3DTA_TEXTURE );
m_pd3dDevice->SetTextureStageState(1, D3DTSS_COLORARG2, D3DTA_CURRENT );
m_pd3dDevice->SetTextureStageState(1, D3DTSS_COLOROP, D3DTOP_ADD);
```

You use the unmodified color of the first texture stage as the output with `D3DTOP_SELECTARG1` in the next texture stage. `D3DTOP_ADD` adds the color of the second texture stage. A multipass version might look like this:

```
// Set texture for the cube
m_pd3dDevice->SetTextureStageState( 0, D3DTSS_COLORARG1, D3DTA_TEXTURE );
m_pd3dDevice->SetTextureStageState( 0, D3DTSS_COLORARG2, D3DTA_SELECTARG1);
m_pd3dDevice->SetRenderState(D3DRS_ALPHABLENDENABLE, FALSE);
m_pd3dDevice->SetTexture( 0, m_pWallTexture);
// draw polygon
// Set darkmap
m_pd3dDevice->SetRenderState(D3DRS_ALPHABLENDENABLE, TRUE);
m_pd3dDevice->SetRenderState(D3DRS_SRCBLEND, D3DBLEND_ONE);
m_pd3dDevice->SetRenderState(D3DRS_DESTBLEND, D3DBLEND_ONE);
m_pd3dDevice->SetTexture(1, m_pEnvTexture);
// draw polygon
```

The alpha-blending formula looks like this:

```
FinalColor = SourcePixelColor * 1.0 + DestPixelColor * 1.0
```

This simulates the `D3DTOP_ADD` functionality in the multitexture code.

Detail Mapping

On newer graphics hardware, you might use an additional texturing pass for detail mapping (see Figure 8.6).

Figure 8.6

Detail mapping

As you see, the wall looks rougher, like a rough plaster. What's the deal with that? Imagine this: You move with your nice little armory through a level. A monster appears, and you crouch behind one of the crates one normally finds on foreign planets. While thinking about your destiny as a hero who saves worlds with a jigsaw, you look at the wall right in front of you, which shows a blurred texture. This texture looked perfectly normal at a foot-step's distance. But if your nose touches the cold, rusted metal that's always on the walls of those foreign-world cellars, the texture blurs.

Back to the real world. You might sharpen the visual appearance of this wall by adding an additional detail texture, which happens to show up in these cases. So what does this detail texture do?

The color of the base map, or the first texture, is used unmodified as the second argument in the second texture stage. The detail texture, which is gray, is added to the base map with D3DTOP_ADDSIGNED. It essentially does an addition, having one of the textures with signed color values (−127...128) instead of the unsigned values (0...255) that you're used to. In the ADDSIGNED texture, −127 is black and 128 is white. It adds the components of the arguments with a −0.5 bias, making the effective range of values from −0.5 through 0.5.

The lighter-gray texels in the detail map will brighten the base map, and the darker-gray texels will darken it. The wall will show a rougher surface and therefore will appear more realistic. You use detail mapping with the following source code piece:

```
m_pd3dDevice->SetTexture( 0, m_pWallTexture);
m_pd3dDevice->SetTextureStageState( 0, D3DTSS_TEXCOORDINDEX, 0 );
m_pd3dDevice->SetTextureStageState( 0, D3DTSS_COLORARG1, D3DTA_TEXTURE );
m_pd3dDevice->SetTextureStageState( 0, D3DTSS_COLOROP, D3DTOP_SELECTARG1);
// Set detail map
```

```
m_pd3dDevice->SetTexture(1, m_pDetailTexture);
m_pd3dDevice->SetTextureStageState(1, D3DTSS_TEXCOORDINDEX, 0 );
m_pd3dDevice->SetTextureStageState(1, D3DTSS_COLORARG1, D3DTA_TEXTURE );
m_pd3dDevice->SetTextureStageState(1, D3DTSS_COLORARG2, D3DTA_CURRENT );
m_pd3dDevice->SetTextureStageState(1, D3DTSS_COLOROP, D3DTOP_ADDSIGNED);
```

Doing the same thing with multipass rendering looks like this:

```
m_pd3dDevice->SetTextureStageState( 0, D3DTSS_COLORARG1, D3DTA_TEXTURE );
m_pd3dDevice->SetTextureStageState( 0, D3DTSS_COLOROP, D3DTOP_SELECTARG1);
m_pd3dDevice->SetRenderState(D3DRS_ALPHABLENDENABLE, FALSE);
m_pd3dDevice->SetTexture( 0, m_pWallTexture);
// draw polygon
// Set darkmap
m_pd3dDevice->SetRenderState(D3DRENDERSTATE_ALPHABLENDENABLE, TRUE);
m_pd3dDevice->SetRenderState(D3DRENDERSTATE_SRCBLEND, D3DBLEND_DESTCOLOR);
m_pd3dDevice->SetRenderState(D3DRENDERSTATE_DESTBLEND, D3DBLEND_ SRCCOLOR);
m_pd3dDevice->SetTexture(1, m_pDetailTexture);
// draw polygon
```

The alpha-blending formula should look like this:

```
FinalColor = SourcePixelColor * DestPixelColor + DestPixelColor * SourcePixelColor
```

D3DTOP_ADDSIGNED is not supported on older graphics hardware. MODULATE2X might be a replacement for this blending mode. A suitable formula for MODULATE2X might look like this:

```
FinalColor = 2 * Arg1 * Arg2
FinalColor = Arg1 * Arg2 + Arg2 * Arg1
FinalColor = SourcePixelColor * DestPixelColor + DestPixelColor * SourcePixelColor
```

Don't forget to switch on and off alpha blending because it is quite expensive computationally on older hardware.

Table 8.3 provides a few constants/settings for the color operations that I have not covered in the source code.

The texture stage operation results in the linear blending of both color operations with the:

- Iterated diffuse alpha
- Current iterated texture alpha
- Scalar alpha (set with D3DRS_TFACTOR)
- Pre-multiplied texture alpha
- Alpha that resulted from the previous stage

ATI uses the D3DTOP_BLENDCURRENTALPHA and the D3DTOP_BLENDFACTORALPHA parameters in its old RADEON 1.3 SDK to show the effect of frosted glass. I haven't found any real-world examples for the other parameters.

TABLE 8.3 Constants and Settings for Additional Color Operations

Constant	Description	Formula
D3DTOP_BLENDDIFFUSEALPHA	Linearly blends this texture stage using the interpolated alpha from each vertex.	$S_{RGBA} = Arg1 * (Alpha) + Arg2 * (1 - Alpha)$
D3DTOP_BLENDTEXTUREALPHA	Linearly blends this texture stage using the alpha from this stage's texture.	$S_{RGBA} = Arg1 * (Alpha) + Arg2 * (1 - Alpha)$
D3DTOP_BLENDFACTORALPHA	Linearly blends this texture stage using a scalar alpha set with the D3DRS_TEXTUREFACTOR render state.	$S_{RGBA} = Arg1 * (Alpha) + Arg2 * (1 - Alpha)$
D3DTOP_BLENDTEXTUREALPHAPM	Linearly blends a texture stage that uses a pre-multiplied alpha.	$S_{RGBA} = Arg1 + Arg2 * (1 - Alpha)$
D3DTOP_BLENDCURRENTALPHA	Linearly blends this texture stage using the alpha taken from the previous texture stage.	$S_{RGBA} = Arg1 * (Alpha) + Arg2 * (1 - Alpha)$

D3DTOP_MODULATEALPHA_ADDCOLOR modulates the color of the second argument using the alpha of the first argument. Then it adds the result to argument 1.

Result = $Arg1_{RGB} + Arg1_{Alpha} * Arg2_{RGB}$

D3DTOP_MODULATEINVALPHA_ADDCOLOR uses the inversed alpha to produce a result.

Result = $Arg1_{RGB} + (1 - Arg1_{Alpha}) * Arg2_{RGB}$

The following two parameters work only with cards with multitexture support for three texture stages. Therefore, they are called *triadic texture-blending members*.

D3DTOP_MULTIPLYADD performs a multiply-accumulate operation. It takes the last two arguments, multiplies them, adds them to the remaining input/source argument, and places that into the result.

```
Result = Arg1 + Arg2 * Arg3
```

D3DTOP_LERP linearly interpolates between the second and third source arguments by a proportion specified in the first source argument.

```
Result = (Arg1) * Arg2 + (1-Arg1) * Arg3
```

Now on to the alpha operations.

Alpha Operations

As with the color operations, I'll concentrate on the alpha operations most cards support. An abstract statement using color operations might look like this:

```
m_pd3dDevice->SetTextureStageState( 1, D3DTSS_ALPHAARG1, arg );
m_pd3dDevice->SetTextureStageState( 1, D3DTSS_ALPHAARG2, arg );
m_pd3dDevice->SetTextureStageState( 1, D3DTSS_ALPHAOP,   op);
```

The op parameter might be

- D3DTOP_DISABLE
- D3DTOP_SELECTARG1
- D3DTOP_SELECTARG2
- D3DTOP_MODULATE
- D3DTOP_MODULATE2X
- D3DTOP_MODULATE4X
- D3DTOP_ADD
- D3DTOP_ADDSIGNED
- D3DTOP_ADDSIGNED2X
- D3DTOP_SUBTRACT
- D3DTOP_MULTIPLYADD
- D3DTOP_LERP

I explained all of these parameters in the previous section on color operations. The alpha operations follow the same idea, so it is easy to adopt the same techniques and put them to use here.

Every alpha operation might get up to three arguments (arg)—D3DTSS_ALPHAARG0, D3DTSS_ALPHAARG1, and D3DTSS_ALPHAARG2. You can set these alpha arguments to any combination of:

- D3DTA_DIFFUSE. Use the diffuse color interpolated from vertex components during Gouraud shading.

- `D3DTA_SPECULAR`. Use the specular color interpolated from vertex components during Gouraud shading.
- `D3DTA_TFACTOR`. Use the texture factor set in a previous call to `SetRenderState()` with the `D3DRS_TEXTUREFACTOR` render-state value.
- `D3DTA_TEXTURE`. Use the texture color for this texture stage.
- `D3DTA_CURRENT`. Use the result of the previous blending stage.
- `D3DTA_TEMP`. Use a temporary register color for read or write.

You can bitwise or in the `D3DTA_COMPLEMENT` modifier flag to invert the argument. You know all of these arguments from the color operations section.

As Direct3D renders a scene, it can integrate color information from several sources—the vertex color, the current material, the texture map, and the color previously written to the render target. It can blend several of these colors. You can use a factor called *alpha*, which can be stored in vertices, materials, and texture maps, to indicate how blending should be weighted. An alpha value of 0 means full transparency; an alpha value of 1 means some level of semitransparency.

If you want to fetch alpha from a texture, use `D3DTA_TEXTURE` as arg. If you want to use an alpha that comes from the color component within a vertex (and interpolated across the polygon), use `D3DTA_DIFFUSE` as `alphaarg` and ensure that `D3DRS_DIFFUSEMATERIALSOURCE = D3DMCS_COLOR1` (the default value). If you want to use an alpha that comes from the material color, use `D3DTA_DIFFUSE` as `alphaarg` and ensure that `D3DRS_DIFFUSEMATERIALSOURCE = D3DMCS_MATERIAL` is set.

```
m_pd3dDevice->SetRenderState(D3DRS_DIFFUSEMATERIALSOURCE , D3DMCS_MATERIAL);
```

If you haven't set a `D3DMCS_x` parameter with `RenderState()`, the material diffuse color is taken as the default. That's the case in the following example of alpha modulation.

Alpha Modulation

You can simulate the view of a night-sight by modulating a green ambient light with the material alpha (see Figure 8.7).

Figure 8.7

Alpha modulation

```
// Set the ambient light.
D3DCOLOR d3dclrAmbientLightColor = D3DRGBA(0.0f,1.0f,0.0f,1.0f);
m_pd3dDevice->SetRenderState(D3DRENDERSTATE_AMBIENT, d3dclrAmbientLightColor);
```

To modulate the ambient color with the texture, you can use the following code:

```
m_pd3dDevice->SetTexture( 0, D3DTextr_GetSurface("wall.bmp"));
m_pd3dDevice->SetTextureStageState( 0, D3DTSS_COLORARG1, D3DTA_TEXTURE );
m_pd3dDevice->SetTextureStageState( 0, D3DTSS_COLORARG2, D3DTA_DIFFUSE );
m_pd3dDevice->SetTextureStageState( 0, D3DTSS_COLOROP, D3DTOP_MODULATE );

m_pd3dDevice->SetTextureStageState( 0, D3DTSS_ALPHAARG1, D3DTA_TEXTURE );
m_pd3dDevice->SetTextureStageState( 0, D3DTSS_ALPHAARG2, D3DTA_DIFFUSE );
m_pd3dDevice->SetTextureStageState( 0, D3DTSS_ALPHAOP, D3DTOP_MODULATE );
```

`SetTexture()` associates the texture map with the first stage. The first `SetTextureStageState()` sets the first color argument to the texture associated with this stage. The second sets the second color argument to diffuse lighting information. The color of the base map and the diffuse color are multiplied. The alpha-blending code takes the alpha value from the texture and multiplies it by the diffuse color. A short description of this process would be BaseMap ∞ DiffuseInterpolation ∞ Alpha ∞ DiffuseInterpolation.

Multitexturing Support

If a program uses multiple textures at once, you have to check the multitexturing support of your 3D hardware in `ConfirmDevice()`.

```
if( pCaps->MaxSimultaneousTextures < 2 )
        return E_FAIL;
```

This code checks the maximum number of supported simultaneous texture-blending stages. It must be higher than 1. If you want to be sure that your multitexturing game is supported on specific hardware, you should check the different texturing possibilities of the user's hardware. The sample program provided for this part of the book checks the following graphic card capabilities.

```
if( (0 == ( pCaps->DestBlendCaps & D3DPBLENDCAPS_INVSRCCOLOR)) &&   // alpha blending
    (0 == ( pCaps->SrcBlendCaps & D3DPBLENDCAPS_SRCCOLOR)) &&
    (0 == ( pCaps->TextureOpCaps & D3DTEXOPCAPS_ADDSIGNED )) &&    // texture blending
    (0 == ( pCaps->TextureOpCaps & D3DTEXOPCAPS_MODULATE )) &&
    (0 == ( pCaps->TextureOpCaps & D3DTEXOPCAPS_MODULATE2X)) &&
    (0 == ( pCaps->TextureOpCaps & D3DTEXOPCAPS_MODULATE4X)) &&
    (0 == ( pCaps->TextureOpCaps & D3DTEXOPCAPS_ADD )) &&
    (0 == ( pCaps->TextureAddressCaps & D3DPTADDRESSCAPS_CLAMP)) && // texture addressing
    (0 == ( pCaps->TextureAddressCaps & D3DPTADDRESSCAPS_BORDER )) &&
    (0 == ( pCaps->TextureAddressCaps & D3DPTADDRESSCAPS_MIRRORONCE)))
return E_FAIL;
```

The first two lines of this code check the support of the alpha-blending parameters that were used in the example program. The remaining lines check the hardware support of all other color operations used by the example program.

Texture Management

If you only have 64 MB of video texture memory in your graphics hardware, you should think about which textures should be loaded or held in memory. Better yet, you can have an algorithm let your computer think about it. So what's the task? You need to track the amount of available texture memory and get an overview of the textures that are needed more often or less often. At the very least, a texture management algorithm has to decide which existing texture resources can be reloaded with another texture image and which surfaces should be destroyed and replaced with new texture resources.

Direct3D has an automatic texture-management system. As you learned earlier, you request its support when you create a texture with `CreateTexture()` and specify the `D3DPOOL_MANAGED` flag for the `Pool` parameter. You cannot use the `D3DPOOL_DEFAULT` or `D3DPOOL_SYSTEMMEM` flags when you create a managed texture.

The texture manager tracks textures with a timestamp that identifies when the texture was last used. It uses the least recently used algorithm to determine which textures should be removed. Texture priorities are used as tiebreakers when two textures are targeted for removal from memory. If they have the same priority, the least recently used texture is removed. If they have the same timestamp, the lower-priority texture is removed first.

You can assign a priority to managed textures by calling the `IDirect3DResource8::SetPriority()` method for the texture surface. Stay with `D3DPOOL_MANAGED` until you know more.

Additional Resources

You can find one of the best articles on multitexturing with DirectX from Mitchell, Tatro, and Bullard at Gamasutra, at http://www.gamasutra.com/features/programming/19981009/multitexturing_01.htm. They have developed a tool to visualize the texture operations… try it. You might find another tool to visualize these operations from NVIDIA, at http://www.nvidia.com. An interesting article is "Multipass Rendering and the Magic of Alpha Rendering" by Brian Hook in *Game Developer* magazine, August 1997, page 12. I've also found the older examples from ATI at http://www.ati.com very interesting.

Check out the following Web pages for an explanation of anisotropic filtering:

- http://whatis.techtarget.com/definition/0,,sid9_gci870037,00.html
- http://www.ping.be/powervr/Anisotropic.htm

Summary

This chapter covered the usage of the multitexturing unit by showing you how to program the most common effects. Because the support of the multitexturing unit in common hardware is inconsistent, it is worth checking the capability bits very carefully.

The market share of DirectX 7 graphic cards will decrease over the next couple of years. If your game does not depend on DirectX 7 graphics hardware, the more flexible pixel shader would be a better way to program these effects.

Part Two Quiz

Q: Why should you use textures?

A: To simulate a rough or irregular surface or to create the illusion that the object consists of more polygons.

Q: How does the addressing scheme of Direct3D work?

A: It uses a normalized addressing scheme in which texture addresses consist of texel coordinates that map to the range of 0.0 to 1.0.

Q: Can you use more than one texture coordinate pair per texture?

A: Yes, you can use up to eight texture coordinate pairs for one texture by declaring them in your vertex definition and defining them in your vertex structure.

Q: What do the so-called texture-addressing modes do?

A: You can generate special effects by using texture addresses outside of the 0.0 to 1.0 range and by using another texture-addressing mode.

Q: What are the names of the default texture-addressing mode and the other modes?

A: Wrap, mirror, clamp, border, and mirroronce.

Q: What is the purpose of the mirror texture-address mode?

A: It mirrors the texture at every integer boundary so that the texels are flipped outside of the 0.0 to 1.0 range.

Q: What is the purpose of the clamp texture-address mode? Why is it useful?

A: It smears the color of the edge pixels to the borders of the window. Bilinear interpolation at the edges sometimes produces artifacts with the wrap mode.

Q: What is the purpose of the border-color address mode? What is its drawback?

A: It sets a border around the texture with the color you've chosen so you can fake larger textures on walls, for example. The drawback is that it's not supported on older hardware.

Q: What is the purpose of the newly introduced mirroronce texture-address mode?

A: It mirrors within the range of −1.0 to 1.0; outside of this range, it is clamped. It's useful for volumetric light maps.

Q: What is texture wrapping and why is it useful?

A: It gives the programmer the option to decide how to interpolate between the texture coordinates. To use a simple example: It's not always useful to interpolate a texture that is wrapped around a cylinder in the shortest way; it is often more useful to cross the boundaries of the texture.

Q: What prevents texture wrapping?

A: Texture-addressing modes, because they make texture coordinates outside of the 0.0 to 1.0 range invalid.

Q: What are texture filtering and texture anti-aliasing?

A: These are methods to decrease the drawbacks of using raster graphics. They prevent staircase, magnification, and minification problems.

Q: What are mipmaps?

A: These are a series of textures in which every mipmap sequence has a height and width that is half of the height and width of the previous level. Direct3D will automatically pick the appropriate mip level from which to texture depending on the width and height of the textured polygon it has to draw.

Q: What is linear texture filtering?

A: It averages the four nearest texels based on the relative distance from the sampling point.

Q: What is trilinear filtering?

A: It's bilinear filtering plus mipmaps.

Q: What is anisotropic filtering? What is its purpose?

A: It averages not only the four nearest texels, but also much more, depending on the support of your graphics card and the quality you choose. It also uses mipmaps. It gives you more depth of detail and a more accurate representation of the texture.

Q: How does full-scene anti-aliasing work?

A: It samples each pixel multiple times. The various samples are blended and output to the screen. This enables a few interesting special effects, such as motion blur, depth of field, reflection blur, and so on.

Q: What is the formula for alpha blending?

A: FinalColor = SourcePixelColor * SourceBlendFactor + DestPixelColor * DestBlendFactor

Q: How does alpha blending work?

A: It blends the pixel currently in the pixel pipeline with the pixel already in the frame buffer, depending on the blending factors used.

Q: What are multipass texturing and multitexturing?

A: Multipass texturing uses more than one pass to map textures on a polygon. Multitexturing renders more than one texture on a single pass on a polygon. The latter is faster.

Q: What is a texture-blending cascade?

A: It's the result of one texture stage used in the next texture stage. It's possible to blend the results of up to eight texture stages.

Q: Why use dark/light mapping?

A: Direct3D lights are generated on a per-vertex basis. Think of a large triangle with a light source close to the surface. As long as the light is close to one of the triangle's vertices, you can see the lighting effect. If the light is in the middle of the triangle, there's very little shining on it. Dark/light maps help to generate the illusion of pixel-based lighting.

Q: How does dark/light mapping work?

A: The colors of two textures are multiplied together.

Q: How can I get a diffuse color?

A: In pseudocode:

```
switch (D3DRS_DIFFUSEMATERIALSOURDE)
case D3DMCS_MATERIAL
  use the diffuse color of the material
break;
case D3DMCS_COLOR1
  use the diffuse color of the vertex. If you haven't chosen one, opaque white is taken.
break;
case D3DMCS_COLOR2
  use the specular color of the vertex. If you haven't chosen one, opaque white is taken.
break;
default:
  use the diffuse color of the material.
```

Q: What is the short description of blending a texture with a material diffuse color?

A: BaseMap + DiffuseInterpolation

Q: What is the difference between the glow mapping and dark mapping effects?

A: In glow mapping you add the two textures, whereas you multiply them in dark mapping.

Q: What is the sufficient replacement for D3DTOP_ADDSIGNED?

A: D3DTOP_MODULATE2X.

Q: Which color/alpha operation parameters need multitexture support for three texture stages?

A: D3DTOP_MULTIPLYADD: Result = Arg1 + Arg2 * Arg3

   D3DTOP_LERP: Result = (Arg1) * Arg2 + (1-Arg1) * Arg3

Q: Where do you get the so-called alpha value for texture-blending operations?

A: From vertices, material, and texture maps. In pseudocode:

```
switch(D3DRS_DIFFUSEMATERIALSOURCE)
case D3DMCS_DIFFUSE:
 use the alpha from the material color + ALPHAARG2 = D3DTA_DIFFUSE
break;
case D3DMCS_COLOR1: (default)
 use the alpha from the color component within a vertex + ALPHAARG2 = D3DTA_DIFFUSE
break;
default:
  use the alpha from material color
```

If you want to use the alpha from the texture, use D3DTA_TEXTURE as the ALPHAARG1.

PART THREE

HARD-CORE
DIRECTX
GRAPHICS
PROGRAMMING

CHAPTER 9

Shader Programming with the High-Level Shader Language

This part of the book features a lot of basic information regarding the most common lighting models and file formats used in current games. Many advanced techniques that will be used in upcoming games, such as any form of image-based lighting, are based on using cube environment maps to fake environment reflection.

In the four chapters in this part of the book, you will learn how to:

- Use the new HLSL (*High-Level Shader Language*) provided with the DirectX 9 SDK to program the most common per-pixel lighting models on the vertex and pixel shader
- Use cube environment maps to simulate reflections from the environment
- Use the most common shadow technique, called shadow volumes, to simulate real-time shadows efficiently
- Store geometry data for a game using the structure of an X file
- Construct a character engine that uses the HLSL shaders developed in this part of the book and a very enhanced *.md3 file format

With the introduction of the second generation of shader-capable hardware, such as the ATI RADEON 9500 and the NVIDIA GeForce FX, several high-level languages for shader programming were released to the public. Until then, shader programming was done only with an assembly-like syntax, which was difficult for non-assembly programmers to read. The new C-like languages help programmers learn shader programming faster and make the shader code easier to read.

All new high-level languages have a similar syntax and provide similar functionality. NVIDIA released Cg (C for graphics); Microsoft's new shader language is HLSL; and the OpenGL ARB is driving the development of glslang.

Because of its wide availibility, I have chosen to use HLSL, which is provided with the DirectX 9 SDK, for this introduction to shader programming with a high-level language. The examples in this chapter should run without any changes in a Cg environment and with minor changes in a glslang environment. For further rapid prototyping of these shaders, I highly recommend ATI's RenderMonkey.

In this chapter, you will learn:

- What you need to get started with HLSL
- How to accomplish some vertex- and pixel-shader tasks
- How to use some of the common lighting formulas implemented with HLSL

What You Need to Jump into HLSL

The only requirement to start HLSL programming with the DirectX SDK is a properly installed HLSL compiler. Make sure you set the right directory path in Tools, Options, Project, VC++ Directories in the Visual .NET IDE. Additionally, you should install the shader debugger provided for Visual .NET (no Visual C/C++ 6 version) from the SDK CD-ROM. This installation is optional and therefore you must explicitly choose it.

To use the Visual Studio .NET shader debugger, you must complete the following steps:

1. Install the shader debugger. This is an option you must select in the DirectX 9 SDK installation routine.

2. Select the Use Debug Version of Direct3D and Enable Shader Debugger check boxes in the DirectX Properties dialog box (see Figure 9.1). (You can access this dialog box by selecting Start, Control Panel, DirectX. You will find the check boxes in question on the Direct3D tab of the dialog box.)

3. Launch the application under Visual Studio .NET by selecting Debug, Direct3D, Start D3D.

4. Switch to the reference rasterizer.

5. Set a breakpoint in the vertex shader or pixel shader.

You can view the shader assembly under Debug, Window, Disassembly and the render targets under Debug, Direct3D, RenderTarget.

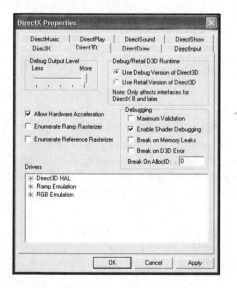

Figure 9.1

DirectX Properties dialog box

Vertex and Pixel Shader Tasks

To estimate the capabilities of vertex and pixel shaders, it is helpful to take a look at their positions in the Direct3D pipeline (see Figure 9.2).

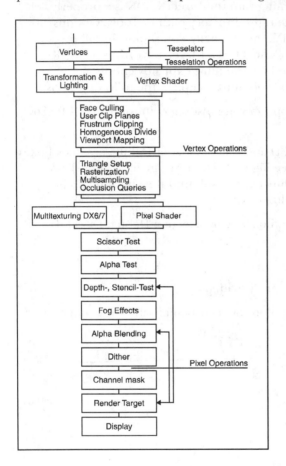

Figure 9.2

Direct3D pipeline

The vertex shader, as the functional replacement of the legacy Transform and Lighting stage (T&L), is located after the tesselation stage and before the culling and clipping stages. The data for one vertex is provided to the vertex shader by the tesselation stage. This vertex might consist of data regarding its position, texture coordinates, vertex colors, normals, and so on. The vertex shader cannot create or remove a vertex. Its minimal output value is the position data of one vertex.

The pixel shader, as the functional replacement of the legacy multitexturing stage, is located after the rasterizer stage. It gets its data from the rasterizer, the vertex shader, the application, and the texture maps. It is important to note that texture maps can store not

only color data, but also all kinds of numbers that are useful for calculating algorithms in the pixel shader. Furthermore, you can write the result of the pixel shader into a render target and set it as the input texture in a second rendering pass. This is called *rendering to the render target*. The output of the pixel shader usually consists of a `float4` value. If the pixel shader renders in several render targets at once, the output might be up to four `float4` values. (This is known as MRT, or *Multiple Render Targets*.)

Common Lighting Formulas Implemented with HLSL

To demonstrate the use of HLSL to program shaders, and also to demonstrate the tasks of the vertex and pixel shaders, the following example programs show the implementation of the common lighting formulas.

Ambient Lighting

In an ambient lighting model, all light beams fall uniformly onto an object from all directions. A lighting model like this, which has no position in space, is also called a *global lighting model*. (Area lighting is an example of a more advanced global lighting model.)

The ambient lighting component can be described with the following formula:

$$I = A_{intensity} * A_{color}$$

The `intensity` value describes the lighting intensity, and the `color` value describes the color of the light. A more complex lighting formula with its ambient terms might look like this:

$$I = A_{intensity} * A_{color} + Diffuse + Specular$$

The `Diffuse` and `Specular` components are placeholders for the diffuse and specular lighting formulas that you will see in the upcoming examples. All high-level languages support shader instructions that are written similar to mathematical expressions, such as multiplication and addition. Therefore, you can write the ambient component in a high-level language as follows:

```
float4 Acolor = {1.0, 0.15, 0.15, 1.0};
float Aintensity = 0.5;
return Aintensity * Acolor;
```

A simplified implementation might look like this:

```
return float4 (0.5, 0.075, 0.075, 1.0);
```

It is quite common to pre-bake the `intensity` and `color` values into one value. This is done in the following example programs for simplicity and readability; otherwise, the HLSL compiler would pre-bake the two constant values together in its output.

The following source code shows a vertex and a pixel shader that display ambient lighting.

```
float4x4 matWorldViewProj;

struct VS_OUTPUT
{
    float4 Pos: POSITION;
};

VS_OUTPUT VS( float4 Pos: POSITION )
{
    VS_OUTPUT Out = (VS_OUTPUT) 0;
    Out.Pos = mul(Pos, matWorldViewProj); // transform Position
    return Out;
}

float4 PS() : COLOR
{
    return float4(0.5,  0.075,  0.075, 1.0);
}
```

The VS_OUTPUT structure at the beginning of the source code describes the output values of the vertex shader. The vertex shader looks like a C function with the return value VS_OUTPUT and the input value in the variable Pos in parentheses after its name (VS).

The input and output values for the vertex shader use the semantic POSITION, which is identified by a colon (:) that precedes it. Semantics help the HLSL compiler bind the correct shader registers for the data. The semantic in the vertex shader input structure identifies the input data to the function as position data. The second semantic identifies the vertex shader return value as position data that will be an input value to the pixel shader. (This is the only obligatory output value of the vertex shader.) There are several other semantics for the vertex shader input and output data, as well as the pixel shader input and output data. The following example programs will show a few of them. Please consult the DirectX 9 SDK documentation for an overview.

The vertex shader transforms the vertex position using the matWorldViewProj matrix provided by the application as a constant; it then outputs the position values.

The pixel shader also follows the C-function-like approach. Its return value is always float4, and this value is always treated as a color value by the compiler because it is marked with the semantic COLOR. Contrary to the vertex shader, the pixel shader gets no explicit input value here (except the obligatory POSITION) because the parentheses after its name (PS) are empty.

The names of the vertex and pixel shader are also the entry point for the high-level language compiler, and you must provide them in its command line.

Figure 9.3 shows the Example program with an ambient lighting model. This program is located in the Chapter9\Example directory on the CD-ROM.

Figure 9.3

Ambient lighting with HLSL shaders

The knob on the top of the teapot is not visible when it is turned toward the viewer because the light beams are coming uniformly from all directions onto the object, and therefore the whole teapot is exactly the same color.

Diffuse Lighting

In a diffuse lighting model, the location of the light is considered. In other words, light has position in space. (This is also known as a *positional* lighting model.) This is the main difference between the diffuse lighting model and the ambient lighting model, in which light has no position in space and is therefore treated as global.

Another characteristic of diffuse lighting is that a reflection is independent of the observer's position. Therefore, the surface of an object used in a diffuse lighting model reflects equally well in all directions. This is why diffuse lighting is commonly used to simulate matte surfaces. Figure 9.4 shows the Example2 program located in the Chapter9\Example2 directory on the CD-ROM.

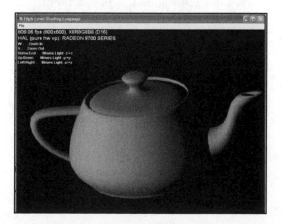

Figure 9.4

Diffuse lighting with HLSL shaders

The diffuse lighting model following Lambert's law is described with the help of two vectors—the light vector L, which describes the position of light, and the normal vector N, which describes the normal of an object's vertex (see Figure 9.5).

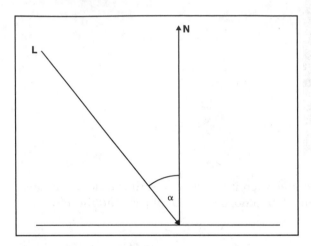

Figure 9.5

Light and normal vectors

The diffuse reflection has its peak (cos α = = 1) when L and N are aligned or, in other words, when the surface is perpendicular to the light beam. The diffuse reflection diminishes for smaller angles. Therefore, light intensity is directly proportional to cos α.

To implement the diffuse reflection in an efficient way, you use a property of the dot-product of two n-dimensional vectors.

```
N.L = ||N|| * ||L|| * cos α
```

If the light and normal vectors are of unit length (normalized), this leads to:

```
N.L = cos α
```

When N.L is equal to cos α, you can describe the diffuse lighting component with the dot-product of N and L. This diffuse lighting component is usually added to the ambient lighting component like this:

```
I = A_intensity * A_color + D_intensity * D_color * N.L + Specular
```

The example uses the following simplified version:

```
I = A + D * N.L + Specular
```

The following source code shows the HLSL vertex and pixel shaders:

```
float4x4 matWorldViewProj;
float4x4 matWorld;
float4 vecLightDir;

struct VS_OUTPUT
{
```

```
        float4 Pos   : POSITION;
        float3 Light : TEXCOORD0;
        float3 Norm  : TEXCOORD1;
};

VS_OUTPUT VS(float4 Pos : POSITION, float3 Normal : NORMAL)
{
    VS_OUTPUT Out = (VS_OUTPUT)0;
    Out.Pos = mul(Pos, matWorldViewProj);          // transform Position
    Out.Light = vecLightDir;                        // output light vector
    Out.Norm = normalize(mul(Normal, matWorld));    // transform Normal and normalize it
    return Out;
}


float4 PS(float3 Light: TEXCOORD0, float3 Norm : TEXCOORD1) : COLOR
{
    float4 diffuse = { 1.0f, 0.0f, 0.0f, 1.0f};
    float4 ambient = {0.1,  0.0,  0.0, 1.0};
    return ambient + diffuse * saturate(dot(Light, Norm));
}
```

Compared to the previous example, the vertex shader also gets a vertex normal as input data. The semantic NORMAL shows the compiler how to bind the data to the vertex shader registers. The world-view-projection matrix, the world matrix, and the light vector are provided to the vertex shader via the constants matWorldViewProj, matWorld, vecLightDir. The application provides all these constants to the vertex shader.

The vertex shader VS also outputs the N and L vectors in the variables Light and Norm here. Both vectors are normalized in the vertex shader with the intrinsic function normalize(). This function returns the normalized vector v = v/length(v). If the length of v is 0, the result is indefinite.

The normal vector is transformed when it is multiplied by the world matrix. This is done using the function mul(a, b), which performs a matrix multiplication between a and b. If a is a vector, it is treated as a row vector. If b is a vector, it is treated as a column vector. The inner dimensions $a_{columns}$ and b_{rows} must be equal. The result has the dimensions a_{rows} * $b_{columns}$. In this example, mul() gets the position vector as the first parameter (so it is treated as a row vector) and the transformation matrix, consisting of 16 floating-point values (float4x4), as the second parameter. Figure 9.6 shows the row vector and the matrix.

You implement the entire lighting formula, consisting of an ambient and a diffuse component, in the return statement. The diffuse and ambient constant values were defined in the pixel shader to make the source code easier to understand. In a real-world application, these values might be loaded from the 3D model file.

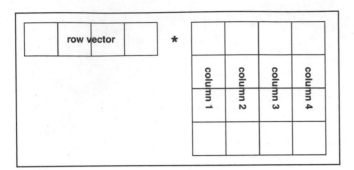

Figure 9.6

Vector with column-matrix multiplication

Specular Lighting

Specular lighting considers the location of the viewer, whereas diffuse lighting considers the location of the light vector and ambient lighting does not consider any location of the light or the viewer. Considering the viewer is useful for simulating smooth, shiny, or polished surfaces. Figure 9.7 shows the Example3 program, located in the Chapter9\Example3 directory on the CD-ROM.

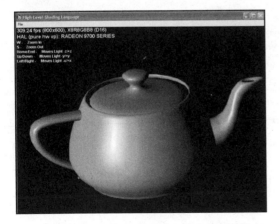

Figure 9.7

Phong lighting

In the specular lighting model developed by Bui Tong Phong, two vectors are used to calculate the specular component—the viewer vector V, which describes the direction of the viewer (or in other words, the camera), and the reflection vector R, which describes the direction of the reflection from the light vector (see Figure 9.8).

The angle between V and R is b. The more V is aligned with R, the brighter the specular light should be. Therefore, you can use cos β to describe the specular reflection (see Figure 9.9). Additionally, you use an exponent n to characterize shiny properties.

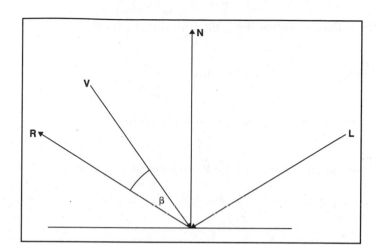

Figure 9.8

Vectors for specular lighting

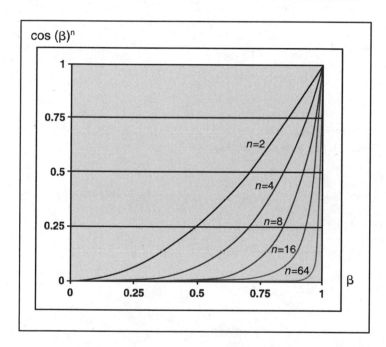

Figure 9.9

Specular power values

Therefore, you can describe the specular reflection with $\cos(\beta)^n$.

In an implementation of a specular lighting model, you can use a property of the dot-product as follows:

```
R.V = ||R|| * ||V|| * cos β
```

If both vectors are of unit length, `R.V` can replace $\cos \beta$. Therefore, you can describe the specular reflection with $(R.V)^n$.

It is quite common to calculate the reflection vector using the following formula:

```
R = 2 * (N.L) * N * L
```

The entire Phong specular lighting formula now looks like this:

$$I = A_{intensity} * A_{color} + D_{intensity} * D_{color} * N.L + S_{intensity} * S_{color} * (R.V)^n$$

Baking some values together and using white as the specular color leads to:

$$I = A + D * N.L + (R.V)^n$$

The following source code shows the implementation of the Phong specular lighting model:

```
float4x4 matWorldViewProj;
float4x4 matWorld;
float4 vecLightDir;
float4 vecEye;

struct VS_OUTPUT
{
    float4 Pos  : POSITION;
    float3 Light : TEXCOORD0;
    float3 Norm : TEXCOORD1;
    float3 View : TEXCOORD2;
};

VS_OUTPUT VS(float4 Pos : POSITION, float3 Normal : NORMAL)
{
    VS_OUTPUT Out = (VS_OUTPUT)0;
    Out.Pos = mul(Pos, matWorldViewProj);                       // transform Position
    Out.Light = vecLightDir;                                    // L
    float3 PosWorld = normalize(mul(Pos, matWorld));
    Out.View = vecEye - PosWorld;                               // V
    Out.Norm = mul(Normal, matWorld);                          // N

    return Out;
}

float4 PS(float3 Light: TEXCOORD0, float3 Norm : TEXCOORD1,
                 float3 View : TEXCOORD2) : COLOR
{
    float4 diffuse = { 1.0f, 0.0f, 0.0f, 1.0f};
    float4 ambient = { 0.1f, 0.0f, 0.0f, 1.0f};

    float3 Normal = normalize(Norm);
    float3 LightDir = normalize(Light);
    float3 ViewDir = normalize(View);
    float4 diff = saturate(dot(Normal, LightDir)); // diffuse component
```

```
// R = 2 * (N.L) * N - L
float3 Reflect = normalize(2 * diff * Normal - LightDir);
float4 specular = pow(saturate(dot(Reflect, ViewDir)), 8); // R.V^n

// I = Acolor + Dcolor * N.L + (R.V)n
return ambient + diffuse * diff + specular;
}
```

The vertex shader input values are the position values and a `normal` vector, much like in the previous example. Additionally, the vertex shader gets as constants the `matWorldViewProj` matrix, the `matWorld` matrix, the position of the eye in `vecEye`, and the light vector in `vecLightDir` from the application.

In the vertex shader, the viewer vector V is calculated by subtracting the vertex position in world space from the eye position. The vertex shader outputs the position, the light, the normal, and the viewer vector. The vectors are also the input values of the pixel shader.

All three vectors are normalized with `normalize()` in the pixel shader, whereas in the previous example vectors were normalized in the vertex shader. Normalizing vectors in the pixel shader is quite an expensive task because every pixel shader version has only a restricted number of assembly instruction slots available for the output of the HLSL compiler to use. If more instruction slots are used than are available, the compiler will display an error message like this:

```
error X4532: cannot map expression to pixel shader instruction set
```

The number of instruction slots available in Direct3D usually corresponds to the number of instruction slots available in the graphics card. The high-level language compiler cannot choose a suitable shader version on its own; the programmer must do it. If the application targets more than the least common denominator of graphics cards in the target market, the programmer must supply several shader versions.

Table 9.1 provides a list of all vertex and pixel shader versions supported by DirectX 9.

You must check the capability bits to obtain the maximum number of instructions supported by a specific card. You can do this in the DirectX Caps viewer or via the `D3DCAPS9` structure in the application. You usually check the availability of specific shader versions when the application starts up. The application can then choose the proper version from a list of already-prepared shaders, or it can put together a shader consisting of already-prepared shader fragments with the help of the shader fragment linker.

NOTE

The examples shown here generally require pixel shader version 2.0 or higher. With some tweaking, you might implement some of the effects using a lower shader version by trading off some image quality, but this is outside the scope of this book. In other words, this book does not cover fallback paths for older graphics hardware.

TABLE 9.1 Vertex and Pixel Shader Versions Supported by DirectX 9

Version	Instruction Slots	Constant Count
vs_1_1	128	At least 96 cap'd (4)
vs_2_0	256	Cap'd (4)
vs_2_x	256	Cap'd (4)
vx_2_sw	Unlimited	8192
vs_3_0	Cap'd (1)	Cap'd (4)
ps_1_1–ps_1_3	12	8
ps_1_4	28 (In two phases)	8
ps_2_0	96	32
ps_2_x	Cap'd (2)	32
ps_3_0	Cap'd (3)	224
ps_3_sw	Unlimited	8192

(1) D3DCAPS9.MaxVertexShader30InstructionSlots
(2) D3DCAPS9.D3DPSHADERCAPS2_0.NumInstructionSlots
(3) D3DCAPS9.MaxPixelShader30InstructionSlots
(4) D3DCAPS9.MaxVertexShaderConst

The pixel shader of the Phong lighting implementation shown earlier calculates the diffuse reflection in the source code line after the lines that are used to normalize the input vectors. The saturate() function is used here to clamp all values to the range 0..1. The reflection vector is retrieved by reusing the result from the diffuse reflection calculation. To get the specular power value, you use the pow() function. It is declared as pow(x, y), and it returns x^y. This function is only available in pixel shaders ps_2_0 and higher. Getting a smooth specular power value in pixel shader versions lower than ps_2_0 is quite a challenge. You can read more about this in Philippe Beaudoin and Juan Guardado's article, "A Non-Integer Power Function on the Pixel Shader," which you will find at http://www.gamasutra.com/features/20020801/beaudoin_01.htm.

The last line, starting with the return statement, corresponds to the implementation of the lighting formula shown earlier.

Self-Shadowing Term

It is common to use a self-shadowing term together with a specular lighting model to receive a geometric self-shadowing effect. Such a term sets the light brightness to 0 if the light vector is obscured by geometry, and allows a linear scaling of the light brightness. This helps reduce pixel popping when you are using bump maps. Figure 9.10 shows an example that uses a self-shadowing term on the right and an example that does not use a self-shadowing term on the left.

Figure 9.10

Self-shadowing term

There are several ways to calculate this term. Example4, located in the Chapter9\Example4 directory on the CD-ROM, uses `S = saturate(4 * N.L)`. (You can read more about the self-shadowing term in Ronald Frazier's article, "Advanced Real-Time Per-Pixel Lighting in OpenGL," which you will find at http://www.ronfrazier.net/apparition/index.asp?appmain=research/advanced_per_pixel_lighting.html.) This implementation just reuses the `N.L` calculation to calculate the self-shadowing term, which leads to the following lighting formula:

```
I = A + S * (D * N.L + (R.V)ⁿ)
```

The self-shadowing term reduces the diffuse and specular components of the lighting model to NULL if the diffuse component is NULL. The diffuse component is used to diminish the intensity of the specular component. This is shown in the following pixel shader:

```
float4 PS(float3 Light: TEXCOORD0, float3 Norm : TEXCOORD1, float3 View : TEXCOORD2) : COLOR
{
    float4 diffuse = { 1.0f, 0.0f, 0.0f, 1.0f};
    float4 ambient = {0.1,  0.0,  0.0, 1.0};

    float3 Normal = normalize(Norm);
    float3 LightDir = normalize(Light);
    float3 ViewDir = normalize(View);
    float4 diff = saturate(dot(Normal, LightDir)); // diffuse component

    // compute self-shadowing term
    float shadow = saturate(4* diff);

    float3 Reflect = normalize(2 * diff * Normal - LightDir);  // R
    float4 specular = pow(saturate(dot(Reflect, ViewDir)), 8); // R.V^n

    // I = ambient + shadow * (Dcolor * N.L + (R.V)n)
    return ambient + shadow * (diffuse * diff + specular);
}
```

Bump Mapping

Bump mapping fakes the existence of geometry (grooves, nodges, and bulges). Figure 9.11 shows the Example5 program located in the Chapter9\Example5 directory on the CD-ROM. This program gives the viewer the illusion that regions with mountains are higher than water regions on Earth.

Figure 9.11

Bump mapping

Whereas a color map stores color values, a bump map is a graphics file (such as *.dds or *.tga) that stores normals that are used instead of the vertex normals to calculate the lighting. These normals are stored in the most common bump-mapping technique, in what is called *texture space* or *tangent space*. The light vector is usually handled in object or world space, which leads to the problem that the light vector must be transformed into the same space as the normals in the bump map to obtain proper results. You do this with the help of a texture or tangent space coordinate system (see Figure 9.12).

The easiest way to obtain such a texture space coordinate system is to use the D3DXComputeNormal() and D3DXComputeTangent() functions provided with the Direct3D utility library Direct3DX. You can find source code implementations of the functionality covered by these functions in the NVMeshMender library, which you can download from the NVIDIA Web

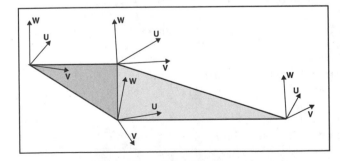

Figure 9.12

Texture space coordinate system

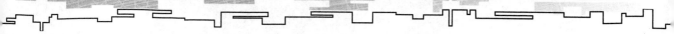
site, at http://developer.nvidia.com. Calculating a texture space coordinate system is much like calculating the vertex normal. For example, if a vertex shares three triangles, you calculate the face normal/face tangent first, and then you add the vectors of all three triangles at the vertex that connects the triangles to form the vertex normal/vertex tangent. This example uses the vertex normal instead of a W vector for the texture space coordinate system and calculates the U vector with the help of the D3DXComputeTangent() function. You retrieve the V vector by calculating the cross-product of the W and U vectors using the cross() function in the vertex shader.

```
struct VS_OUTPUT
{
    float4 Pos  : POSITION;
    float2 Tex : TEXCOORD0;
    float3 Light : TEXCOORD1;
    float3 View : TEXCOORD2;
};

VS_OUTPUT VS(float4 Pos : POSITION, float2 Tex : TEXCOORD, float3 Normal : NORMAL, float3
Tangent : TANGENT )
{
    VS_OUTPUT Out = (VS_OUTPUT)0;
    Out.Pos = mul(Pos, matWorldViewProj);          // transform Position

    // compute the 3x3 transform matrix
    // to transform from world space to tangent space
    float3x3 worldToTangentSpace;
    worldToTangentSpace[0] = mul(Tangent, matWorld);
    worldToTangentSpace[1] = mul(cross(Tangent, Normal), matWorld);
    worldToTangentSpace[2] = mul(Normal, matWorld);

    Out.Tex = Tex.xy;

    Out.Light.xyz = mul(worldToTangentSpace, vecLightDir);          // L
    float3 PosWorld = normalize(mul(Pos, matWorld));
    float3 Viewer = vecEye - PosWorld;                              // V
    Out.View = mul(worldToTangentSpace, Viewer);

    return Out;
}

float4 PS(float2 Tex: TEXCOORD0, float3 Light : TEXCOORD1,
float3 View : TEXCOORD2) : COLOR
{
    float4 color = tex2D(ColorMapSampler, Tex); // fetch color map
    float3 bumpNormal = 2 * (tex2D(BumpMapSampler, Tex) - 0.5); // bump map
```

```
float3 LightDir = normalize(Light);      // L
float3 ViewDir = normalize(View);        // V

float4 diff = saturate(dot(bumpNormal, LightDir)); // diffuse comp.

float shadow = saturate(4 * diff); // compute self-shadowing term

float3 Reflect = normalize(2 * diff * bumpNormal - LightDir);  // R

// gloss map in color.w restricts spec reflection
float4 spec = min(pow(saturate(dot(Reflect, ViewDir)), 3), color.w);

return 0.2 * color + shadow * (color * diff + spec);
}
```

You create the 3x3 matrix, consisting of the U, V, and W (== N) vectors, in the vertex shader and use it there to transform L and V to texture space.

Compared to the previous example, the major differences in the pixel shader are the use of a color map and a bump map, which are fetched with tex2D(). The tex2D() function is declared as tex2D(s, t), where s is a sampler object and t is a 2D texture coordinate. Please consult the DirectX 9 documentation for many other texture sampler functions (for example, texCUBE(s, t), which is used to fetch a cube map).

You use the normal from the bump map here, instead of the normal from the vertex throughout the whole pixel shader. It is fetched from the normal map by biasing (–0.5) and scaling (* 2.0) its values. You must do this because the normal map was stored in an unsigned texture format with a value range of 0..1 to allow older hardware to operate correctly; therefore, you must expand the normals back to their signed range.

Compared to the previous examples, this pixel shader also restricts the region where a specular reflection might occur on the water regions of the Earth model. This is accomplished with the help of the min() function and a gloss map that is stored in the alpha values of the color map. min() is defined as min(a, b), and it selects the lesser of a and b.

In the return statement, the ambient term is replaced by an intensity-decreased color value from the color map. This way, if the self-shadowing term reduces the diffuse and specular lighting components, at least a very dark Earth is still visible.

Point Lights

Example6 is the last example; it is located in the Chapter9\Example6 directory on the CD-ROM. Example6 adds a per-pixel point light to the previous example. Contrary to the parallel light beams of a directional light source, the light beams of a point light spread out uniformly in all directions from the position of the point light (see Figure 9.13).

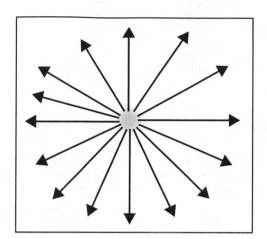

Figure 9.13

Point light

In his article on the NVIDIA developer Web site, Sim Dietrich shows that the following function delivers reasonable results:

```
attenuation = 1 - d * d // d = distance
```

This stands for:

```
attenuation = 1 - (x * x + y * y + z * z)
```

In his book *Real-Time Rendering Tricks and Techniques in DirectX* (Premier Press, 2002), Kelly Dempski divides the squared distance by a constant, which stands for the range of distance, in which the point light attenuation effect should occur.

$$attenuation = 1 - ((x/r)^2 + (y/r)^2 + (z/r)^2)$$

Take the x/r, y/r, and z/r values to the pixel shader via a TEXCOORDn channel and multiply them there with the help of the mul() function. The relevant source code to do this is

```
VS_OUTPUT VS(float4 Pos : POSITION, float2 Tex : TEXCOORD,
float3 Normal : NORMAL, float3 Tangent : TANGENT )
{
...
    float LightRange = 1.0;

    // point light
    Out.Att = Light * LightRange;
...
}

float4 PS(float2 Tex: TEXCOORD0, float3 Light : TEXCOORD1,
float3 View : TEXCOORD2, float3 Att : TEXCOORD3) : COLOR
{
...
```

```
// attenuation
float4 Attenuation = mul(Att, Att);

// colormap * (self-shadow-term * diffuse + ambient) + self-shadow-term * // specular
return (color * (shadow * diff + ambient) + shadow * spec) * (1 -Attenuation);
}
```

Decreasing the `LightRange` parameter increases the range of light, whereas increasing this value leads to a shorter range. The attenuation value is multiplied by itself in the pixel shader because it is more efficient than using the exponent 2. In the last line of the pixel shader, the attenuation value is multiplied by the result of the lighting computation to decrease or increase light intensity depending on the distance of the light source.

Summary

This chapter covered the syntax and some of the intrinsic functions of HLSL by showing you how to implement some common lighting formulas. It introduced you to six working (and generally concise) code examples to get you ready to generate your own shaders. To move on from here, I recommend that you look at the RenderMonkey examples on ATI's Web site (http://www.ati.com) and play around with the source code. You will also find an interactive RenderMonkey tutorial on my Web site (http://www.direct3d.info).

CHAPTER 10

MORE ADVANCED SHADER EFFECTS

This chapter features a technique called *cube environment mapping*, which reflects the environment of an object in its surface. Most current graphic cards support this technique, and it is gaining in popularity. Understanding the idea behind this technique will open many doors to more advanced gaming techniques that might be implemented in the next couple years.

This chapter also covers the shadowing technique that, in the next couple years, will be used as the standard for creating realistic depictions of dynamic shadows in a scene.

In this chapter, you'll learn how to:

- Generate, access, and implement cube maps
- Use dynamic refractive and reflective environment mapping
- Work with shadows and shadow volumes

Working with Cube Maps

One thing that has been missing in the examples so far is the idea of reflection. Creating photorealistic "virtual environments" requires surfaces that are capable of reflecting light as they would in the natural world. Therefore, the term *reflection mapping* is sometimes used interchangeably with the term *environment mapping*.

The surfaces of real-life objects are characterized by the degree to which light is absorbed, reflected, or transmitted. To replicate the visual richness of natural objects, the eye must perceive that light is accurately reflected off objects in real-time, without objectionable artifacts. The complexity involved in modeling the physical behavior of light by explicitly tracing secondary light rays throughout a scene, however, has led to alternative techniques to simulate realistic reflections. Environment mapping is an efficient technique to compute reflections in computer-synthesized environments without tracing a myriad of secondary rays. By using pre-defined images cast as a geometric map shape that surrounds an object, you can define reflections for a single point in space. The most common pre-defined images that surround an object are called *cube environment maps* or simply *cube maps*. All recent graphics cards support them.

Generating Cube Maps

Conceptually, cube maps represent the environment as six sides of a cube that surrounds one or more of the objects in your scene. To generate a cube map, replace the object on which you want to put reflections with a camera at the object's position, and take snapshots in six directions (positive x, negative x, positive y, negative y, positive z, and negative z). Each snapshot should have a 90-degree field-of-view and a square aspect ratio, so that the six cube faces seam tightly to create an omnidirectional panorama. Use these images as the six faces of your cube map (see Figure 10.1).

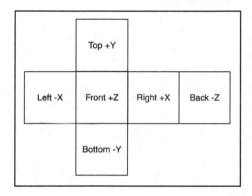

Figure 10.1

A cube environment map unfolded, illustrating its sides

The process of generating a cube map is done in the first two example programs as a pre-processing step. In the last two example programs, the process is done dynamically by the application.

Accessing Cube Maps

You access a cube map much like you created a cube map. Think of the texture coordinate as a 3D vector pointing from the center of the cube out toward the sides. The point where the vector intersects a cube wall is the matching texel for that texture coordinate. You create the vector R, which is used to access the cube map, with the help of the incident ray vector. This vector is the negated eye vector. Please note that the reflection vector in Figure 10.2 is not the same reflection vector used in the Phong equation in the previous chapter. It is calculated with the following formula, where I is the vector from eye to vertex (the opposite of the eye vector, which goes from vertex to eye).

```
R = I - 2 * N * (I.N)
```

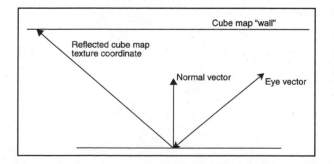

Figure 10.2

Vector tracing the reflection of a ray onto a cube map

You can find a mathematical proof for R on many Web sites and in numerous textbooks. A geometrical proof by inspection might look like Figure 10.3.

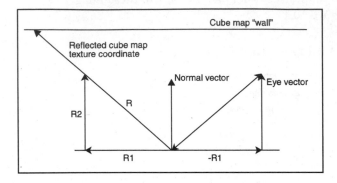

Figure 10.3

Reflection vector

```
R = R1 + R2
R1 = I - R2
```

This leads to:

```
R = I - 2 * R2
R2 =  N  * (I.N)
```

This leads to:

```
R = I - 2 * N * (I.N)
```

Implementation

The first example program, named CubeMap, which you will find in the directory Chapter10\CubeMap on the CD-ROM, demonstrates environment mapping in its simplest form. It shows a teapot that was given a chrome-like appearance by the environment map (see Figure 10.4).

This is the bare-bones application of the technique, yet it already produces nice results. In this example, the vertex shader computes the incident and the reflection vector and passes the reflection vector to the pixel shader. The value from the cube environment map is fetched in the pixel shader and used there as the output value.

```
float4x4 matWorldViewProj;
float4x4 matWorld;
float4x4 matView;
float4 vecEye;


texture CubeMap;
samplerCUBE CubeMapSampler = sampler_state
{
```

Figure 10.4

Cube environment mapping

```
    Texture = <CubeMap>;
    MinFilter = Linear;
    MagFilter = Linear;
    AddressU  = Wrap;
    AddressV  = Wrap;
};


struct VS_OUTPUT
{
    float4 Pos   : POSITION;
    float3 Reflect: TEXCOORD4;
};


VS_OUTPUT VS(float4 Pos : POSITION, float2 Tex : TEXCOORD, float3 Normal : NORMAL)
{
    VS_OUTPUT Out = (VS_OUTPUT)0;
    Out.Pos = mul(Pos, matWorldViewProj);        // transform Position
    float3 Norm = normalize(mul(Normal, matWorld));

    // get a vector toward the camera/eye -> V
    float3 PosWorld = normalize(mul(Pos, matWorld));
    float3 Incident = normalize(PosWorld - vecEye);

    // Reflection Vector for cube map: R = I - 2 * N * (I.N)
    Out.Reflect = normalize(reflect(Incident, Norm));
    // Out.Reflect = normalize(Incident - 2 * Norm * dot(Incident, Norm));
```

```
        return Out;
}


float4 PS(float3 Ref : TEXCOORD4) : COLOR
{
        return texCUBE(CubeMapSampler, Ref);
}
```

As in the examples in the previous chapter, the position of the vertex is transformed with the concatenated world, view, and projection matrixes, and the normal is transformed with the world matrix. The incident ray I is calculated by subtracting the eye position from the position of the vertex in world space. The normalized reflection vector is calculated with the help of the reflect() function provided with the common high-level language compiler. An implementation of this function might look like this:

```
float3 reflect(float3 I, float3 N)
{
        return I - 2 * N * dot(I, N);
}
```

reflect() returns the reflection vector R, given the entering ray direction I and the surface normal N. In the pixel shader, the function texCUBE() samples a texel from a cube map and outputs it. The 3D look-up vector provided as the second parameter is the reflection vector calculated in the vertex shader.

Refractive and Reflective Environment Mapping

Now that you have learned how to implement basic environment mapping, you should add a refraction effect to the previous example. In the real world, light rays that pass through one medium into another are bent at the interface between the two mediums. This is called *refraction*. The most common example of this is when you stand at the edge of the water and look at a fish below the surface. The light rays reflected off of the fish bend as they leave the water. The light also bends differently as the shape of the water's surface changes. Figure 10.5 shows a similar effect from the example program.

The CubeMap 2 example program, which you will find in the Chapter10\CubeMap 2 directory on the CD-ROM, shows a partly reflective and partly refractive teapot. In this example, the refraction effect is only approximated by reusing the reflection equation and a scaled, not re-normalized, normal vector. You can read more about this topic in Kelly Dempski's *Real-Time Rendering Tricks and Techniques in DirectX* (Premier Press, 2002). Shortening the normal leads to a bend vector that might look like an extension of the eye vector (see Figure 10.6).

Figure 10.5

Refractive and reflective environment mapping

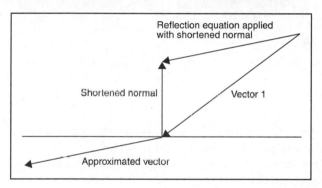

Figure 10.6

Refracted vector

If the normal is shortened to a zero length, the refraction vector will be the same as the vector I. With a longer normal, the refraction vector is bent more to the surface.

The following shader fetches the cube map twice—first with the reflection vector, and then with an approximated refracted vector as the 3D texture coordinate.

```
struct VS_OUTPUT
{
    float4 Pos   : POSITION;
    float3 Reflect: TEXCOORD4;
    float3 Reflect2: TEXCOORD5;
};


VS_OUTPUT VS(float4 Pos : POSITION, float2 Tex : TEXCOORD, float3 Normal : NORMAL)
{
    VS_OUTPUT Out = (VS_OUTPUT)0;
    Out.Pos = mul(Pos, matWorldViewProj);        // transform Position
```

```
    float3 Norm = normalize(mul(Normal, matWorld));

    // get a vector toward the camera/eye -> V
    float3 PosWorld  = normalize(mul(Pos, matWorld));
    float3 Incident = normalize(PosWorld  - vecEye);

    // Reflection Vector for cube map: R = I - 2*N * (I.N)
    Out.Reflect = normalize(reflect(Incident, Norm));

    float3 ShortNorm = mul(Norm, 0.4);

    // Reflection Vector for cube map: R = I - 2*N * (I.N)
    Out.Reflect2 = normalize(reflect(Incident, ShortNorm));

   return Out;
}

float4 PS(float3 Ref : TEXCOORD4, float3 Ref2 : TEXCOORD5) : COLOR
{
    float4 tex1 = texCUBE(CubeMapSampler, Ref);
    float4 tex2 = texCUBE(CubeMapSampler, Ref2);

    return tex2 * 0.5 + tex1;
}
```

The normal is shortened and stored in the ShortNorm variable in the vertex shader. You then use this variable with the reflect() function to calculate the refraction vector. Using a higher value of the constant (near 1.0) results in something that looks very much like reflection, whereas lower values (near zero) are closer to the vector I and might cause a zooming effect. Just play around with this value.

The reflection and refraction values are then sent to the pixel shader, where they are used to fetch the same cube map twice. The resulting color value of the cube map fetched with the refraction vector is reduced in its intensity by multiplying it by 0.5. It is then added to the value fetched with the reflection vector.

Dynamic Refractive and Reflective Environment Mapping

The main improvement to the following example (CubeMap 3, which you will find in the Chapter10\CubeMap 3 directory on the CD-ROM) is the dynamic updating process of the cube map. In other words, the content of the cube map is changed every frame. To highlight this dynamic update, an airplane is flying around the teapot. Its reflection on the teapot is visible by projecting the cube map onto the teapot. The source code for the airplane and most parts of the cube-map rendering is taken from the DirectX 9 SDK Cube map example (see Figure 10.7).

Figure 10.7

Dynamic cube map

You use the following function to update a cube map dynamically every frame:

```
HRESULT CMyD3DApplication::RenderSceneIntoEnvMap()
{
    HRESULT hr;

    // Set the projection matrix for a field of view of 90 degrees
    D3DXMATRIXA16 matProj;
    D3DXMatrixPerspectiveFovLH( &matProj, D3DX_PI * 0.5f, 1.0f, 0.5f, 1000.0f );

    // Get the current view matrix, to concat it with the cubemap view vectors
    D3DXMATRIXA16 matViewDir( m_matView );
    matViewDir._41 = 0.0f; matViewDir._42 = 0.0f; matViewDir._43 = 0.0f;

    // Render the six cube faces into the environment map
    if( m_pCubeMap )
        hr = m_pRenderToEnvMap->BeginCube( m_pCubeMap );

    if(FAILED(hr))
        return hr;

    for( UINT i = 0; i < 6; i++ )
    {
        m_pRenderToEnvMap->Face( (D3DCUBEMAP_FACES) i, 0 );

        // Set the view transform for this cubemap surface
        D3DXMATRIXA16 matView;
        matView = D3DUtil_GetCubeMapViewMatrix( (D3DCUBEMAP_FACES) i );
        D3DXMatrixMultiply( &matView, &matViewDir, &matView );
```

```
        // Render the scene (except for the teapot)
        RenderScene( &matView, &matProj, FALSE );
    }


    m_pRenderToEnvMap->End( 0 );
    return S_OK;
}
```

The source code shows how the projection matrix is set by the function
D3DXMatrixPerspectiveFovLH(). The camera gets a field of view of 90 degrees, and the aspect
ratio is set as a square. The next two lines show how the camera is positioned in the center
of the scene. Then the camera is rotated in the six directions of the cube map, and the
scene is rendered onto each cube-map face. The RenderScene() function does the rendering;
it renders the scene onto the cube map as well as to the output window. The Boolean variable bRenderTeapot prevents the teapot from being rendered onto the cube map.

```
HRESULT CMyD3DApplication::RenderScene( CONST D3DXMATRIXA16 *pView,
CONST D3DXMATRIXA16 *pProject,
                                       BOOL bRenderTeapot )
{
    // Render the Skybox
    {
        D3DXMATRIXA16 matWorld;
        D3DXMatrixScaling( &matWorld, 10.0f, 10.0f, 10.0f );

        D3DXMATRIXA16 matView(*pView);
        matView._41 = matView._42 = matView._43 = 0.0f;

        m_pd3dDevice->SetTransform( D3DTS_WORLD, &matWorld );
        m_pd3dDevice->SetTransform( D3DTS_VIEW, &matView );
        m_pd3dDevice->SetTransform( D3DTS_PROJECTION, pProject );

        m_pd3dDevice->SetTexture(0, m_pCubeMap);
        m_pd3dDevice->SetTextureStageState( 0, D3DTSS_COLORARG1, D3DTA_TEXTURE );
        m_pd3dDevice->SetTextureStageState( 0, D3DTSS_COLOROP,    D3DTOP_SELECTARG1 );
        m_pd3dDevice->SetSamplerState( 0, D3DSAMP_MINFILTER, D3DTEXF_LINEAR );
        m_pd3dDevice->SetSamplerState( 0, D3DSAMP_MAGFILTER, D3DTEXF_LINEAR );
        if( (m_d3dCaps.TextureAddressCaps & D3DPTADDRESSCAPS_MIRROR)
== D3DPTADDRESSCAPS_MIRROR )
        {
            m_pd3dDevice->SetSamplerState( 0, D3DSAMP_ADDRESSU,  D3DTADDRESS_MIRROR );
            m_pd3dDevice->SetSamplerState( 0, D3DSAMP_ADDRESSV,  D3DTADDRESS_MIRROR );
        }

        // Always pass Z-test, so we can avoid clearing color and depth buffers
        m_pd3dDevice->SetRenderState( D3DRS_ZFUNC, D3DCMP_ALWAYS );
        m_pSkyBox->Render( m_pd3dDevice );
```

```
        m_pd3dDevice->SetRenderState( D3DRS_ZFUNC, D3DCMP_LESSEQUAL );
}


// Render the Airplane
{
    m_pd3dDevice->SetTransform( D3DTS_WORLD, &m_matAirplane );
    m_pd3dDevice->SetTransform( D3DTS_VIEW, pView );
    m_pd3dDevice->SetTransform( D3DTS_PROJECTION, pProject );

    m_pd3dDevice->SetTextureStageState( 0, D3DTSS_COLORARG1, D3DTA_TEXTURE );
    m_pd3dDevice->SetTextureStageState( 0, D3DTSS_COLOROP,   D3DTOP_SELECTARG1 );
    m_pd3dDevice->SetSamplerState( 0, D3DSAMP_MINFILTER, D3DTEXF_LINEAR );
    m_pd3dDevice->SetSamplerState( 0, D3DSAMP_MAGFILTER, D3DTEXF_LINEAR );
    m_pd3dDevice->SetSamplerState( 0, D3DSAMP_ADDRESSU,  D3DTADDRESS_WRAP );
    m_pd3dDevice->SetSamplerState( 0, D3DSAMP_ADDRESSV,  D3DTADDRESS_WRAP );

    m_pAirplane->Render( m_pd3dDevice );

    m_pd3dDevice->SetTransform( D3DTS_WORLD, &m_matWorld);
}

// Render the environment-mapped ShinyTeapot
if( bRenderTeapot )
{
    //Rotate the object
    D3DXMatrixRotationY(&m_matWorld, (float)GetTickCount() / 1000.0f);

    D3DXMATRIX mWorldViewProj;
    D3DXMatrixMultiply(&mWorldViewProj,&m_matWorld, pView);
    D3DXMatrixMultiply(&mWorldViewProj, &mWorldViewProj, pProject);
    m_pEffect->SetMatrix( "matWorldViewProj", &mWorldViewProj );
    m_pEffect->SetMatrix( "matWorld", &m_matWorld);
    m_pEffect->SetMatrix( "matView", pView);
    m_pEffect->SetVector( "vecEye", &m_vEyePos);

    UINT nPasses;
    UINT iPass;

    if( m_pEffect != NULL )
    {
        D3DXHANDLE hTechnique = m_pEffect->GetTechniqueByName( "TShader" );
            m_pEffect->SetTechnique( hTechnique );

    m_pEffect->SetTexture("CubeMap", m_pCubeMap);
    m_pEffect->Begin( &nPasses, 0 );
```

```
        for( iPass = 0; iPass < nPasses; iPass ++ )
        {
                m_pEffect->Pass( iPass );
                m_pD3DXMesh->DrawSubset( 0 );
        }
        m_pEffect->End();
        }
    }
    return S_OK;
}
```

The fixed-function pipeline renders the environment and the airplane. The environment (here the skybox, airplane, and teapot) use their own transformation matrix. The cube map is rendered from the center of the scene, at the same point where its content is rendered into it. The airplane flies around the teapot and is rendered with the Render() function of the file utility library function in d3dfile.cpp. The teapot is rendered here with the help of a vertex and pixel shader in an effect file, as with all shader examples in this book.

When RenderScene() is called from within the Render() function, the variable bRenderTeapot is set to TRUE. When the function is called from within the RenderSceneIntoEnvMap() function, this variable is set to FALSE.

Bumped Dynamic Refractive and Reflective Environment Mapping

The CubeMap 4 example combines the functionality of the bump-mapping example in the previous chapter with the dynamic reflection/refraction example shown earlier in this chapter. You will find this example program in the Chapter10\CubeMap 4 directory on the CD-ROM. The combination of bump mapping and a dynamically updated cube map leads to quite a long shader.

```
struct VS_OUTPUT
{
    float4 Pos  : POSITION;
    float2 Tex : TEXCOORD0;
    float3 Light : TEXCOORD1;
    float3 View : TEXCOORD2;
    float3 Reflect: TEXCOORD3;
    float3 Reflect2: TEXCOORD4;
};

VS_OUTPUT VS(float4 Pos : POSITION, float2 Tex : TEXCOORD, float3 Normal : NORMAL,
float3 Tangent : TANGENT  )
{
    VS_OUTPUT Out = (VS_OUTPUT)0;
    Out.Pos = mul(Pos, matWorldViewProj);        // transform Position
```

```
    // compute the 3x3 transform matrix
    // to transform from world space to tangent space
    float3x3 worldToTangentSpace;
    worldToTangentSpace[0] = mul(Tangent, matWorld);
    worldToTangentSpace[1] = mul(cross(Tangent, Normal), matWorld);
    float3 Norm = mul(Normal, matWorld);
    worldToTangentSpace[2] = Norm;

    Out.Tex = Tex.xy;

    // output light vector
    float3 Light = normalize(vecLightDir);
    Out.Light.xyz = mul(worldToTangentSpace, Light);

    // get a vector toward the camera/eye -> V
    float3 PosWorld = normalize(mul(Pos, matWorld));
    float3 Incident = normalize(PosWorld  - vecEye);

    // view vector for bump map
    float3 Viewer2 = normalize(vecEye - PosWorld);
    Out.View = mul(worldToTangentSpace, Viewer2);

    // Reflection Vector for cube map: R = I - 2*N * (I.N)
    Out.Reflect = normalize(reflect(Incident, Norm));

    float3 ShortNorm = mul(Norm, 0.4);

    // Reflection Vector for cube map: R = I - 2*N * (I.N)
    Out.Reflect2 = normalize(reflect(Incident, ShortNorm));

  return Out;
}

float4 PS(float2 Tex: TEXCOORD0, float3 Light : TEXCOORD1,
float3 View : TEXCOORD2, float3 Ref : TEXCOORD3,
float3 Ref2 : TEXCOORD4) : COLOR
{
    float4 color = tex2D(ColorMapSampler, Tex);                  // fetch color map
    float4 bumpNormal = 2 * (tex2D(BumpMapSampler, Tex) - 0.5); // fetch bump map
    float4 tex1 = texCUBE(CubeMapSampler, Ref);
    float4 tex2 = texCUBE(CubeMapSampler, Ref2);

    // light vector
    float3 LightDir = normalize(Light);
    float3 ViewDir = normalize(View);
```

```
// diffuse component
float4 diff = saturate(dot(bumpNormal, LightDir));

// compute self-shadowing term
float shadow = saturate(4 * diff);

// compute R vector
float3 Reflect = normalize(2 * diff * bumpNormal - LightDir);

// gloss map in color.w used to restrict specular reflection on non-glossy regions
float4 spec = min(pow(saturate(dot(Reflect, ViewDir)), 15), color.w);

    return 0.2 * color + shadow * ((color * diff + spec)+ ((tex2 * 0.5 + tex1) * 0.05));
}
```

At the beginning of the vertex shader, you create the texture space coordinate system with the help of the Tangent vector, the Normal vector, and the Binormal vector that is created from the cross-product of the Tangent and Normal vectors. The resulting 3×3 matrix is used to transform the light vector L and the viewer vector V in tangent space. Additionally, the reflection vector and the refraction vector are sent to the pixel shader in world space. The return statement should look familiar to you. The result of the reflection/refraction example is simply added to the result of the bump-mapping example. This example provides you with several parameters to tweak. Just play around with them. Figure 10.8 shows a shot of this example.

To play with this example, you might put a higher weight on the reflection/refraction part, or use only the self-shadowing term to dump the diffuse and specular lighting components and not the reflection/refraction component.

Figure 10.8

Bumped reflection/refraction cube mapping

Following are a few tips to help you create an effective implementation of cubic environment maps:

- Use one environment map for all objects.
- Use static cube maps instead of dynamic ones when possible.
- If you need a dynamic cube map, write only every fifth frame.
- Cube maps do not work on flat reflective surfaces.
- Switch off cube mapping based on distance.

Working with Shadows

As much as lighting can create a mood in a scene, it's often the rendered shadows that further define that mood and give an object more lifelike qualities. Shadows are an important element in creating realistic images and in providing the user with visual cues about object placement. Furthermore, shadows can be a vital part of the game design. For example, the player might be a thief who has to take cover in the shadows to hide.

As hard as it is to create and apply realistic and appropriate lighting to a scene, it can be equally challenging to render convincing shadows. There are several very different techniques to create shadows. They all have in common the description of the anatomy of a shadow. A shadowed scene needs a light source that is calculated per-vertex or per-pixel, an object that casts a shadow (called the *occluder*), and a surface onto which the shadow is being cast (called the *receiver*). Figure 10.9 shows that shadows themselves have two parts—the *umbra*, which is the hard inner part of the shadow, and the softer *penumbra*, which is composed of the outer and border portions of the shadow.

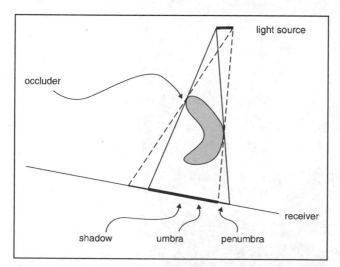

Figure 10.9

Shadow terminology: light source, occluder, receiver, umbra, and penumbra

Courtesy of Tomas Akenine-Möller/Eric Haines, Real-Time Rendering, 2nd edition

The penumbra creates the difference between hard and soft shadows. With hard shadows, the shadow ends abruptly and looks unnatural, whereas with soft shadows, the penumbra transitions from the color of the shadow (usually black) to the adjacent pixel color, creating a more realistic effect.

There are numerous ways to create shadows in a game. I would like to feature one newer method available in DirectX 8 and in an optimized form on DirectX 9 graphics hardware—shadow volumes with a stencil buffer.

Shadow Volumes

Shadow volumes should be the preferred technique in the next two years for creating shadows in upcoming games. The example Shadow Volume program, which is located in the directory Chapter10\Shadow Volume on the CD-ROM, uses the two-sided stencil buffer, introduced in DirectX 9, and falls back to the legacy one-sided stencil buffer on older graphics cards (see Figure 10.10).

The example program shows a room in which two boxes are located. The light source is located under the roof, and both boxes throw shadows. The shadows of the two boxes occupy a given volume of space. Anything outside of the shadow volume is lit, and anything within the volume is not.

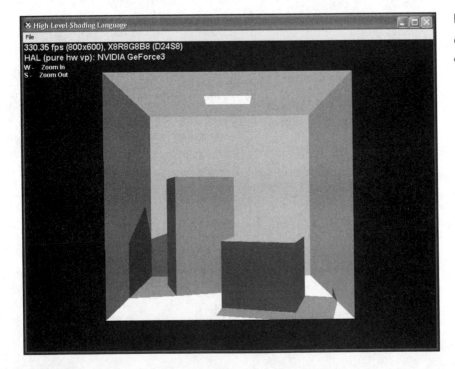

Figure 10.10

Cornell box with two cubes with shadows

Figure 10.11 shows the same scene in the ATI RadeonShadowShader example available on ATI's Web site (http://www.ati.com/developer). The right side of the figure shows two shadow volumes from the two light sources. Please note the volumes of the light and the shadow. The object cuts off all light beams.

Figure 10.11

Shadow volumes in the ATI RadeonShadowShader example

One of the challenges of shadow volumes is cutting off the light beams in the right way. To do so, you need to detect the silhouette edges of the mesh from the perspective of the light. A silhouette edge is an edge of the object where one polygon faces toward the light and the other faces away from it. To make such an edge detectable by the vertex shader, the source geometry must be preprocessed so that it is possible to form a shadow volume in any direction, without needing to create new geometry on the fly.

In this preprocessing step, degenerate quads replace shared edges of the objects. Figure 10.12 depicts the preprocessing of the source geometry that forms a cube and shows only the front faces for simplicity. The shared edges of the faces are filtered out, and degenerate quads are inserted to replace them. The two edges that form the opposing sides of each degenerate quad have the same positional values but different face normals. This chapter's example uses a preprocessing technique that was used by Imagire Takashi in his shadow volume example at http://www.t-pot.com.

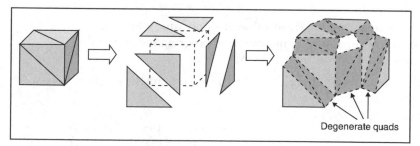

Degenerate quads

Figure 10.12

You need to replace shared edges on flat surfaces with degenerate quads.

Figure courtesy of Hun Yen Kwoon

I will briefly run through the preprocessing algorithm for you.

1. Step through all the faces in the source mesh.

2. Compute the face normals for each face.

3. Step through the three edges of each face.

4. Insert each edge into a checklist.

5. If two vertices of the same two faces share an edge, follow one of these two steps:

   a. If the normals of the faces sharing the edge are not parallel, change the direction of the face.

   or

   b. Generate a degenerated quad.

First the face normals of all faces are calculated, to see which direction the face points. Then vertices that share one edge are searched; if two vertices of one face share two vertices with another face, a degenerated quad is inserted. This quad helps the vertex shader create the shadow volume independent of the location of the light source.

Note that the pre-processing technique used here indiscriminately inserts degenerate quads into every shared edge in the preprocessing step. Checking whether a shared edge would have a good chance of becoming a silhouette edge might reduce the polygon count. If a shared edge has almost no chance of becoming a silhouette edge, then there is really no need to insert a degenerate quad to replace that edge. A simple way to determine the chances of an edge forming part of a silhouette is to test the parallelism of the normals of the faces that share it. If the two faces have normals that are almost parallel, then the shared edge is on a flat surface and would have little chance of becoming part of a silhouette.

One other thing to note is that the source mesh should be a closed mesh. Any seams or holes (formed by T-junctions, for example) will greatly complicate the silhouette determination algorithm in the vertex shader. Additionally, non-closed front faces will throw the stencil counting off balance.

You can find the Create() function that performs this preprocessing step in the CShadowVolume.cpp file in the Shadow Volume example program located in the Chapter10\Shadow Volume directory on the CD-ROM.

```
HRESULT CShadowVolume::Create( LPDIRECT3DDEVICE9 pd3dDevice, LPD3DXMESH pSrcMesh )
{
    HRESULT ret = S_OK;
    SHADOW_VOLUME_VERTEX* pVertices;        // local copy of the vertex buffer
    WORD*        pIndices;                  // local copy of the index buffer
    DWORD i, j, k, l, face;
    LPD3DXMESH pMesh;
```

```cpp
    if( FAILED( pSrcMesh->CloneMeshFVF(D3DXMESH_SYSTEMMEM,
                                    D3DFVF_XYZ | D3DFVF_NORMAL,
                                    pd3dDevice, &pMesh ) ) )
        return E_FAIL;

DWORD dwNumFaces    = pMesh->GetNumFaces();

// four times the number of faces and
// three times the number of vertices.
m_dwNumFaces = 4 * dwNumFaces;
m_pVertices = new SHADOW_VOLUME_VERTEX[3*m_dwNumFaces];

// lock buffers
pMesh->LockVertexBuffer( 0L, (LPVOID*)&pVertices );
pMesh->LockIndexBuffer ( 0L, (LPVOID*)&pIndices );

// allocate space for normal
D3DXVECTOR3 *vNormal = new D3DXVECTOR3[dwNumFaces];
if(NULL==vNormal)
{
    m_dwNumFaces = 0;
            ret = E_OUTOFMEMORY;
    goto end;
}

// compute face normals for each face
for( i=0; i < dwNumFaces; i++ )
{
    D3DXVECTOR3 v0 = pVertices[pIndices[3*i+0]].p;
    D3DXVECTOR3 v1 = pVertices[pIndices[3*i+1]].p;
    D3DXVECTOR3 v2 = pVertices[pIndices[3*i+2]].p;

    // calculate normal
    D3DXVECTOR3 vCross1(v1-v0);
    D3DXVECTOR3 vCross2(v2-v1);
    D3DXVec3Cross( &vNormal[i], &vCross1, &vCross2 );

    // store faces
    m_pVertices[3*i+0].p = v0;
    m_pVertices[3*i+1].p = v1;
    m_pVertices[3*i+2].p = v2;
    m_pVertices[3*i+0].n = vNormal[i];
    m_pVertices[3*i+1].n = vNormal[i];
    m_pVertices[3*i+2].n = vNormal[i];
}
```

```
// step through the three edges of each face
face = dwNumFaces;
for( i = 0  ; i < dwNumFaces; i++ )
{
    for( j = i + 1; j < dwNumFaces; j++ )
    {
        DWORD id[2][2];         // checklist
        DWORD cnt=0;

        for(k = 0; k < 3; k++)
         {
         for(l = 0; l < 3; l++)
           {
             D3DXVECTOR3 dv;
             D3DXVec3Subtract( &dv, &pVertices[pIndices[3*i+k]].p,
                               &pVertices[pIndices[3*j+l]].p);

             // if two vertices from two different faces form one edge
             // put them into checklist and increment counter
             if( D3DXVec3LengthSq( &dv ) < 0.001f )
             {
                 // cnt counts until two …
                 id[cnt][0] = 3*i+k;
                 id[cnt][1] = 3*j+l;
                 cnt++;
             }
           }
         }

        // if two times two vertices from two faces share one edge …
        if(2 == cnt)
        {
            // if one face has a different direction than the other face …
            // alternative: check if the face normals are parallel,
            // if not insert degenerate quad
            // else exit if statement
            if(id[1][0] - id[0][0]!=1)
            {
              // … adjust direction of face
              DWORD tmp = id[0][0];
              id[0][0] = id[1][0];
              id[1][0] = tmp;                 // swap id[0][0] and id[1][0]
              tmp = id[0][1];
              id[0][1] = id[1][1];
              id[1][1] = tmp;                 // swap id[0][1] and id[1][1]
            }
```

```
        // insert degenerated quadrilateral
        // the face normals are used for the vertex normals
        m_pVertices[3*face+0].p = pVertices[pIndices[id[1][0]]].p;
        m_pVertices[3*face+2].p = pVertices[pIndices[id[0][1]]].p;
        m_pVertices[3*face+1].p = pVertices[pIndices[id[0][0]]].p;
        m_pVertices[3*face+0].n = vNormal[i];
        m_pVertices[3*face+2].n = vNormal[j];
        m_pVertices[3*face+1].n = vNormal[i];
        face++;
        m_pVertices[3*face+0].p = pVertices[pIndices[id[1][0]]].p;
        m_pVertices[3*face+2].p = pVertices[pIndices[id[1][1]]].p;
        m_pVertices[3*face+1].p = pVertices[pIndices[id[0][1]]].p;
        m_pVertices[3*face+0].n = vNormal[i];
        m_pVertices[3*face+2].n = vNormal[j];
        m_pVertices[3*face+1].n = vNormal[j];
      face++;
    }
  }
  }
  assert(face == m_dwNumFaces);

  delete[] vNormal;
  end:

  // unlock buffers
  pMesh->UnlockVertexBuffer();
  pMesh->UnlockIndexBuffer();

  pMesh->Release();

 return ret;
}
```

A local copy of the original geometry is stored in pVertices, and a global copy is stored in m_ pVertices. The latter holds the shadow volume geometry at the end. After calculating the face normals, you search for four vertices that share two edges from two triangles. If these two edges are found, the direction of the faces is checked. If one face has a different direction than the other, this direction is changed.

Now that you have the extended geometry, the question is, how do you render the shadow volume? The answer is, with the help of the stencil buffer. Consider a single pixel. Assuming the camera is not in the shadow volume, there are four possibilities for the corresponding point in the scene. If the ray from the camera to the point does not intersect with the shadow volume, then no shadow polygons will have been drawn there and the stencil buffer will still be zero. Otherwise, if the point lies in front of the shadow volume, the shadow polygons will be z-buffered out, and the stencil will again remain unchanged. If the point lies behind the shadow volume, then the same number of front shadow faces as back faces will have been rendered, and the stencil will be zero, having been incremented as many times as decremented. The final possibility is that the point lies inside the shadow volume. In this case, the back face of the shadow volume will be z-buffered out (but not the front face), so the stencil buffer will be a non-zero value. The result is that portions of the frame buffer lying in shadow will have a non-zero stencil value. To achieve this functionality, the example program performs the following steps:

1. Clear the render target, z-buffer, and stencil buffer.

2. Render the scene into the color buffer and the z-buffer.

3. Disable color-buffer writes and z-buffer writes, activate the stencil buffer, and switch on flat-shading mode.

4. Pass the stencil buffer. When the stencil test passes or fails, increment the stencil buffer.

5. If the depth test fails:

   a. If a two-sided stencil buffer is supported, switch it on.

      1) Decrement the second side of the stencil buffer when the depth test fails.

      2) Switch off back face culling.

      3) Render the shadow volumes, filling up the two-sided stencil buffer, and go to Step 6.

   b. If a two-sided stencil buffer is not supported:

      1) Render front-facing polygons.

      2) Reverse the culling order so the back sides can be written to the stencil buffer.

      3) Decrement the stencil buffer. When the depth tests fails, render the back-facing polygons.

6. Repeat Steps 4 and 5 for every light source.

7. Switch on Gouraud shading, color writes, and z-buffer writes; deactivate the stencil buffer; and switch off the z-buffer.

8. Where the stencil value is greater than or equal to 1, render your scene into a shadow mask.

9. Alpha blend #8 with #2 (optional).

The key to this and other volumetric stencil buffer effects is the interaction between the stencil buffer and the z-buffer. A scene with a shadow volume is rendered in three stages. First, the scene without the shadow is rendered as usual, using the z-buffer. Next, the shadow is marked out in the stencil buffer. The front faces of the shadow volume are drawn using invisible polygons, with z-testing enabled, z-writes disabled, and the stencil buffer incremented at every pixel passing the z-test. The back faces of the shadow volume are rendered similarly, but with the stencil value decremented instead.

The first render in Steps 1 and 2 in the preceding set of steps renders the scene into the color- and z-buffers. Then the setup for the stencil buffer occurs. You don't need Gouraud shading or to write color to fill up the stencil buffer with values; therefore, you use the cheaper flat shading. Because you don't need to render geometry, the z-buffer is switched off.

The value in the stencil buffer should be passed when the stencil buffer passes or fails, and it should be incremented when the depth test fails. Depending on the support of two-sided stencil buffers, Step 5a or 5b is executed. If a two-sided stencil buffer is supported, the second side of the stencil buffer is decremented in case the depth test fails. To render the shadow volumes according to the content of both sides of the stencil buffer, back face culling is switched off.

If a two-sided stencil buffer is not available, Step 5b is executed. Because everything was set up for a stencil buffer write in Step 4, the stencil buffer values for the front-facing polygons can be rendered in Step 5b. Because the legacy stencil buffer has no back side, you need to reverse culling and configure the stencil buffer so that it decrements when the depth test fails. Then you can fill up the stencil buffer a second time by rendering the back-facing values. Steps 4 and 5 must be repeated as often as there are light sources.

Incremented values left in the stencil buffer correspond to pixels that are in the shadow. These remaining stencil-buffer contents are used as a mask, to alpha-blend a large, all-encompassing black quad into the scene. With the stencil buffer as a mask, the pixels that are in the shadows are darkened. Here is the source code:

```
//------------------------------
//  Step 2: Render the scene into color and z-buffer
//------------------------------
D3DXMatrixIdentity( &matWorld);
m_pd3dDevice->SetTransform( D3DTS_WORLD,  &matWorld);
m_pMeshBG->Render( m_pd3dDevice );


// scale, rotate, translate and render the box on the right
D3DXMatrixScaling( &matScale, 1.82f,1.65f, 1.82f );
D3DXMatrixRotationY( &matRotate, 0.59f * D3DX_PI );
D3DXMatrixTranslation( &matTranslate, 2.73f-1.85f, 0.f ,1.69f);
matTemp = matScale * matRotate * matTranslate;
m_pd3dDevice->SetTransform( D3DTS_WORLD,  &matTemp );
m_pMeshBox->Render( m_pd3dDevice );


// scale, rotate, translate and render the box on the left
D3DXMatrixScaling( &matScale, 1.69f, 3.30f, 1.69f );
D3DXMatrixRotationY( &matRotate, 0.91f * D3DX_PI );
D3DXMatrixTranslation( &matTranslate, 2.73f-3.685f, 0, 3.51f );
matTemp = matScale * matRotate * matTranslate;
m_pd3dDevice->SetTransform( D3DTS_WORLD,  &matTemp);
m_pMeshBox->Render( m_pd3dDevice );
```

```
//------------------------------------
// ------------------------------------
// Step 3: Disable color writes, z-buffer writes, activate
// stencil buffer, switch on flat shading mode
//------------------------------------
m_pd3dDevice->SetRenderState( D3DRS_ZWRITEENABLE,  FALSE );

// prevent the update of the color buffer
m_pd3dDevice->SetRenderState( D3DRS_COLORWRITEENABLE,  FALSE );

//  switch on flat shading
m_pd3dDevice->SetRenderState( D3DRS_SHADEMODE, D3DSHADE_FLAT );

// switch on stencil buffer
m_pd3dDevice->SetRenderState( D3DRS_STENCILENABLE, TRUE );

// The comparison function is used to compare the reference
// value to a stencil buffer entry. This comparison applies
// only to the bits in the reference value and stencil buffer
// entry that are set in the stencil mask (set by the
// D3DRS_STENCILMASK render state). If TRUE, the stencil test
// passes.
m_pd3dDevice->SetRenderState(D3DRS_STENCILFUNC, D3DCMP_ALWAYS);

// An int reference value for the stencil test. The default
// value is 0.
m_pd3dDevice->SetRenderState( D3DRS_STENCILREF, 0x1 );

// Mask applied to the reference value and each stencil buffer
// entry to determine the significant bits for the stencil
// test. The default mask is 0xFFFFFFFF.
m_pd3dDevice->SetRenderState( D3DRS_STENCILMASK, 0xffffffff);
m_pd3dDevice->SetRenderState(D3DRS_STENCILWRITEMASK,
0xffffffff);

//------------------------------------
//  Step 4: pass stencil buffer, when the stencil test passes or
//  fails
//------------------------------------
m_pd3dDevice->SetRenderState( D3DRS_STENCILPASS,
D3DSTENCILOP_KEEP);
m_pd3dDevice->SetRenderState( D3DRS_STENCILFAIL,
D3DSTENCILOP_KEEP);

//------------------------------------
// Step 5: increment stencil buffer, when the depth test fails
//------------------------------------
```

```
m_pd3dDevice->SetRenderState( D3DRS_STENCILZFAIL,
D3DSTENCILOP_INCR );


//--------------------------------------
// Step 6: if the two-sided stencil buffer is supported by
// hardware
//--------------------------------------
if( ( m_d3dCaps.StencilCaps & D3DSTENCILCAPS_TWOSIDED ) != 0 )
{

        // same for the second side of the stencil buffer ...
        m_pd3dDevice->SetRenderState( D3DRS_TWOSIDEDSTENCILMODE,
TRUE );
        m_pd3dDevice->SetRenderState( D3DRS_CCW_STENCILFUNC,
D3DCMP_ALWAYS );


//--------------------------------------
// Step 6. a): decrement the second side of the stencil
// buffer, when the depth test fails
//--------------------------------------
        m_pd3dDevice->SetRenderState( D3DRS_CCW_STENCILZFAIL,
D3DSTENCILOP_DECR );

        //--------------------------------------
// Step 6. b): switch off backface culling
        //--------------------------------------
        m_pd3dDevice->SetRenderState( D3DRS_CULLMODE,
D3DCULL_NONE );

        //--------------------------------------
        // Step 6. c): Render shadow volume
        //--------------------------------------
        if( m_pEffect != NULL )
        {
                D3DXHANDLE hTechnique =
m_pEffect->GetTechniqueByName( "TShader" );
                m_pEffect->SetTechnique( hTechnique );
                m_pEffect->Begin( NULL, 0 );
                m_pEffect->Pass( 0 );

                // scale, rotate and translate the shadow of the
// box on the right
                D3DXMatrixScaling( &matScale, 1.82f,1.65f, 1.82f);
                D3DXMatrixRotationY( &matRotate, 0.59f * D3DX_PI);
                D3DXMatrixTranslation( &matTranslate, 2.73f-1.85f,
0.f , 1.69f );
```

```
            matWorld = matScale * matRotate * matTranslate;
            matTemp = matWorld * m_matView * m_matProj;
            m_pEffect->SetMatrix("matWorldViewProj",&matTemp);
            D3DXMatrixInverse( &matTemp, NULL, &matWorld);
            D3DXVec3Transform( &vVector, &m_LighPos,&matTemp);
            m_pEffect->SetVector("vLightPos", &vVector);
            m_pShadowBox->Render( m_pd3dDevice );

            // scale, rotate and translate the shadow of the
// box on the left
            D3DXMatrixScaling( &matScale, 1.69f, 3.30f, 1.69f );
            D3DXMatrixRotationY( &matRotate, 0.91f * D3DX_PI );
            D3DXMatrixTranslation(&matTranslate, 2.73f-3.685f,
0, 3.51f );
            matWorld = matScale * matRotate * matTranslate;
            matTemp = matWorld * m_matView * m_matProj;
            m_pEffect->SetMatrix("matWorldViewProj",&matTemp);
            D3DXMatrixInverse( &matTemp, NULL, &matWorld);
            D3DXVec3Transform( &vVector, &m_LighPos,
&matTemp );
            m_pEffect->SetVector("vLightPos", &vVector );
            m_pShadowBox->Render( m_pd3dDevice );

            m_pEffect->End();
    }
    m_pd3dDevice->SetRenderState( D3DRS_TWOSIDEDSTENCILMODE,
FALSE );
}


//-----------------------------------
// Step 7: else if two-sided stencil buffer is not supported
// (non-DX9 hardware)
//-----------------------------------
else
{
//----------------------------
// Step 7. a): render front-facing polygons
//----------------------------
    if( m_pEffect != NULL )
    {
            D3DXHANDLE hTechnique =
m_pEffect->GetTechniqueByName( "TShader" );
            m_pEffect->SetTechnique( hTechnique );
            m_pEffect->Begin( NULL, 0 );
            m_pEffect->Pass( 0 );
```

```
                // scale, rotate and translate the shadow of the box
                // on the right
                D3DXMatrixScaling( &matScale, 1.82f,1.65f, 1.82f );
                D3DXMatrixRotationY( &matRotate, 0.59f * D3DX_PI );
                D3DXMatrixTranslation( &matTranslate, 2.73f-1.85f,
  0.f , 1.69f );
                matWorld = matScale * matRotate * matTranslate;
                matTemp = matWorld * m_matView * m_matProj;
                m_pEffect->SetMatrix("matWorldViewProj", &matTemp);
                D3DXMatrixInverse( &matTemp, NULL, &matWorld);
                D3DXVec3Transform( &vVector, &m_LighPos, &matTemp);
                m_pEffect->SetVector("vLightPos", &vVector);
                m_pShadowBox->Render( m_pd3dDevice );

                // scale, rotate and translate the shadow of the
                // box on the left
                D3DXMatrixScaling(&matScale, 1.69f, 3.30f, 1.69f);
                D3DXMatrixRotationY(&matRotate, 0.91f * D3DX_PI);
                D3DXMatrixTranslation(&matTranslate, 2.73f-3.685f,
  0, 3.51f );
                matWorld = matScale * matRotate * matTranslate;
                matTemp = matWorld * m_matView * m_matProj;
                m_pEffect->SetMatrix("matWorldViewProj", &matTemp);
                D3DXMatrixInverse( &matTemp, NULL, &matWorld);
                D3DXVec3Transform( &vVector, &m_LighPos, &matTemp );
                m_pEffect->SetVector("vLightPos", &vVector );
                m_pShadowBox->Render( m_pd3dDevice );

                m_pEffect->End();
}


//------------------------------------
// Step 7. b): reverse culling order so the back sides can be
// written to stencil buffer
//------------------------------------
m_pd3dDevice->SetRenderState( D3DRS_CULLMODE, D3DCULL_CW );


//------------------------------------
// Step 7. c): decrement stencil buffer, when depth test fails
//------------------------------------
        m_pd3dDevice->SetRenderState( D3DRS_STENCILZFAIL,
D3DSTENCILOP_DECR );


//------------------------------------
// Step 7. d): render back-facing polygons
//------------------------------------
```

```
            if( m_pEffect != NULL )
            {
                    D3DXHANDLE hTechnique =
m_pEffect->GetTechniqueByName( "TShader" );
                    m_pEffect->SetTechnique( hTechnique );
                    m_pEffect->Begin( NULL, 0 );
                    m_pEffect->Pass( 0 );

                    // scale, rotate and translate the shadow of the box on
                    // the right
                    D3DXMatrixScaling( &matScale, 1.82f,1.65f, 1.82f );
                    D3DXMatrixRotationY( &matRotate, 0.59f * D3DX_PI );
                    D3DXMatrixTranslation(&matTranslate, 2.73f-1.85f, 0.f,
    1.69f );
                    matWorld = matScale * matRotate * matTranslate;
                    matTemp = matWorld * m_matView * m_matProj;
                    m_pEffect->SetMatrix("matWorldViewProj", &matTemp);
                    D3DXMatrixInverse( &matTemp, NULL, &matWorld);
                    D3DXVec3Transform( &vVector, &m_LighPos, &matTemp);
                    m_pEffect->SetVector("vLightPos", &vVector);
                    m_pShadowBox->Render( m_pd3dDevice );

                    // scale, rotate and translate the shadow of the
                    // box on the left
                    D3DXMatrixScaling( &matScale, 1.69f, 3.30f, 1.69f );
                    D3DXMatrixRotationY( &matRotate, 0.91f * D3DX_PI );
                    D3DXMatrixTranslation(&matTranslate, 2.73f-3.685f,
    0, 3.51f );
                    matWorld = matScale * matRotate * matTranslate;
                    matTemp = matWorld * m_matView * m_matProj;
                    m_pEffect->SetMatrix("matWorldViewProj",&matTemp);
                    D3DXMatrixInverse( &matTemp, NULL, &matWorld);
                    D3DXVec3Transform(&vVector, &m_LighPos, &matTemp);
                    m_pEffect->SetVector("vLightPos", &vVector );
                    m_pShadowBox->Render( m_pd3dDevice );

                    m_pEffect->End();
            }

    }
```

If the new two-sided stencil buffer is not supported, the shadow geometry is drawn twice per light source, putting pressure on the vertex throughput of the GPU. The two-sided stencil feature was designed to mitigate this situation. The advantage of the two-sided stencil buffer is that it reduces this process to one rendering pass.

You render the shadow volumes by performing the following steps:

1. Cast a light ray from the light source.

2. To find out whether a vertex is facing the light or pointing away from it, store the dot-product of the light ray and the normal (L.N).

3. Depending on the value of L.N, store 0 or 1 in the variable scale.

4. Reduce the position value of the shadow geometry slightly, so that the shadow does not overlap the edges of the objects.

5. Scale the direction of the light ray and subtract it from the position value. (This process is also called *extruding* the shadow volume geometry.) When the shadow volume geometry position is not extended in the direction of the light source (scale == 0), it is hidden by the object because it is smaller than the object.

The example source code is quite simple.

```
VS_OUTPUT VS (float4 Pos: POSITION, float3 Normal : NORMAL)
{
    VS_OUTPUT Out = (VS_OUTPUT)0;

    // light to vertex ray
    float4 dir = vLightPos - Pos;

    // dot ray and normal
    float LN = dot( Normal, dir );

    // scale is 0 for light facing or 1 for non-light facing
    float scale = (LN >=  0) ? 0.0f : 1.0f;

    // reduce position slightly of shadow volume geometry
    Pos.xyz -= 0.001f*Pos;

    // reduced position - scale * light direction
    Out.Pos = mul( Pos - scale * dir, matWorldViewProj );

    return Out;
}
```

By commenting out the line that starts with Pos.xyz, you can see how the position is slightly reduced. There are several other ways to implement such a technique. Please consult Eric Lengyel's article "The Mechanics of Robust Stencil Shadows" at http://www.gamasutra.com/features/20021011/lengyel_pfv.htm for further ideas.

Things to Consider When Using Shadow Volumes

Please note that the example application does not have to choose a specific light source from several light sources because there is only one. Additionally, a real-world application would determine the objects that should cast shadows in the visible region to reduce the shadow generation only on the visible objects.

You could further improve this example by using Direct3D's depth-biasing capabilities to overcome the reduced depth precision with increasing distance from the camera. This leads to a visible flickering when you are zooming in and out using the W and S keys. DirectX 9.0 offers the `D3DRS_DEPTHBIAS` and `D3DRS_SLOPESCALEDEPTHBIAS` render states to calculate an offset. This offset is used to position the front capping of the shadow volume behind the occluder's front-facing geometries. You accomplish this by adding the offset to the fragment's interpolated depth value, which is used to create the final depth value for depth testing. To check out these new capabilities, use the values of `D3DPRASTERCAPS_DEPTHBIAS` and `D3DPRASTERCAPS_SLOPESCALEDEPTHBIAS`. If this functionality is not supported, the fallback path is to use the legacy `D3DRS_DEPTHBIAS` render state.

You can reduce the shadow geometry data set by being more selective regarding the insertion of quads. You might accomplish this by checking the direction of the normal, as described previously. Additionally, a low-polygon model of the occluder might be sufficient to compute the shadow-volume geometry.

Remember that a closed volume mesh is one of the requirements for shadow volumes. Otherwise, any gaps within the mesh would potentially throw the stencil counting off balance, and thus break the shadow-volume implementation. Such a requirement mandates the need for modelers and designers to alter their workflow and modeling styles to avoid compromising the graphics engine.

Another thing to remember is that it is quite complicated to use shadow volumes together with skinned meshes. Chris Brennan describes a solution for this in *Direct3D ShaderX: Vertex and Pixel Shader Tips and Tricks* (Wordware Publishing, 2002).

Summary

This chapter covered two very important techniques that are currently used in games and will likely continue to be used for the next few years. A basic understanding of how cube maps work will be helpful for understanding more advanced techniques that are currently being developed. The stencil shadow volume technique showed you how you can use the stencil buffer to track regions of a scene. Understanding this concept will also help you with many other techniques.

CHAPTER 11

WORKING WITH FILES

There are a lot of file formats out there. However, you can distinguish between file formats typically used by graphic artists and formats typically used in game engines. File formats used by 3D tools include .3ds, .max, and .cof, and they are produced by those tools. These formats have a lot of information in them, and they are not optimized for use in real-time environments like game engines. Games use faster and simpler file formats, which differ between game genres and are generally unique to one game.

One of the most challenging economical considerations in game production is to build a proper workflow for the graphic information that must be exchanged between the 3D graphic artist and the game engine programmer. The typical solution to this problem is to write custom tools, which import, for example, the 3D Studio Max file and export it, after modification, in the game engine format.

The game engine formats used in id Software's *Quake* series are widely used because many game companies license the *Quake* engines. Therefore, I'll concentrate on the Microsoft X file format used in DirectX in this chapter, and *Quake 3*'s .md3 model format in the following chapter. I think these are easy to learn. If you know these two formats, you should be able to understand and use other formats as well.

In this chapter, you'll learn how to:

- Work with 3D file formats
- Use transformation matrices
- Work with X files

3D File Formats

3D scene file formats present two fundamental problems—how to store the objects that will make up the scene, and how to store the relationships between these objects. User-defined data types are necessary. Scene data requires hierarchical relationships, such as parent, child, and sibling relationships, and associational relationships, such as meshes attached to frames, materials attached to meshes, and so on. In addition, a file format design should be robust enough to handle forward and backward compatibility.

The X file format handles all of these tasks, so it's a good solution to show the loading of 3D models into a game engine in this book.

The X File Format

The Direct3D X file format was built for the legacy retained mode of Direct3D and expanded with the advent of DirectX 6.0 for Immediate Mode. Take a look at how the X file format solves the problems described in the previous section on an abstract level.

- **User-defined data types**. X files are driven by templates, which can be defined by the user. A *template* is the definition of how a data object should be stored. The predefined templates are contained in the directory headers rmxftmpl.h in d3dfile.cpp and rmxftmpl.x in x:\mssdk\include, and their identification signatures are in rmxfguid.h, which is also included in d3dfile.cpp, one of the common files.

- **Hierarchical relationships.** Data types allowed by the template are called *optional members.* These optional members are saved as children of the data object. The children can be another data object, a reference to an earlier data object, or a binary object.

OK, let's dive into the X file format with a sample—a square, which is located in square.x. To try out and play with the following files, use the MeshViewer provided with the DirectX 9 SDK (see Figure 11.1).

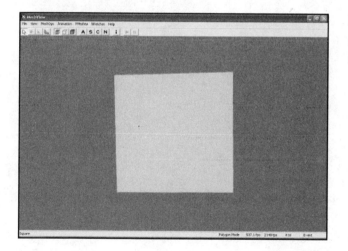

Figure 11.1

Square.x in the DX9 MeshViewer

And here's the source:

```
xof 0303txt 0032

// square
Mesh Square {
// front face and back face
 8;                          // number of vertices
 1.0; 1.0; 0.0;,             // vertice 0
```

```
-1.0; 1.0; 0.0;,        // vertice 1
-1.0;-1.0; 0.0;,        // vertice 2
 1.0;-1.0; 0.0;         // vertice 3
 1.0; 1.0; 0.0;,        // vertice 4
 1.0;-1.0; 0.0;,        // vertice 5
-1.0;-1.0; 0.0;,        // vertice 6
-1.0; 1.0; 0.0;;        // vertice 7
 4;                     // number of triangles
 3;0,1,2;,              // triangle #1
 3;0,2,3;,              // triangle #2
 3;4,5,6;,              // triangle #3
 3;4,6,7;;              // triangle #4

MeshMaterialList {
  1;                    // one material
  4;                    // four faces
  0,                    // face #0 use material #0
  0,                    // face #1 use material #0
  0,                    // face #2 use material #0
  0;;                   // face #3 use material #0
Material {              // material #0
    0.0;1.0;0.0;1.0;;   // face color
    0.0;                // power
    0.0;0.0;0.0;;       // specular color
    0.0;0.0;0.0;;       // emissive color
  }
 }
}
```

Header

The magic 4-byte number is xof. The major version number is 03, and the minor version number is 03. The file format is txt for text or bin for a binary format.

Additionally, the legacy *.x file format supported by the legacy Direct3D retained mode uses a template called Header. Its declaration can be found in rmxftmpl.x, like the declaration of all other templates.

Other possible file formats are tzip and bzip, which stand for MSZip compressed text or binary files, respectively. The floating-point data type is set to 0032 instead of 0064.

As you can see in the code, comments are set with either the double slash (as in C++) or the hash symbol (#).

Mesh

Most of the sample file consists of a Mesh template and its integrated templates:

```
template Mesh {
 <3D82AB44-62DA-11cf-AB39-0020AF71E433>
 DWORD nVertices;
 array Vector vertices[nVertices];
 DWORD nFaces;
 array MeshFace faces[nFaces];
 [...]
}
```

The Mesh template needs the Vector and MeshFace templates because Mesh refers to them:

```
template Vector {
 <3D82AB5E-62DA-11cf-AB39-0020AF71E433>
 FLOAT x;
 FLOAT y;
 FLOAT z;
}
template MeshFace {
 <3D82AB5F-62DA-11cf-AB39-0020AF71E433>
 DWORD nFaceVertexIndices;
 array DWORD faceVertexIndices[nFaceVertexIndices];
}
```

Templates consist of four parts. The unique name, which consists of numbers, characters, and the underscore, is the first part. It shouldn't start with a number. The second part is the UUID (*Universally Unique Identifier*), and the third part consists of the data types of the entries. The last part regulates the degree of restriction; a template can be open, closed, or restricted. Open templates can contain every other data type, closed templates contain no other data types, and restricted templates can only integrate specific other data types.

```
// square
Mesh Square {
// front face and back face
 8;                           // number of vertices
 1.0; 1.0; 0.0;,              // vertice 0
-1.0; 1.0; 0.0;,              // vertice 1
-1.0;-1.0; 0.0;,              // vertice 2
 1.0;-1.0; 0.0;               // vertice 3
 1.0; 1.0; 0.0;,              // vertice 4
 1.0;-1.0; 0.0;,              // vertice 5
-1.0;-1.0; 0.0;,              // vertice 6
-1.0; 1.0; 0.0;;              // vertice 7
 4;                           // number of triangles
 3;0,1,2;,                    // triangle #1
```

```
3;0,2,3;,                   // triangle #2
3;4,5,6;,                   // triangle #3
3;4,6,7;;                   // triangle #4
```

Here, the first number is the number of vertices used. After that, the vertices are set. The front face uses four vertices consisting of two triangles, as shown in Figure 11.2. You have to define a front and a back face.

The Mesh template is an open template because it uses open brackets [. . .] at the end. Therefore, it can contain every other data type.

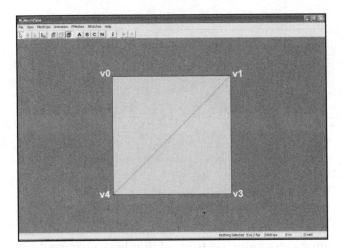

Figure 11.2

The two triangles consisting of four vertices of Square.x

MeshMaterialList

MeshMaterialList is a child object of the Mesh object and is incorporated in the Mesh object. It needs the number of faces and materials, and it concatenates one face with one or more materials.

```
MeshMaterialList {
  1;                        // one material
  2;                        // two faces
  0,                        // face #0 use material #0
  0;;                       // face #1 use material #0
  Material {                // material #0
    0.0;1.0;0.0;1.0;;       // face color
    0.0;                    // power
    0.0;0.0;0.0;;           // specular color
    0.0;0.0;0.0;;           // emissive color
  }
}
```

The template in rmxftmpl.x looks like:

```
template MeshMaterialList {
 <f6f23f42-7686-11cf-8f52-0040333594a3>
 DWORD nMaterials;
 DWORD nFaceIndexes;
 array DWORD faceIndexes[nFaceIndexes];
 [Material]
}
```

The first variable holds the number of materials used by this sample. The second variable holds the number of faces. The square uses the front and back faces, so the variable has to be set to 2. The concatenation of the materials with the faces happens with the faceIndexes array. Every face is concatenated with a material by naming the material number. The X file reader knows the proper face by counting the number of faces provided.

Beneath that array, you could integrate Material templates. The MeshMaterialList template is a restricted template because only specified templates can be integrated.

```
template Material {
 <3D82AB4D-62DA-11cf-AB39-0020AF71E433>
 ColorRGBA faceColor;
 FLOAT power;
 ColorRGB specularColor;
 ColorRGB emissiveColor;
 [...]
}
```

This template incorporates the following two templates:

```
template ColorRGBA {
 <35FF44F0-6C7C-11cf-8F52-0040333594A3>
 FLOAT red;
 FLOAT green;
 FLOAT blue;
 FLOAT alpha;
}
template ColorRGB {
 FLOAT red;
 FLOAT green;
 FLOAT blue;
}
```

The Material data object holds the material color, power, specular color, and emissive color. The open brackets show that it can integrate other data objects. You can reference the Material data object by MeshMaterialList. The file square2.x shows two referenced Material data objects.

xof 0303txt 0032

```
Material GreenMat {          // material #0
  0.0;1.0;0.0;1.0;;
  0.0;
  0.0;0.0;0.0;;
  0.0;0.0;0.0;;
  }
 Material RedMat {           // material #1
  1.0;0.0;0.0;1.0;;
  0.0;
  0.0;0.0;0.0;;
  0.0;0.0;0.0;;
  }
// square
Mesh Square {
 // front face and back face
 8;                          // number of vertices
 1.0; 1.0; 0.0;,             // vertice 0
-1.0; 1.0; 0.0;,             // vertice 1
-1.0;-1.0; 0.0;,             // vertice 2
 1.0;-1.0; 0.0;              // vertice 3
 1.0; 1.0; 0.0;,             // vertice 4
 1.0;-1.0; 0.0;,             // vertice 5
-1.0;-1.0; 0.0;,             // vertice 6
-1.0; 1.0; 0.0;;             // vertice 7
 4;                          // number of triangles
 3;0,1,2;,                   // triangle #1
 3;0,2,3;,                   // triangle #2
 3;4,5,6;,                   // triangle #3
 3;4,6,7;;                   // triangle #4
MeshMaterialList {
  2;                         // two material
  4;                         // four faces
  0,                         // face #0 use material #0
  0,                         // face #1 use material #0
  1,                         // face #0 use material #0
  1;;                        // face #1 use material #0
  {GreenMat}
  {RedMat}
  }
  VertexDuplicationIndices {
   8;
   8;
   0,
   1,
   2,
   3,
```

```
      4,
      5,
      6,
      7;
    }
  }
```

{GreenMat} and {RedMat} are the references for the Material objects. The template VertexDuplicationIndices is instantiated on a per-mesh basis, holding information about which vertices in the mesh are duplicates of each other. Duplicates result when a vertex sits on a smoothing group or material boundary. The purpose of this template is to allow the loader to determine which vertices exhibiting different peripheral parameters are actually the same vertices in the model. Certain applications (mesh simplification, for example) can use this information. Figure 11.3 shows the file square2.x in the MeshViewer.

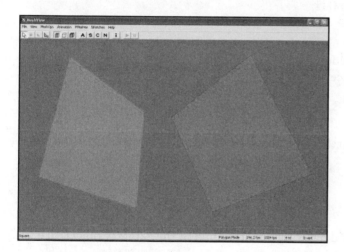

Figure 11.3

Rendering a polygon with two materials— the left side uses the material GreenMat, and the right side uses RedMat

Normals

You need normals to calculate lighting models. There are face normals and vertex normals, as you learned earlier. To calculate a lighting model on a per-vertex basis, you need vertex normals. Usually vertex normals are calculated so that the face normals of the faces that share one vertex are added and the resulting normal is normalized. The normals in file square3.x are defined like this:

```
MeshNormals {
  8;
  0.000000;0.000000;1.000000;,
  0.000000;0.000000;1.000000;,
  0.000000;0.000000;1.000000;,
  0.000000;0.000000;1.000000;,
  0.000000;0.000000;-1.000000;,
```

```
    0.000000;0.000000;-1.000000;,
    0.000000;0.000000;-1.000000;,
    0.000000;0.000000;-1.000000;;
    4;
    3;0,1,2;,      // vertex normals on faces
    3;0,2,3;,
    3;4,5,6;,
    3;4,6,7;;
    }
template MeshNormals {
<f6f23f43-7686-11cf-8f52-0040333594a3>
 DWORD nNormals;
 array Vector normals[nNormals];
 DWORD nFaceNormals;
 array MeshFace faceNormals[nFaceNormals];
}
```

As you can see, there are eight vertex normals positioned on the faces. Their order is shown following the line 4;, which I have bolded in the code. For example, the vertex normals 4, 6, and 7 are positioned on the fourth face.

Textures

You can reference textures in a TextureFilename data object as child objects of the Material object.

```
template TextureFilename {
 STRING filename;
}
```

The reference to the texture file name has to be incorporated in the Material object, like this:

```
  Material GreenMat {   // material #0
    0.0;1.0;0.0;1.0;;
    0.0;
    0.0;0.0;0.0;;
    0.0;0.0;0.0;;
    TextureFilename{"wall.bmp";}
  }
```

Additionally, you need to specify texture coordinates:

```
template MeshTextureCoords {
 <f6f23f40-7686-11cf-8f52-0040333594a3>
 DWORD nTextureCoords;
 array Coords2d textureCoords[nTextureCoords];
}
```

```
template Coords2d {
 <f6f23f44-7686-11cf-8f52-0040333594a3>FLOAT u;
 FLOAT v;
}
```

The first variable holds the number of vertices that have to be used in conjunction with the texture coordinates. The following array holds the tu/tv pairs of the textures. To map a texture to that square, you could use the following texture coordinates. If you want to map one texture on the whole square, you have to use this:

```
MeshTextureCoords {
    4;                          // 4 texture coords
    1.0; 1.0;,                  // coord  0
    1.0; 0.0;,                  // coord  1
    0.0; 0.0;,                  // coord  2
    0.0; 1.0;;                  // coord  3
  }
```

The bottom-right corner is (1.0f, 1.0f) and the upper-left corner is (0.0f, 0.0f), regardless of the actual size of the texture—even if the texture is wider than it is tall.

To get four textures, use the following coordinates:

```
MeshTextureCoords {
 4;
 // four textures
 1.0; 1.0;,                     // coord  0
-1.0; 1.0;,                     // coord  1
-1.0;-1.0;,                     // coord  2
 1.0;-1.0;;                     // coord  3
}
```

This example is driven by the default texture-wrapping mode that I explained in Part Two. The complete file square3.x looks like this:

```
xof 0303txt 0032

  Material GreenMat {            // material #0
    0.0;1.0;0.0;1.0;;
    0.0;
    0.0;0.0;0.0;;
    0.0;0.0;0.0;;

    TextureFilename {
     "wall.bmp";                 // texture map to use
    }
  }

// square
```

```
Mesh Square {
 // front face and back face
 8;                          // number of vertices
 1.0; 1.0; 0.0;,             // vertice 0
-1.0; 1.0; 0.0;,             // vertice 1
-1.0;-1.0; 0.0;,             // vertice 2
 1.0;-1.0; 0.0;              // vertice 3

 1.0; 1.0; 0.0;,             // vertice 4
 1.0;-1.0; 0.0;,             // vertice 5
-1.0;-1.0; 0.0;,             // vertice 6
-1.0; 1.0; 0.0;;             // vertice 7

 4;                          // number of triangles
 3;0,1,2;,                   // triangle #1
 3;0,2,3;,                   // triangle #2
 3;4,5,6;,                   // triangle #3
 3;4,6,7;;                   // triangle #4

  MeshNormals {
   8;
   0.000000;0.000000;1.000000;,
   0.000000;0.000000;1.000000;,
   0.000000;0.000000;1.000000;,
   0.000000;0.000000;1.000000;,
   0.000000;0.000000;-1.000000;,
   0.000000;0.000000;-1.000000;,
   0.000000;0.000000;-1.000000;,
   0.000000;0.000000;-1.000000;;
   4;
   3;0,1,2;,
   3;0,2,3;,
   3;4,5,6;,
   3;4,6,7;;
  }

  MeshTextureCoords {
   8;                        // 4 texture coords
   1.0; 1.0;,                // coord  0
   1.0; 0.0;,                // coord  1
   0.0; 0.0;,                // coord  2
   0.0; 1.0;;                // coord  3

   1.0; 1.0;,                // coords 4
   1.0;-1.0;,                // coords 5
  -1.0;-1.0;,                // coords 6
```

```
  -1.0; 1.0;;                 // coords 7
  }

MeshMaterialList {
  1;                          // one material
  4;                          // one face
  0,                          // face #0 use material #0
  0,                          // face #1 use material #0
  0,                          // face #2 use material #0
  0;;                         // face #3 use material #0

  {GreenMat}
}

  VertexDuplicationIndices {
   8;
   8;
   0,
   1,
   2,
   3,
   4,
   5,
   6,
   7;
  }
}
```

As shown in Figure 11.4, the front face displays four textures, and the back face displays one texture. All textures are modulated by the MeshViewer with the green material color.

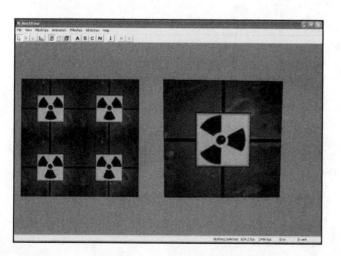

Figure 11.4

Texture-mapped square with four textures on the front and one texture on the back

I prepared a bigger example with the vertex data used by the examples in Chapter 5. Just open the file boidy.x in the MeshViewer from the directory for this chapter on the CD-ROM. Figure 11.5 shows the boid object in an X file.

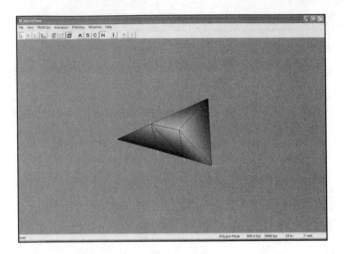

Figure 11.5

The boid object from
Chapter 5 in an X file

Figure 11.5 shows the faces, vertices, and vertex normals used by the example. Here is the source code:

```
xof 0302txt 0064

// boid
Mesh boid {
  // vertices
  7;                        // number of vertices
  0.00; 0.00; 0.50;,        // vertice 0
  0.50; 0.00;-0.50;,        // vertice 1
  0.15; 0.15;-0.35;,        // vertice 2
 -0.15; 0.15;-0.35;,        // vertice 3
  0.15;-0.15;-0.35;,
 -0.15;-0.15;-0.35;,
 -0.50; 0.00;-0.50;;

  10;                       // number of triangles
  3;0,1,2;,                 // triangle #1
  3;0,2,3;,                 // triangle #2
  3;0,3,6;,                 // triangle #3
  3;0,4,1;,                 // ...
  3;0,5,4;,
  3;0,6,5;,
  3;1,4,2;,
  3;2,4,3;,
```

```
   3;3,4,5;,
   3;3,5,6;;


MeshMaterialList {
  1;                     // one material
  10;                    // ten faces
  0,0;;                  // face #1 use material #0
  0,0;;                  // face #2 use material #0
  0,0;;                  // face #3 use material #0
  0,0;;                  // face #4 use material #0
  0,0;;                  // face #5 use material #0
  0,0;;                  // face #6 use material #0
  0,0;;                  // face #7 use material #0
  0,0;;                  // face #8 use material #0
  0,0;;                  // face #9 use material #0
  0,0;;                  // face #10 use material #0

  Material {             // material #0
   1.0;0.92;0.0;1.0;;
   1.0;
   0.0;0.0;0.0;;
  0.0;0.0;0.0;;
  }


MeshNormals {
  7;
  0.000000;0.000000;1.000000;,
  0.984784;0.000000;0.173785;,
  0.192491;0.971619;-0.137493;,
 -0.185863;0.938163;-0.292070;,
  0.185863;-0.938163;-0.292070;,
 -0.192491;-0.971619;-0.137493;,
 -0.984784;0.000000;0.173785;;
  10;
  3;0,1,2;,
  3;0,2,3;,
  3;0,3,6;,
  3;0,4,1;,
  3;0,5,4;,
  3;0,6,5;,
  3;1,4,2;,
  3;2,4,3;,
  3;3,4,5;,
  3;3,5,6;;
```

```
    }
  }
}
```

The seven vertices have seven vertex normals, and these normals are placed on the 10 faces.

Because of the small number of vertices, the lighting effect is not very realistic. Diffuse lighting is calculated in the MeshViewer on a per-vertex basis. Having fewer vertices leads to diffuse lighting problems like this. The object can be tesselated in the MeshViewer by following the menu path N-Patches, N-Patches Selected, Snapshot to Mesh. This way, vertices are inserted via the N-Patch algorithm. Additionally, you must recalculate the normals after each tesselation process. Doing this four times makes the object look like Figure 11.6.

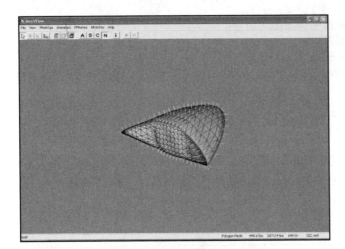

Figure 11.6

The boid object with a much higher tesselation

This object is lighted uniformly. You can see the greater number of faces, vertices, and vertex normals. Just play around with the MeshViewer to get to know its functionality.

So now that you have the big picture on creating X file geometry manually, it's time to delve a little deeper into the requirements for animation.

Transformation Matrices

To transform parts of an object independently from each other, you have to divide the model into different frames. For example, a tank could turn its cannon up and down and to the left or right. Its chains and wheels will turn when it drives through the wild enemy terrain. Therefore, there is a frame for the hull, turret, cannon, chains, and wheels. Every frame will hold the matrix for the specified part of the tank. A Frame data object is expected to take the following structure:

```
Frame Hull {
 FrameTransformMatrix {
```

```
    1.000000, 0.000000, 0.000000, 0.000000,
    0.000000, 1.000000, 0.000000, 0.000000,
    0.000000, -0.000000, 1.000000, 0.000000,
    206.093353, -6.400993, -31.132195, 1.000000;;
   }
  Mesh Hull {
    2470;
    41.310013; -26.219450; -113.602348;,
    ...
  Frame Wheels_L {
   FrameTransformMatrix {
    1.000000, 0.000000, 0.000000, 0.000000,
    0.000000, 1.000000, -0.000000, 0.000000,
    0.000000, 0.000000, 1.000000, 0.000000,
    -56.020325, -31.414078, 3.666503, 1.000000;;
   }
   Mesh Wheels_L {
     2513;
     -4.642166; -11.402874; -98.607910;,
...
Frame Wheels_R {
   FrameTransformMatrix {
    1.000000, 0.000000, 0.000000, 0.000000,
    0.000000, 1.000000, -0.000000, 0.000000,
    0.000000, 0.000000, 1.000000, 0.000000,
    56.687805, -31.414078, 3.666503, 1.000000;;
   }
  Mesh Wheels_R {
     2513;
     4.642181; -11.402874; -98.607910;,
Frame Turret {
   FrameTransformMatrix {
    1.000000, 0.000000, 0.000000, 0.000000,
    0.000000, 1.000000, 0.000000, 0.000000,
    0.000000, 0.000000, 1.000000, 0.000000,
    -2.077148, 84.137527, 29.323750, 1.000000;;
   }
   Mesh Turret {
     2152;
     52.655853; -36.225544; -16.728998;,
...
```

The templates used in this sample in rmxftmpl.x are

```
template Frame {
 <3D82AB46-62DA-11cf-AB39-0020AF71E433>
 [...]
```

```
}
template FrameTransformMatrix {
 Matrix4x4 frameMatrix;
}
template Matrix4x4 {
 array FLOAT matrix[16];
}
```

As an old DirectX Graphics programming freak, you might notice the use of 4×4 matrices as described in Chapter 6. Another simple sample you should look at is the file car.x in the c:\dxsdk\samples\Media directory. Here's an advanced version of the X file of the sample program boidsy2.x:

```
xof 0302txt 0064

Frame BOID_Root {
 FrameTransformMatrix {
  1.000000, 0.000000, 0.000000, 0.000000,
  0.000000, 1.000000, 0.000000, 0.000000,
  0.000000, 0.000000, 1.000000, 0.000000,
  0.000000, 0.000000, 0.000000, 1.000000;;
 }

// boid
Mesh boid {
 // vertices
 7;                          // number of vertices
 0.00; 0.00; 0.50;,          // vertice 0
 0.50; 0.00;-0.50;,          // vertice 1
 0.15; 0.15;-0.35;,          // vertice 2
-0.15; 0.15;-0.35;,          // vertice 3
 0.15;-0.15;-0.35;,
-0.15;-0.15;-0.35;,
-0.50; 0.00;-0.50;;

 10;                         // number of triangles
 3;0,1,2;,                   // triangle #1
 3;0,2,3;,                   // triangle #2
 3;0,3,6;,                   // triangle #3
 3;0,4,1;,                   // ...
 3;0,5,4;,
 3;0,6,5;,
 3;1,4,2;,
 3;2,4,3;,
 3;3,4,5;,
 3;3,5,6;;
```

```
MeshMaterialList {
  1;                        // one material
  10;                       // ten faces
  0,0;;                     // face #1 use material #0
  0,0;;                     // face #2 use material #0
  0,0;;                     // face #3 use material #0
  0,0;;                     // face #4 use material #0
  0,0;;                     // face #5 use material #0
  0,0;;                     // face #6 use material #0
  0,0;;                     // face #7 use material #0
  0,0;;                     // face #8 use material #0
  0,0;;                     // face #9 use material #0
  0,0;;                     // face #10 use material #0

  Material {                // material #0
   1.0;0.92;0.0;1.0;;
   1.0;
   0.0;0.0;0.0;;
  0.0;0.0;0.0;;
   }


MeshNormals {
  7;
  0.000000;0.000000;1.000000;,
  0.984784;0.000000;0.173785;,
  0.192491;0.971619;-0.137493;,
 -0.185863;0.938163;-0.292070;,
  0.185863;-0.938163;-0.292070;,
 -0.192491;-0.971619;-0.137493;,
 -0.984784;0.000000;0.173785;;
  10;
  3;0,1,2;,
  3;0,2,3;,
  3;0,3,6;,
  3;0,4,1;,
  3;0,5,4;,
  3;0,6,5;,
  3;1,4,2;,
  3;2,4,3;,
  3;3,4,5;,
  3;3,5,6;;
  }

 }
 }
 }
```

Animation

To animate an X file, you have to provide a set of animations with a reference to the proper frame matrix. The example file square4.x shows a simple animation that moves the quad on its x-axis. Load this file into the MeshViewer by choosing File, Open MeshFile.

```
xof 0303txt 0032

Frame SQUARE_Root {
 FrameTransformMatrix {
      1.000000, 0.000000, 0.000000, 0.000000,
      0.000000, 1.000000, 0.000000, 0.000000,
      0.000000, 0.000000, 1.000000, 0.000000,
      0.000000, 0.000000, 0.000000, 1.000000;;
 }
 Material GreenMat {               // material #0
   0.0;1.0;0.0;1.0;;
   0.0;
   0.0;0.0;0.0;;
   0.0;0.0;0.0;;

   TextureFilename{"wall.bmp";} // the texture map
  }

// square
Mesh Square {
 // front face and back face
 8;                          // number of vertices
 1.0; 1.0; 0.0;,             // vertice 0
-1.0; 1.0; 0.0;,             // vertice 1
-1.0;-1.0; 0.0;,             // vertice 2
 1.0;-1.0; 0.0;              // vertice 3

 1.0; 1.0; 0.0;,             // vertice 4
 1.0;-1.0; 0.0;,             // vertice 5
-1.0;-1.0; 0.0;,             // vertice 6
-1.0; 1.0; 0.0;;             // vertice 7

 4;                          // number of triangles
 3;0,1,2;,                   // triangle #1
 3;0,2,3;,                   // triangle #2
 3;4,5,6;,                   // triangle #3
 3;4,6,7;;                   // triangle #4

 MeshMaterialList {
  1;                         // one material
```

```
4;                          // one face
0,                          // face #0 use material #0
0,                          // face #1 use material #0
0,                          // face #2 use material #0
0;;                         // face #3 use material #0

{GreenMat}
}

 MeshTextureCoords {
  8;                         // 4 texture coords
  1.0; 1.0;,                 // coord   0
  1.0; 0.0;,                 // coord   1
  0.0; 0.0;,                 // coord   2
  0.0; 1.0;;                 // coord   3

  1.0; 1.0;,                 // coords 4
  1.0;-1.0;,                 // coords 5
 -1.0;-1.0;,                 // coords 6
 -1.0; 1.0;;                 // coords 7
  }

MeshNormals {
 8;
 0.000000;0.000000;1.000000;,
 0.000000;0.000000;1.000000;,
 0.000000;0.000000;1.000000;,
 0.000000;0.000000;1.000000;,
 0.000000;0.000000;-1.000000;,
 0.000000;0.000000;-1.000000;,
 0.000000;0.000000;-1.000000;,
 0.000000;0.000000;-1.000000;;
 4;
 3;0,1,2;,
 3;0,2,3;,
 3;4,5,6;,
 3;4,6,7;;
}
VertexDuplicationIndices {
 8;
 8;
 0,
 1,
 2,
 3,
 4,
```

```
      5,
      6,
      7;
    }
  }


}

AnimationSet MoveX{
 Animation {
      AnimationKey {
      4;                  // Position keys
      5;                  // 5 keys
     0;16;1.0,0.0,0.0,0.0,
            0.0,1.0,0.0,0.0,
            0.0,0.0,1.0,0.0,
            0.1,0.0,0.0,1.0;;,
    80;16;1.0,0.0,0.0,0.0,
            0.0,1.0,0.0,0.0,
            0.0,0.0,1.0,0.0,
            0.2,0.0,0.0,1.0;;,
    160;16;1.0,0.0,0.0,0.0,
             0.0,1.0,0.0,0.0,
             0.0,0.0,1.0,0.0,
             0.3,0.0,0.0,1.0;;,
    240;16;1.0,0.0,0.0,0.0,
             0.0,1.0,0.0,0.0,
             0.0,0.0,1.0,0.0,
              0.2,0.0,0.0,1.0;;,
    320;16;1.0,0.0,0.0,0.0,
             0.0,1.0,0.0,0.0,
             0.0,0.0,1.0,0.0,
              0.1,0.0,0.0,1.0;;,
     }
        {SQUARE_Root}
   }
 }

AnimationSet MoveY{
 Animation {
      AnimationKey {
      4;                  // Position keys
      5;                  // 5 keys
     0;16;1.0,0.0,0.0,0.0,
            0.0,1.0,0.0,0.0,
            0.0,0.0,1.0,0.0,
```

```
         0.0,0.1,0.0,1.0;;,
80;16;1.0,0.0,0.0,0.0,
         0.0,1.0,0.0,0.0,
         0.0,0.0,1.0,0.0,
         0.0,0.2,0.0,1.0;;,
160;16;1.0,0.0,0.0,0.0,
         0.0,1.0,0.0,0.0,
         0.0,0.0,1.0,0.0,
         0.0,0.3,0.0,1.0;;,
240;16;1.0,0.0,0.0,0.0,
          0.0,1.0,0.0,0.0,
          0.0,0.0,1.0,0.0,
          0.0,0.2,0.0,1.0;;,
320;16;1.0,0.0,0.0,0.0,
          '0.0,1.0,0.0,0.0,
          0.0,0.0,1.0,0.0,
          0.0,0.1,0.0,1.0;;,
    }
        {SQUARE_Root}
  }
}
```

This small example shows you the use of two different animation sets named MoveX and MoveY. You can choose them in the MeshViewer by clicking on Animation, Animation. These two sets use five animation keys, each consisting of a 4×4 matrix. The only value that changes is the first value in the fourth row—as you already know, the x-position of the square. {SQUARE_ROOT} is the reference to the frame matrix. The 4 indicates that you are using matrix keys. It's the so-called keyType. The DirectX 8.0 and 9.0 SDK documentation indicate that the keyType member specifies whether the keys are rotation, scale, position, or matrix keys. The numbers to specify the correct keyType range in the documentation from 0 to 3, whereas the tiny.x example in the media directory uses 4 as the number to indicate the use of matrix keys.

Using X Files

All the examples in this book use similar functions to load X files. For instance, the loading function I used in the cube map example is

```
HRESULT CMyD3DApplication::LoadXFile(TCHAR* name)
{
    HRESULT      hr;
    LPD3DXMESH   pMeshSysMem = NULL, pMeshSysMem2 = NULL;

    if (FAILED (D3DXLoadMeshFromX(name, D3DXMESH_SYSTEMMEM,
        m_pd3dDevice, NULL, NULL, NULL, NULL, &pMeshSysMem)))
```

```
        return E_FAIL;

    D3DVERTEXELEMENT9 decl[]=
    {
            // stream, offset, type, method, semantic type (for example normal), ?
            {0, 0, D3DDECLTYPE_FLOAT3, D3DDECLMETHOD_DEFAULT, D3DDECLUSAGE_POSITION, 0},
            {0, 12, D3DDECLTYPE_FLOAT2, D3DDECLMETHOD_DEFAULT, D3DDECLUSAGE_TEXCOORD,
0},

            {0, 20, D3DDECLTYPE_FLOAT3, D3DDECLMETHOD_DEFAULT, D3DDECLUSAGE_NORMAL, 0},
            D3DDECL_END()
    };

    hr = pMeshSysMem->CloneMesh(D3DXMESH_MANAGED, decl, m_pd3dDevice, &pMeshSysMem2);

    // compute the normals
    hr = D3DXComputeNormals(pMeshSysMem2,NULL);
    if(FAILED(hr))
            return E_FAIL;

    D3DVERTEXELEMENT9 decl2[]=
    {
            // stream, offset, type, method, semantic type (for example normal), ?
            {0, 0, D3DDECLTYPE_FLOAT4, D3DDECLMETHOD_DEFAULT, D3DDECLUSAGE_POSITION, 0},
            {0, 16, D3DDECLTYPE_FLOAT2, D3DDECLMETHOD_DEFAULT, D3DDECLUSAGE_TEXCOORD, 0},
            {0, 24, D3DDECLTYPE_FLOAT3, D3DDECLMETHOD_DEFAULT, D3DDECLUSAGE_NORMAL, 0},
            D3DDECL_END()
     };

     hr = pMeshSysMem2->CloneMesh(D3DXMESH_MANAGED, decl2, m_pd3dDevice,
&m_pD3DXMesh);

    // cleanup
    SAFE_RELEASE(pMeshSysMem);
    SAFE_RELEASE(pMeshSysMem2);

    return S_OK;
}
```

To load an X file, you use the function D3DXLoadMeshFromX() from the Direct3DX library. The declaration of this function looks like this:

```
HRESULT D3DXLoadMeshFromX(
    LPCTSTR pFilename,
    DWORD Options,
    LPDIRECT3DDEVICE9 pDevice,
    LPD3DXBUFFER* ppAdjacency,
    LPD3DXBUFFER* ppMaterials,
```

```
    LPD3DXBUFFER* ppEffectInstances,
    DWORD* pNumMaterials,
    LPD3DXMESH* ppMesh
);
```

The first parameter, pFilename, should get a pointer to the path of the file. The examples load the *.x file with the help of the Direct3D utility function DXUtil_FindMediaFileCb().

```
TCHAR strFile[160];
DXUtil_FindMediaFileCb(strFile, sizeof(strFile),_T("teapot.x"));
LoadXFile(strFile);
```

This function searches through the file system to find a file. Options, the second parameter of the D3DXLoadMeshFromX() function, defines the memory pool and some other flags for the vertex and index buffers. The example uses D3DXMESH_SYSTEMMEM, but a better choice might be D3DXMESH_MANAGED. The combination D3DXMESH_MANAGED | D3DXMESH_WRITEONLY will not work here because the function CloneMesh() will also read from the vertex and index buffers.

The third parameter takes the pointer to the device. You don't need any data on the neighbors of faces, so the fourth paramter is set to NULL. Because you also don't need a pointer to a buffer containing material data or data on effect instances, the next three parameters are NULL. The last parameter returns a pointer to the mesh object that is used to clone the mesh and compute normals later. Please note that the D3DXComputeNormal() function, which is responsible for calculating the normals of the mesh, only accepts a position input value that consists of three floats. The two CloneMesh() functions are used to create a clone of the original mesh, which holds the data in the way defined by the D3DVERTEXELEMENT9 structures. The first time the original mesh is cloned to get a data layout that fits the expected data layout of the D3DXComputeNormal() function. The second time the already-cloned mesh is cloned again to get a data layout with a position value consisting of four float values.

Loading non-animated objects is a simple task compared to loading an animated X file. Check out the SkinnedMesh example from the DirectX 9 SDK to see how to load an X file that uses skinning to animate a figure.

Extending X Files

One of the most fascinating aspects of the concept behind X files is extensibility. You might recall the file rmxftmpl.x, which holds the definitions of the templates. You might define your own templates in it and make your own X file format this way. For example, a shader template with all of the texturing functionality explained in Part Two might be implemented this way with different parameters and so on. Your files can hold their own shader classes, collision detection parameters, physics, specialized animations, paths to sound files, and more.

If you take a look at the following section, you'll get an idea of what has been done already in this area. I'm sure you'll be thinking of building your own file format in the next few hours, with this in mind!

Additional Resources

This section includes some Web sites you might want to check out to do a little further reading on some of the topics covered in this chapter.

X File Format

The DirectX 9 documenation provides excellent material to search for details. There is also an X file dump provided by Rich Thompson at http://www.xmission.com/~legalize/book/snippets/index.html#12.

Skinned Meshes

There is an article at http://www.flipcode.com/articles/article_dx9skinmeshmod.shtml on how to modularize the skinned mesh example in the DX9 SDK.

You will find an article that explains how skinning works at http://www.gamedev.net/reference/articles/article1835.asp

There is a Spanish Web site that shows a few variations of the skinned mesh example at http://atc1.aut.uah.es/~infind/Programming/Programming.htm.

Furthermore, there are a few excellent articles on skinning written by Jeff Lander in *GameDeveloper* magazine. Check out the May 1998 and April 2001 issues.

Additionally, the article from Eike F. Anderson at http://ncca.bournemouth.ac.uk/newhome/alumni/docs/CharacterAnimation.pdf is very helpful. Michael Putz and Klaus Hufnagl describe a more advanced approach at http://www.cg.tuwien.ac.at/studentwork/CESCG/CESCG-002/MPutzKHufnagl/paper.pdf.

Summary

This chapter taught you all you ever wanted to know about transformation matrices and Microsoft's X file format. Okay, maybe not...but it gave you a good start! And I'm sure you can't wait to learn all about the *.md3 file format used by the *Quake 3* engine, so turn the page and let's move on!

CHAPTER 12

USING
*.MD3 FILES

This chapter describes the *.md3 file format used by the *Quake 3* engine, and contains an example program that demonstrates how to use this format, together with per-pixel lighting, bump mapping, and an efficient shading system with HLSL shaders.

The .md3 format is an often-used file format, which has been tested extensively and has proven to be an excellent model format in *Quake 3* and many other games. When you dive into the .md3 format, you'll dive also into the *Quake 3* coding universe. It's very impressive to learn how *Quake 3* was made by looking at the models, and it doesn't hurt to take a quick look at an approved model file spec before you start your own.

Quake 3 uses 800 to 900 faces in the highest level of detail, approximately 500 faces in the middle level, and 300 faces in the least-detailed level. There is no limit to the number of faces you can use.

These model files store animations in frames with fixed names, different lengths, and different speeds for every move. Using key frames is an inexpensive way to handle animations. However, the drawback to key-frame animation is the high amount of memory needed for high-tesselated models.

Most of the *Quake 3* models own different skins—a.k.a. different texture maps—that can be loaded on demand. You might use the same geometry for a static statue, a soldier, and an officer with a golden helmet, for example.

Files of the Trade

An .md3 model is normally made of three body parts and the weapon model. So you have to open three model files and put them together. (If you are using a weapon, you have to open four.) In *Quake 3* they are called head.md3, upper.md3, and lower.md3, as shown in Figure 12.1.

Inside the .md3 files, you can have any number of components. For example, in the DOOM marine's head.md3, there is a mesh called h_helmet and one called h_visor. You can apply different textures or shader effects to certain components of the model. There's no limit to the number of components, but they have to follow the naming convention, which is h_ for head components, u_ for torso components, and l_ for lower components.

The .md3 files store the character animations in *key frames*. To visualize key-frame animation, it helps to imagine the use of sprites in old sprite engines. These were long lists of pictures called one after another so the viewer got the impression of a moving object, like in those old celluloid films. The same thing happens in .md3 files with the vertices of poly-

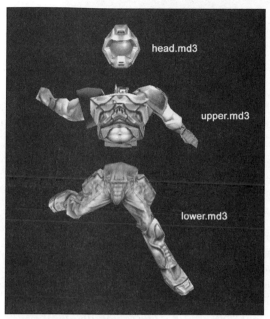

Figure 12.1

DOOM marine (original model of Quake 3)

Courtesy of id Software

gons. There's no limit for frames in the engine, but a maximum of 300 might be a good number to keep the rendering fast and the image quality reasonable. Using more would lead to quite a large memory footprint. The file that stores the animation data is called animation.cfg, and it directs the call of the key frames.

You can provide three different levels of detail with three different .md3 files for each model. The naming convention of the files used in *Quake 3* for the three levels of detail is as follows. For the lowest-detail level, a 2 is placed after the file name; for the middle-detail level, a 1 is placed after it; the highest-detail level gets no additional number. So the file names head.md3, head1.md3, and head2.md3 would be interpreted as highest, middle, and lowest detail, respectively.

The head, torso, and lower body parts are attached to each other by so-called *tags*. Every tag is just a one-face geometry. The long pointy end of the triangle must face the front. The base of the triangle is the actual pivot point. It determines where the respective model will be rotated. This tag does not have material, so it's not visible.

There can be three tags in every .md3 model, and the tag name corresponds to its location (see Figure 12.2). The base of the neck is attached to the upper torso with tag_head. At the base of the spine, the torso is attached to the legs with tag_torso. The weapon is attached to the hand of the model with tag_weapon. Each model has at least one tag. head.md3 has tag_head; upper.md3 has tag_head, tag_torso, and tag_weapon; and lower.md3 has tag_torso.

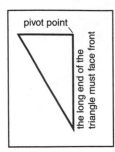

pivot point

the long end of the
triangle must face front

Figure 12.2

The tags that connect
.md3 models

You need to place `tag_head` at the pivot point of the head bone, `tag_torso` at the pivot point of the base spine bone, and so on. The tag used to connect the .md3 file is determined by an entry into the *.skin file. You can attach the .md3 models any way you like.

The *.skin file also helps to attach skins—texture maps of .tga or .jpg files—to geometry. This way, it's easy to use different skins on the same geometry. (For example, the model is used as a statue looking out of ivory, and another model is a soldier fighting his way through the levels.) With these kind of skin files came another visual advancement in *Quake 3*—32-bit textures. Instead of being restricted to 8-bit palettes or to just one skin, you can use 32-bit color power and as many skins as you want. In the *Quake 3* engine, texture sizes will work best as a power of 2, as a square size, and with a limit of 256×256-pixel skins. (The example accompanying this chapter can open any texture size.) Please note that every component of a model might get its own skin.

The *Quake 3* engine also uses shader files for the .md3 models. This was one of its most exciting features when it was released. With shader effects, you can control texture mapping, transparency, many light parameters, and much more. *Quake 3* uses one shader file called models.shader, which handles all these parameters.

Additionally, the *Quake 3* engine made it possible to attach different sounds to your .md3 file format by using .wav files with 22.5-KHz, 16-bit, 1-channel (mono) format in any length (theoretically).

Table 12.1 summarizes the file formats and the names of the files used by a standard *Quake 3* .md3 model.

The .md3 files contain the geometry of the model, whereas the .tga or .jpg files hold the textures on a per-mesh basis for the .md3 files. The shader file controls the mapping of the texture and a lot more. With the help of the .skin file, you might tag more than one .md3 file together to form a model and define specialized skins—.tga or .jpg files—with it. To animate the model's different parts stored in their own .md3 files, there is an animation.cfg file. To hear your models speaking or shooting, you might provide .wav files with the proper sounds.

To analyze .md3 files on your own, you need to be able to look into the *Quake 3* pak0.pk3 file, which is located in one of the *Quake 3* directories after the game is installed. You have

TABLE 12.1 File Formats Used by a Standard *Quake 3* Model

File Format	File Names
.md3 file	Normally head.md3, upper.md3, and lower.md3
Icon file	icon_default.tga
Animation file	animation.cfg
Skin file	.tga or .jpg
Tag file	.skin
Shader file	models.shader, for example
Sound file	.wav

to rename it pak0.zip and use a Zip utility to see the directories and files. The files for the Biker .md3 model are stored in the following directories:

- The .md3 files, animation.cfg, .tga, and .skin are in models/players/biker.
- The models.shader file for all models is in the directory scripts.
- The .wav files are in sound/player/biker.

To see the contents of a typical directory that holds a *Quake 3* model, you might look at the models directories. You'll find at least the following files:

- animation.cfg
- head.md3
- upper.md3
- lower.md3
- head_default.skin
- upper_default.skin
- lower_default.skin
- At least one texture map—.tga or .jpg
- icon_default.tga (a 64×64-pixel, 24-bit image with an alpha mask)

If you want to use the model in a Capture the Flag mode, you need additional CTF skins as well.

- head_blue.skin
- head_red.skin
- upper_blue.skin
- upper_red.skin
- lower_blue.skin
- lower_red.skin
- At least two texture maps, one for each color—.tga or .jpg
- icon_blue.tga
- icon_red.tga

To create your own *Quake 3* models, the names of the files must follow these conventions:

- head_charactername.skin
- upper_charactername.skin
- lower_charactername.skin
- The textures for the characters
- icon_charactername.tga

Now let's examine the details of the different files.

Animation.cfg

The animation of *Quake 3* models works with the so-called key frames. For this kind of animation, the same model is saved in different positions. The model is drawn as a series of different models.

In the case of the *Quake 3* models, the different positions of a model are saved in different vertices and tags. So if a model supports 246 different frames, in every .md3 file there must be 246 different vertex groups in every mesh of the model, as well as 246 different tags that connect the .md3 files. The torso, for example, often has three tags, so there has to be 738 (3×246) different tags connected with the torso geometry.

Animations in *Quake 3* files can generally be any length and any frame rate. The naming convention must be exactly the same. The animation.cfg file of the Biker model looks like this:

NOTE

Contrary to key-frame animation, a skeleton-based animation system used in the DirectX X file format, *Half-Life, F.A.K.K.*[2], or the newer *Unreal 2* and *DOOM III* engines works by giving a model a skeleton, which is set up with joints or bones to determine how the unit will animate. Such an animation system consumes less memory at run time, but requires more computational power.

```
// animation config file
sex       m
// first frame, num frames, looping frames, frames per second, name of animation


headoffset -4 0 0
footsteps boot
0          30         0          25         // BOTH_DEATH1
29         1          0          25         // BOTH_DEAD1
30         30         0          25         // BOTH_DEATH2
59         1          0          25         // BOTH_DEAD2
60         30         0          25         // BOTH_DEATH3
89         1          0          25         // BOTH_DEAD3

90         40         0          20         // TORSO_GESTURE

130        6          0          15         // TORSO_ATTACK
136        6          0          15         // TORSO_ATTACK2

142        5          0          20         // TORSO_DROP
147        4          0          20         // TORSO_RAISE

151        1          0          15         // TORSO_STAND
152        1          0          15         // TORSO_STAND2

153        9          9          20         // LEGS_WALKCR
162        8          8          20         // LEGS_WALK
170        13         13         24         // LEGS_RUN
183        10         10         24         // LEGS_BACK
193        10         10         15         // LEGS_SWIM

203        7          0          15         // LEGS_JUMP
210        5          0          17         // LEGS_LAND

215        8          0          15         // LEGS_JUMPB
223        4          0          17         // LEGS_LANDB

227        10         10         15         // LEGS_IDLE
237        9          9          15         // LEGS_IDLECR

246        7          6          15         // LEGS_TURN
```

As far as I can see, any animation.cfg file is built like this. sex can be m for masculine, f for feminine, or n for none (in the case of machines, for example). sex determines how the game will display messages about the characters (for example, he or she) and which sounds will be used in the absence of custom sounds.

There are two optional variables named footsteps and headoffset. Setting the variables boot, normal, energy, mech, or flesh leads to a specific sound for the footsteps of the character. headoffset is the offset of the HUD in x, y, and z coordinates.

Farther down comes the frame-based animation script. The numbers in the first four columns change, but not the number of rows or paragraphs. The first column shows the first frame—where the animation with the name after the double-slash starts. The second column shows the number of frames; it's the length of the animation. A few animations are so-called *looping animations*. The third column contains the number of frames that will be looped. The fourth column shows the speed of the animation, and the last column shows the name of the animation. The names of the animations are the same in every model.

The BOTH_DEATH* animations are for both the legs and upper-torso objects. The last frame of a death animation is located in the BOTH_DEAD* animation.

The TORSO_* animations are for the—you guessed it—torso object. TORSO_GESTURE can be any length, and it even has its own sound. TORSO_ATTACK is the attack animation for ranged weapons. In *Quake 3*, it must be exactly six frames long because it is synced to the weapon firing. The first frame of the animation is the aim, the second frame is the fire and recoil, and the rest recovers to the first frame. TORSO_ATTACK2 must be a six-frame attack sequence showing the attack with the gauntlet. The first frame is the anticipation of the punch, the second frame is the punch itself, and the rest is recovery. TORSO_DROP is the first part of the weapon switch; it must be exactly five frames long in *Quake 3*. The second part of the weapon switch is TORSO_RAISE, which must be five frames long as well. The static pose holding a ranged weapon is animated by TORSO_STAND, whereas TORSO_STAND2 is the static pose holding the gauntlet.

The LEGS_* animations are for the legs. LEGS_WALKCR is the crouch walking cycle. There are walk (LEGS_WALK), run (LEGS_RUN), swim (LEGS_SWIM), jump forward (LEGS_JUMP), land forward (LEGS_LAND), jump back (LEGS_JUMPB), land back (LEGS_LANDB), and backpedal or run backward cycles (LEGS_BACK). There are idle (LEGS_IDLE), idle for crouching (LEGS_IDLECR), and a turn animation when the player rotates far enough for the legs to rotate (LEGS_TURN).

Usually, all of the animation frames are stored in arrays. You can call the proper animation by providing the frame number to that array.

The .skin File

All of the necessary tag and texture info is kept in the .skin files provided in your model directory. (Please note that the example program CharacterEngine in the Chapter12\CharacterEngine directory uses a different *.skin file format than the original *Quake 3* *.md3 format.) These text files hold the tags to which the model is attached, as well as the skins. The name of the .skin file corresponds to the name of the .md3 file that uses it. Here are the _default.skin files of the Biker model:

- head_default.skin:
  ```
  tag_head,
  h_head,models/players/biker/biker_h.tga
  ```

- upper_default.skin:
  ```
  tag_head,
  tag_weapon,
  u_larm,models/players/biker/biker.tga
  u_rarm,models/players/biker/biker.tga
  u_torso,models/players/biker/biker.tga
  tag_torso,
  ```

- lower_default.skin:
  ```
  l_legs,models/players/biker/biker.tga
  tag_torso,
  ```

The head .skin file describes the only tag that is provided with the head.md3 file and the texture that should be used for the head. The upper .skin file describes three meshes and three tags; the three meshes should be textured with the same .tga file. The last mesh in lower.md3 will be textured with the biker.tga bitmap file; it holds only one tag.

Textures are located in the same directory where the .md3 files reside. You can also find the names of the default textures in the .md3 file, as you will see in a few moments. If you want to use custom textures, they have to be declared in a custom .skin file.

Textures and the Shader File

The textures used for the .md3 files can have an RGB color depth of 32 bits. In the case of the *Quake 3* engine, textures should be a power of 2 in width and height, and they should be limited to 256 pixels in either direction. Textures are shaded with the commands of the shader file, which is located in the Scripts directory. (Please note that the example program uses a different shader file format than the original *Quake 3* file format.) Every mesh of a model can have its own texture and shader properties.

The shader file is a text file, like the animation.cfg and the .skin files, which you can manipulate with a text editor. It's written in its own language with a ton of commands. Shaders are simple scripts that the *Quake 3* engine uses to determine the properties of the polygon surfaces and how they are rendered. The most common use of shaders is to control the properties of walls in levels. Shaders control the texturing of objects by providing commands that are similar to the texturing commands of OpenGL, the 3D API that is used in the *Quake* series. You'll find the Direct3D equivalents of these texturing commands in Part Two of this book. You also might browse around in the models.shader file in the scripts directory of your *Quake 3* pak file.

Here's the anatomy of a shader file:

```
// a comment
[the shader name]
{
        [surface attributes]

        // a stage
        {
                [stage attributes]
        }

        [more stages]
}
```

As you might suppose, comments are set with the standard C++ double-slash. Every shader starts with its name, consisting of fewer than 64 characters and lowercase letters. Slashes must be forward slashes, and the shader body is contained in curly brackets.

There are three attribute types. The *surface* attributes control the behavior of the overall polygon surface to which the shader is linked (for example, if the surface is water or lava). *Stage* or *content* attributes control the look of a surface. *Deformation* attributes deform the vertices of a surface in some way.

With the .md3 models, you might concentrate on the stage or content attributes. As far as I can see, the models.shader file uses only these. To get a reference for all the shader commands used by id Software in *Quake 3*, you might check ftp.idsoftware.com/idstuff/quake3/tools/Q3Ashader_manual.doc. This is the official shader document written by id Software.

Let's examine the commands for the DOOM marine in the model.shader file. I've copied the shader scripts for the DOOM models from this file.

```
models/players/doom/phobos_f
{
        {
                map textures/effects/tinfx.tga
                tcGen environment
                blendFunc GL_ONE GL_ZERO
                rgbGen lightingDiffuse
        }
        {
                map models/players/doom/phobos_f.tga
                blendFunc GL_SRC_ALPHA GL_ONE_MINUS_SRC_ALPHA
                rgbGen lightingDiffuse
        }
}
```

```
models/players/doom/phobos
{
        {
                map models/players/doom/phobos_fx.tga
                blendFunc GL_ONE GL_ZERO
                tcmod scale 7 7
                tcMod scroll 5 -5
                tcmod rotate 360
                rgbGen identity
        }
        {
                        map models/players/doom/phobos.tga
                        blendFunc GL_SRC_ALPHA GL_ONE_MINUS_SRC_ALPHA
                        rgbGen lightingDiffuse
        }
}

models/players/doom/f_doom
{
        {
                        map models/players/doom/f_doom.tga
        }
        {
                        map models/players/doom/fx_doom.tga
                        tcGen environment
                        rgbGen lightingDiffuse
                        blendfunc gl_ONE gl_ONE
        }
}

models/players/doom/doom_f
{
        {
                map models/players/doom/doom_f.tga
                rgbGen lightingDiffuse
        }
        {
                        map models/players/doom/doom_fx.tga
                        tcGen environment
                        rgbGen lightingDiffuse
                        blendfunc gl_ONE gl_ONE
        }
}
```

The geometry of the DOOM model is used with four different texture packs. Start by examining the phobos_f model.

The line

```
map textures/effects/tinfx.tga
```

tells you that you must use the texture map shown in Figure 12.3 for the model.

Figure 12.3

The environment map

This texture is a global effect texture, which is accessible by many models, walls, and so on. The next line tells the renderer to produce the texture coordinates that are necessary for environment mapping.

```
tcGen environment
```

To blend the texture with diffuse lighting, these lines hold the OpenGL blending parameters:

```
blendFunc GL_ONE GL_ZERO
rgbGen lightingDiffuse
```

The blend functions are the keyword commands that tell the *Quake 3* graphic engine's renderer how graphic layers—a.k.a. different texture maps or texture maps with diffuse color or lighting, for example—should be mixed.

`blendFunc` (or in other words, the blending function) is the equation at the core of processing shader graphics. The alpha-blending formula is as follows:

```
FinalColor = SourcePixelColor * SourceBlendFactor + DestPixelColor * DestBlendFactor
```

Source is usually the RGB color data in a texture .tga file modified by any rgbgen and alphagen. In the shader, the source is generally identified by the command MAP followed by the name of the image. Dests is the color data currently existing in the frame buffer.

As you learned in Chapter 8, each texturing pass or stage of blending is combined in a cumulative manner with the color data passed to it by the previous stage. How that data combines depends on the values you choose for the source and destination blends at each stage. In the *Quake 3* engine, any value for srcBlend other than GL_ONE or GL_SRC_ALPHA (where the alpha channel is entirely white) will cause the source to become darker. There are many values for the srcBlend parameters. These commands are used by OpenGL as the blending parameters for texture mapping. Please check the shader manual for the different meanings of these parameters and every OpenGL reference (search for glBlendFunc()). Keep in mind that Direct3D provides equivalent parameters.

With the parameter GL_ONE used here, the value of the source color information doesn't change when multiplied by source. The parameter for destination blending, dstBlend, is GL_ZERO. This is the value 0. Therefore, multiplied by the destination, all RGB data in the destination becomes 0, or black.

Next you add the product of the source side of the equation to the product of the destination side. You then place the sum into the frame buffer to become the destination for the next stage. rgbGen lightingdiffuse illuminates the object by using the vertex normals.

So this first stage tells the renderer to blend the texture tinfx.tga by illuminating it with diffuse lighting. The texture coordinates for environment mapping are also created here.

Now on to the next stage. You need to blend a second texture, phobos_f.tga, with the first texture (see Figure 12.4).

```
map models/players/doom/phobos_f.tga
```

Alpha blending should occur with the following OpenGL parameters:

```
blendFunc GL_SRC_ALPHA GL_ONE_MINUS_SRC_ALPHA
```

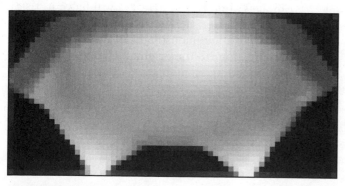

Figure 12.4

The visor of the Quake 3 DOOM model

Courtesy of id Software

These are similar to the following Direct3D parameters:

`D3DBLEND_SCRALPHA D3DBLEND_INVSRCALPHA`

Check out the multitexturing section in Chapter 8 for a description of these parameters.

The last attribute, `rgbGen`, tells the renderer to multiply alpha blending by a value generated by applying Gouraud-shaded directional light to the surface.

Okay, this was a first look at the phobos_f model. Now it's time to examine the phobos model.

You should blend a texture map called phobos_fx.tga, shown in Figure 12.5, with the `GL_ONE` and `GL_ZERO` parameters, which are similar to the `D3DBLEND_ONE` and `D3DBLEND_ZERO` commands in Direct3D.

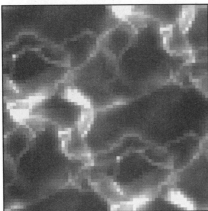

Figure 12.5

The effects texture map of the DOOM/Phobos model of Quake 3

Courtesy of id Software

The command `tcMod scale 7 7` resizes (enlarges or shrinks) the texture coordinates by multiplying them by the given factors. The formula scales the stage along the appropriate axis by 1/n. `tcMod scale. 0.5 0.5` will double your image, while `tcMod scale 2 2` will halve it. `tcMod scroll` continuously scrolls the stage by the given x and y offsets per second. The scroll speed is measured in textures per second; a texture is the dimension of the texture being modified and includes any previous shader modifications to the original .tga. A negative x value scrolls the texture to the left. A negative y value scrolls the texture down. So `tcMod scroll 0.5 -0.5` moves the texture down and to the right at the rate of a half texture each second of travel.

`tcMod rotate` rotates the stage by the given number of degrees per second. A positive number rotates clockwise; a negative number rotates counterclockwise. The stage here is rotated 360 degrees in a second with `tcMod rotate 360`. The parameter `rgbGen` means to leave the RGB values unchanged.

To sum up, the first stage loads an effect texture, and then scales, scrolls, and rotates it. In the next stage, the default texture map phobos.tga is loaded and lit by diffuse lighting. This texture map is blended with the map used in the first stage. The destination where the texture map from the first stage resides is multiplied by GL_ONE_MINUS_SRC_ALPHA and added to the source where the texture map from this stage resides, which is multiplied by GL_SRC_ALPHA.

The whole alpha blending formula looks like this:

```
FinalColor = SourcePixelColor * GL_SRC_ALPHA + DestPixelColor * GL_ONE_MINUS_SRC_ALPHA
```

In Direct3D the first parameter corresponds to D3DBLEND_INVSRCALPHA, and the second corresponds to D3DBLEND_SRCALPHA.

As you might notice, the shader language in *Quake 3* is a very powerful scripting language that maps directly onto the OpenGL commands used by the *Quake 3* rendering engine.

I hope you got the big picture on using *Quake 3* shaders. The example program that accompanies this chapter uses the DirectX 9 SDK effect file format, which has similar tasks to the original *Quake 3* shader file format but is much more advanced.

Custom Sounds

You need to put sounds in the sounds/player/modelname directory. In *Quake 3* the .wav files should be in the 22.5-KHz, 16-bit, one-channel (mono) format. The *Quake 3* engine needs a specific number of sound files with particular names. These files can be any length, but—as always—performance issues might come up with longer files. If a model doesn't provide its custom sound files, the default files are the sound files of the sarge or major model, depending on the sex of your model. Table 12.2 lists the sound files required by the *Quake 3* engine.

For all the models there are sound files located in the sounds/player/footsteps directory. Depending on the footsteps parameter provided with the animation.cfg file, the proper files are chosen. There are always four files per chosen footstep sound. If you choose energy in your animation.cfg file, the files are energy1.wav to energy4.wav.

Let's move on with the internals of the .md3 file format. To find out more about *Quake 3* .md3 files, you must now unwrap your scalpel.

The .md3 Format

The .md3 file format has not been officially documented by id Software until recently. As far as I know, a few points have changed over time, so this explanation might be subject to change.

There are different ways to build your own .md3 files. For example, http://www.planetquake.com/polycount and other *Quake 3* modification Web sites offer free downloads of .md3 files. These Web sites always cover a list of tools that you can use for this purpose.

TABLE 12.2 Sound Files Required by the *Quake 3* Engine

File	Description
death1.wav	Death sound
death2.wav	Death sound
death3.wav	Death sound
drown.wav	Death by drowning
gasp.wav	Gasping for breath after being underwater
falling1.wav	Falling from something
fall1.wav	Impact from a fall or big jump
jump1.wav	Jump sound
pain100.wav	Pain sounds dependent on health
pain75_1.wav	Pain with 75% of health
pain50_1.wav	Pain with 50% of health
pain25_1.wav	Pain with 25% of health
taunt.wav	Sound played during a gesture

You'll find many exporters for 3D Studio Max and other modeling software tools. If you're familiar with these tools, that's the best way to go. If you're like me and you're not familiar with these tools, I would suggest using MilkShape 3D, which helps you build your .md3 file with animation. It's a shareware tool, and its only purpose is to build models for the various 3D shooters. After you download the software, you can register it online using your credit card. Last I knew it was $25. Check out the MilkShape Web site for tutorials (http://www.swissquake.ch/chumbalum-soft/index.html).

You'll make your skins—.tga or .jpg files—with your preferred graphics-painting tool, such as Adobe Photoshop or Jasc Paint Shop Pro.

To take a look at your creations, you might use the Java MD3 Model Viewer at http://fragland.net/md3view/download.html. At the moment, it seems like the best program for the job. It's a little bit tricky to install, so watch for the installation instructions.

You can divide the content of an .md3 file into the following categories:

- .md3 header
- .md3 boneframes
- .md3 tags
- .md3 meshes

Every .md3 mesh consists of the following components:

- Mesh header
- Mesh texture names
- Mesh triangles
- Mesh texture coordinates
- Mesh vertices

The order of the different pieces shows the read-in order from the .md3 file.

Md3.h

The .md3 header holds all the information for the entire .md3 file. The md3.h file of the provided source package contains a structure holding this information.

```
typedef struct
{
            char id[4];             // id of file, always "IDP3"
            int iVersion;           // version number
            char cFileName[68];
            int iBoneFrameNum;      // Number of animation key frames in the whole
                                       model=every mesh
            int iTagNum;            // Number of tags
            int iMeshNum;           // Number of meshes
            int iMaxTextureNum;     // maximum number of unique textures used in a md3
                                       model
            int iHeaderSize;        // size of header
            int iTagStart;          // starting position of tag frame structures
            int iMeshStart;         // starting position of mesh structures
            int iFileSize;
} MD3HEADER;
```

The iVersion variable should hold 15 as a version number, and iHeaderSize should always be 108 bytes. The number of animation key frames of the whole model should equal the number of animation key frames of every mesh of this model. As far as I can see, iMaxTextureNum is always 0, so it seems that it's not used. The starting points of the different file contents are useful to check the correct read length of your .md3 file reader.

After checking the header structure, you need to read the boneframe structure from the .md3 file.

```
typedef struct
{
        FLOAT    mins[3];            // first corner of the bounding box
        FLOAT    maxs[3];            // second corner of the bounding box
        FLOAT    position[3];        // position/origin of the bounding box
        FLOAT    scale;              // radius of bounding sphere
        char     name[16];           // name of frame ASCII character string, NULL terminated
} MD3BONEFRAME;
```

Every boneframe structure holds a bounding box for a single animation frame. The bounding box values are used for collision detection. The array name is the name of the frame from which the bounding box was created. As the header shows, there are iBoneFrameNum number of key frames in the whole model.

As you might recall, a key-framed model is saved in different positions, so it's drawn as a series of different models. In an .md3 file, the different positions of the model are saved in different tags, bounding boxes, and vertices.

Every stored position of the model is called a *frame*. Every mesh holds the same number of frames with tags, bounding boxes, and vertices for each animation. A model with one mesh with 12 key frames and one tag (for example, mesh[12]) consists of:

- 12 bounding boxes
- 12 tags
- 12 vertex groups

Now on to the tags. There are at least as many tags as boneframes:

```
typedef struct
{
        char     name[64];
        FLOAT    position[3];        // position of tag relative to the model that contains
                                        the tag
        FLOAT    rotation[3][3];      // the direction the tag is facing
} MD3TAG;
```

The direction the tag is facing is stored in the 3×3 matrix, whereas the position is stored in three float values.

After the tags, which connect the parts of a model, come the meshes—the most important part of the .md3 model. Every .md3 model can consist of as many different meshes as you want. Normally the number of meshes corresponds to the need for specialized texturing for different meshes. For example, the helmet of the DOOM marine consists of two meshes, the visor and the rest of the helmet. You can texture the visor with a visor texture map and an environment texture map, and the rest of the helmet with the default texture map.

Now on to the mesh headers, which you need to load the texture names, triangles, texture coordinates, and vertices of this mesh.

```
typedef struct
{
  char cId[4];
  char cName[68];
  int iMeshFrameNum;     // number of frames in mesh
  int iTextureNum;       // number of textures=skins in this mesh
  int iVertexNum;        // number of vertices in this mesh
  int iTriangleNum;      // number of triangles
  int iTriangleStart;    // start of triangle data, rel. to MD3MESHFILE
  int iHeaderSize;       // Headersize = starting position of texture data
  int iTecVecStart;      // starting position of the texture vector data
  int iVertexStart;      // starting position of the vertex data
  int iMeshSize;
} MD3MESHFILE;
```

Most of the variable names are self-explanatory. The texture names start at the end of iHeaderSize, which normally means 108. If you multiply the number of textures by 68, you get the starting point of the triangle data, iTriangleStart. If you multiply iTriangleNum by the size of the TRIANGLEVERT data type and add it to iTriangleStart, you should get the starting point of the texture coordinates, iTecVecStart. By multiplying the number of vertices by the size of the TEXCOORDS structure, you get the starting point of the vertex data, iVertexStart. Because the file will hold vertex groups for every frame, you have to multiply the number of vertices by the number of frames, multiplied by the size of the vertex data, to reach the end of the mesh.

```
typedef struct
{
    SHORT vec[3];
    UCHAR unknown;
} MD3VERTEX;
```

The MD3VERTEX structure holds one array of shorts and an unknown UCHAR, which is probably used to round up to four bytes.

The CharacterEngine Example Program

The CharacterEngine example program, which is located in the Chapter12\CharacterEngine directory on the CD-ROM, is shown in Figure 12.6. This sample program demonstrates the following techniques:

- How you can load and animate the geometry of a complete *Quake 3* model
- How you can enhance this file format
- How you can use vertex and pixel shaders to animate and shade the model
- How you can implement a Level of Shading (LOS) model for an .md3 model

Figure 12.6

*The CharacterEngine
example program*

Please note that the railgun model is provided courtesy of Lee David Ash (available at http://www.planetquake.com/polycount), and the dragon model was created by Michael "Magarnigal" Mellor (available at http://www.planetquake.com/polycount).

Figure 12.7 shows all possible animations for the upper and lower model in the upper-left corner (press A). You can choose the animation using the J, L, K, and I keys.

You can access all other options using the O key, as shown in Figure 12.8. You can switch on and off the weapons using the G key, switch on and off the wireframe mode using the W key, and cycle through the different shader profiles using the + and – keys on the number pad.

You can move the light source by pressing P and then using the arrow keys.

The light position is marked by a yellow sphere, as shown in Figure 12.9. Moving it around shows how the light is reflected from the surface of the example.

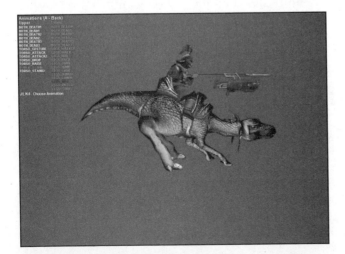

Figure 12.7

Animation menu system

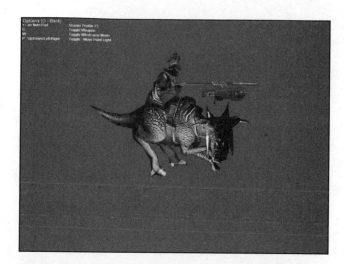

Figure 12.8

The Options menu

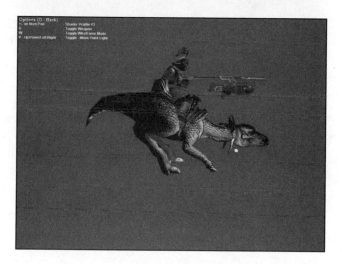

Figure 12.9

Movable light source

The following sections will take you through these features step by step.

Loading and Animating an .md3 Model

You can find all the code used to load, animate, and shade .md3 files in md3.h and md3.cpp. The code consists of two classes. The Q3Player class is a level of abstraction above the CMD3Model class. It covers all functionality necessary for one model consisting of four .md3 files (in this example, three for the dragon and the rider and one for the weapon).

The methods of the Q3Player class are

```
class Q3Player
{
public:
      Q3Player();
      ~Q3Player();

      VOID LoadPlayerGeometry(TCHAR *path);
      VOID DeletePlayerGeometry(VOID);

      VOID LoadSkins(LPDIRECT3DDEVICE9 m_pd3dDevice, char *path, char *skin);
      VOID FreeSkins();

      VOID LoadPlayerShaders(LPDIRECT3DDEVICE9 m_pd3dDevice, char *cPath, char *cSkin);
      VOID FreePlayerShaders(LPDIRECT3DDEVICE9 m_pd3dDevice);
      VOID LoadPlayerShaderProfile(char *pcFileName);

      HRESULT CreateVertexNIndexBuffer(LPDIRECT3DDEVICE9 m_pd3dDevice);
      VOID DeleteVertexNIndexBuffer();

      VOID Draw(LPDIRECT3DDEVICE9 m_pd3dDevice);

      VOID Update(FLOAT time);
      VOID LoadAnim(TCHAR *filename);
      VOID SetLowerAnim(int iAnimNumber);
      VOID SetUpperAnim(int iAnimNumber);
      VOID DumpAnimInfo();

      VOID LoadWeaponGeometry(char *cPath);
      VOID DeleteWeaponGeometry();

      VOID LoadWeaponSkins(LPDIRECT3DDEVICE9 m_pd3dDevice, char *cPath, char *skin);
      VOID FreeWeaponSkins();

      VOID LoadWeaponShaders(LPDIRECT3DDEVICE9 m_pd3dDevice, char *cPath, char *skin);
      VOID FreeWeaponShaders(LPDIRECT3DDEVICE9 m_pd3dDevice);
      VOID LoadWeaponShaderProfile(char *pcFileName);

      VOID SetWorldMatrix(D3DXMATRIX &matW) { matWorld=matW;}
      VOID SetViewProjMatrix(D3DXMATRIX matVP) { matViewProj=matVP; }

      CMD3Model                    md3Lower, md3Upper, md3Head, md3Weapon;

      LPDIRECT3DVERTEXDECLARATION9 m_pVertexDeclaration;
```

```
private:
        MD3ANIM                         playerAnim[25];

        int                             playerAnimLower;
        int                             playerAnimUpper;

        LPDIRECT3DINDEXBUFFER9   m_pIB;
        LPDIRECT3DVERTEXBUFFER9 m_pVB;

        D3DXMATRIX matViewProj;
        D3DXMATRIX matWorld;
};
```

After the constructor and destructor, the LoadPlayerGeometry() and DeletePlayerGeometry() functions load and delete the geometry of the dragon and its rider. All textures are loaded and freed with the LoadSkins() and FreeSkins() functions. Three functions load and free all shader-related items. LoadPlayerShaders() and FreePlayerShaders() load and free all vertex and pixel shaders used by the dragon with its rider, and LoadPlayerShaderProfile() loads the shader profiles. These profiles define for each shader level a specific pair of shaders per mesh. CreateVertexNIndexBuffer() and DeleteVertexNIndexBuffer() create and delete the vertex and index buffer. All geometry is written dynamically every frame into one vertex and index buffer. The Draw() function handles all the necessary commands to draw the model. Update() updates the animation time. LoadAnim() loads all animations from animation.cfg, and the SetLowerAnim() and SetUpperAnim() functions set the specific animations. The last animation function, DumpAnimInfo(), dumps all animation data to the log file. All functions with the word Weapon in their names are equivalent to the player functions. The SetWorldMatrix() and SetViewProjMatrix() functions deliver the matrices to the main application. The four different .md3 files are stored in the md3Lower, md3Upper, md3Head, and md3Weapon classes. Please note that this is hard-coded in the Q3Player class. There might be a reason to extend the viewer so that it is able to load one .md3 file model or three or more .md3 files. There is only one vertex declaration for all vertex shaders. This declaration corresponds to the vertex buffer. The CMD3Model class handles all the low-level stuff.

The following class shows the low-level functions called by the functions of the Q3Player class.

```
class CMD3Model
{
public:
        CMD3Model();
        ~CMD3Model();

        int  LoadModelGeometry (TCHAR *filename);
        VOID DeleteModelGeometry(VOID);
        VOID DumpGeometryInfo(VOID);
```

```
        VOID UpdateFrameTime (FLOAT fTime);

        VOID DrawSkeleton (CMD3Model *md3Model,
                  LPDIRECT3DDEVICE9 m_pd3dDevice,
                  LPDIRECT3DINDEXBUFFER9 m_pIB,
                  LPDIRECT3DVERTEXBUFFER9 m_pVB,
                  D3DXMATRIX *viewProj,
                  D3DXMATRIX *world,
                  LPDIRECT3DVERTEXDECLARATION9 m_pVertexDeclaration);

        int  LinkModel (TCHAR *cTagName, CMD3Model *mod);
        VOID UnLinkModel (TCHAR *cTagName);

        VOID LoadSkins (LPDIRECT3DDEVICE9 m_pd3dDevice, TCHAR *filename, TCHAR *imagepath);
        VOID DeleteSkins(VOID);
        VOID DumpSkinInfo(VOID);

        VOID LoadShaders(LPDIRECT3DDEVICE9 m_pd3dDevice, char *pcFileName, char *pcShaderPath);
        VOID DeleteShaders(LPDIRECT3DDEVICE9 m_pd3dDevice);
        VOID DumpShaderInfo(VOID);

        VOID CalculateNormals2(MD3MESH *MD3Mesh);

        VOID ComputeDuDv(const D3DXVECTOR3& v0_pos, const D3DXVECTOR2& v0_uv,
                            const D3DXVECTOR3& v1_pos, const D3DXVECTOR2& v1_uv,
                            const D3DXVECTOR3& v2_pos, const D3DXVECTOR2& v2_uv,
                            TANGENTS& meshTangents);
        VOID AverageTriangles(int index, int tri_count, int frame, MD3MESH *MD3Mesh);
        VOID GenerateTangent(MD3MESH *MD3Mesh);



        int                 iFrame;             // current frame to draw
        int                 iNextFrame;         // next frame to draw
        int                 iFps;               // frames per second

        int                 iStartFrame;
        int                 iEndFrame;

        MD3MESH             *md3Meshes;
        MD3HEADER            modelHeader;

private:
        TCHAR               cModelName[512];    // name for the md3 file
        MD3BONEFRAME        *md3BoneFrames;
        D3DTAG              *d3dTag;             // Direct3D specific
```

```
CMD3Model              **md3Links;

FLOAT                  fOldTime;
FLOAT                  fNewTime;

IDirect3DTexture9* pMiniTextureCache[MAXTEXTURESPERMESH];
};
```

The geometry is loaded with the functions that contain the word Geometry in their names; the textures are loaded with functions that contain the word Skin in their names; and the shaders are loaded with functions that contain the word Shader in their names. The CalculateNormals2(), ComputeDuDv(), AverageTriangles(), and GenerateTangent() functions create the normals and a tangent vector to create the texture space coordinate system. GenerateTangent() calls the ComputeDuDv() and AverageTriangles() functions.

All the following structures in the MD3Model class are defined in the md3.h file and described in the previous section. Please note that this example uses a texture cache, which is used to track texture changes. This texture-caching technique guarantees that the SetTexture() function is not called as long as the texture for the mesh does not change.

The following sections cover the most important functions of the CMD3Model class, including LoadModelGeometry(), LoadShaders(), and DrawSkeleton().

LoadModelGeometry()

The LoadModelGeometry() function loads all the geometry of one .md3 file. It calculates the normals and tangents and stores them in a compressed format in *.n and *.tan files. The function reads in the geometry in the following order. You can divide the contents of an .md3 file into the following categories:

- md3 header
- md3 boneframes
- md3 tags
- md3 meshes
  - Mesh header
  - Mesh texture names
  - Mesh triangles
  - Mesh texture coordinates
  - Mesh vertices

The entire function looks like this:

```
1: int CMD3Model::LoadModelGeometry(char *filename)
2:{
3:     FILE               *md3file;
4:     int                i, j;
```

```
5:
6:      // check if file exist
7:      if ( CheckFile(filename) == 0)
8:       return -1;
9:
10:      // open file
11:      md3file = fopen(filename, "rb");
12:
13:      // copy name
14:      _tcscpy(cModelName, filename);
15:
16://
17://     read header
18://
19:      fread(&modelHeader, 1, sizeof(MD3HEADER), md3file);
20:
21:      static char ver[4];
22:      wsprintf(ver, "%c%c%c%c", modelHeader.id[0], modelHeader.id[1],
                 modelHeader.id[2], modelHeader.id[3]);
23:
24:      if ( strcmp(ver, "IDP3") || modelHeader.iVersion != 15)
25:      {
26:          fclose(md3file);
27:          return -2;
28:      }
29:
30://
31://     read boneframes
32://
33:      md3BoneFrames = (MD3BONEFRAME *) malloc(sizeof(MD3BONEFRAME) *
                 modelHeader.iBoneFrameNum);
34:      fread(md3BoneFrames, sizeof(MD3BONEFRAME), modelHeader.iBoneFrameNum, md3file);
35:
36://
37://     read tags
38://
39:      MD3TAG *tempTag;
40:      tempTag = (MD3TAG *) malloc(sizeof(MD3TAG) *
                 modelHeader.iBoneFrameNum * modelHeader.iTagNum);
41:      d3dTag = (D3DTAG *) malloc(sizeof(D3DTAG) *
                 modelHeader.iBoneFrameNum * modelHeader.iTagNum);
42:      fread(tempTag, sizeof(MD3TAG), modelHeader.iBoneFrameNum *
                 modelHeader.iTagNum, md3file);
43:
44:      for (i=0; i < modelHeader.iBoneFrameNum * modelHeader.iTagNum; i++)
45:      {
```

```
46:            _tcscpy (d3dTag[i].name, tempTag[i].name);
47:            d3dTag[i].matTag(0, 0) = tempTag[i].rotation[0][0];
48:            d3dTag[i].matTag(0, 1) = tempTag[i].rotation[0][1];
49:            d3dTag[i].matTag(0, 2) = tempTag[i].rotation[0][2];
50:            d3dTag[i].matTag(0, 3) = 0.0f;
51:            d3dTag[i].matTag(1, 0) = tempTag[i].rotation[1][0];
52:            d3dTag[i].matTag(1, 1) = tempTag[i].rotation[1][1];
53:            d3dTag[i].matTag(1, 2) = tempTag[i].rotation[1][2];
54:            d3dTag[i].matTag(1, 3) = 0.0f;
55:            d3dTag[i].matTag(2, 0) = tempTag[i].rotation[2][0];
56:            d3dTag[i].matTag(2, 1) = tempTag[i].rotation[2][1];
57:            d3dTag[i].matTag(2, 2) = tempTag[i].rotation[2][2];
58:            d3dTag[i].matTag(2, 3) = 0.0f;
59:            d3dTag[i].matTag(3, 0) = tempTag[i].position[0];
60:            d3dTag[i].matTag(3, 1) = tempTag[i].position[1];
61:            d3dTag[i].matTag(3, 2) = tempTag[i].position[2];
62:            d3dTag[i].matTag(3, 3) = 1.0f;
63:        }
64:    delete tempTag;
65:
66://
67://    init links
68://
69:    md3Links = (CMD3Model **) malloc(sizeof(CMD3Model) *
                    modelHeader.iTagNum);
70:
71:    for (i=0; i<modelHeader.iTagNum; i++)
72:        md3Links[i] = NULL;
73:
74://
75://    read meshes
76://
77:    md3Meshes = (MD3MESH *) malloc(sizeof(MD3MESH) *
                    modelHeader.iMeshNum);
78:
79:    LONG lMeshOffset = ftell(md3file);
80:
81:    for (i=0; i<modelHeader.iMeshNum; i++)
82:    {
83:        fseek(md3file, lMeshOffset, SEEK_SET);
84:        fread(&md3Meshes[ i ].meshHeader, sizeof(MD3MESHHEADER), 1, md3file);
85:
86:        // ----------------------
87:        md3Meshes[ i ].meshSkins = (MD3SKIN *)
                    malloc(sizeof(MD3SKIN) * md3Meshes[ i ].meshHeader.iTextureNum);
```

```
88:            fread(md3Meshes[ i ].meshSkins, sizeof(MD3SKIN),
                   md3Meshes[ i ].meshHeader.iTextureNum, md3file);
89:
90:            // -----------------------
91:            fseek(md3file, lMeshOffset+md3Meshes[ i ].meshHeader.iTriangleStart,
                      SEEK_SET);
92:            md3Meshes[ i ].meshTriangles = (MD3TRIANGLE *) malloc(sizeof(MD3TRIANGLE) *
93:                           md3Meshes[ i ].meshHeader.iTriangleNum);
94:            fread(md3Meshes[ i ].meshTriangles, sizeof(MD3TRIANGLE),
                   md3Meshes[ i ].meshHeader.iTriangleNum,
95:                md3file);
96:
97:            // -----------------------
98:            fseek(md3file, lMeshOffset+md3Meshes[ i ].meshHeader.iTecVecStart, SEEK_SET);
99:            md3Meshes[ i ].meshTexCoord = (MD3TEXCOORD *) malloc(sizeof(MD3TEXCOORD) *
100:                            md3Meshes[ i ].meshHeader.iVertexNum);
101:           fread(md3Meshes[ i ].meshTexCoord, sizeof(MD3TEXCOORD),
                      md3Meshes[ i ].meshHeader.iVertexNum,
102:                   md3file);
103:
104:            // -----------------------
105:            fseek(md3file, lMeshOffset+md3Meshes[ i ].meshHeader.iVertexStart, SEEK_SET);
106:            md3Meshes[ i ].meshVertices = (MD3VERTEXEX *) malloc(sizeof(MD3VERTEXEX) *
107:            md3Meshes[ i ].meshHeader.iVertexNum *
                   md3Meshes[ i ].meshHeader.iMeshFrameNum);
108:
109:            MD3VERTEX *meshTempVertices;
110:            meshTempVertices = (MD3VERTEX *) malloc(sizeof(MD3VERTEX) *
                          md3Meshes[ i ].meshHeader.iVertexNum *
111:                          md3Meshes[ i ].meshHeader.iMeshFrameNum);
112:            fread(meshTempVertices, sizeof(MD3VERTEX),
                   md3Meshes[ i ].meshHeader.iMeshFrameNum *
113:               md3Meshes[ i ].meshHeader.iVertexNum, md3file);
114:
115:            for (j = 0; j < md3Meshes[ i ].meshHeader.iVertexNum *
                       md3Meshes[ i ].meshHeader.iMeshFrameNum; j++)
116:            {
117:                // The /64 is a constant scale factor that is used to convert the md3
118:                // model verts from shorts to floats.
119:                md3Meshes[ i ].meshVertices [ j ].vVector[0] =
                          (FLOAT) meshTempVertices[j].sVector[0] / 64;
120:                md3Meshes[ i ].meshVertices [ j ].vVector[1] =
                          (FLOAT) meshTempVertices[j].sVector[1] / 64;
121:                md3Meshes[ i ].meshVertices [ j ].vVector[2] =
                          (FLOAT) meshTempVertices[j].sVector[2] / 64;
122:
```

```
123:            /*
124:            The normal information in the md3 file is stored as two unsigned
                   chars to save space.
125:            These chars contain the spherical coordinates of the normal.
126:
127:            The first byte is longitude and the second byte is latitude. You may find
128:            This information in mathlib.c in the NormalToLatLong() function
129:            in the Quake3 tools source code.
130:            */
131:            //   md3Meshes[ i ].meshVertices [ j ].vNormal =
132:            //        fCalcNormals[meshTempVertices[j].cNormal[0]]
                //          [meshTempVertices[j].cNormal[1]];
133:            }
134:            //-----------------------------------
135:            //
136:            // Calculate Normals and Tangents
137:            // store them in files for faster startup
138:            //
139:            //-----------------------------------
140:            FILE              *File;
141:            DWORD              dwNumberOfVertices;
142:            TCHAR             cMeshName[68];
143:
144:            dwNumberOfVertices = md3Meshes[i].meshHeader.iMeshFrameNum *
                   d3Meshes[i].meshHeader.iVertexNum;
145:
146:            // allocate memory for tangents
147:            md3Meshes[i].meshTangents = (TANGENTS *) malloc (sizeof(TANGENTS) *
                   dwNumberOfVertices);
148:
149:            // Calculate Normals
150:            // store the normals in a file with the extension *.nor
151:               // read normals from this file to speed things up
152:            int z = 0;
153:
154:            // read in for example hunter\ when cModelName stores hunter\head.md3
155:            while (!(cModelName[z - 1] == '\\'))
156:                cMeshName[z] = cModelName[z++];
157:
158:            // adds to hunter\ for example legs_l: hunter\legs_l
160:            for (int y = 0; y < strlen(md3Meshes[i].meshHeader.cName); y++)
161:                cMeshName[z++] = md3Meshes[i].meshHeader.cName[y];
162:
163:            // saves mesh name in an extra array and adds the terminating \0
164:            TCHAR cNormalName[68];
165:            memcpy (cNormalName, cMeshName, sizeof(cNormalName) );
```

```
166:              cNormalName[z] = '\0';
167:
168:          // add the appendix .n
169:          strcat (cNormalName, ".n");
170:
171:          // check if file exists
172:          if ( CheckFile(cNormalName) == 0)
173:          {
174:                  CalculateNormals2(&md3Meshes[i]);
175:
176:                  // open file
177:                  File = fopen(cNormalName, "w+b");
178:
179:                  for(int y = 0; y < dwNumberOfVertices; y++)
180:                       fwrite(&md3Meshes[i].meshVertices[y].uiCompressedVertexNormal,
                                   sizeof(UINT), 1, File);
181:
182:                  // close file
183:                  fclose (File);
184:          }
185:          else
186:          {
187:                  // open file
188:                  File = fopen(cNormalName, "rb");
189:
190:                  for(int y = 0; y < dwNumberOfVertices; y++)
191:                       fread(&md3Meshes[i].meshVertices[y].uiCompressedVertexNormal,
                                   sizeof(UINT), 1, File);
192:
193:                  // close file
194:                  fclose(File);
195:          }
196:
197:          // Calculate tangent
198:          // store the tangent in a file with the extension *.tan
199:               // read tangents from this file to speed things up
200:          // check if file exists
201:          TCHAR cTangentName[68];
202:          memcpy (cTangentName, cMeshName, sizeof(cTangentName) );
203:          cTangentName[z] = '\0';
204:
205:          // add the appendix .t
206:          strcat (cTangentName, ".t");
207:
208:          // check if file exists
209:          if ( CheckFile(cTangentName) == 0)
```

```
210:             {
211:                     GenerateTangent(&md3Meshes[i]);
212:
213:                     // open file
214:                     File = fopen(cTangentName, "w+b");
215:
216:                     // write tangents into file
217:                     for(int y = 0; y < dwNumberOfVertices; y++)
218:                         fwrite(&md3Meshes[i].meshTangents[y].vCompressedTangent,
                                    sizeof(UINT), 1, File);
219:
220:                     // close file
221:                     fclose (File);
222:             }
223:         else
224:             {
225:                     // open file
226:                     File = fopen(cTangentName, "rb");
227:
228:                     // read tangents
229:                     for(int y = 0; y < dwNumberOfVertices; y++)
230:                         fread(&md3Meshes[i].meshTangents[y].vCompressedTangent,
                                   sizeof(UINT), 1, File);
231:
232:                     // close file
233:                     fclose(File);
234:             }
235:
236:         delete meshTempVertices;
237:
238:         lMeshOffset += md3Meshes[ i ].meshHeader.iMeshSize;
239:         md3Meshes[i].iNumTextures = NULL;
240:
241:         for (j = 0; j < MAXSHADERPROFILE; j++)
242:         {
243:                 md3Meshes[i].iChoosedShaderLevel[j] = NULL;
244:         }
245:
246:         for (j = 0; j < MAXSHADERLEVELINMESH; j++)
247:         {
248:                 md3Meshes[i].pVertexShader[j] = 0;
249:                 md3Meshes[i].pPixelShader[j] = 0;
250:         }
251:
252:         for (j = 0; j < MAXTEXTURESPERMESH; j++)
253:         {
```

```
254:                    md3Meshes[i].pTexturesInterfaces[j] = 0;
255:              }
256:        }
257:
258:        // close file
259:        fclose(md3file);
260:
261:        // note: the last frame for the quake3 model is header.numBoneFrames - 1
262:        modelHeader.iBoneFrameNum -= 1;
263:
264:        // set the start, end frame
265:        iStartFrame = 0;
266:        iEndFrame = modelHeader.iBoneFrameNum;
267:
268:        return 1;
269:}
```

The first 14 lines check the existence of the .md3 file. The MD3HEADER structure is filled with data in lines 16 through 28. The identification number is always IDP3, and the latest known version number is 15. If the identification number or the version number of the file is incorrect, the function returns a "bad header" return value. The memory for the number of bone frames (iBoneFrameNum) specified in the model header is allocated in lines 30 through 34. The MD3BONEFRAME structure in the md3.h file was presented earlier, in the section on the .md3 header file. Every mesh must have the same number of boneframes, which is provided in the header of the model.

The memory for all the tags that are used to align separate .md3 objects in the game is allocated in lines 36 through 42, and the tags are read in. The tags are converted to a customized D3DTAG structure in lines 44 through 64. This structure stores the 3×3 rotation matrix and the position value of the original MD3TAG format.

The memory for the so-called links is allocated in lines 66 through 72. The links are used to build up a linked list of all .md3 objects. This list is searched for the next model. For example, the weapon is linked to the hand (or in the case of this model, to the spear). DrawSkeleton() goes through this list by recursively drawing one .md3 object after another; it breaks out when the model does not link to another model.

The next section of the code reads in the mesh data with the help of the MD3MESHHEADER structure. Lines 74 through 133 read in all the members of the MD3MESH structure. The structure looks like this:

```
typedef struct
{
     MD3MESHHEADER              meshHeader;
     MD3SKIN                    *meshSkins;
     MD3TRIANGLE                *meshTriangles;
     MD3TEXCOORD                *meshTexCoord;
```

```
MD3VERTEXEX              *meshVertices;
TANGENTS                 *meshTangents;
int                       iNumTextures;
LPDIRECT3DTEXTURE9       pTexturesInterfaces[MAXTEXTURESPERMESH];
LPDIRECT3DVERTEXSHADER9  pVertexShader[MAXSHADERLEVELINMESH];
LPDIRECT3DPIXELSHADER9   pPixelShader[MAXSHADERLEVELINMESH];
int                       iChoosedShaderLevel[MAXSHADERPROFILE];
} MD3MESH;
```

The structure stores the header data, the triangle, texture coordinate and vertex data, the tangents, the interfaces for the texture, and vertex shader and pixel shader data. Additionally, it stores the shader level you chose for this mesh. There are two things you should note. First, the original vertex data is stored in three 16-bit values. The example program converts this data to 32-bit float values and decompresses it by dividing by 64. This makes the data easier to handle, and it is more instructive for an example program. Nevertheless, a more elegant solution would have been to send the 16-bit values to the vertex shader and decompress the data there. The second thing to note is that the example program does not use the normals provided with the meshes. It even computes the normal completely from scratch using the `CalculateNormals2()` function. It recalculates the normals because the normals necessary for the example program are not used to calculate per-vertex lighting; they are only used to build up a texture-space coordinate system together with the tangents, in order to transform the light and other vectors into texture space. This would not have worked with the tweaked normals provided with the model.

The normals and tangents are created and stored in their own files in lines 134 through 234. Before they are stored, the normals and tangents are compressed to 32-bit int values with the help of the `QuantiseVector()` function. This is done in the `CalculateNormals2()` and `GenerateTangent()` functions.

The rest of the code in the source snippet is for housekeeping purposes.

LoadShaders()

The `LoadShaders()` function loads the files with the extension *.sha. These files hold the references to shader files and the level of shading. The content of the lower_default.sha file looks like this:

```
lower_mesh01,shaders/ColorNOneTexture.vsh,shaderlevel0
lower_mesh02,shaders/ColorNOneTexture.vsh,shaderlevel0
l_legs01,shaders/ColorNOneTexture.vsh,shaderlevel0
lower_mesh01,shaders/OnlyOneTexture.psh,shaderlevel0
lower_mesh02,shaders/OnlyOneTexture.psh,shaderlevel0
l_legs01,shaders/OnlyOneTexture.psh,shaderlevel0
lower_mesh01,shaders/diffuse.vsh,shaderlevel1
lower_mesh02,shaders/diffuse.vsh,shaderlevel1
l_legs01,shaders/ColorNOneTexture.vsh,shaderlevel1
lower_mesh01,shaders/diffuse.psh,shaderlevel1
```

```
lower_mesh02,shaders/diffuse.psh,shaderlevel1
l_legs01,shaders/OnlyOneTexture.psh,shaderlevel1
lower_mesh01,shaders/diffspec.vsh,shaderlevel2
lower_mesh02,shaders/diffspec.vsh,shaderlevel2
l_legs01,shaders/ColorNOneTexture.vsh,shaderlevel2
lower_mesh01,shaders/diffspec.psh,shaderlevel2
lower_mesh02,shaders/diffspec.psh,shaderlevel2
l_legs01,shaders/OnlyOneTexture.psh,shaderlevel2
```

The first column (separated by commas) shows the names of the meshes. lower.md3 consists of three meshes: lower_mesh01, lower_mesh02, and l_legs01. The entire file must be read from right to left. For shader level 0, these three meshes use the vertex shader in the file ColorNOneTexture.vsh and the pixel shader in OnlyOneTexture.psh. In shader level 1, the three meshes use the vertex shader in diffuse.vsh, the pixel shader in diffuse.psh, and so on. This way, in every shader level, each mesh can get a specific vertex and pixel shader.

Additionally, the dragon_shader.profiles file holds another level of abstraction.

```
shaderprofile0
head01,shaderlevel1
lower_mesh01,shaderlevel0
lower_mesh02,shaderlevel0
l_legs01,shaderlevel0
upper_mesh01,shaderlevel1

shaderprofile1
head01,shaderlevel1
lower_mesh01,shaderlevel0
lower_mesh02,shaderlevel0
l_legs01,shaderlevel1
upper_mesh01,shaderlevel1

shaderprofile2
head01,shaderlevel1
lower_mesh01,shaderlevel0
lower_mesh02,shaderlevel1
l_legs01,shaderlevel1
upper_mesh01,shaderlevel1

shaderprofile3
head01,shaderlevel1
lower_mesh01,shaderlevel1
lower_mesh02,shaderlevel1
l_legs01,shaderlevel1
upper_mesh01,shaderlevel1
```

```
shaderprofile4
head01,shaderlevel1
lower_mesh01,shaderlevel2
lower_mesh02,shaderlevel2
l_legs01,shaderlevel1
upper_mesh01,shaderlevel1

shaderprofile5
head01,shaderlevel0
lower_mesh01,shaderlevel1
lower_mesh02,shaderlevel0
l_legs01,shaderlevel1
upper_mesh01,shaderlevel0

shaderprofile6
head01,shaderlevel0
lower_mesh01,shaderlevel0
lower_mesh02,shaderlevel0
l_legs01,shaderlevel0
upper_mesh01,shaderlevel0
```

This file chooses one of the shader levels defined in the *.sha files for a specific mesh. For example, in shaderprofile5, the mesh lower_mesh01 gets the vertex and pixel shaders connected with the shader level 1, whereas lower_mesh02 gets the vertex and pixel shaders connected with the shader level 0. Specifying a specific shader profile in the *.shader file connects a mesh with a specific shader level. The shader level is connected in the *.sha file with a specific vertex and pixel shader. Figure 12.10 shows this relationship.

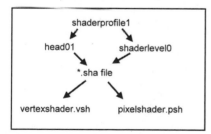

Figure 12.10

Level-of-shading system

The application can cycle through the shader profiles and choose a combination of vertex and pixel shaders for each mesh depending on the shader level. This might occur depending on the distance of the entire model from the camera. Therefore, you can use this system to implement a level-of-shading system.

The loading of the vertex and pixel shaders from the *.sha files occurs in the LoadShaders() function, and the loading of the shader profiles is done with the LoadPlayerShaderProfile() function, which is a member of the Q3Player class.

The LoadShaders() function gets the name of the *.sha file and the path to the directory in which this file is located. The following source code loads one vertex shader and one pixel shader per shader level.

```
1:void CMD3Model::LoadShaders(LPDIRECT3DDEVICE9 m_pd3dDevice, char *pcFileName, char
*pcShaderPath)
2:{
3:      LOGFUNC("LoadShaders()");
4:
5:      FILE    *ShaderFile;
6:      CHAR    cMeshName[16];
7:      CHAR    cShaderName[256];
8:      CHAR    strToken[1024], cPath[1024];
9:      CHAR    pcTextLine[1024];
10:     BOOL    bMesh, bTag, bShader, bShaderLevel;
11:     int     iShaderLevel;
12:
13:     //
14:     // open *.sha file
15:     //
16:     if ( CheckFile(pcFileName) == 0)
17:         return;
18:
19:     ShaderFile=fopen(pcFileName, "rt");
20:
21:     while ( !feof(ShaderFile) )
22:     {
23:         bMesh = FALSE;
24:         bTag = FALSE;
25:         bShader = FALSE;
26:         bShaderLevel = FALSE;
27:
28:         // scans a whole text line
29:         fscanf(ShaderFile, "%s", pcTextLine);
30:
31:         while (pcTextLine && pcTextLine[0])
32:         {
33:             // returns in strToken a word of a textline
34:             // returns in pcTextLine the next word of this textline
35:             // Reads only words consisting of chars, numbers,
                   // points and underscores
36:             ParseTextLine(pcTextLine, strToken);
37:
38:             // get mesh name
39:             if (bMesh == 0 && bShaderLevel == 0)
40:             {
```

```
41:                              _tcscpy(cMeshName, _strlwr(strToken));
42:                         bMesh = 1;
43:                }

44:
45:                else if ( (strstr(_strlwr(strToken), ".vsh") ||
46:                         strstr(strToken, ".psh")) && bMesh == 1 && bShader == 0)
46:                {
47:                         _tcscpy(cShaderName, strToken);
48:                         bShader = 1;
49:                }

50:
51:                // get shaderlevel
52:                else if ((strstr(strToken, "shaderlevel")) &&
                         bShaderLevel == 0 && bMesh == 1 && bShader == 1)
53:                {
54:                         iShaderLevel = ParseNumber(strToken);
55:                         bShaderLevel = 1;
56:                }
57:           }

58:
59:       //
60:       // create vertex and pixel shaders
61:       //
62:       if (bShader)
63:       {
64:            wsprintf(cPath, "%s\\%s", "shaders", cShaderName);

65:
66:            // Quest for the right mesh
67:            int i = 0;
68:            while (!strstr(md3Meshes[ i++ ].meshHeader.cName, cMeshName))
69:            {
70:                 if (modelHeader.iMeshNum < i)
71:                 {
72:                      LOG("Didn't find a Mesh with the Name: "
                                + string(cMeshName), Logger::LOG_ERR);
73:                      fclose(ShaderFile);
74:                   return;
75:                 }
76:            }
77:            i--;

78:
79:            if (strstr(cShaderName, ".vsh"))
80:            {

81:
82:                 TCHAR strVertexShaderPath[512];
83:                 LPD3DXBUFFER pCode;
```

```
84:                    HRESULT hr;
85:
86:                    DWORD dwFlags = 0;
87:
88:#if defined( _DEBUG ) || defined( DEBUG )
89:                    dwFlags |= D3DXSHADER_DEBUG;
90:#endif
91:
92:            hr = DXUtil_FindMediaFileCb(strVertexShaderPath,
                        sizeof(strVertexShaderPath), cShaderName);
93:            hr = D3DXAssembleShaderFromFile(strVertexShaderPath,
                        NULL, NULL, dwFlags, &pCode, NULL)
94:            hr = m_pd3dDevice->CreateVertexShader((DWORD*)pCode->GetBufferPointer(),
95:                                &md3Meshes[i].pVertexShader[iShaderLevel]);
96:
97:                if(!(FAILED(hr)))
98:                {
99:                    CHAR strData[128];
100:                   wsprintf(strData,"Created Vertex Shader: %s for Mesh: %s with
                          handle #%d",
101:                        cShaderName,
102:                        cMeshName,
103:                        md3Meshes[i].pVertexShader[iShaderLevel]);
104:                   LOG(string(strData), Logger::LOG_DATA);
105:                }
106:               else
107:                {
108:                   LOG ("Could not load Vertex Shader " + string(cShaderName) + "
                            for Mesh " +
109:                        string(cMeshName), Logger::LOG_ERR);
110:                        md3Meshes[i].pVertexShader[iShaderLevel] = 0;
111:                }
112:            }
113:         if (strstr(cShaderName, ".psh"))
114:         {
115:             TCHAR strPixelShaderPath[512];
116:             LPD3DXBUFFER pCode;
117:             HRESULT hr;
118:
119:             hr = DXUtil_FindMediaFileCb(strPixelShaderPath,
                        sizeof(strPixelShaderPath), cShaderName);
120:             hr = D3DXAssembleShaderFromFile(strPixelShaderPath,
                        NULL, NULL,NULL, &pCode,
121:                            NULL);
122:             hr = m_pd3dDevice->CreatePixelShader(
                        (DWORD*)pCode->GetBufferPointer(),
```

```
123:                                    &md3Meshes[i].pPixelShader[iShaderLevel]);
124:
125:                  if(!(FAILED(hr)))
126:                  {
127:                      CHAR strData[128];
128:                      wsprintf(strData,"Created Pixel Shader: %s for Mesh: %s
                                   with handle #%d",
129:                                          cShaderName,
130:                                          cMeshName,
131:                                      md3Meshes[i].pPixelShader[iShaderLevel]);
132:                      LOG(string(strData), Logger::LOG_DATA);
133:                  }
134:              else
135:                  {
136:                      LOG ("Could not load Pixel Shader " + string(cShaderName) +
                                   " for Mesh " +
137:                              string(cMeshName), Logger::LOG_ERR);
138:                      md3Meshes[i].pPixelShader[iShaderLevel] = 0;
139:                  }
140:              }
141:          }
142:      }
143:      fclose(ShaderFile);
144:}
```

The shader file is loaded in lines 16 through 21. In line 21, the text parser reads in a line from the shader file with `fscanf()`. The `ParseTextLine()` function, which you can find in the utility.cpp file, outputs this text line word by word. It reads only words consisting of chars, numbers, points, and underscores. The string `lower_mesh01,shaders/OnlyColor.vsh,shaderlevel0` is parsed like this:

```
in cTokenString:                          in pcTextLine:
first call:       lower_mesh01            ,shaders/OnlyColor.vso,shaderlevel0
second call:      ,                       shaders/OnlyColor.vso,shaderlevel0
third call:       shaders                 /OnlyColor.vso,shaderlevel0
fourth call:      /                       OnlyColor.vso,shaderlevel0
fifth call:       OnlyColor.vso           ,shaderlevel0
six call:         ,                       shaderlevel0
seventh call:     shaderlevel0            " "
```

This function is used to parse every ASCII text file in the entire example program. The words returned by `ParseTextLine()` are analyzed in lines 39 through 56. In this example, three words are scanned from the text line—the mesh name, the shader name, and the shader level. The mesh name is always the same word, so it's easy to find. The shader name is identified by the extension *.vsh or *.psh; afterward, the shader level is read in by searching for the read-in word after the term `shaderlevel`. This parser is used to parse all *.sha, *.skin, and *.profile files.

Before the vertex or pixel shader is created, the mesh is searched in the .md3 object in lines 68 through 77. The vertex or pixel shader handle and the shader level are stored in the mesh structure of the type MD3MESH. This example compiles assembly shaders instead of HLSL shaders, although the HLSL compiler generates the assembly. This way, you can optimize the code on the assembly level, in case the HLSL compiler didn't produce the best-optimized code. To use a vertex or pixel shader without using the effect file format, which I used in all previous examples, you need to perform the following steps:

- Search for the shader using DXUtil_FindMediaFileCb().
- Assemble the file using D3DXAssembleShaderFromFile().
- Create the vertex or pixel shader using CreateVertexShader() or CreatePixelShader().
- Set the vertex shader declaration using SetVertexDeclaration().
- Set the vertex or pixel shader constants using SetVertexShaderConstant*() or SetPixelShaderConstant*().
- Set the vertex or pixel shader using SetVertexShader() or SetPixelShader().

Please note that the LOG() function writes into the file app.log. You can find the entire logging class in the file logger.cpp. Its creator, Paul Nettle, released this file into the public domain.

The LoadSkins() function and some of the Load*() functions in the Q3Player class follow the same pattern.

DrawSkeleton()

DrawSkeleton() sets all mesh data of a model in the display buffer by using DrawIndexedPrimitive(). The function is called recursively with a link to the content of the next .md3 file. The recursion stops with head.md3 because this model has no link to another model.

The function provides to the vertex shader the interpolation value, the worldviewproj matrix, the world matrix, blended position values, two compressed normals, and two compressed tangents.

```
1:void CMD3Model::DrawSkeleton(CMD3Model *md3Model, LPDIRECT3DDEVICE9 m_pDevice,
2:                    LPDIRECT3DINDEXBUFFER9 m_pIB, LPDIRECT3DVERTEXBUFFER9 m_pVB,
3:                    D3DXMATRIX *matViewProj, D3DXMATRIX *matWorld,
4:                    LPDIRECT3DVERTEXDECLARATION9 m_pVertexDeclaration)
5:{
6:      //---------------------
7:      // draw one of the up to four md3 models
8:      //
9:      // 1. lower.md3
10:      // 2. upper.md3
11:      // 3. optional: railgun.md3
12:      // 4. head.md3
13:      //---------------------
```

```
14:     D3DXMATRIX matClip, matTemp;
15:     int i, j;      // counter
16:     int iCurrMesh, iCurrOffsetVertex, iNextCurrOffsetVertex;
17:
18:     // interpolation factor
19:     FLOAT fPol = md3Model->iFps * (md3Model->fNewTime - md3Model->fOldTime);
20:
21:     // interpolation constant
22:     D3DXVECTOR4 intpol(fPol, 1.0f , 0.5f, 1.0f);
23:     m_pDevice->SetVertexShaderConstantF(37, (float*)&intpol, 1);
24:
25:     for (iCurrMesh = 0;  iCurrMesh < md3Model->modelHeader.iMeshNum;  iCurrMesh++)
26:     {
27:         MD3VERTEXBUFFERSTRUCT* pVertexBuffer;
28:       m_pVB->Lock(0, 0, (VOID**)&pVertexBuffer, D3DLOCK_DISCARD);
29:
30:       WORD *pIndices;        // fill index buffer
31:       m_pIB->Lock(0, 0, (VOID **)&pIndices, D3DLOCK_DISCARD);
32:       DWORD dwIndexBufferCounter = 0;
33:
34:       iCurrOffsetVertex = md3Model->iFrame * md3Model->
                    md3Meshes[iCurrMesh].meshHeader.iVertexNum;
35:       iNextCurrOffsetVertex = md3Model->iNextFrame * md3Model->
                    md3Meshes[iCurrMesh].meshHeader.iVertexNum;
36:
37:
38:       // fill index buffer
39:       for (i = 0; i < md3Model->md3Meshes[iCurrMesh].meshHeader.iTriangleNum; i++)
40:        for (j = 0; j < 3; j++)
41:          pIndices[dwIndexBufferCounter++] = (WORD) md3Model->
                    md3Meshes[iCurrMesh].meshTriangles[i].index[j];
42:
43:       for(i = 0; i < md3Model->md3Meshes[iCurrMesh].meshHeader.iVertexNum; i++)
44:       {
45:         // interpolated vertices -------------------
46:         // pseudo code: CurrVertex.vPosition +  fPol * (NextVertex.vPosition -
                //CurrVertex.vPosition);
47:         pVertexBuffer[i].vPosition =
48:             md3Model->md3Meshes[iCurrMesh].meshVertices[iCurrOffsetVertex +
49:             i].vVector + fPol *
50:             (md3Model->md3Meshes[iCurrMesh].meshVertices
                [iNextCurrOffsetVertex + i].vVector-
51:             md3Model->md3Meshes[iCurrMesh].meshVertices
                [iCurrOffsetVertex + i].vVector);
52:
53:         pVertexBuffer[i].uiCompressedVertexNormal =
```

```
54:          md3Model->md3Meshes[iCurrMesh].meshVertices
                   [iCurrOffsetVertex + i].uiCompressedVertexNormal;
55:          pVertexBuffer[i].uiCompressedVertexNormal2 =
56:          md3Model->md3Meshes[iCurrMesh].meshVertices
                   [iNextCurrOffsetVertex + i].uiCompressedVertexNormal;

57:
58:          // texture coordinates ---------------
59:          pVertexBuffer[i].vTexCoord = md3Model->
                        md3Meshes[iCurrMesh].meshTexCoord[i].texvec;

60:
61:          // tangent vectors
62:          // two for interpolation
63:          pVertexBuffer[i].vCompressedTangent =
64:          md3Model->md3Meshes[iCurrMesh].meshTangents
                   [iCurrOffsetVertex + i].vCompressedTangent;
65:          pVertexBuffer[i].vCompressedTangent2 =
66:          md3Model->md3Meshes[iCurrMesh].meshTangents
                   [iNextCurrOffsetVertex + i].vCompressedTangent;
67:            }
68:
69:       m_pVB->Unlock();
70:       m_pIB->Unlock();
71:
72:       // world * view * proj matrix
73:       D3DXMATRIX  matTemp;
74:         D3DXMatrixMultiply(&matClip, matWorld, matViewProj);
75:       D3DXMatrixTranspose(&matTemp,&matClip);
76:       m_pDevice->SetVertexShaderConstantF(8, (float*)&matTemp, 4);
77:
78:       // world matrix
79:       D3DXMatrixTranspose(&matTemp, matWorld);
80:       m_pDevice->SetVertexShaderConstantF(0, (float*)&matTemp, 4);
81:
82:       m_pDevice->SetVertexDeclaration( m_pVertexDeclaration );
83:
84:       //
85:       // set vertex shader
86:       //
87:         m_pDevice->SetVertexShader(md3Model->
                        md3Meshes[iCurrMesh].pVertexShader[md3Model
88:              ->md3Meshes[iCurrMesh].iChoosedShaderLevel[iShaderProfile]]);
89:
90:       //
91:       // texture caching
92:       //
93:       if(md3Model->md3Meshes[iCurrMesh].iNumTextures > 0)
```

```
94:          {
95:              for (i = 0; i < md3Model->md3Meshes[iCurrMesh].iNumTextures; i++)
96:              {
97:                  if( pMiniTextureCache[i] != md3Model->
                            md3Meshes[iCurrMesh].pTexturesInterfaces[i])
98:                  {
99:                      pMiniTextureCache[i] = md3Model->
                            md3Meshes[iCurrMesh].pTexturesInterfaces[i];
100:                     m_pDevice->SetTexture(i, pMiniTextureCache[i] );
101:                 }
102:             }
103:         }
104:
105:         //
106:         // set pixel shader
107:         //
108:         m_pDevice->SetPixelShader(md3Model->md3Meshes
                [iCurrMesh].pPixelShader[md3Model
109:             ->md3Meshes[iCurrMesh].iChoosedShaderLevel[iShaderProfile]]);
110:
111:
112:
113:         // set the vertex buffer
114:         // == specify the source of stream 0
115:         m_pDevice->SetStreamSource( 0, m_pVB, 0, sizeof(MD3VERTEXBUFFERSTRUCT));
116:
117:         // set the index buffer
118:         m_pDevice->SetIndices(m_pIB);
119:
120:         // ... rendering
121:         m_pDevice->DrawIndexedPrimitive(D3DPT_TRIANGLELIST,
122:                         0,
123:                         0,
124:                         // number of vertices
125:                         md3Model->md3Meshes[iCurrMesh].meshHeader.iVertexNum,
126:                         0,
127:                         // number of primitives
128:                         md3Model->md3Meshes[iCurrMesh].meshHeader.iTriangleNum);
129:     }
130:
131:     //
132:     // interpolate position of tags of lower.md3 (md3lower),
            // upper.md3 (md3upper) and optional railgun.md3 (md3weapon)
133:     // Not: head.md3
134:     //
135:     CMD3Model *modelLink;
```

```
136:
137:      D3DXQUATERNION quatFromMatrix, quatFromMatrix2, quatResult;
138:      D3DXMATRIX matFrame, matNextFrame;
139:
140:      int iModelFrame = md3Model->iFrame * md3Model->modelHeader.iTagNum;
141:      int iModelNextFrame = md3Model->iNextFrame * md3Model->modelHeader.iTagNum;
142:
143:      for (i=0; i < md3Model->modelHeader.iTagNum; i++)
144:      {
145:          // pointer to a model class
146:          modelLink = md3Model->md3Links[i];
147:
148:          if (modelLink)
149:          {
150:              // rotation matrix
151:              matFrame = &md3Model->d3dTag[ iModelFrame + i].matTag.m[0][0];
152:              matNextFrame = &md3Model->d3dTag[ iModelNextFrame + i].matTag.m[0][0];
153:
154:              // quaternion slerp interpolation
155:              D3DXQuaternionRotationMatrix(&quatFromMatrix, &matFrame);
156:              D3DXQuaternionRotationMatrix(&quatFromMatrix2, &matNextFrame);
157:              D3DXQuaternionSlerp(&quatResult, &quatFromMatrix, &quatFromMatrix2, fPol);
158:              D3DXMatrixRotationQuaternion(&matTemp, &quatResult);
159:
160:              // interpolated position vector
161:              // Pseudo code: Position[0] + fPol * (nextPosition[0] - Position[0]);
162:              matTemp[12] = md3Model->d3dTag[ iModelFrame + i].matTag.m[3][0] + fPol *
163:                        (md3Model->d3dTag[ iModelNextFrame + i].matTag.m[3][0] -
164:                            md3Model->d3dTag[ iModelFrame + i].matTag.m[3][0]);
165:
166:              matTemp[13] = md3Model->d3dTag[ iModelFrame + i].matTag.m[3][1] + fPol *
167:                        (md3Model->d3dTag[ iModelNextFrame + i].matTag.m[3][1] -
168:                            md3Model->d3dTag[ iModelFrame + i].matTag.m[3][1]);
169:
170:              matTemp[14] = md3Model->d3dTag[ iModelFrame + i].matTag.m[3][2] + fPol *
171:                        (md3Model->d3dTag[ iModelNextFrame + i].matTag.m[3][2] -
172:                            md3Model->d3dTag[ iModelFrame + i].matTag.m[3][2]);
173:              matTemp[15] = 1.0f; matTemp[3] = matTemp[7] = matTemp[11] = 0;
174:
175:              D3DXMatrixMultiply(&matTemp ,&matTemp, matWorld);
176:              DrawSkeleton(modelLink, m_pDevice, m_pIB, m_pVB, matViewProj, &matTemp,
177:                      m_pVertexDeclaration);
178:          }
179:      }
180:}
```

The reference to the texture object is cached in the pMiniTextureCache array in lines 93 through 103. This reduces the amount of SetTexture() calls.

The position of the models is SLERP-interpolated (*Spherical Linear Interpolation*) with a quaternion in the lines 150 – 172. This is accomplished by interpolating the position of the tag that links the different parts of the model.

The recursive call of the DrawSkeleton() function occurs in lines 176 and 177.

Please note that the interpolation of the position vector in lines 45 through 51 is done on the CPU, whereas the interpolation of the compressed normals and tangents is done in the vertex shader (and therefore on the GPU) after decompression. Handling the position values in a similar way would be a nice enhancement of this example. In his article "Vertex Decompression in a Shader," which you can find in *Direct3D ShaderX: Vertex and Pixel Shader Tips and Tricks* (Wordware, 2002), Dean Calver desribes a technique that compresses the position value with the help of the bounding box.

HLSL Shaders

The example program uses assembly shaders in ASCII files that are created by the HLSL compiler fxc.exe from HLSL shaders. Getting an assembly output from the HLSL compiler gives the programmer the chance to optimize the shaders and—more importantly—control the output from the compiler.

The compiler is called in the custom build menu via:

```
fxc.exe /T vs_1_1 /E VS /Fc diffuse.vsh $(InputName).fx
```

This line tells the compiler to create the file diffuse.vsh with the compiler option /Fc diffuse.vsh by using the HLSL file $(InputName).fx. The macro $(InputName).fx inserts the name of the input file. The /E option tells the compiler that the entry point of the HLSL shader is named VS, and the /T option requests a vs_1_1 vertex shader profile. All HLSL shaders are compiled with a similar command line.

diffuseSpecular.fx and diffuseSpecular.fxp are taken straight from the CharacterEngine example in Chapter 12, located in the Chapter12\CharacterEngine directory (originally from Chapter 9). The HLSL shaders in diffuse.fx and diffuse.fxp are just reduced version of these shaders; I removed the specular lighting code. All other HLSL shaders are reduced versions of the shaders shown in Chapter 9.

Taking a closer look at the assembly shaders created by the HLSL compiler might give you a starting point to learn assembly shader programming. I would like to recommend the assembly shader tutorials I wrote for http://www.gamedev.net. That said, I would like to point out that learning assembly shader programming is no longer necessary because the available HLSL compiler generates fantastic assembly code, and the HLSL C-like syntax is easier to read.

Further Improvements

There are a lot of improvements that you could make to this model viewer. An obvious one would be to reduce the memory footprint of the application. Here is a list of some other possible improvements:

- Handle original .md3 position data and decompress it in the vertex shader, or use a better compression scheme to handle it.
- Perform higher compression of normals and tangents.
- Use Cook-Torrance lighting on the helmet and the armor.
- Use an energy plasma shader on the weapon.
- Use a cartoon shader for the whole model to give it a cartoonish look and feel.

Additional Resources

You will find the best .md3 file viewer at http://fragland.net/md3view/index.html.

You will find the best description of the .md3 file format at http://linux.ucla.edu/~phaethon/q3a/formats/md3format.html.

Summary

In this chapter you learned a wealth of information about the *Quake 3* .md3 file format. And now that you've reached the end of the book, you should have a pretty good basis for programming with Direct3D. But wait—there's more! Check out the appendixes for some helpful additional information, including a C++ primer and a mathematics primer. And don't miss Appendix E, "Game Programming Resources," for a list of Web sites you can check out to learn more about some of the topics covered in this book. Happy programming!

PART FOUR

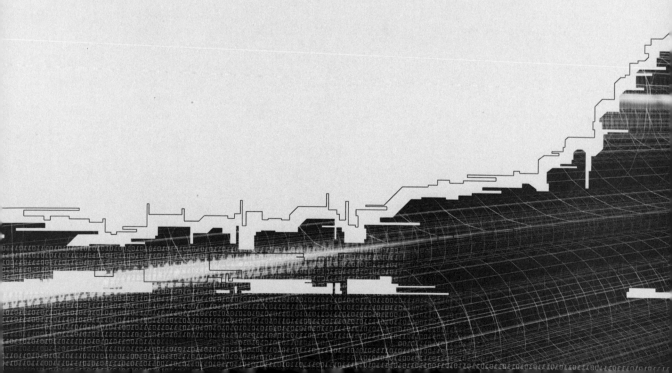

APPENDIX A

WINDOWS GAME PROGRAMMING FOUNDATION

What do game programmers have to do with Windows programming? Well... to be honest, not much. I think a game programmer mainly needs to know three topics for Windows programming:

- How to create a window
- How to use the window message procedure
- How to use resources (icons, menus, shortcuts, and so on) with the help of Visual C/C++

There are many articles and books that will help you understand this stuff. Take a look in the "Additional Resources" section at the end of this appendix for some places to start. For now, let's start investigating some of these topics.

How to Look through a Window

You are interested in programming a game that can be used in full-screen or windowed mode. I will describe the programming of both modes here, but before you set up the code for the first window that will present your game output, you have to learn a few general Windows concepts.

How Windows 95/98/Me/NT/2000/XP Interacts with Your Game

A DOS game requests such things as resources, input, and output. It doesn't have to share resources or ask someone before it takes them. However, a Windows-based game has to wait until it is sent a message by Windows. This message is passed to your program through a special function called by Windows. Once a message is received, your program is expected to take an appropriate action. Messages arrive randomly, so every Windows game has to check for new messages constantly.

Windows not only initiates the activity, it also grants the right to use resources (such as the graphics card, hard disk, and so on). You must consider this when you program windowed or full-screen applications. There are ways to get full control over the hardware from Windows, especially for full-screen games. So the resources of your game are only shared in windowed mode.

Before you move on to specific aspects of Windows programming, I need to define a few important concepts.

The Components of a Window

Every window has a border that defines its limits and is used to resize the window. There is also a title bar, containing the system menu at the far left and the minimize, maximize, and close boxes at the far right. Figure A.1 shows the FaceMorph example from ATI.

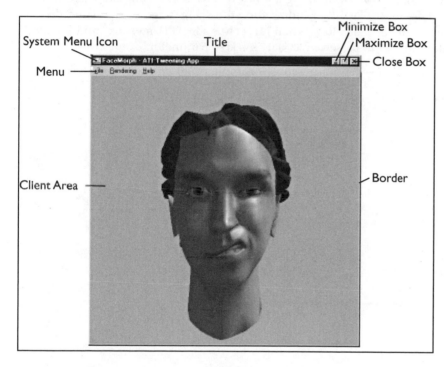

Figure A.1

Components of a window

Your world-class game is shown in the client area.

A Window Skeleton

Now I want to have you develop a Windows application that provides the necessary features common to all Windows applications. This Windows program will contain two functions:

- WinMain()
- A window procedure such as WndProc()

The `WinMain()` function performs the following general steps:

1. Define a window class.

2. Register that class with Windows.

3. Create a window of that class.

4. Display the window.

5. Begin running the message loop.

`WinMain()` initializes the application by defining a window class, registering that class, and creating the window. Then it displays the window and enters a message retrieval and dispatch loop. It terminates the message loop when it receives a `WM_QUIT` message, and it exits your game by returning the value passed in `WM_QUIT`'s `wParam` parameter.

Figure A.2 shows the first (somewhat unattractive) example program, called winskel.exe.

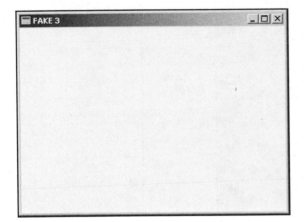

Figure A.2

Window skeleton

Here's the source:

```
#include <windows.h>
LRESULT CALLBACK WndProc(HWND, UINT, WPARAM, LPARAM);
char szWinName[] = "Crusher"; /* name of window class */
int WINAPI WinMain(HINSTANCE hThisInst, HINSTANCE hPrevInst,
                   LPSTR lpszArgs, int nWinMode)
{
        HWND hwnd;
        MSG msg;
    /* Step 1: Define a window class. */
      WNDCLASS wcl;
      wcl.hInstance = hThisInst; /* handle to this instance */
      wcl.lpszClassName = szWinName; /* window class name */
      wcl.lpfnWndProc = WndProc; /* window function */
```

```
     wcl.style = 0; /* default style */
     /* icon style */
     wcl.hIcon = LoadIcon(NULL, MAKEINTRESOURCE( IDI_APPLICATION));
     wcl.hCursor = LoadCursor(NULL, IDC_ARROW); /* cursor style */
     wcl.lpszMenuName = NULL; /* no menu */
     wcl.cbClsExtra = 0; /* no extra */
     wcl.cbWndExtra = 0; /* 0 information needed */
     /* Make the window background white. */
     wcl.hbrBackground = (HBRUSH) GetStockObject(WHITE_BRUSH) ;
     /* Step 2: Register the window class. */
     if(!RegisterClass (&wcl))
             return 0;
     /* Step 3: Now that a window class has been registered,
        a window can be created. */
     hwnd = CreateWindow(szWinName, /* name of window class */
                 "FAKE 4", /* title */
                 WS_OVERLAPPEDWINDOW, /* window style - normal */
                 CW_USEDEFAULT, /* X coordinate - let Windows decide */
                 CW_USEDEFAULT, /* y coordinate - let Windows decide */
                 CW_USEDEFAULT, /* width - let Windows decide */
                 CW_USEDEFAULT, /* height - let Windows decide */
                 HWND_DESKTOP, /* no parent window */
                 NULL, /* no menu */
                 hThisInst, /* handle of this instance of the program */
                 NULL /* no additional arguments */
                 );
     /* Step 4: Display the window. */
     ShowWindow(hwnd, nWinMode);

     /* Step 5: Create the message loop. */
     while (GetMessage(&msg, NULL, 0, 0))
     {
                 TranslateMessage(&msg); /* allow use of keyboard */
                 DispatchMessage(&msg); /* return control to Windows */
     }
     return msg.wParam;
}


//------------------------------------------
// Name: WndProc
// Desc: This function is called by Windows and is passed
//                       messages from the message queue
//------------------------------------------
LRESULT CALLBACK WndProc(HWND hwnd, UINT message,
                    WPARAM wParam, LPARAM lParam)
{
```

```
switch (message)
{
        case WM_DESTROY: /* terminate the program */
                PostQuitMessage(0);
          break;
        default: /* Let Windows process any messages not
                    specified in the preceding switch statement. */
            return DefWindowProc(hwnd, message, wParam, lParam);
}
    return 0;
}
```

The window function used by this program is called WndProc(). It is the function that Windows calls to communicate with your program. To indicate this call, it's declared as a callback function. Program execution starts with WinMain(), which is passed four parameters.

```
int WINAPI WinMain(
   HINSTANCE hInstance,        // handle to current instance
   HINSTANCE hPrevInstance,    // handle to previous instance
   LPSTR lpCmdLine,            // command line
   int nCmdShow                // show state
);
```

hInstance refers to the current instance of your game. hPrevInstance is obsolete with the newer Windows versions. So for a Win32-based application, this parameter is always NULL.

lpCmdLine is a pointer to a string that holds any command line arguments specified when the application was begun. It excludes the program name. To retrieve the entire command line, use the GetCommandLine() function. nCMDShow specifies how the window is to be shown.

NOTE

What are handles and why are they used so often in Windows-based programs? In Windows, a handle is a pointer to a pointer, so it points to an address stored in a table or list. You can use the address to which the handle points to access the object associated with the handle. This kind of indirect access is necessary because the memory manager often moves objects around in memory—for example, to compact memory—without notifying your application that the address of the object has changed. The memory manager ensures that the object's handle is still valid.

Windows uses many different kinds of objects through handles. These objects are named Windows objects; the name has nothing to do with the C++ objects. You can use Windows objects in programs based on the C language as well as in C++-based programs.

Table A.1 shows the typical flags.

TABLE A.1 Typical Flags

Flag	Description
SW_HIDE	Hides the window and activates another window
SW_MAXIMIZE	Maximizes the specified window
SW_MINIMIZE	Minimizes the window
SW_RESTORE	Restores the window to its original size and position from a maximized or minimized position

As usual, take a look at your Win32 documentation provided with Visual C/C++ or at http://msdn.microsoft.com for more flags. Now let's work through the five steps needed to show you a window.

Step 1: Define a Window Class

Your Windows program first must register a window class. When you register a window class, you are telling Windows about the form and function of the window you need. The word "class" is not used in its C++ sense; rather, it means style or type.

The hInstance field is assigned the current instance handle as specified in hThisInst. The name of the window class is pointed by lpszClassName, which points to the string Crusher in this case. The address of the window function is assigned to lpfnWndProc. No default style is specified, and the application icon and arrow cursor are used when the mouse is in the client area. You don't want to use a menu, but you would like to have a white background in the client area.

You can use different class styles in the WNDCLASS structure. To assign a style to a window class, assign the style to the style member of the WNDCLASS structure. Game programmers won't use many of these. The more interesting ones are

- CS_NOCLOSE, which disables Close on the window menu.
- CS_DROPSHADOW, which enables the drop-shadow effect on a window. This effect is turned on and off by SPI_SETDROPSHADOW and is supported by the next-generation Windows operating system with the code name Whistler.

The other styles don't seem to be of any benefit for your purposes.

You must always define a default shape for the mouse cursor and the application's icon. You can define your own versions of these resources, or you can use one of the built-in styles, as this skeleton does. LoadIcon() loads the style of the icon; its prototype is shown here:

```
HICON LoadIcon (HINSTANCE hInst, LPCSTR lpIconName);
```

The first parameter is a handle to the instance of the module whose executable file contains the icon to be loaded. This parameter must be NULL when a standard icon is being loaded, as it is here. The second parameter is a NULL-terminated string that contains the name of the icon resource to be loaded. Alternatively, this parameter can contain the resource identifier in the low-order word and 0 in the high-order word. Use the MAKEINTRESOURCE macro to create the value.

To use one of the predefined icons, set the hInst parameter to NULL and the lpIconName parameter to one of the values shown in Table A.2.

> **NOTE**
>
> LoadIcon() can only load an icon whose size conforms to the SM_CXICON and SM_CYICON system metric values.

TABLE A.2 lpIconName Parameter Values

Value	Description
IDI_APPLICATION	Default application icon
IDI_ASTERISK	Same as IDI_INFORMATION
IDI_ERROR	Hand-shaped icon
IDI_EXCLAMATION	Same as IDI_WARNING
IDI_HAND	Same as IDI_ERROR
IDI_INFORMATION	Asterisk icon
IDI_QUESTION	Question mark icon
IDI_WARNING	Exclamation point icon
IDI_WINLOGO	Windows logo icon

The icons you might make on your own are more interesting...we'll get to those in just a few seconds.

If `LoadIcon()` succeeds, the return value is a handle to the newly loaded icon. If it fails, the return value is NULL.

To load the mouse cursor, use `LoadCursor()`. This function has the following prototype:

```
HCURSOR LoadCursor (HINSTANCE hInst, LPCSTR lpCursorName);
```

The first parameter is, as usual, the handle to the instance of the module whose executable file contains the cursor to be loaded. The second parameter is a pointer to a NULL-terminated string that contains the name of the cursor resource to be loaded. Alternatively, this parameter can consist of the resource identifier in the low-order word and 0 in the high-order word. Use the `MAKEINTRESOURCE` macro to create this value.

To use one of the predefined cursors, the application must set the `hInstance` parameter to NULL and the `lpCursorName` parameter to one of the values shown in Table A.3.

TABLE A.3 Predefined Cursors

Value	Description
IDC_APPSTARTING	Standard arrow and small hourglass
IDC_ARROW	Standard arrow
IDC_CROSS	Crosshair
IDC_HAND	Hand (Windows 2000 only)
IDC_HELP	Arrow and question mark
IDC_IBEAM	I-beam
IDC_ICON	Obsolete for applications marked version 4.0 or later
IDC_NO	Slashed circle
IDC_SIZE	Obsolete for applications marked version 4.0 or later; use IDC_SIZEALL
IDC_SIZEALL	Four-pointed arrow pointing north, south, east, and west
IDC_SIZENESW	Double-pointed arrow pointing northeast and southwest
IDC_SIZENS	Double-pointed arrow pointing north and south
IDC_SIZENWSE	Double-pointed arrow pointing northwest and southeast
IDC_SIZEWE	Double-pointed arrow pointing west and east
IDC_UPARROW	Vertical arrow
IDC_WAIT	Hourglass

In this example, you obtain a handle to the background color brush using `GetStockObject()`. A brush is a resource that paints the screen using a predetermined size, color, or pattern. This function can retrieve a handle to one of the stock pens, brushes, fonts, or palettes.

```
HGDIOBJ GetStockObject(int fnObject);
```

`fnObject` specifies the type of stock object. Game programmers won't use this method very often. Table A.4 shows a few flags that might be useful.

TABLE A.4 Brushes

Flag	Description
BLACK_BRUSH	Black brush
DKGRAY_BRUSH	Dark-gray brush
GRAY_BRUSH	Gray brush
LTGRAY_BRUSH	Light-gray brush
NULL_BRUSH	Null brush
WHITE_BRUSH	White brush

Windows Data Types

The skeleton program does not extensively use C/C++ data types, such as int or char *. Instead, all data types used by Windows have been typedefed within the windows.h include file or its related include files. You must include this header file in all Windows programs.

Some of the most common data types are HANDLE (32-bit int), HWND, BYTE (8-bit sized), WORD (16-bit unsigned short integer), DWORD (32-bit unsigned long integer), UINT (32-bit unsigned integer), LONG (32-bit long), BOOL (integer), LPSTR (pointer to a string), LPCSTR (const pointer to a string), and HANDLE. As you see, there are a number of handle types that start with an H, but they are all the same size as HANDLE. A HANDLE is simply a value that identifies some resources.

Windows defines several structures, such as MSG and WNDCLASS. As you will see in a few moments, MSG holds a Windows message.

Back to our skeleton code. Once the window class has been fully specified, it is registered with Windows using RegisterClass().

Step 2: Register the Window Class

RegisterClass() registers a window class for subsequent use in calls to CreateWindow() or CreateWindowEx(). All window classes that an application registers are unregistered when it terminates.

CAUTION

If an application calls CreateWindow() to create an MDI (*Multiple Document Interface*) client window, lpParam must point to a CLIENTCREATESTRUCT structure.

```
ATOM RegisterClass(CONST WNDCLASS *lpWndClass);
```

The function returns a value that identifies the window class. ATOM is a typedef that means WORD.

Step 3: Create a Window of That Class

Once you have defined and registered a window class, your game can actually create a window of that class with CreateWindow().

```
HWND CreateWindow(
  LPCTSTR lpClassName,              // registered class name
  LPCTSTR lpWindowName,             // title of window
  DWORD dwStyle,                    // window style
  int x,                            // horizontal position of window
  int y,                            // vertical position of window
  int nWidth,                       // window width
  int nHeight,                      // window height
  HWND hWndParent,                  // handle to parent or owner window
  HMENU hMenu,                      // menu handle or child identifier
  HINSTANCE hInstance,              // handle to application instance
  LPVOID lpParam                    // window-creation data
);
```

You can default or specify as NULL many of the parameters to CreateWindow(). In fact, most of the x, y, nWidth, and nHeight parameters will simply use the macro CW_USEDEFAULT in most applications, which tells Windows to select an appropriate size and location for the window. However, in a game application you want to set the window with a predefined width and height. As you will see, AdjustWindowRect() can help by calculating the required size of the window rectangle based on the desired client rectangle size.

You must specify the handle to the parent window hWndParent as HWND_DESKTOP. If the window will not contain a menu, then hMenu must be NULL. If no additional information is required, as is most often the case, then lpParam is NULL.

You must set the remaining four parameters explicitly for your game. lpClassName must point to the name of the window class. The title of the window is a string pointed by lpWindowName. The style of the window is actually created by the value of dwStyle. The macro WS_OVERLAPPEDWINDOW specifies a standard window that has a system menu; a border; and minimize, maximize, and close boxes. As a game programmer, you will set the styles on your own in a more differentiated manner. For example, you won't use a Close box if your game only uses the Esc key to quit, and you won't use a minimize/maximize button if your game only supports 640×480 or 800×600 windows, because these are the rectangles for which it is optimized.

> **TIP**
>
> What's the difference between CreateWindow() and CreateWindowEx()? The latter creates windows with an extended window style.

Table A.5 presents a selection of the different window styles.

TABLE A.5 Window Styles

Value	Description
WS_BORDER	Creates a window that has a thin border.
WS_CAPTION	Creates a window that has a title bar (includes the WS_BORDER style).
WS_CHILD	Creates a child window. A window with this style cannot have a menu bar. This style cannot be used with the WS_POPUP style.
WS_CHILDWINDOW	Same as the WS_CHILD style.
WS_DISABLED	Creates a window that is initially disabled. A disabled window cannot receive input from the user. To change this after a window has been created, use EnableWindow.
WS_DLGFRAME	Creates a window that has a border of the style typically used for dialog boxes. A window with this style cannot have a title bar.
WS_ICONIC	Creates a window that is initially minimized. Same as the WS_MINIMIZE style.
WS_MAXIMIZE	Creates a window that is initially maximized.
WS_MAXIMIZEBOX	Creates a window that has a maximize button. Cannot be combined with the WS_EX_CONTEXTHELP style. The WS_SYSMENU style must also be specified.
WS_MINIMIZE	Creates a window that is initially minimized. Same as the WS_ICONIC style.

TABLE A.5 Window Styles *(continued...)*

Value	Description
WS_MINIMIZEBOX	Creates a window that has a minimize button. Cannot be combined with the WS_EX_CONTEXTHELP style. The WS_SYSMENU style must also be specified.
WS_OVERLAPPED	Creates an overlapped window. An overlapped window has a title bar and a border. Same as the WS_TILED style.
WS_OVERLAPPEDWINDOW	Creates an overlapped window with the WS_OVERLAPPED, WS_CAPTION, WS_SYSMENU, WS_THICKFRAME, WS_MINIMIZEBOX, and WS_MAXIMIZEBOX styles. Same as the WS_TILEDWINDOW style.
WS_POPUP	Creates a pop-up window. This style cannot be used with the WS_CHILD style.
WS_POPUPWINDOW	Creates a pop-up window with WS_BORDER, WS_POPUP, and WS_SYSMENU styles. The WS_CAPTION and WS_POPUPWINDOW styles must be combined to make the window menu visible.
WS_SIZEBOX	Creates a window that has a sizing border. Same as the WS_THICKFRAME style.
WS_SYSMENU	Creates a window that has a window menu on its title bar. The WS_CAPTION style must also be specified.
WS_THICKFRAME	Creates a window that has a sizing border. Same as the WS_SIZEBOX style.
WS_TILED	Creates an overlapped window. An overlapped window has a title bar and a border. Same as the WS_OVERLAPPED style.
WS_TILEDWINDOW	Creates an overlapped window with the WS_OVERLAPPED, WS_CAPTION, WS_SYSMENU, WS_THICKFRAME, WS_MINIMIZEBOX, and WS_MAXIMIZEBOX styles. Same as the WS_OVERLAPPEDWINDOW style.
WS_VISIBLE	Creates a window that is initially visible.

This style can be turned on and off using ShowWindow or SetWindowPos.

The styles used in the common files in d3dapp.cpp are

```
m_dwWindowStyle = WS_POPUP | WS_CAPTION | WS_SYSMENU | WS_THICKFRAME |
                  WS_MINIMIZEBOX | WS_VISIBLE;
```

If you remove WS_THICKFRAME, the window is not resizable. The WS_VISIBLE flag indicates that this window should be visible after creation and not after a call to ShowWindow(). A title bar is used because of WS_CAPTION. There's no WS_MAXIMIZEBOX, so the maximize button is grayed out.

CreateWindow() returns the handle of the window it creates, or NULL if the window cannot be created. If you haven't set the WS_VISIBLE flag, you must make your window visible with a call to ShowWindow().

Step 4: Display the Window

If you want to determine when your window shows up, you might use ShowWindow().

```
BOOL ShowWindow(HWND hWnd, int nCmdShow);
```

The handle of the window to display is specified in hWnd. nCmdShow specifies how the window is to be shown. The first time the window is displayed, you will want to pass WinMain()'s nCmdShow as the nCmdShow parameter. In subsequent calls, you can use one of the values in Table A.6, for example.

The ShowWindow() function returns the previous display status of the window. If the window was displayed, then nonzero is returned. If the window has not been displayed, 0 is returned.

TABLE A.6 Shown Properties

Value	Description
SW_FORCEMINIMIZE	Minimizes a window even if the thread that owns the window is hung. This flag should only be used when minimizing windows from a different thread (Windows 2000 only).
SW_HIDE	Hides the window and activates another window.
SW_MAXIMIZE	Maximizes the specified window.
SW_MINIMIZE	Minimizes the specified window and activates the next top-level window in the Z order.
SW_RESTORE	Activates and displays the window. If the window is minimized or maximized, the system restores it to its original size and position. An application should specify this flag when restoring a minimized window.
SW_SHOW	Activates the window and displays it in its current size and position.

Step 5: Create the Message Loop

The final part of `WinMain()` is the message loop. It receives and processes messages sent by Windows. When an application is running, it is continually sent messages, which are stored in the application's message queue until they can be read and processed. Each time your application is ready to read another message, it must call `GetMessage()`.

```
BOOL GetMessage(
  LPMSG lpMsg,              // message information
  HWND hWnd,               // handle to window
  UINT wMsgFilterMin,      // first message
  UINT wMsgFilterMax       // last message
);
```

The message is received by `lpMsg`. All Windows messages are of structure type `MSG`, shown here:

```
typedef struct tagMSG
{
  HWND hwnd;
  UINT message;
  WPARAM wParam;
  LPARAM lParam;
  DWORD time;
  POINT pt;
} MSG, *PMSG;
```

You will find the message data in `message` with additional information in `wParam` and `lParam`. In its `hwnd` and `message` fields, a `MSG` structure identifies the message being referred to by the window that the message affects. In its `wParam` and `lParam` fields, this structure stores information about the kind of event the message refers to and the event's source. For example, if the event is caused by keyboard input, the `wParam` and `lParam` fields identify the key being pressed and also reveal whether a command key was pressed at the same time. There is a time stamp in milliseconds in `time`, and `pt` holds the coordinates of the mouse in a `POINT` structure.

```
typedef struct tagPOINT
{
  LONG x, y;
} POINT;
```

`wMsgFilterMin` and `wMsgFilterMax` specify a range of messages that will be received. If you want your application to receive all of the messages, you will specify both `min` and `max` as 0.

`GetMessage()` returns 0 when the user terminates the program, causing the message loop to terminate; otherwise, it returns nonzero.

> **NOTE**
> Javier F. Otaegui has another interesting approach to get rid of the window message pump. (See http://www.gamedev.net/reference/articles/article1249.asp.) He uses a second thread that handles the window message routine.

You won't use GetMessage() in all situations; there are several situations in which you will use PeekMessage().

```
BOOL PeekMessage(
    LPMSG lpMsg,              // message information
    HWND hWnd,                // handle to window
    UINT wMsgFilterMin,       // first message
    UINT wMsgFilterMax,       // last message
    UINT wRemoveMsg           // removal options
);
```

There's one additional parameter—wRemoveMsg. It specifies how messages are handled. Table A.7 lists the possible values for this parameter.

You should generally use PM_REMOVE. By default, all message types are processed. One of the more interesting features that came with the advent of Windows 98, Me, and 2000 is the ability to specify that only a certain message should be processed. Table A.8 lists some more PeekMessage() flags.

Table A.7 PeekMessage() Flags

Value	Description
PM_NOREMOVE	Messages are not removed from the queue after processing by PeekMessage().
PM_REMOVE	Messages are removed from the queue after processing by PeekMessage().

Table A.8 PeekMessage() II Flags

Value	Description
PM_QS_INPUT	Process mouse and keyboard messages.
PM_QS_PAINT	Process paint messages.
PM_QS_POSTMESSAGE	Process all posted messages, including timers and hot keys.
PM_QS_SENDMESSAGE	Process all sent messages.

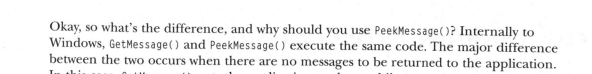

Okay, so what's the difference, and why should you use `PeekMessage()`? Internally to Windows, `GetMessage()` and `PeekMessage()` execute the same code. The major difference between the two occurs when there are no messages to be returned to the application. In this case, `GetMessage()` puts the application to sleep, while `PeekMessage()` returns to the application with a NULL value. You don't want your game to sleep until the next message arrives in the message queue, so it's better to use `PeekMessage()` when the game is active and `GetMessage()` when the game pauses. Pseudocode might look like this:

```
BOOL bGotMsg;
MSG msg;
While(WM_QUIT != msg.message)
{
    if (m_bActive)
        bGotMsg = PeekMessage(&msg, NULL, OU, OU, PM_REMOVE);
    else
        bGotMsg = GetMessage(&msg, NULL, OU, OU);
...
```

In the `while(GetMessage ...)` routine, there are two more function calls:

```
...
TranslateMessage(&msg); /* allow use of keyboard */
DispatchMessage(&msg); /* return control to Windows */
...
```

`TranslateMessage()` translates virtual key codes generated by Windows into character messages. Once the message has been read and, if necessary, translated, `DispatchMessage()` will send the message to the window procedure, which in this case is `WndProc()`. Figure A.3 shows you the relationship between the message queue, the message pump in `WinMain()`, and the window procedure. GetMessage stands for `GetMessage()` and `PeekMessage()`.

Once the message loop terminates, `WinMain()` returns the value of `msg.wParam` to Windows. This value contains the return code generated when your program terminates.

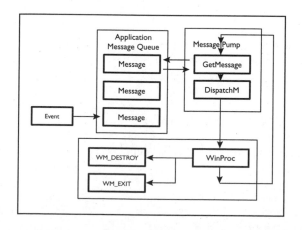

Figure A.3

Message pump

The Window Procedure

The second function in the skeleton is the window procedure. Its name is provided to the window class function. (I chose WndProc().) This procedure receives the first four members of the MSG structure as parameters. The skeleton window procedure responds to only one message—WM_DESTROY. This message is sent when the user terminates the program. PostQuitMessage() causes a WM_QUIT message to be sent to your application, which causes GetMessage()/PeekMessage() to return FALSE, thus stopping the program. msg.wParam will return with the WM_QUIT value if nothing goes wrong.

Any other messages received by WinProc() are passed to Windows via a call to DefWindowProc(). It calls the default window procedure to provide processing for any window messages that an application does not process. This function ensures that every message is processed.

A Window Skeleton Optimized for Games

After digging through the default window skeleton that is shown in nearly every window-programming book, you will undoubtedly want to take a look at a game-optimized version.

```
#include <windows.h>
#include "resource.h"
LRESULT CALLBACK WndProc(HWND, UINT, WPARAM, LPARAM);
VOID Render();
char szWinName[] = "MyWin"; /* name of window class */
BOOL bActive = TRUE;
int WINAPI WinMain(HINSTANCE hThisInst, HINSTANCE hPrevInst,
                   LPSTR lpszArgs, int nWinMode)
{
        HWND hwnd;
        MSG msg;
        /* Step 1: Define a window class. */
        WNDCLASS wcl;
        wcl.hInstance = hThisInst; /* handle to this instance */
        wcl.lpszClassName = szWinName; /* window class name */
        wcl.lpfnWndProc = WndProc; /* window function */
        wcl.style = 0; /* default style */
        /* icon style */
        wcl.hIcon = LoadIcon(hThisInst, MAKEINTRESOURCE(IDI_ICON1));
        /* cursor style */
        wcl.hCursor = LoadCursor( hThisInst, MAKEINTRESOURCE(IDC_HULLA)) ;
        wcl.lpszMenuName = NULL; /* no menu */
        wcl.cbClsExtra = 0; /* no extra */
        wcl.cbWndExtra = 0; /* information needed */
```

```
/* Make the window background white. */
wcl.hbrBackground = (HBRUSH) GetStockObject(WHITE_BRUSH) ;
/* Step 2: Register the window class. */
if(!RegisterClass (&wcl))
            return 0;
DWORD dwWindowStyle = WS_SYSMENU;
DWORD dwCreationWidth = 640;
DWORD dwHeight = 480;
RECT rc;
SetRect(&rc, 0, 0, dwWidth, dwHeight);
AdjustWindowRect(&rc, dwWindowStyle, TRUE);
/* Step 3: Now that a window class has been registered,
                                    a window can be created. */
hwnd = CreateWindow(szWinName, /* name of window class */
                    "FAKE 4", /* title */
                    dwWindowStyle, /* window style - normal */
                      /* X coordinate - let Windows decide */
                    CW_USEDEFAULT,
                       /* y coordinate - let Windows decide */
                     CW_USEDEFAULT,
                    (rc.right - rc.left), /*   */
                    (rc.bottom - rc.top), /*   */
                    HWND_DESKTOP, /* no parent window */
                     NULL, /* no menu */
                       /* handle of this instance of the program */
                    hThisInst,
                     NULL /* no additional arguments */
                    );
/* Step 4: Display the window. */
ShowWindow(hwnd, nWinMode);
BOOL bGotMsg;
/* Step 5: Create the message loop. */
while (WM_QUIT != msg.message)
{
        if( bActive)
                bGotMsg = PeekMessage (&msg, NULL,
                                    OU, OU, PM_REMOVE);
        else
                bGotMsg = GetMessage (&msg, NULL,
                                    OU, OU);
        if(bGotMsg)
        {
                /* allow use of keyboard */
                TranslateMessage(&msg);
                /* return control to Windows */
                DispatchMessage(&msg);
```

```
                    }
                    else
                    {
                            if(bActive)
                                Render();
                    }
            }
            return msg.wParam;
}
//------------------------------------------------
// Name: WndProc
// Desc: This function is called by Windows and is passed
//                      messages from the message queue
//------------------------------------------------
LRESULT CALLBACK WndProc(HWND hwnd, UINT message,
                        WPARAM wParam, LPARAM lParam)

{
        switch (message)
        {
                case WM_DESTROY: /* terminate the program */
                        PostQuitMessage(WM_QUIT);
                 break;
                case WM_KEYDOWN:
                {
                            switch (wParam)
                            {
                            case VK_ESCAPE:
                                    PostQuitMessage(WM_QUIT);
                             break;
                            case VK_F1:
                            {
                             bActive = FALSE;
                             MessageBox( hwnd,
"Here comes your help text",
                                "Help for FAKE 4", MB_ICONQUESTION|
MB_OK | MB_SYSTEMMODAL );
                             bActive = TRUE;
                            }
                            break;
                            }
                }
        }
   return DefWindowProc(hwnd, message, wParam, lParam);
}
//------------------------------------------------
// Name: Render
```

```
// Desc: dummy function to show the use of the enhanced skeleton
//-------------------------------------------------
VOID Render()
{
};
```

You will find the first enhancements just before Step 3.

```
DWORD dwWindowStyle = WS_POPUP | WS_CAPTION;
DWORD dwWidth = 640;
DWORD dwHeight = 480;
RECT rc;
SetRect(&rc, 0, 0, dwWidth, dwHeight);
AdjustWindowRect(&rc, dwWindowStyle, TRUE);
```

You define a window style only with a title bar. It should be 640×480 pixels. SetRect() sets the coordinates of the specified rectangle. AdjustWindowRect() calculates the required size of the window rectangle, based on the desired client rectangle size, so you really get a client window size of 640×480. The real stuff is located in the message loop in Step 5.

```
/* Step 5: Create the message loop. */
while (WM_QUIT != msg.message)
{
      if( bActive)
              bGotMsg = PeekMessage (&msg, NULL, OU, OU, PM_REMOVE);
      else
              bGotMsg = GetMessage (&msg, NULL, OU, OU);
      if(bGotMsg)
      {
              TranslateMessage(&msg); /* allow use of keyboard */
              DispatchMessage(&msg); /* return control to Windows */
      }
      else
      {
              if(bActive)
              Render();
      }
}
```

When the application is active, PeekMessage() returns to the application with NULL when there is no message in the message queue. When the application is inactive, GetMessage() puts the application to sleep when there is no message in the message queue. TranslateMessage() and DispatchMessage() are only called when a message has worn out. Render() is only called when the application is active. I made a small example for cases when the application is not active (see Figure A.4).

```
case VK_F1:
{
      bActive = FALSE;
```

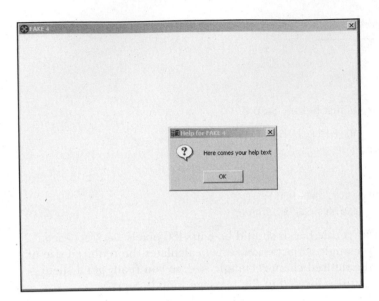

Figure A.4

Window skeleton 2

```
            MessageBox( hwnd, "Here comes your help text",
                "Help for FAKE 4", MB_ICONQUESTION|MB_OK | MB_SYSTEMMODAL );
            bActive = TRUE;
    }
        break;
```

If the message box appears, bActive is FALSE and Render() is not called.

That's it. I hope you got the idea of how to set up window code for use in games. You will not use much window code because in full-screen games you must build all the dialog boxes by hand. Usually window dialog boxes don't fit into games.

Windows Resources

In the beginning of Windows programming, all programmers had to set resources by hand. Nowadays, the Visual C/C++ integrated development environment helps a lot. You have to work through the following steps to build and include resources:

1. Select File, New, Resource Script.

2. Give your script a nice name, such as winskel (see Figure A.5). Click on OK. The new resource file will be named winskel.rc.

3. Now click on the Resource View tab in your workspace, then right-click on winskel resources.

4. Click on Insert (see Figure A.6). A dialog box will appear so you can choose a resource (see Figure A.7).

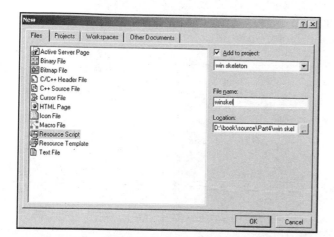

Figure A.5

Creating a resource script

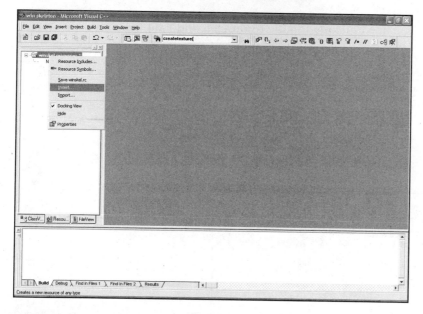

Figure A.6

Insert a resource

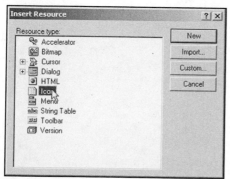

Figure A.7

Create an icon

I produced an icon with the help of the standard directx.ico by using a blue color as the background and transparent for the foreground color (see Figure A.8).

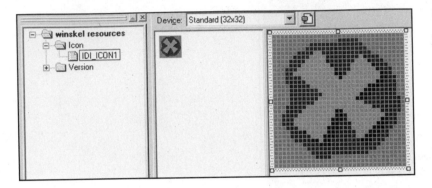

Figure A.8

Coloring an icon

5. To load the icon, you must include the file resource.h and load the icon with

    ```
    wcl.hIcon = LoadIcon(hThisInst, MAKEINTRESOURCE(IDI_ICON1)); /* icon style */
    ```

6. I also chose to create a version control resource (see Figure A.9). Using a version control resource helps you arrange different versions of your program and hold your copyright information in the .exe file.

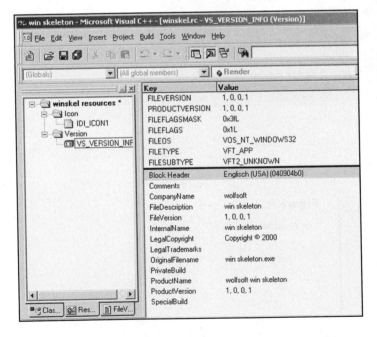

Figure A.9

Creating a version control resource

7. Oh yes, a special cursor would be nice. Click on the Resource View tab in your work-space, right-click on winskel resources, and then choose Cursor (see Figure A.10).

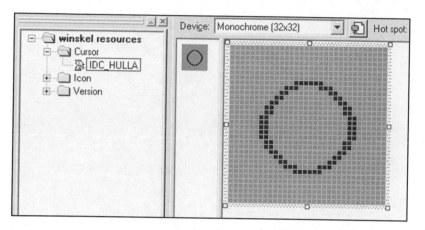

Figure A.10

Cursor production

So you have three resources for your simple skeleton (see Figure A.11).

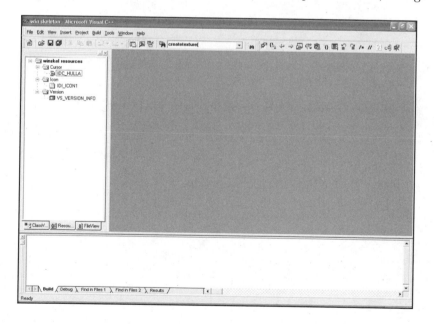

Figure A.11

Three resources

So now you know how to build your first skeleton with resources. Whereas you have to enter all of the skeleton code by hand in the Visual C/C++ editor, you get a lot of help when you create resources from the IDE.

APPENDIX B

C++ PRIMER

A few years ago, there were a lot of discussions going around in the newsgroups about using C or C++ in games. One faction said that C produces faster code and named games such as *Quake* and *Unreal* as proof. The other faction said that C++ is more elegant, helps structure your game better, and is economically cheaper when used by production teams.

Practice—as always—leads to the practical solution: Take the speed of C and the ability to structure game code from C++. I suppose many game programmers don't use much C++ stuff. If you take a look at the examples in the DirectX SDK, you will see a lot of C++ code and traditional C code.

This appendix covers a host of topics, including:

- A brief explanation of the uses and features of object-oriented programming
- An overview of some C++ keywords and data types that aren't available in C or that are used differently in C++ and C
- Creating and using classes, or how the C-language structure has evolved into the C++ class—one of the cornerstones of object-oriented programming in C++
- Other C++ programming techniques such as access specifiers; operators for accessing member methods and member variables of classes, constructors, and destructors; copy constructors; and the this pointer

What Is Object-Oriented Programming?

In an object-oriented view of programming, a program describes a system of objects interacting. This is contrary to a procedure-oriented view of programming, in which a program describes a series of steps to be performed.

Object-oriented programming involves a few key concepts. The most basic of these is abstraction, which simplifies writing large programs. Another is encapsulation, which makes it easier to change and maintain a program. The concept of class hierarchies is a powerful classification tool that can make a program easily extensible.

To understand C++ as an object-oriented language, you have to understand how C++ takes advantage of these concepts.

Abstraction

Abstraction is the process of ignoring details in order to concentrate on essential things. A so-called high-level programming language supports a high level of abstraction. The usual example is the comparison of a program written in assembly and one written in C. The assembly source contains a very detailed description of what the computer does to perform the task, whereas the C source gives a much more abstract description of what the computer does; that abstraction makes the program clearer and easier to understand.

All procedural languages support procedural abstraction, in which a piece of source code is put into a function and reused this way. For example, consider matrix multiplication:

```
FLOAT  pM[16];
    ZeroMemory( pM, sizeof(D3DXMATRIX) );
    for( WORD i=0; i<4; i++ )
        for( WORD j=0; j<4; j++ )
            for( WORD k=0; k<4; k++ )
                pM[4*i+j] +=  pM1[4*i+k] * pM2[4*k+j];
    memcpy( pOut, pM, sizeof(D3DXMATRIX) );
```

You wouldn't want to write this piece of code every time two 4×4 matrices have to be multiplied. Instead, you abstract it by embedding it in a function call like this:

```
D3DXMATRIX* D3DXMatrixMultiply (D3DXMATRIX* pOut,

                                              CONST D3DXMATRIX* pM1,
                                              CONST D3DMATRIX* pM2)
{
    FLOAT  pM[16];
    ZeroMemory( pM, sizeof(D3DXMATRIX) );
    for( WORD i=0; i<4; i++ )
        for( WORD j=0; j<4; j++ )
            for( WORD k=0; k<4; k++ )
                pM[4*i+j] +=  pM1[4*i+k] * pM2[4*k+j];
    memcpy( pOut, pM, sizeof(D3DXMATRIX) );
  return (pOut);
}
```

Using D3DXMatrixMultiply() will lead to more readable and understandable source code and will save you a lot of typing.

You already know about data abstraction, which lets you ignore details of how a data type is represented. The C language provides data types like int or float, which let you type in something like 42.5, rather than hexadecimal bytes. Thankfully, floating-point arithmetic performed in binary is something that C programmers don't have to worry about. On the other hand, C does not support the abstraction of strings because it requires you to manipulate strings as a series of characters.

But C supports user-defined data abstraction through structures and typedefs. Programmers might use structures to manipulate several pieces of information as a unit instead of individually.

```
Struct Mesh
{
   char cName[68];                  // 65 chars, 32-bit aligned == 68 chars in file
   int iNumVertices;                // Mesh vertices
   int iMeshFrameNum;               // animation frames in mesh
   VMESHFRAME *vMeshFrames;         // stores vertices per animation frame in
                                    // vertices[FrameNum][VertexNum]
   int iNumTriangles;               // Mesh triangles
   TRIANGLEVERT *pTriangles;
   int iNumTextures;                // Mesh textures
   TEXNAMES *pTexNames;
   LPDIRECT3DTEXTURE8* pTexturesInterfaces;
   TEXCOORDS *pfTextureCoords;      // Mesh tex coordinates
   TEXCOORDS *pfEnvTextureCoords;   // not used here
};
```

This user-defined data type lets you manipulate the variables in a more understandable way. For example:

```
Mesh.iNumVertices = 5;
```

But there is no conceptual advantage. You get a better data abstraction by defining data types and data structures with typedef.

```
typedef int TRIANGLEVERT[3];
typedef char TEXNAMES[68];
typedef D3DXVECTOR3 *VMESHFRAME;
typedef struct
{
   float u;
   float v;
} TEXCOORDS;
typedef struct
{
char cName[68];                     // 65 chars, 32-bit aligned == 68 chars in file
int iNumVertices;                   // Mesh vertices
int iMeshFrameNum;                  // animation frames in mesh
VMESHFRAME *vMeshFrames;            // stores vertices per animation frame in\
                                    // vertices[FrameNum][VertexNum]
   int iNumTriangles;               // Mesh triangles
   TRIANGLEVERT *pTriangles;
   int iNumTextures;                // Mesh textures
   TEXNAMES *pTexNames;
```

```
LPDIRECT3DTEXTURE8* pTexturesInterfaces;
TEXCOORDS *pfTextureCoords;          // Mesh tex coordinates
TEXCOORDS *pfEnvTextureCoords;       // not used here
} MD3MESH;
```

Now MD3MESH is an abstract data type that might be used in combination with functions as their parameter. These functions handle the details of filling the specific fields.

This traditional procedural approach lets you view data abstraction and procedural abstraction as two distinct techniques. A more elegant way would be to link them. The following section describes the object-oriented programming approach, which uses classes.

Classes

A class combines procedural and data abstraction by describing everything about a high-level entity at once. Think of the CMD3 class, for example, which holds all of the geometry data and texture interface pointers for as many .md3 models as you want.

```
class CMD3Model
{
 private:
    int                    iNumMeshes;
    MD3MESH                *pMd3Meshes;
    MD3BONEFRAM            *md3BoneFrame;
    MD3TAG                 **md3Tags;
    FILE *LogFile;                         // the log file for md3 geometry data.txt
                                           // and md3 textures.txt
    LPDIRECT3DVERTEXBUFFER8 m_pVB;         // Buffer to hold vertices
    long ReadLong(FILE* File);            // file i/o helper
    short ReadShort(FILE* File);
    FLOAT ReadFloat(FILE* File);
    void CreateVB(LPDIRECT3DDEVICE8 lpD3Ddevice);          // vertex buffer system
    void DeleteVB();
    void CreateTextures(LPDIRECT3DDEVICE8 lpD3Ddevice);  // texture system
    void DeleteTextures();
 public:
    // class methods
    BOOL CreateModel( char *fname, LPDIRECT3DDEVICE8 lpD3Ddevice);
    void DeleteModel();
    void InitDeviceObjects(LPDIRECT3DDEVICE8 lpD3Ddevice);
    void DeleteDeviceObjects();
    void Render(LPDIRECT3DDEVICE8 lpD3Ddevice);
      CMD3Model();                         // constructor/destructor
     ~CMD3Model();
};
```

Classes make it easy for you to create an additional layer of separation between your program and the computer. The high-level entities you define have the same advantages that floating-point numbers and print statements have when compared to bytes and MOV instructions.

This class is only accessible through five methods: CreateModel(), DeleteModel(), InitDeviceObjects(), DeleteDeviceObjects(), and Render(). There is no way to access variables from outside the class. This leads to another advantage of object-oriented programming—encapsulation.

> **NOTE**
> The keyword-protected label enables you to make members visible to derived classes but not to the user. You can give derived classes more information about your class than you give users.

Encapsulation

Encapsulation is the process of hiding the internal workings of a class to support or enforce abstraction. This requires drawing a sharp distinction between a class's interface, which has public visibility, and its implementation, which has private visibility. These are expressed by the private: and public: labels.

A class interface describes what a class can do, while its implementation describes how it does it. A user views an object in terms of the operations it can perform, not in terms of its data structure.

> **NOTE**
> The C++ encapsulation does not provide a guarantee of safety. A programmer who is intent on using a class's private data can always use the & and * operators to gain access to it.

A truly encapsulated class surrounds or hides its data with its functions so that you can access the data only by calling the functions. An illustration might look like Figure B.1. On the left are the public data members, and on the right are the private data members.

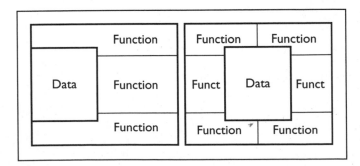

Figure B.1

Data encapsulation with functions (public vs. private data members)

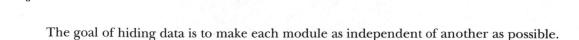

The goal of hiding data is to make each module as independent of another as possible. Ideally, a module has no knowledge of the data structures used by other modules, and it refers to those modules only through their interfaces.

As you saw earlier, this is the case in the CMD3 class. Even if the class interface changes in the future, it is still a good idea to use an encapsulated class rather than accessible data structures. You can add the changes to the interface through the existing interface. For example, if the older interface is Direct3D7, you might add Direct3D8. Any code that uses the old interface still works correctly.

After all this theory, you probably want a little bit of practice.

Declaring a Class

Let's start where we left off in Appendix A, by building a C++ version of the window skeleton program. As usual, you start with a piece of source:

```
#ifndef APP_H
#define APP_H
class Capp
{
protected:
            TCHAR* m_strWindowTitle;
            DWORD m_dwWidth;
            DWORD m_dwHeight;
private:
            BOOL m_bActive;
            HRESULT Render();
public:
            // used in Fake.cpp to create, run and pause fake
            virtual HRESULT Create (HINSTANCE hInstance);
            virtual LRESULT MsgProc (HWND hWnd, UINT uMsg,
                                     WPARAM wParam, LPARAM lParam);
            virtual WPARAM Run();
            virtual VOID Pause(BOOL bPause);
            // internal constructor
            CApp();
};
#endif
```

You will find the class declaration in the app.h header file, which you can find in the win skeleton++ directory in the example source code directories.

The

```
#ifndef APP_H
#define APP_H
...
#endif
```

preprocessor directives are used for conditional compilation. This prevents multiple inclusions of header files in a multi-module program. The class declaration looks similar to a structure declaration, except that its members include both functions and data, instead of just data. It declares the following:

- The contents of each instance of CApp, including the window title, width and height, and the status of rendering
- The prototypes of five methods that you can use with the data

I supplied the definitions of the member functions in App.cpp:

```cpp
#define STRICT
#include <windows.h>
#include <windowsx.h>
#include <tchar.h>
#include "App.h"
#include "resource.h"
//-------------------------------------------
// global this pointer
//-------------------------------------------
static CApp* g_pCApp = NULL;
//-------------------------------------------
// Name: FAKEApp()
// Desc: Constructor
//-------------------------------------------
CApp::CApp()
{
            g_pCApp = this;
            m_bActive = FALSE;
            m_strWindowTitle = _T("FAKE 4");
            m_dwWidth = 640;
            m_dwHeight = 480;
}
//-------------------------------------------
// Name: WndProc()
// Desc: static msg handler which passes messages to the application class
//                              in the fake.cpp file
//-------------------------------------------
LRESULT CALLBACK WndProc (HWND hWnd, UINT uMsg, WPARAM wParam, LPARAM lParam)
{
            return g_pCApp->MsgProc (hWnd, uMsg, wParam, lParam);
}
//-------------------------------------------
// Name: Create()
// Desc: static msg handler which passes messages to the application class
//                              in the fake.cpp file
//-------------------------------------------
```

```
HRESULT CApp::Create(HINSTANCE hThisInst)
{
  HWND hwnd;
  /* Step 1: Define a window class. */
  WNDCLASS wcl;
  wcl.hInstance = hThisInst; /* handle to this instance */
  wcl.lpszClassName = _T("Crusher") ; /* window class name */
  wcl.lpfnWndProc = WndProc; /* window function */
  wcl.style = 0; /* default style */
  /* icon style */
  wcl.hIcon = LoadIcon(hThisInst, MAKEINTRESOURCE(IDI_ICON1));
  /* cursor style */
  wcl.hCursor = LoadCursor( hThisInst, MAKEINTRESOURCE(IDC_HULLA));
  wcl.lpszMenuName = NULL; /* no menu */
  wcl.cbClsExtra = 0; /* no extra */
  wcl.cbWndExtra = 0; /* information needed */
  /* Make the window background white. */
  wcl.hbrBackground = (HBRUSH) GetStockObject(WHITE_BRUSH) ;
  /* Step 2: Register the window class. */
  if(!RegisterClass (&wcl))
            return 0;
  DWORD dwWindowStyle = WS_POPUP | WS_CAPTION | WS_VISIBLE | WS_SYSMENU;
  RECT rc;
  SetRect(&rc, 0, 0, m_dwWidth, m_dwHeight);
  AdjustWindowRect(&rc, dwWindowStyle, TRUE);
  /* Step 3: Now that a window class has been registered,
              a window can be created. */
  hwnd = CreateWindow(_T("Crusher"), /* name of window class */
            m_strWindowTitle, /* title */
            dwWindowStyle, /* window style - normal */
            CW_USEDEFAULT, /* X coordinate - let Windows decide */
            CW_USEDEFAULT, /* y coordinate - let Windows decide */
            (rc.right - rc.left), /*   */
            (rc.bottom - rc.top), /*   */
            HWND_DESKTOP, /* no parent window */
            NULL, /* no menu */
            hThisInst, /* handle of this instance of the program */
            NULL /* no additional arguments */
            );
  /* Step 4: Display the window. */
  //ShowWindow(hwnd, nWinMode); // obsolete because of the use of WS_VISIBLE
  return S_OK;
}
//-------------------------------------
// Name: MsgProc()
// Desc: Message handling function
```

```
//--------------------------------------
LRESULT CApp::MsgProc(HWND hWnd, UINT message, WPARAM wParam, LPARAM lParam)
{
  switch (message)
  {
    case WM_CLOSE:
    case WM_DESTROY:
            PostQuitMessage(WM_QUIT);
      break;
  }
  return DefWindowProc(hWnd, message, wParam, lParam);
}
//--------------------------------------
// Name: Render()
// Desc: Render the app
//--------------------------------------
VOID CApp::Render()
{
            // do anything
}
//--------------------------------------
// Name: Pause()
// Desc: Sets bActive
//--------------------------------------
VOID CApp::Pause(BOOL bPause)
{
            m_bActive = bPause? 0 : 1;
}
//--------------------------------------
// Name: Run()
// Desc: Message Loop and render method
//--------------------------------------
WPARAM CApp::Run()
{
            BOOL bGotMsg;
            MSG msg;
            PeekMessage (&msg, NULL, OU, OU, PM_REMOVE);
            /* Step 5: Create the message loop. */
            while (WM_QUIT != msg.message)
            {
                  if( m_bActive)
                        bGotMsg = PeekMessage (&msg, NULL, OU, OU, PM_REMOVE);
                  else
                        bGotMsg = GetMessage (&msg, NULL, OU, OU);
                        if(bGotMsg)
                        {
```

```
                    TranslateMessage(&msg); /* allow use of keyboard */
                    DispatchMessage(&msg); /* return control to Windows */
                    }
                    else
                    {
                        if(m_bActive)
                                Render();
                    }
                }
            return msg.wParam;
}
```

As you might have noticed, I used Pause() to encapsulate the m_bActive variable. But now let's move on to the constructor.

The Constructor

The constructor ensures that objects always contain valid values. A *constructor* is a special initialization function that is called automatically whenever an instance of your class is declared. It prevents errors resulting from the use of uninitialized objects and checks whether a value is out of range. It must have the same name as the class itself. You aren't required to use constructors, but it is generally a good idea.

I initialized all members—g_pCApp, m_bActive, m_strWindowTitle, m_dwWidth, and m_dwHeight—in CApp(). Constructors create objects and do not return values.

You can declare more than one constructor for a class if each constructor has a different parameter list. These are called *overloaded constructors*, and they are useful if you want to initialize your object in more than one way. I will show you how to overload constructors in a few seconds.

The Destructor

The counterpart to the constructor is the *destructor*. Its purpose is to perform any cleanup work necessary before an object is destroyed. The destructor's name is the class name with a tilde (~) as a prefix. It is a member function that is called automatically when a class object goes out of scope.

What is scope? I will give you a simple example.

```
int number = 123;
VOID ShowMeANumber()
{
    int number = 456;
    Showme (::number);
    Showme (number);
}
```

You will see

```
123
456
```

as an output. There is a global variable called *number* and a local variable called *number*. In both cases, C will use the local variable. You might use the scope operator : : to get the global variable in C++. So scope is the range of the class.

The scope operator is also used to access member functions, so it appears between the name of the class and the name of a function in a C++ program:

```
VOID CApp::Render()
```

This means that the specified function is a member of the specified class.

Now back to destructors. I have not used a destructor here because they are usually required for more complicated classes, where they are used to release dynamically allocated resources. A destructor cannot be overloaded. It takes no parameters and has no return value.

The this Pointer

There's one interesting variable in the constructor of win skeleton++—g_pCApp. It is used as a so-called this pointer. When you call a member function for an object, the compiler assigns the address of the object to the this pointer, and then calls the function. Every time a member function accesses one of the class's data members, it is implicitly using the this pointer. Type in the following code to build an example:

```
void CApp::Render (BOOL active)
{
    BOOL bPause;
    bPause = active;
}
myApp.Render(FALSE);
```

This is equivalent to

```
void CApp::Render (BOOL active)
{
    BOOL bPause;
    this->bPause = active;
// or (*this).pause = active
}
myApp.Render(FALSE);
```

Both statements in Render() are equivalent. Why do you need a this pointer? The answer lies in WinProc(). You want to call MsgProc() in any derived class. Because you can't know the name of a class used in the future, you have to use the this pointer. The derived class' MsgProc() will override the MsgProc() in the base class. In this example, MsgProc() is located in the MyFrame class, so the calling order would look like Figure B.2.

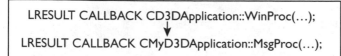

Figure B.2

Message procedures

This is also called *static binding*, and it is a possible way to avoid virtual functions that you will smell in a few seconds.

You might also use a `this` pointer to avoid self-assignment. For example:

```
void String::operator= (const String &other)
{
  if (&other == this)
    return;
...
}
```

This method exits without doing anything if a self-assignment is attempted. To summarize this piece of code, you can say that to encapsulate all of the data, the variables are labeled private, so every variable must be accessed by a member function. To be sure that every variable has a valid value, you use a constructor that initializes them. The `this` pointer is used to access functions in derived classes.

This brings you to the next fundamental principle of object-oriented programming, class hierarchies and inheritance.

Class Hierarchies and Inheritance

One standalone feature of object-oriented programming is class hierarchy. In C++ you can define one class as a subtype or special category of another class by deriving them all from one base class. This is not possible with C, which treats all types as completely independent of one another.

The benefits of defining a class hierarchy are code sharing and interface sharing. The derived class shares the code and/or the interface of the base class. The example program uses both.

Inheriting Code

You might reduce redundant code by deriving a class from a base class. An example of inheriting code is a program that maintains a database of all the aliens in a game.

It would not be a good idea to use a C structure called `alien` because each type of alien requires slightly different information. You wouldn't define a structure type for each type of alien; it would be a waste of space to include all possible fields in one structure. Unions would help, but the resulting C program would be difficult to read and maintain.

It's easier to do this in C++ with a base class and derived classes. The following pseudocode provides an example:

```
class CAlien
{
public:
     CAlien();
     VOID Attack(HUMAN human);
     VOID RunTo(WAYPOINT waypoint);
     VOID SetHealth(DWORD dwHealth);
     DWORD GetHealth ();
Private:
     char cName[32];
     DWORD dwHealth;
}
```

> **NOTE**
> With the keyword `private`, the public and protected members of the base class are private members of the derived class, so they are only accessible to the derived class.

For simplicity, this `CAlien` class stores only a few values; in real life, there might be many more. Assume that there are different aliens that can fly, only crouch, only swim, or teleport. Some of them bite, fire weapons at humans, or perform magic.

```
class CMagician : public CAlien
{
public:
    Magician();
    VOID SetGlow(BOOL bGlow);
private:
    BOOL bGlow;
}
or
class CFrankenstein : class CAlien
{
public:
    Frankenstein();
    VOID StruckByLightning(BOOL bStruck);
private:
    BOOL bStruck;
}
```

`CMagician` and `CFrankenstein` are derived classes from the base class `CAlien`. To declare a derived class, you follow its name with a colon and the keyword `public`, followed by the name of its base class.

In the declaration of the derived class, you declare the members that are specific to it by describing the additional qualities that distinguish it from the base class. Each instance of `CFrankenstein` contains all of the `CAlien` data members in addition to its own (see Figure B.3).

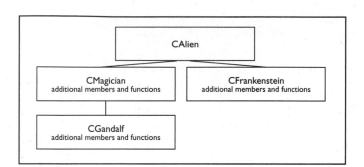

Figure B.3

Class hierarchy

The member functions of a derived class do not have access to the private members of its base class, so the derived class has to use the base class's public interface to access the private members of its base class.

If you use different magicians with, for example, different levels and kinds of magic, you might derive special magicians from CMagician.

```
class CGandalf : CMagician
{
public:
    CGandalf();
    VOID TellWisdoms(HUMAN bHuman);
    SetWeakness(WORD wWeakness);
private:
    char cWisdoms[32][128];
    WORD wWeakness;
}
```

This means that CMagician is both a derived and a base class. It derives from the CAlien class and serves as the base for the CGandalf class. You can define as many levels of inheritance as you want. In the win skeleton++ example, you only derive CMyFrame from CApp in Fake.cpp:

```
#define STRICT
#include <windows.h>
#include <tchar.h>
#include "App.h"
//-------------------------------------------
// Name: class App
// Desc: Main class to run this application. Most functionality is inherited
//       from the App base class.
//-------------------------------------------
class CMyFrame : public CApp
{
public:
    LRESULT MsgProc (HWND hWnd, UINT uMsg, WPARAM wParam, LPARAM lParam);
    CMyFrame();  // constructor
};
```

```
//--------------------------------------------
// Name: WinMain()
// Desc: Entry point to the program. Initializes everything, and goes into a
//        message-processing loop. Idle time is used to render the scene.
//--------------------------------------------
INT WINAPI WinMain( HINSTANCE hInst, HINSTANCE, LPSTR, INT )
{
    CMyFrame d3dApp;
    if( FAILED( d3dApp.Create( hInst ) ) )
        return 0;
    return d3dApp.Run();
}
//--------------------------------------------
// Name: CMyD3DApplication()
// Desc: Constructor
//--------------------------------------------
CMyFrame::CMyFrame()
{
    // Override base class members
    m_strWindowTitle    = _T("Fake 4 ++");
    m_dwWidth = 400;
    m_dwHeight = 300;
}
//--------------------------------------------
// Name: MsgProc()
// Desc: message procedure
//--------------------------------------------
LRESULT CMyFrame::MsgProc(HWND hWnd, UINT message, WPARAM wParam, LPARAM lParam)
{
    if (message == WM_KEYDOWN)
    {
        switch (wParam)
        {
            case VK_ESCAPE:
                PostQuitMessage(WM_QUIT);
            break;
            case VK_F1:
            {
                    Pause(TRUE);
                    MessageBox( hWnd, "Here comes your help text",
                            "Help for FAKE 4++", MB_ICONQUESTION|MB_OK |
                                            MB_SYSTEMMODAL );
                                    Pause(FALSE);
            }
            break;
        }
```

```
        }
    return CApp::MsgProc( hWnd, message, wParam, lParam );
}
```

CFrame uses its own MsgProc() and its own constructor. Three base class members are over-written there.

A class hierarchy designed for code sharing has most of its code in the base classes. This way, many classes can reuse the code. The derived classes represent specialized or extended versions of the base class.

Inheriting an Interface

You might inherit just the names of the base class's member functions, not the code. This is called inheriting an interface. What's the idea behind that?

Think of the CAlien class, which is used to inherit all of those different alien classes. You might be able to use the derived alien classes as generic CAlien objects when all of the derived classes share its interface.

That's as far as I'm going to go with classes and inheritance. I don't want to dig deeper into this kind of stuff. There are a few things I left out; try to invest time to learn them using the resources in the "Additional Resources" section at the end of this appendix.

Virtual Functions

When you call a virtual function through a pointer to a base class, the derived class's version of the function is executed. This is the opposite behavior of ordinary member functions.

A pointer to a derived class object may be assigned to a base class pointer and a virtual function called through the pointer. If the function is virtual and occurs both in the base class and the derived class, the correct function will be picked up based on what the base class pointer really points at.

You declare a virtual function by placing the keyword virtual before the declaration of the member function in the base class. All of the public interface methods in d3dapp.h of the common files framework are virtual functions.

```
virtual HRESULT ConfirmDevice(D3DCAPS8*,DWORD,D3DFORMAT)    { return S_OK; }
virtual HRESULT OneTimeSceneInit()                         { return S_OK; }
virtual HRESULT InitDeviceObjects()                        { return S_OK; }
virtual HRESULT RestoreDeviceObjects()                     { return S_OK; }
virtual HRESULT FrameMove()                                { return S_OK; }
virtual HRESULT Render()                                   { return S_OK; }
virtual HRESULT InvalidateDeviceObjects()                  { return S_OK; }
virtual HRESULT DeleteDeviceObjects()                      { return S_OK; }
virtual HRESULT FinalCleanup()                             { return S_OK; }
```

They are called from the derived class in your main file. This could be, for example, .md3viewer.cpp.

```
HRESULT CMyD3DApplication::RestoreDeviceObjects()
{
   return S_OK;
}
```

This method is called in d3dapp.cpp by the base class.

```
HRESULT CD3DApplication::Resize3DEnvironment()
{
...
// Initialize the app's device-dependent objects
hr = RestoreDeviceObjects();
if( FAILED(hr) )
     return hr;
...
     return S_OK;
}
```

So calling `RestoreDeviceObjects()` in the base class method `Resize3Denvironment()` leads to a call to the derived class function `RestoreDeviceObjects()` in .md3viewer.cpp.

The `virtual` keyword is only necessary in the declaration in the base class.

Using virtual functions is also called *dynamic binding* because the compiler must evaluate the statement at run time, when it can tell what type of object it gets.

You're probably asking yourself a typical question: "Well that's nice, but how much overhead is involved?" Calling a virtual function takes only slightly longer than calling a normal function.

A trick to reduce the overhead is to use static binding. I have done that with the `MsgProc()` function.

```
static CApp* g_pCApp = NULL;
CApp::CApp()
{
           g_pCApp = this;
...
}
LRESULT CALLBACK WndProc (HWND hWnd, UINT uMsg, WPARAM wParam, LPARAM lParam)
{
           return g_pCApp->MsgProc (hWnd, uMsg, wParam, lParam);
}
```

To summarize: Virtual functions are an elegant way to call functions in the derived class from within base class. The dynamic binding used comes with a small overhead. The inelegant but efficient way is to use static binding with no overhead.

Polymorphism

The ability to call member functions for an object without specifying the object's exact type is called *polymorphism.* This means that a single statement can invoke many different functions. Let's build an example. Suppose you are interested in checking the health of all aliens so you can compare their health with the health of all humans.

In C you have to use a `switch` statement to find the exact type of alien. This might look like the following code:

```
DWORD ComputeHealth (struct ALIEN *alien)
{
        switch (alien->type)
        {
           case Magician:
               return alien.dwhealth;
           break;

           case Frankenstein:
             return alien.dwhealth;
           break;

           …
        };
}
```

In C++ you can call the following function:

```
DWORD ComputeHealth (CALIEN *alien)
{
    return alien->GetHealth();
}
```

The C++ version of `ComputeHealth()` calls the appropriate function automatically, without requiring you to examine the type of object that alien points to. There is a tiny amount of overhead, as described in the section on virtual functions, but no `switch` statement is needed.

Inline Functions

Game programmers can optimize performance by using `inline` functions. The `inline` keyword causes a new copy of the function to be inserted in each place it is called. If you call an `inline` function from 21 places in your program, the compiler will insert 21 copies of that function into your .exe file.

`Inline` eliminates the overhead of calling a function. This makes your program run faster, but having multiple copies of a function can make the program larger. `Inline` is similar to macros declared with the `#define` directive. The difference is that the compiler recognizes `inline` functions, and macros are implemented by a simple text substitution. But `inline` functions are more powerful. The compiler performs type-checking, and an `inline` function behaves just like an ordinary function, without any side effects that macros might have. An example might be:

```
#define MAX (A, B) ((A) > (B)? (A) : (B))
inline int max (int a, int b)
{
if (a > b)
  return a;
return b;
}
```

This is one of your favorite C++ features, isn't it? Well, experience has shown that all the things you like need more work and attention. This is also the case with the `inline` keyword.

Inlining only occurs if the compiler's cost/benefit analysis shows it to be profitable. A `_forceinline` keyword overrides the cost/benefit analysis and relies on the judgment of the programmer instead, but this might lead to performance losses if it's not properly used.

You cannot force the compiler to `inline` a function with `_forceinline` when conditions other than cost/benefit analysis prevent it. You cannot `inline` a function if:

- The function or its caller is compiled with /Ob0 (the default option for debug builds).
- The function and the caller use different types of exception handling (such as C++ exception handling in one and structured exception handling in the other).
- The function has a variable argument list.
- The function uses `inline` assembly and is not compiled with /Og, /Ox, /O1, or /O2.
- The function returns an unwindable object by value and is not compiled with /GX, /EHs, or /EHa.
- The function receives a copy-constructed object passed by the value when compiled with /GX, /EHs, or /EHa.
- The function is recursive and is not accompanied by `#pragma(inline_recursion, on)`. With the `pragma`, recursive functions can be `inlined` to a default depth of eight calls. To change the inlining depth, use `#pragma(inline_depth, n)`.

Check out your Visual C/C++ Compiler Reference for the meaning of the compiler directives. If the compiler cannot `inline` a function declared `_forceinline`, it will generate a Level 1 warning (4714).

You can find a typical example of how `inline` is used in the file d3dfont.cpp.

```
inline FONT2DVERTEX InitFont2DVertex( const D3DXVECTOR4& p, D3DCOLOR color,
                                      FLOAT tu, FLOAT tv )
{
    FONT2DVERTEX v;    v.p = p;    v.color = color;    v.tu = tu;
v.tv = tv;     return v;
}
```

This was the first one of the language enhancements of C++. Read on to take a look at a few others.

C++ Enhancements to C

C++ introduces some simple enhancements and improvements to C. I will explain the following C++ enhancements in this section:

- Default function arguments
- More flexible placement of variable declarations
- The const keyword
- Enumerations
- Function and operator overloading

Default Function Arguments

A C++ function prototype can list default values for some of the parameters.

```
VOID Pause(BOOL TRUE);
```

You might declare this in the header file. If you provide your own arguments, the compiler will use them instead of the declared defaults.

If you use a more complex example, it might look like this:

```
VOID DoSomething (DWORD w = 2; FLOAT f = 1.5);
```

You might call it in the following way:

```
DoSomething ( , 2.5);
```

In this example, the first value (w) is 2, and the second value (f) is 2.5. Another way to call it is like this:

```
DoSomething (3);
```

The first value (w) is 3, and the second value (f) is 1.5. Be careful: Syntax like this is error-prone and makes reading and writing function calls more difficult.

Placement of Variable Declarations

There is a big improvement in C++, about which I suspect you already know. C requires you to declare variables at the beginning of a block. C++ gives you the ability to declare variables anywhere in the code. A pseudocode function with C would look like this:

```
VOID Myfunction ()
{
  int z;
  AnotherFunction (d);
```

```
   doSomethingWith(z);
}
The same function with C++:
VOID Myfunction ()
{
  AnotherFunction (d);
  int z;
  doSomethingWith(z);
}
```

That's a big improvement because it is much easier to read the code when the variable and function are near each other. Another nice expression that is often used in C++ is

```
for (int z = 0; z < 5; z++)
{
// do something
}
```

But it is not possible to use the following statements:

```
if (int z == 0)
;
while (int j == 0)
```

Besides, they are meaningless!

Const Variable

As a rule of thumb, you can assume that wherever you can use a constant expression or would define a #define expression, you can use a const variable.

There is a difference between the const qualifier used by C and the one used in C++. In C you can initialize the const qualifier and use it in place of its value in your program. In C++ you can use consts in many different ways with pointers, references, and functions.

Most C programs define constant values using the #define preprocessor directive.

```
#define MAX_HEIGHT 800
```

The drawback is that the #define directive does not generate type-safe constants because it is just a preprocessor directive, not a compiler statement. When you generate a constant using #define, your constant has no data type, so your compiler has no way to ensure that operations on the constant are carried out properly—at design time, at run time, or even at debugging time.

In contrast, when you define a const in a C++ program, you execute a real compiler statement, such as this one:

```
const int MAX_HEIGHT 800
```

You can also use const in pointer declarations:

```
char *const ptr = cString;
```

You can change the value to which ptr points:

```
*ptr = 'a';
```

But you can't change the const value:

```
ptr = cString2;
```

It is another case if the pointer points to a constant:

```
Const char *ptr = cString;
ptr = cString2;
*ptr = 'a';
```

It's okay to change the pointer in the second row, but changing the value will give you an error message. You might use the const qualifier to prevent changing a parameter in a function.

```
int readonly (const struct NODE *nodeptr);
```

As you have seen, const is a powerful qualifier to make your programs more type-safe, so use it often.

Enumeration

An *enumeration* is an integral data type that defines a list of named constants. Each element of an enumeration has an integer value that, by default, is one greater than the value of the previous element. The first element has the value 0, unless you specify another value. The following example demonstrates how a C++ program can reference an enumeration:

```
enum color {yellow, orange, red, green };  // values 0, 1, 2, 4
enum day {Monday, Tuesday, Wednesday, Thursday = 8, Friday};  // values 0, 1, 2, 8, 9
```

You can convert an enumeration into an integer, but you cannot reverse conversion unless you use a cast. Casting an integer into an enumeration is not safe. If the integer is outside the range of the enumeration, or if the enumeration contains duplicate values, the result of the cast is undefined.

Function and Operator Overloading

C++ uses two kinds of overloading—function overloading and operator overloading. Both of these are major—and beneficial—features of the C++ language.

Function Overloading

To implement function overloading, you use two or more functions that share the same name but have different argument lists. The compiler decides which version to call by using argument matching. It compares the number of arguments and the types of arguments that are passed to the function.

Function overloading is often used in C++ because it imposes almost no run-time penalty and requires practically no overhead.

A special case of function overloading is constructor overloading. You find the following code snippet in d3dvec.inl:

```
inline
_D3DVECTOR::_D3DVECTOR(D3DVALUE f)
{
    x = y = z = f;
}
inline
_D3DVECTOR::_D3DVECTOR(D3DVALUE _x, D3DVALUE _y, D3DVALUE _z)
{
    x = _x; y = _y; z = _z;
}
inline
_D3DVECTOR::_D3DVECTOR(const D3DVALUE f[3])
{
    x = f[0]; y = f[1]; z = f[2];
}
```

Typical function overloading is used in the D3DXVECTOR3 initialization in d3dmath.inl.

```
D3DXINLINE
D3DXVECTOR3::D3DXVECTOR3( CONST FLOAT *pf )
{
#ifdef D3DX_DEBUG
    if(!pf)
        return;
#endif
    x = pf[0];
    y = pf[1];
    z = pf[2];
}
D3DXINLINE
D3DXVECTOR3::D3DXVECTOR3( CONST D3DVECTOR& v )
{
    x = v.x;
    y = v.y;
    z = v.z;
}
D3DXINLINE
D3DXVECTOR3::D3DXVECTOR3( FLOAT fx, FLOAT fy, FLOAT fz )
{
    x = fx;
    y = fy;
    z = fz;
}
```

These overloaded functions pursue the same target by using different parameters. You have to fill three variables—x, y, and z—with a value.

Complete vector/math libraries are built using function and operator overloading. By using function overloading, you can give the same name to member functions that perform different, but similar, operations. You can even give the same name to entire groups of functions.

Operator Overloading

With operator overloading, you can customize operators, such as the addition operator (+), the subtraction operator (–), the assignment operator (=), the increment and decrement operators (++ and ––), and many more to make the operators behave differently when they are used with objects of different classes. Such a self-defined operator is a dressed-up function.

To overload an operator in C++, you must define an operator overloading function (usually a member function). A function that overloads an operator always contains the keyword operator.

The syntax for operator overloading is

```
ReturnType operator @ (arguments)
                      {
                      // code
                      } // global function


ReturnType classname::operator @ (arguments)
                                 {
                                 // code
                                 } // class function
```

The @ sign is a replacement for the operator. The syntax

```
z = x @ y
```

is replaced by

```
z = operator @ (x, y)
```

or by

```
z = x.operator @(y);
```

A real-world example might look like this:

```
D3DXINLINE D3DXVECTOR3&
D3DXVECTOR3::operator += ( CONST D3DXVECTOR3& v )
{
    x += v.x;
    y += v.y;
    z += v.z;
    return *this;
}
```

This one adds the `D3DXVECTOR3` `v` structure to the `D3DVECTOR3` that stands on the left of the +=
operator.

```
z += v;
```

The operator += produces a new `D3DXVECTOR3` structure, which is returned. This temporary
structure is destroyed as soon as it is no longer needed.

Another nice example is

```
D3DXINLINE D3DXVECTOR3
operator * ( FLOAT f, CONST struct D3DXVECTOR3& v )
{
    return D3DXVECTOR3(f * v.x, f * v.y, f * v.z);
}
```

The syntax prototype of this one looks like this:

```
z = operator * (f, v)
```

The return value `D3DXVECTOR3(f * v.x, f * v.y, f * v.z)` is also a temporary structure.
Here you use the so-called returned value optimization. The compiler builds the object
directly into the location of the outside return value.

OK…I think you've got it. Take a look at the d3dxmath.inl file to play around with many
more examples.

You've reached the end of this short C++ primer. I tried to concentrate on the most important C++ features for game programmers. I left many things unsaid, and you should be sure
to look at the use of references and multi-inheritance. So…keep on learning.

Additional Resources

There is a free C++ book in HTML/PDF/PalmPilot format at http://www.mindview.net/
Books/TICPP/ThinkingInCPP2e.html.

Other C++ tutorials online are at http://www.intap.net/~drw/cpp/index.htm,
http://www.cplusplus.com/doc/tutorial, and
http://devcentral.iftech.com/articles/C++/default.php.

APPENDIX C

MATHEMATICS PRIMER

This appendix provides supplemental information to augment your understanding of the math and 3D concepts introduced in Parts One and Two of the book. I will jump-start the process of understanding mathematics for 3D by showing you how to rotate points in 3D.

Points in 3D

First imagine a point rotating in 2D space. The two axes make a plane that is like a piece of paper. This plane is called the x-y plane because it is defined by the two principal axes (see Figure C.1)

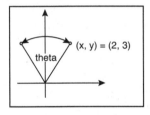

Figure C.1

Two-dimensional

coordinate system

To rotate a point counterclockwise by theta radians, you use the following formula:

```
x_new = x * cos(theta) - y * sin(theta)
y_new = x * sin(theta) + y * cos(theta)
```

OK, now let's jump into 3D…just add a third axis. Call it z; I think that's a nice name for an axis. The difference between 2D and 3D is that the z-axis introduces two new principal planes—the x-z plane and the y-z plane. Now the essence: You perform a full 3D rotation by rotating by a specified angle one plane at a time. Figure C.2 depicts the same rotation as shown in Figure C.1, only this time it's in 3D.

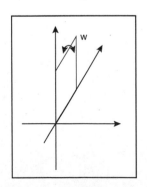

Figure C.2

Three-dimensional

coordinate system

To rotate a point w (x, y, z) counterclockwise by theta radians in a 3D system, you use the following formula:

```
x_new = x * cos(theta) - y * sin(theta)
y_new = x * sin(theta) + y * cos(theta)
z_new = z
```

It's nearly the same formula as earlier, but there is an additional z value.

The resulting point x_{new}, y_{new}, z_{new} is used as the source point for the next rotation. The next rotation might happen about the x-axis (see Figure C.3).

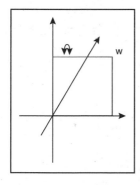

Figure C.3

Rotating about the

x-axis

To rotate a point w (x, y, z) by theta radians about the x-axis, you use the following formula:

```
x_new = x
y_new = y * cos(theta) - z * sin(theta)
z_new = y * sin(theta) + z * cos(theta)
```

Now take a look at a rotation about the y-axis (see Figure C.4).

To rotate a point w (x, y, z) by theta radians about the y-axis, you use the following formula:

```
x_new = x * cos(theta) - z * sin(theta)
y_new = y
z_new = x * sin(theta) + z * cos(theta)
```

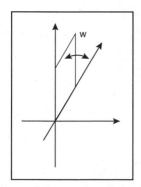

Figure C.4

Rotating about the

y-axis

To rotate a point w (x, y, z) in 3D space, you:

1. Rotate it in the x-y plane and store the results in x_{new}, y_{new}, z_{new}.

2. Rotate the resulting point around the y-z plane and store the results in x_2, y_2, z_2.

3. Rotate the resulting point around the z-x plane and store the results in x_{new}, y_{new}, and z_{new}.

A piece of pseudocode might look like this:

```
Xnew = x * cos(theta) - y * sin(theta)
Ynew = x * sin(theta) + y * cos(theta)
Znew = z
X2 = Xnew
Y2 = Ynew * cos(theta) - Znew * sin(theta)
Z2 = Ynew * sin(theta) + Znew * cos(theta)
Xnew = X2 * cos(theta) - Z2 * sin(theta)
Ynew = Y2
Znew = X2 * sin(theta) + Z2 * cos(theta)
```

To summarize 3D point rotation: To rotate a point in 3D, you have to rotate it around the three axes, one after another.

The translation of a point in 3D is much easier. Moving a point in a direction simply requires adding three offsets (representing the direction) to that point—one offset each for x, y, and z. For example, translating the point (2, 3, 0) to (8, 7, 0) requires adding (6, 4, 0) to each component.

Vectors

Vectors are mathematical entities that describe a direction and a magnitude (which might be speed). This is the difference between vectors and scalars, which describe a magnitude alone. A typical scalar value is, for example, the temperature 32 degrees Celsius. This information tells you everything about the temperature at that point. It is more difficult to describe the direction of an airplane and how fast it is going; this would be a job for a vector.

You can differentiate between a general-purpose, or *bound*, vector and the so-called *free* vector used in games.

Bound Vector

A bound vector V, as shown in Figure C.5, has the following attributes:

- A starting point
- A final point
- A direction
- A magnitude

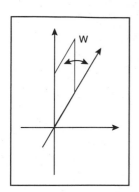

Figure C.5

Bound vector

A bound vector might look like Figure C.6 in the coordinate system.

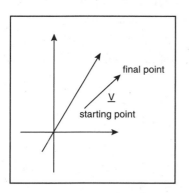

Figure C.6

A bound vector in coordinate system

A bound vector consists of two coordinates. You can see the direction of these vectors by drawing a line between the two coordinates; the distance between the points represents the magnitude. The first coordinate is called the starting point, and the second is the final point.

Free Vector

For game programmers, a vector has no starting point. If all points are moving in the same direction at the same speed, it would be inefficient to use a vector for each point. It is enough to describe the speed and direction for one vector that is used with all points. Therefore, you don't have to represent a starting point for a free vector.

By definition, the starting points of all free vectors are in the origin, so only three numbers are required to describe a free vector (see Figure C.7).

Oops...you might say, "That sounds like a point in 3D." To which I'd say, "That's an important remark." So what's the difference between a point and a vector in 3D? A free vector, as shown in Figure C.7, is represented additionally by magnitude and direction. The magnitude of a vector (2, 3, 2) is the distance between the origin (0, 0, 0) and the final point (2, 3, 2).

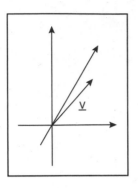

Figure C.7

Free vector in a coordinate system

If you only need the final point, then it is a 3D point. If you need magnitude and direction as well, then it is a vector. You might say a free vector describes a 3D point, but that is a more philosophical point of view. A 3D point might also be described as a null vector with magnitude 0.

Just like real values, you can use arithmetic operations on vectors. For example, you can add, subtract, and multiply them.

Vector Addition: U + V

To add two vectors, you have to add their components:

```
U (1, 3, 2) + V (2, 1, 2)
= Z (1 + 2, 3 + 1, 2 + 2)
= Z (3, 4, 4)
```

You can visualize this addition more easily in 2D space, so I'll skip the z value to keep it simple.

If you want to add vectors, as shown in Figure C.8, in a more visual way, you can lay the second vector V with its starting point at the final point of the vector U and draw the sum U + V between the starting point of U and the final point of V (see Figure C.9).

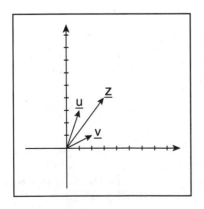

Figure C.8

Vector addition

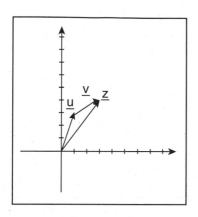

Figure C.9

Vector addition graphically

Vector additions are useful to show, for example, the drift you get if you are sailing a ship. Adding more vectors works the same way. Yet another important arithmetic function you can perform is subtraction.

Vector Subtraction: U – V

You subtract vectors by subtracting one vector's component from the other. Vector subtraction undoes vector addition. For example:

```
U (1, 3, 2) - V (2, 1, 2)
= Z (1 - (-2), 3 - 1, 2 - 2)
= Z (-1, 2, 0)
```

Simplified by using only the x and y values, that equation might look like Figure C.10.

If you want to subtract the two vectors in a visual way, you might multiply the vector V by –1 and add that to U (see Figure C.11).

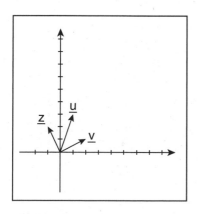

Figure C.10

Vector subtraction

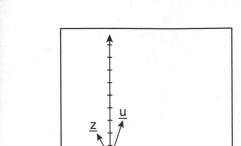

Figure C.11

Vector subtraction graphically

You use vector subtraction to remove the effect of vector addition.

Vector Multiplication

There are three kinds of vector multiplication:

- Scalar-product
- Dot-product
- Cross-product

Scalar-Product

Multiplication of a vector by a scalar (real number) changes the vector's magnitude. It changes the distance between its starting and final points.

```
U (1, 3, 2) * 2
= Z (1 * 1, 3 * 2, 2 * 2)
= Z (2, 6, 4)
```

A simplified picture might look like Figure C.12.

Z has double the magnitude of U, so the scalar-product results in a vector.

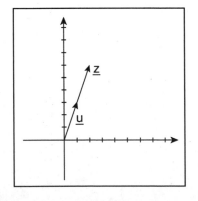

Figure C.12

Scalar-product

Dot-Product

The dot-product of two vectors is designated by the dot symbol *. It results in a real value. This is defined as:

```
U * V
```

Suppose you would like to get the angle between two 2D vectors U and V (see Figure C.13).

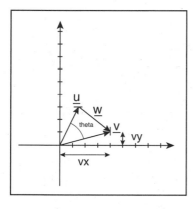

Figure C.13

Angle of dot-product

The enclosed angle between U and the x-axis should be alpha. The enclosed angle between V and the x-axis should be beta. So you can say:

```
cosalpha = ux / ||U||
sinalpha = uy / ||U||
cosbeta  = vx / ||V||
sinbeta  = vy / ||V||
```

You can calculate the magnitude of vectors by using the Pythagorean theorem, which states that the sum of the squares of the sides of a right triangle is equal to the square of the hypotenuse. Mathematically, this is represented as $a^2 + b^2 = c^2$. Or, using x and y for the sides and m for the hypotenuse, it is represented as $x^2 + y^2 = m^2$.

So the length (magnitude) of the vector is retrieved by

```
||V|| = sqrt (x² + y²)
```

The angle between U and V is the difference between alpha and beta.

```
theta = alpha - beta
```

The law of cosines states that for a triangle such as the one formed by the vectors U, V, and W, where ||U||, ||V||, and ||W|| are the lengths of the sides of the triangle, the following is true:

```
U * V = ||U|| * ||V|| * cos(alpha - beta)
= ||U|| * ||V|| * (cos alpha * cos beta + sin alpha * sin beta)
= ||U|| * ||V|| * (ux / ||U|| * vx / ||V|| + uy / ||U|| * vy / ||V||)
= ||U|| * ||V|| * (ux * vx + uy * vy) / (||U|| * ||V||)
= ux * vx + uy * vy
```

I would like to solve this equation for the angle between the two vectors.

```
cos(theta) = U * V / ||U|| * ||V||
U (1.5, 3)
V (4, 1)
||U|| = sqrt(ux²+ uy²)
= sqrt (2.25 + 9)
= 3.4
||V|| = sqrt(vx² + vy²)
= sqrt (16 + 1)
= 4.12
U * V = ux * vx + uy * vy
= 1.5 * 4 + 3 * 1
= 9
cos (theta) = 9 / 3.4 * 4.12
cos (theta) = 0.64
theta = 49.99°
```

Now let's do that for a 3D vector. For a triangle such as the one formed by the vectors U, V, and W, where ||U||, ||V||, and ||W|| are the lengths of the sides of the triangle, the following is true:

```
W = U - V
U - V = U² + V² - 2* U * V
```

To solve it after U −V:

```
2 * U * V = U² + V² - (U - V)
```

To find the magnitude of the vectors, the following is true:

```
||U||² = ux² + uy² + uz²
||V||² = vx² + vy² + vz²
||U - V||² = (ux - vx)² + (uy - vy)² + (uz - vz)²
```

Let's solve the above equation in terms of the dot-product, like this:

```
2 * U * V = ux  + uy² + uz² + vx² + vy² + vz² - (ux - vx)² - (uy - vy)² - (uz - vz)²
= ux² + uy² + uz² + vx² + vy² + vz² - ux² - vx² + 2 * ux * vx - uy² - vy² + 2 * ux * vy -
uz² - vz² + 2 * uz * vz
= 2 * ux * vx + 2 * uy * vy + 2 * uz * vz
= 2 * (ux * vx + uy * vy + uz * vz)
```

That leads to:

```
U * V = ux * vx + uy * vy + uz * vz
```

To get the angle between those vectors you might use

```
cos(theta) = U * V / ||U|| * ||V||
U (1.5, 3, 4)
V (4, 1 ,2)
```

```
||U|| = sqrt(ux² + uy² + uz²)
= sqrt (2.25 + 9 + 16)
= 4
||V|| = sqrt(vx² + vy² + vz²)
= sqrt (16 + 1 + 2)
= 4.4
U * V = ux * vx + uy * vy + uz * vz
= 1.5 * 4 + 3 * 1 + 4 * 2
= 17
cos (theta) = 17 / 4 * 4.4
cos (theta) = 0.96
theta = 15.00°
```

You use the dot-product to find the angle between two vectors; as such, it is used to shade polygons and produce many other effects.

Cross-Product

Taking the cross-product of any two vectors forms a third vector perpendicular to the plane formed by the first two. This vector is called a *normal* vector, and it points in the direction of the plane formed by the other two vectors.

You use the cross-product to determine which way polygons are facing. It uses two of the polygon's edges to generate a normal. Thus, you can use the cross-product to generate a normal for any surface for which you have two vectors that lie within the surface. Unlike the dot-product, the cross-product is not commutative.

```
U x V = - (V x U)
```

The magnitude of the cross-product of U and V, ||U x V||, is given by ||U||*||V||*sin(theta). The direction of the resultant vector is perpendicular to both U and V (see Figure C.14).

You get the sine value if you divide the cross-product by the magnitudes of both vectors.

```
sin (theta) = U x V / ||U|| * ||V||
```

You shouldn't use this to find an angle between the two vectors because the dot-product is faster.

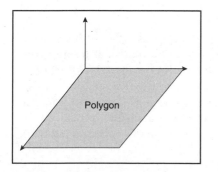

Figure C.14

Cross product

Unit Vector

There is another class of vectors that is important to know—the unit vector. A unit vector has a magnitude of 1. If you combine that with the free vector, you get a vector with all possible directions and a magnitude of 1. All possible free and unit vectors form a sphere with their final points. If you define the starting point as the origin of, for example, a camera, you might rotate that camera by altering the vector values.

How do you calculate a unit vector or normalize a vector? To calculate a unit vector, divide the vector by its magnitude or length.

```
N = V / ||V||
```

And you can calculate the magnitude of these vectors by using the 3D version of the distance formula based on the Pythagorean theorem.

```
x²+y²+z² = m²
```

The length of the vector is retrieved by:

```
||V|| = sqrt (x² + y² + z²)
```

The final length is the square root of the sum of squares (Pythagorean theorem). The magnitude of a vector has a special symbol in mathematics, a capital letter designated with two vertical bars: $||V||$. A function performing this task might look like this:

```
D3DXVECTOR3* D3DXVec3Normalize(D3DXVECTOR3* v1, D3DXVECTOR3* v2)
{
    D3DXVECTOR3 tv1 = (D3DXVECTOR3)*v1;
    D3DXVECTOR3 tv2 = (D3DXVECTOR3)*v2;
    tv1 = tv2/(float) sqrt(tv2.x * tv2.x + tv2.y * tv2.y + tv2.z * tv2.z);
    v1 = &tv1;
  return (v1);
}
```

It divides the vector by its magnitude, which is retrieved by the square root of the Pythagorean theorem.

Matrices

Matrices are rectangular arrays of numbers. These numbers can represent anything you want, such as equations or constants. Additionally, you can think of a matrix as a set of row vectors or a set of column vectors. For our purposes, we are mostly concerned with using matrices as a compact form to write general 3D transformations, so the discussions in this book will focus on matrices as representations of transformations such as the world, camera, and projection. For example, a 4×4 world matrix contains four vectors, which represent the world-space coordinates of the x, y, and z unit axis vectors, and the world-space coordinate, which is the location of these axis vectors.

```
ux uy uz 0
vx vy vz 0
wx wy wz 0
tx ty tz 1
```

The u, v, and w vectors represent the so-called *rigid body*. This is the matrix that defines the mapping from object space to world space. Graphically, it looks like Figure C.15.

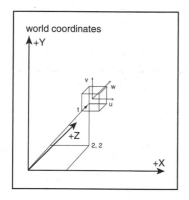

Figure C.15

The u, v, and w vectors

To describe the position of this cube, the matrix has to look like:

```
1, 0, 0, 0
0, 1, 0, 0
0, 0, 1, 0
2, 2, 2, 1
```

The cube is oriented like the coordinate system. The first row contains the world-space coordinates of the local x-axis. The second row contains the local y-axis, and the third row contains the world-space coordinates of the local z-axis. The vectors are unit vectors whose magnitudes are 1. The last row contains the world-space coordinates of the object's origin. You might translate the cube with these.

A special matrix that has 1s along the main diagonal is the identity matrix:

```
1 0 0 0
0 1 0 0
0 0 1 0
0 0 0 1
```

The identity matrix represents a set of object axes that are aligned with the world axes. The world x-coordinate of the local x-axis is 1, the world y- and z-coordinates of the local x-axis are 0, and the origin vector is (0, 0, 0). Therefore, the local model x-axis lies directly on the world x-axis. The same is true for the local y- and z-axes, so it's a "get back to the roots" matrix. If an object's position in model space corresponds to its position in world space, simply set the world transformation matrix to the identity matrix. This matrix and all other matrices in Direct3D can be accessed like this:

```
D3DMATRIX mat;
mat._11 = 1.0f; mat._12 = 0.0f; mat._13 = 0.0f; mat._14 = 0.0f;
mat._21 = 0.0f; mat._22 = 1.0f; mat._23 = 0.0f; mat._24 = 0.0f;
mat._31 = 0.0f; mat._32 = 0.0f; mat._33 = 1.0f; mat._34 = 0.0f;
mat._41 = 0.0f; mat._42 = 0.0f; mat._43 = 0.0f; mat._44 = 1.0f;
```

Multiplication of a Matrix by a Vector

A typical transformation operation is a 4×4 matrix multiplication operation. A transformation engine multiplies a vector representing 3D data, typically a vertex or a normal vector, by a 4×4 matrix. The result is the transformed vector. This is done with standard linear algebra:

```
Transform      Original                                   Transformed
Matrix         Vector                                     Vector

a b c d          x           ax + by + cy + dw              x'
e f g h     x    y     =     ex + fy + gz + hw       =      y'
i j k l          z           ix + jy + kz + lw              z'
m n o p          w           mx + ny + oz + pw              w'
```

Before you can transform a vector, you must construct a transform matrix. This matrix holds the data to convert the vector data to the new coordinate system. You must create such an interim matrix for each action (scaling, rotation, and transformation) that will be performed on the vector. Those matrices are multiplied to create a single matrix that represents the combined effects of all of those actions (matrix concatenation). You can use this single matrix, called the *transform matrix,* to transform one vector or a million vectors. The time to set it up is made worthwhile by the ability to reuse it.

Matrix Addition and Subtraction

It is simple to add two matrices. You just add the first number in the first column of the first matrix to the first number in the first column of the second matrix, and so on. It works the same with subtraction.

```
 1  2  3  4        17 18 19 20        18 20 22 24
 5  6  7  8   +    21 22 23 24   =    26 28 30 32
 9 10 11 12        25 26 27 28        34 36 38 40
13 14 15 16        29 30 31 32        42 44 46 48
```

Matrix Multiplication

To explain matrix multiplication, it's best to show an example.

```
 1  2  3  4        17 18 19 20
 5  6  7  8        21 22 23 24
```

```
 9 10 11 12    *     25 26 27 28
13 14 15 16          29 30 31 32
```

The idea is to multiply the first row of the left matrix by the first column of the second row and add the result. You do the same with the second column of the second matrix, and then with the third, and with the fourth.

```
1 * 17 + 2 * 21 + 3 * 25 + 4 * 29    1 * 18 + 2 * 22 + 3 * 26 + 4 * 30 etc.
```

Next you start multiplying the second row of the first matrix by the first column of the second matrix, and add the result. You continue by multiplying the second row of the first matrix by the second column of the second matrix and so on. In the end, you will get the 16 values of the 4×4 matrix.

Translation Matrix

To move an object in 3D space, you normally manipulate the fourth row of the world matrix of the object (object matrix) or multiply the world matrix by a translation matrix.

```
1 0 0 0
0 1 0 0
0 0 1 0
x y z 1
```

Instead of holding the coordinate, a translation matrix holds how far the object must be moved. The object matrix is used to store x-, y-, and z-values.

Scaling Matrix

This type of matrix will scale a coordinate, so it's useful to make an object smaller or bigger.

```
x 0 0 0
0 y 0 0
0 0 z 0
0 0 0 1
```

It's also possible to manipulate the three values directly, without using a matrix, by using mat._11, mat._22, and mat._33 to access them.

Rotation Matrices

There are three rotation matrices to rotate around the y-, x-, and z-axes.

Rotation around the Y-Axis

The Direct3D function D3DXMatrixRotationY() rotates around the y-axis. I don't have the source, but it might look like the following code:

```
VOID D3DXMatrixRotationY( D3DXMATRIX* mat, FLOAT fRads )
{
    D3DXMatrixIdentity(mat);
    mat._11 =  cosf( fRads );
    mat._13 = -sinf( fRads );
    mat._31 =  sinf( fRads );
    mat._33 =  cosf( fRads );
}
```
=

cosf fRads	0	-sinf fRads	0
0	0	0	0
sinf fRads	0	cosf fRads	0
0	0	0	0

Rotation around the X-Axis

D3DXMatrixRotationX() rotates the objects around the x-axis, where fRads equals the amount you want to rotate. It might look like this in source:

```
VOID D3DXMatrixRotationX( D3DXMATRIX* mat, FLOAT fRads )
{
    D3DXMatrixIdentity(mat);
    mat._22 =  cosf( fRads );
    mat._23 =  sinf( fRads );
    mat._32 = -sinf( fRads );
    mat._33 =  cosf( fRads );
}
```
=

1	0	0	0
0	cos fRads	sin fRads	0
0	-sin fRads	cos fRads	0
0	0	0	0

Rotation around the Z-Axis

D3DXMatrixRotationZ() rotates the objects around the z-axis, where fRads equals the amount you want to rotate. Source code for this function might look like this:

```
VOID D3DXMatrixRotationZ( D3DXMATRIX* mat, FLOAT fRads )
{
    D3DXMatrixIdentity(mat);
    mat._11 =  cosf( fRads );
    mat._12 =  sinf( fRads );
    mat._21 = -sinf( fRads );
    mat._22 =  cosf( fRads );
}
```
=

cosf fRads	sinf fRads	0	0
-sinf fRads	cos fRads	0	0
0	0	0	0
0	0	0	0

These matrices are concatenated by Direct3D. It is very important to remember that matrix multiplication is not commutative. That means ([a] * [b]) is not equal to ([b] * [a]) in most cases. The formula for transformation is

|W| = |M| * |T| * |X| * |Y| * |Z|

where M is the model's matrix, T is the translation matrix, and X, Y, and Z are the rotation matrices. Direct3D uses the resulting matrix W internally.

Summary

This appendix provided you with the knowledge necessary to understand all of the mathematical stuff in this book. Nevertheless, there is much more out there you need to learn to become a more advanced game programmer. Mathematics is the key to most game-programming-related problems. Having a good background in mathematics is a must for a good game programmer.

APPENDIX D

CREATING A TEXTURE WITH D3DXCREATE TEXTUREFROM FILEEX()

Most examples in this book use the D3DUtil_CreateTexture() function found in the d3dutil.cpp library file to create a texture. This function actually puts a thin layer of abstraction on a much more complex function named D3DXCreateTextureFromFileEx(). This function is so overwhelming that you might get lost in all its parameters. D3DUtil_CreateTexture() feeds most of these parameters with a "works-in-most-cases" value. So you can reach a more advanced level of creating textures for Direct3D devices, this appendix features the parameters of D3DXCreateTextureFromFileEx().

```
HRESULT D3DXCreateTextureFromFileEx(
    LPDIRECT3DDEVICE9 pDevice,        // pointer to device interface
    LPCTSTR pSrcFile,                 // pointer to string with filename
    UINT Width,                       // width in pixels
    UINT Height,                      // height in pixels
    UINT MipLevels,                   // number of mip levels requested
    DWORD Usage,                      // usage of texture
    D3DFORMAT Format,                 // describes requested pixel format
    D3DPOOL Pool,                     // memory class
    DWORD Filter,                     // how the texture is filtered
    DWORD MipFilter,                  // how the texture is mip filtered
    D3DCOLOR ColorKey,                // color to replace with transparent black
    D3DXIMAGE_INFO *pSrcInfo,         // info structure regarding texture
    PALETTEENTRY *pPalette,           // 256 color palette
    LPDIRECT3DTEXTURE9 *ppTexture     // pointer to texture interface
);
```

pDevice represents the device to be associated with the texture. pSrcFile holds an ANSI string that specifies the file from which the texture should be created. You might specify a width and height of the texture. By providing 0 or D3DX_DEFAULT—as in the d3dutil.cpp— you take the dimensions from the source file.

This method could even produce mipmaps for you. A series of mipmaps consists of the same texture in different resolutions. The textures differ by a power of two in their dimensions. Why would you use the same texture in different resolutions? You wouldn't want to use a texture with the highest resolution if a player was very far from the object on which the texture was mapped, because the player can't see the texture in detail at this distance. So it's cheaper performance-wise to give the player the smallest texture scaled at the proper size for the farthest distance, a middle-sized texture for the middle distance, and the biggest and most detailed texture for the short distances. Direct3D can produce and use these textures automatically for you; you only have to tell it your favorite API. You do this in the MipLevels parameter. Providing 0 or D3DX_DEFAULT as the MipLevels will lead to a complete mipmap chain built from the source file. With any other number, the requested

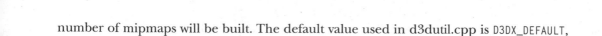

number of mipmaps will be built. The default value used in d3dutil.cpp is D3DX_DEFAULT, which builds and uses in your engine a complete mipmap chain.

The Usage parameter shows the Direct3D engine whether a texture surface will be used as a render target. There are impressive effects you can accomplish with rendering onto a texture surface. One of the most common examples in the DirectX SDK is rendering a video on a rotating cube. You might provide 0 or D3DUSAGE_RENDERTARGET as the parameters. If you want to render on a texture surface, you have to check the capabilities of your graphics hardware with CheckDeviceFormat(), set Pool to default with D3DPOOL_DEFAULT, and later set the render target with SetRenderTarget(). The D3DUtil_CreateTexture() function of d3dutil.cpp uses 0 as the default value.

The Format parameter defines the surface format you want to use, so the format of the returned texture might have a different format than the source file. If the format is unknown, it's taken from the source file. You can provide the desired format in D3DXCreateTextureFromFileEx(). If you don't provide a parameter here, the format of the source file is used.

The Pool parameter defines the memory class in which the texture should reside. One of the common files, d3dutil.cpp, uses D3DPOOL_MANAGED, the handiest memory class.

With Filter, you can control how the image is filtered (that is, how the pixels are sampled from the source image, which affects the picture quality). This is useful when the texture should have a different size than the source file. If the dimensions of the texture should be half of those in the source file, you might provide D3DX_FILTER_BOX, which computes the pixel in the texture by averaging a 2×2 box from the source image. If the dimensions of the texture should be a quarter of the dimensions of the source file, it would be wise to use D3DX_FILTER_LINEAR, which computes the pixel in the texture by averaging a 4×4 box. This is one of the killer features of this method. The method call of D3DXCreateTextureFromFileEx() in D3DUtil_CreateTexture() uses the same size for the texture as for the source file, so it uses D3DX_FILTER_TRIANGLE|D3DX_FILTER_MIRROR. This tells the Direct3D engine that every pixel in the source file contributes equally to the texture, and that the mirror filter, which mirrors the u, v, and w values, should be used.

The same parameters for Filter work for the MipFilter parameter. Handling visual quality in different dimensions of textures is even more important when you are using mipmaps. D3DUtil_CreateTexture() uses the same parameters here as Filter.

The ColorKey parameter helps in setting, for example, transparent regions in a texture. It's a D3DCOLOR value that replaces a provided color with transparent black. I don't use transparent regions here by default.

pSrcInfo might give you back a pointer with a D3DXIMAGE_INFO structure, which holds the width, height, number of mip levels, and the format of the source file. It's not used in the call to D3DUtil_CreateTexture().

If you use palettized textures (256 colors), pPalette will give you back the palette entries in a PALETTEENTRY structure. Using 32-bit textures gives you a higher visual quality. You might see the difference between *Quake 2* and *Quake 3* models: Whereas the first one could only use 8-bit textures, the latter has the ability to handle the smoother-looking 32-bit textures. I aim for 32-bit quality, so the D3DXCreateTextureFromFileEx() in D3DUtil_CreateTexture() call doesn't need to give back a palette structure.

The ppTexture pointer will give you the pointer to the texture interface IDirect3Dtexture9, representing the created texture.

If D3DXCreateTextureFromFileEx() succeeds, it will return D3D_OK.

Summary

It is worth taking a closer look at the D3DXCreateTextureFromFileEx() function and playing around with it. It offers a tremendous amount of possibilities for altering textures. You will be surprised how much source you would have to write to replace this function with your own code.

APPENDIX E

GAME PROGRAMMING RESOURCES

I would like to recommend a few Internet resources, which you might want to check out on a regular basis to be in sync with the fast development of game programming.

General

http://www.voodooextreme.com. Gives you a lot of info and screen shots of the newest games. This might help you keep an eye on what is possible in game programming. Sometimes it provides you with leaked drivers and information on game development, but it's not for developers only.

http://www.bluesnews.com. Follows the same rules as Voodoo Extreme. Both are nice sites; they are like your daily newsletter, entertaining and informative.

http://www.realtimerendering.com. A list of interesting links for graphics programming.

DirectX Graphics

http://msdn.microsoft.com/directx. This is the source. Read the articles of Philip Taylor.

http://www.direct3D.info. This is the accompanying Web site for this book. You will find updates and corrections here. Besides, there are always a few interesting tutorials on Direct3D.

http://www.gamedev.net. You will find a lot of DirectX Graphics tutorials here. A few of them were written by me.

http://www.flipcode.com. A Web site for game programmers. Every day I look at the image, code, and tip of the day.

http://hometown.aol.com/billybop7/index.htm. The Web site of William Chin, alias billybop, who, together with Peter Kovach, has written the road-rage engines used in *Inside Direct3D* (Microsoft Press, 2000).

http://www.zen-x.net. ZEN-X is a DirectX Graphics engine with source. You can learn a lot by checking the provided source.

http://www.cbloom.com. The Web site of Charles Bloom, who provides a few very interesting papers and demos to download.

http://www.mrgamemaker.com. Great Direct3D tutorials.

http://www.swissquake.ch/chumbalum-soft. The home of MilkShape 3D, the best modeling tool you can get.

http://discuss.microsoft.com/archives/directxdev.html. The most important know-how database you can use.

APPENDIX F

WHAT'S ON THE CD

You've read the book; now it's time to check out the software! This book's CD-ROM contains the source code to every one of the sample programs in the book, as well as a handful of useful utilities and applications that I used to create the effects mentioned in this book.

If you haven't already done so, tear open that CD-ROM sleeve and plop the disc in your computer's CD drive. If Autorun is enabled, you should be greeted with an interface that will guide you through the CD-ROM's contents. If Autorun is disabled, you can still run the interface by following these steps:

1. Insert the CD-ROM into your computer's CD drive.

2. Right-click on My Computer and select Open from the menu.

3. Click on your CD drive in the list of drives.

4. In the list of the CD's contents, double-click on the Start_Here.html file. After reading the licensing agreement, click I Agree if you accept the terms (or click I Disagree to quit the interface).

If you accepted the licensing terms and clicked on the I Agree button, you'll be presented with the Premier Press user interface. From there you can browse the contents of the CD-ROM or select from a number of applications to install. Following is a list of the applications you will find on the CD-ROM.

DirectX 9.0 SDK

The main application is Microsoft's DirectX 9 SDK. Used in all the projects in this book, the SDK is the first thing you should install. For help installing the DirectX 9.0 SDK, consult the Introduction.

ATI RenderMonkey

The CD includes a beta version of ATI's fantastic RenderMonkey software, which you can use to create awesome real-time shader effects.

NVIDIA Cg Toolkit

Cg is NVIDIA's new high-level language for graphics programming. The Cg Toolkit is based on the Cg language, and it allows programmers to create amazing visual effects using real-time pixel and vertex shaders.

Flash Movies

The CD also includes some Flash movies I created to help you set up Visual C/C++ 6 and Visual C++ .NET so you can start programming your Direct3D applications.

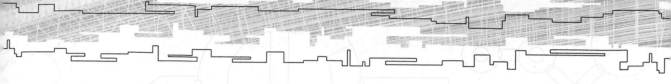

Index

GAME DEVELOPMENT.
IT'S SERIOUS BUSINESS.

"Game programming is without a doubt the most intellectually challenging field of Computer Science in the world. However, we would be fooling ourselves if we said that we are 'serious' people! Writing (and reading) a game programming book should be an exciting adventure for both the author and the reader."

—André LaMothe,
Series Editor

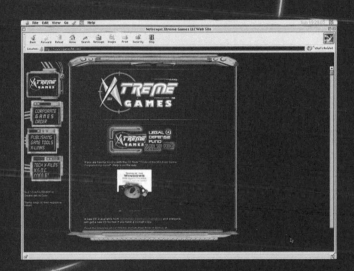

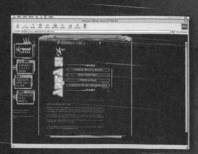

License Agreement/Notice of Limited Warranty

By opening the sealed disc container in this book, you agree to the following terms and conditions. If, upon reading the following license agreement and notice of limited warranty, you cannot agree to the terms and conditions set forth, return the unused book with unopened disc to the place where you purchased it for a refund.

License:
The enclosed software is copyrighted by the copyright holder(s) indicated on the software disc. You are licensed to copy the software onto a single computer for use by a single user and to a backup disc. You may not reproduce, make copies, or distribute copies or rent or lease the software in whole or in part, except with written permission of the copyright holder(s). You may transfer the enclosed disc only together with this license, and only if you destroy all other copies of the software and the transferee agrees to the terms of the license. You may not decompile, reverse assemble, or reverse engineer the software.

Notice of Limited Warranty:
The enclosed disc is warranted by Premier Press to be free of physical defects in materials and workmanship for a period of sixty (60) days from end user's purchase of the book/disc combination. During the sixty-day term of the limited warranty, Premier Press will provide a replacement disc upon the return of a defective disc.

Limited Liability:
THE SOLE REMEDY FOR BREACH OF THIS LIMITED WARRANTY SHALL CONSIST ENTIRELY OF REPLACEMENT OF THE DEFECTIVE DISC. IN NO EVENT SHALL PREMIER PRESS OR THE AUTHORS BE LIABLE FOR ANY OTHER DAMAGES, INCLUDING LOSS OR CORRUPTION OF DATA, CHANGES IN THE FUNCTIONAL CHARACTERISTICS OF THE HARDWARE OR OPERATING SYSTEM, DELETERIOUS INTERACTION WITH OTHER SOFTWARE, OR ANY OTHER SPECIAL, INCIDENTAL, OR CONSEQUENTIAL DAMAGES THAT MAY ARISE, EVEN IF PREMIER AND/OR THE AUTHORS HAVE PREVIOUSLY BEEN NOTIFIED THAT THE POSSIBILITY OF SUCH DAMAGES EXISTS.

Disclaimer of Warranties:
PREMIER AND THE AUTHORS SPECIFICALLY DISCLAIM ANY AND ALL OTHER WARRANTIES, EITHER EXPRESS OR IMPLIED, INCLUDING WARRANTIES OF MERCHANTABILITY, SUITABILITY TO A PARTICULAR TASK OR PURPOSE, OR FREEDOM FROM ERRORS. SOME STATES DO NOT ALLOW FOR EXCLUSION OF IMPLIED WARRANTIES OR LIMITATION OF INCIDENTAL OR CONSEQUENTIAL DAMAGES, SO THESE LIMITATIONS MIGHT NOT APPLY TO YOU.

Other:
This Agreement is governed by the laws of the State of Indiana without regard to choice of law principles. The United Convention of Contracts for the International Sale of Goods is specifically disclaimed. This Agreement constitutes the entire agreement between you and Premier Press regarding use of the software.